THE MEDIÆVAL HISTORY OF DENBIGHSHIRE.

THE RECORDS OF DENBIGH

AND ITS

LORDSHIP:

BEARING UPON
THE GENERAL HISTORY OF THE COUNTY OF DENBIGH
SINCE THE CONQUEST OF WALES;
ILLUSTRATED
WITH MANY GEMS OF WELSH MEDIÆVAL POETRY
NEVER BEFORE PUBLISHED.

BY JOHN WILLIAMS,
(GLANMOR,)
AUTHOR OF "ANCIENT AND MODERN DENBIGH," "AWSTRALIA A'R
CLODDFEYDD AUR," ETC.

VOL. I.

WREXHAM:
PRINTED AND PUBLISHED BY GEORGE BAYLEY, HOPE STREET.
MDCCCLX.

ADVERTISEMENT.

Volume II. to contain UCHALED and UCHDULAS.—Antiquities of the Vale of Conway, and the hill country of Hiraethog; with THE RECORDS OF RUTHIN AND ITS LORDSHIP, &c. Vol. III., THE RECORDS OF BROMFIELD AND YALE, Antiquities of the eastern and southern parts of the County.

The completion and perfection of the plan must, however, depend upon circumstances,—the reception of the present volume—the prompt assistance and support of the local antiquary and patriot. The whole to be confined to historical and documentary facts, antiquities, traditions, and mediæval poems. It will, of course, be optional with Subscribers to this volume whether they take the rest or withdraw their names.

THE AUTHOR.

Gwersyllt School, Wrexham.

THE RECORDS OF DENBIGH
AND ITS LORDSHIP.

From an Original Portrait in the Hall of the Worshipful Company of Goldsmiths.

INTRODUCTION.

THE change which the world undergoes in the course of a few centuries is really marvellous, as the following Records convince us. What a mighty revolution the last five hundred years have brought about in the value of property, the tenure of land, the state of society, the distinction of class or *caste*, the character, language, and religion of the inhabitants of districts! The following pages carry us back, as it were in a dream, to times when England planted her colonies, not along the shores of the Pacific and Indian Oceans, but among the hills and valleys of Wales;—times when great military lords fortified themselves on the tops of the highest eminences, and when there were few or no landed gentry, or great commercial men, the present staff and stay of society. Nay, these Records bring us, in reflection, to those primitive simple times when princes actually took their revenue in kind—just in so many lambs, or thraves of oats—the chief grain then raised—so many dishes of meal, couples of fowl, dozens of eggs, or pots of butter; so many days ploughing and harrowing in spring and reaping in autumn; or so many "meals of meat," nights' lodging, or other provision, for the king's servants, horses, and dogs.

These Records also illustrate the ancient Welsh laws, and system of political economy, and bring to light a great fact not found in the common "histories" of our country; viz.:—that great numbers of the Welsh, the legitimate proprietors of the soil, either "died contrary to the peace," or fled their country for ever, during the reigns of "the Three Edwards," A.D. 1284—1334. So far as the Lordship of Denbigh may be taken as a sample of the whole "state of Wales" there were few, very few, or no great Welsh proprietors left after the complete Conquest of the Principality. Montacute drew nearly four times as much revenue as De Lacy received from this Lordship.

Another remarkable fact is the futile attempt of victorious

England to eradicate or supplant the Welsh race and tongue, and the gradual disappearance, decay, and extinction of the exclusive "*English*" element in our municipalities.

The *Poems*, which of themselves form a striking feature of the work, are not only fine specimens of mediæval Welsh, but a parcel of the history itself. Compared with the Anglo-Saxon, the Welsh tongue has undergone no change for a thousand years; so that the poetical effusions of three or four centuries back, must, with the notes given, be perfectly intelligible to ordinary Welsh scholars. It will, however, be seen that some words which were then current have become obsolete, others have assumed a different signification. Some verbs have lost their active voice, whilst a marked change has taken place in the use of the verb "*to be*," particularly in the third person singular, indicative mood; and also in the power and government of conjunctions and prepositions. "*I*" was then used both as a singular and plural pronoun—for the present "*ei*" and "*eu*;" "eb" and "yd," for *heb* and *hyd*; "yn" for *ein;* "no" for *na*, &c. We have no such expressions now as—

"Ni'th *ery* no thŷ no thŵr."

That is, "neither house nor tower can withstand thee." *Aros* now makes *erys*, not "ery;" and it no longer signifies *to abide*, but simply *to await*.

"Anos yw dy *aros* di
Nog aros naw o gowri."

"It is more difficult to withstand thee than to withstand nine giants." The pronoun "*ef*" is now the objective case of "*efe*;" the former answering to the English "*him*," the latter to "*he*." Such expressions as the following are now obsolete:—

"Ef a'm llas i a'm nasiwn,
Yn awr y llas yr iarll hwnn."

We are particularly struck with the frequent use of English words and expressions by the Welsh poets of the middle ages, a proof that the English language was even then understood and spoken in conjunction with the Welsh. The written Welsh of the present day is, in this respect, "purer," having less foreign admixture; but the syntax and idiom of those times came much nearer to the terse elliptical expressiveness of the Latin, and the

" order " of the words, in the formation of sentences, kept closer to the construction of the classic tongues. The adjective was frequently separated from its noun by an interjectional or other clause, as—

> " Yn y *tân* yr enaid *dic.*"

The present Welsh, with its thousands of new words, the natural produce of more extensive cultivation, has, like its English ally, become a far more prosy tongue. Even the verb itself was, with the ancients, frequently omitted, by an elegant ellipsis; and so was the relative pronoun—

> " Nid tew dail ond dy dylwyth
> Sy winllan ffres yn llawn ffrwyth."—*Tudur Aled.*

The auxiliary verb *to be* (" *sy,*" Welsh; *est, esse,* Lat.; *is,* Engl.) was very frequently " dropt," as—

> " Llin *Don* yn llenwi dy wedd;
> Llwyn *Venabyl* llawn o vonedd."—*Idem.*

The whole scheme of mediæval orthography will be found in the following lines :—

> " Canknu aur Nanconwy cait,
> Cottvm wirion Coetmoriait;
> Blodeu Rros, oed blait Rrys Wynn,
> Brynfanigyl, Brân a Phenwyn.
> Bualiait, gwaet y blait gynt,
> Bro Clwyt a bric Iâl yttynt."

There was less Extravagance in the use of the letter *y,* as, " Die Estwyll distill y Gwiliau,"—" Nos dowell ar ben monydd."

Neither were the *mutations* of the initials carried so far as at present. Whilst the tongue has become more euphonious to the ear, the orthography is more uncouth to the eye. But few old writers, however, followed the rule ; being led astray by caprice and poetical accident.

Another remarkable feature of (Welsh) mediæval poetry is the frequent allusion to ancient British, Roman, Grecian, and Sacred history, heathen mythology, &c., which proves the poets of that age to have been men of some classical acquirements and general intelligence. But we value their effusions chiefly as pictures of their own times, as historical evidence sometimes bearing upon great national events. They lived in an age when the pride of ancestry

A

ran high, and courage was esteemed the greatest of all human virtues; when physical and military training went for the highest or most useful branches of education, and the first gentlemen in the land took a pride in wrestling and fencing, and other "athletic sports," as our poet says of Robert Salusbury, Esq., of Yale — .

> " Cwympo rhai 'mhob camp yr wyd."

Nay, the "gentlemen" of those times often engaged in fierce fights with sticks and cudgels, in fairs, markets, and sporting assemblies, and so did our poet's hero, as he says—

> " O fyn'd i ffair fwn dy ffon
> Yr äi'r bwlch ar wŷr beilchion,
> Odid i feilch o doy di' fann
> Oedi angau, o diengan'."

In their friendships such men, according to our poet, were "gentile as lambs;" in their animosities "fierce as bulls."

> " Ymlaen dic mal ŵyn y don'
> Mal teirw yn ymlid dewrion;
> Cynnyrch gweilch cawn ar awch gwŷr,
> Cynnarwch cowion eryr."

And when such attention was paid to the developement of the physical powers, to the cultivation of muscular strength, from generation to generation, no wonder that we should find some individuals of gigantic stature and strength in those ages; as Syr John y Bodiau, Syr Risiart Hir, and others, alluded to in this work. Such were those mediæval giants who commonly wore—

> " Aerwyau mawr o aur a main;"

Great torques of gold and precious stones.

The poems of these ages also exhibit a strange belief in astrology and fatalism, intermingled with popish sentiments. All the sorrows of life, and death itself, are attributed to the evil influence of the planets :—

> " Blin ydyw gan blaenedau
> Yn trin oes dyn i'n tristau."

Appeals to the protection and "cognizance" of the Blessed Virgin abound in these effusions, whilst the Romish purgatory forms a prominent feature of the poet's creed, as—

> " Nid ä i'r nef, rhaid yw 'n wir
> Ffinio dros y korff anwir,
> A thalu 'r ffin Gatholic

Yn y tân yr enaid dic.
Krist ni dderbyn o'r krasdân
Enaid yw law ond yn lân."—*Gutto'r Glynn*.

They often exhibit a blind lamentable reliance upon human
merits :—

" Klud i'r korff, klodvawr i kaid
O phrynodd ffafr yw enaid."—*Idem*.

The pomp and splendour of the Romish form of worship, the
sacrifice of the mass, invocation of saints, images, &c., are also
ably depicted in a fine poem (found at Denbigh) dedicated to Rhys
of Ystrad Towy :—

" Y kôr ef a'i koweiriawdd,
A dorau tec o wydr tawdd.
Aeth hanner gwerth i ynys
I wydro hon wedy, Rhys.
Ystratfflur ar waith kuras,
A gynau plwm i gan plas.

* * * *

Tec yw swn byrdwnn lle bo,
Trebl '*Amen*' trwy blwm yno.
Be baen' vil bawb yn i vedd
Yn veirw'n hon o frenhinedd,
Y mae rhwng i muriau hi
Erw i gladdu arglwyddi.

* * * *

Gwiscwyd oll, gwysc hyd allawr,
Gwëau plwm am gypplau mawr.
Ergyd saeth o dderwgoed serth
Yw i chrib uwch yr *aberth*.
Un dydd ni rifwn oe dôr
Y derw oll hyd yr allor.
Y mae 'r derw rh'om a'r dwyrain
O rif myrdd ar fwäau main.

* * * *

Klochdy mawr, kalchisd murwyñ,
Kwarterau gwaith kaer Twr Gwynn.
Pwy a edrych, pob hydref,
Golwc uwch no'i geilioc ef ?
Be bae 'r dw'r ugain gwrhyd,
Heb un bont uwch ben y byd,
Gallai hwnn, o argau lluw,
Gadw 'r *delwau* rhac dw'r Diluw.—*D. Nanmor*.

Still, the Abbot exercised as much munificence and hospitality,
and indulged in as much luxury as any baron :—

" Ni bu air, mwy no barwn,
Am leihau saic ymhlas hwnn.

> Mae 'n kostiaw iddaw ar wydd,
> Ben Tŷ Benet, bunt beunydd ;
> A chan punt gyrch i win per,
> Eblaw ammod i blymmer."—*Idem.*

How affectually the old monks must have mortified the flesh by
" faring sumptuously every day !" And no doubt they were very
hospitable, and charitable withal, as Gutto'r Glynn says of another
holy abbot—

> " Tri bwrdd a bair droi yw borth,
> Tair siambr yn trwssio ymborth.
>
>   *   *   *   *
>
> A'i law yntau val Antwn,
> A'i laif rrudd—i lyfr yw hwnn
> I ladd y *saith* (lewaidd Sion !)
> Marwol *bechodau mowrion.*
> *Saith rinwedd,* a sathr yna—
> Eglwys_Duw yn i glôs da.
>
>   *   *   *   *
>
> Kynnal y mae'r kard'nal ku
> Kost y llys , Kastell Jessu.
>
>   *   *   *   *
>
> Gwledd echdoe a doe'n i dŷ
> Gwledd kanhanedd kynn hynny.
>
>   *   *   *   *
>
> Ty'r vendith, ty'r gwenith gwynn,
> Tref wendec tra vo undyn ;
> Ty *Sulio* i lwyddo'r wledd,
> *Trinio* a gatwo'r annedd."

Other poems might have been quoted to show that morality was
then at a low ebb among some worshippers of the muse. Indeed,
the lamp of gospel truth, though at no period quite extinct in this
land, burnt so dimly during the middle ages, as to exhibit little
more than a painful lack of vital Christianity. Notwithstanding, it
is said the Welsh never submitted quietly to the authority of Rome.
There were always some who protested against her superstitions.

According to " *Sir Roger Twysden's Vindication,*" the clergy did
secretly contract marriage until towards the end of Edward the
Third's reign; and in the following Records we have a priest's
wife among the tenants of Nantglyn in the eighth year of that
monarch.

Henry of Lincoln and Thomas of Lancaster (who figure in these
Records) and Guy of Warwick, were the three greatest and most

popular earls of the fourteenth century. They were also considered the greatest defenders of the rights of the laity, in opposition to the assumptions of the Pope and the hierarchy.

The lists of Members of Parliament for the boroughs and county, High Sheriffs, &c., must, it is presumed, be considered valuable as ready " reference and index " to the political and civil history of Denbighshire. And the municipal records of Denbigh, during a period of nearly three hundred and fifty years, not only form important addenda to the author's former work, but, throw more or less light upon the general history of the county.

The hitherto unpublished letters of the celebrated Hugh Myddelton are not only interesting in themselves, but must contribute to satisfy the curiosity of those literary and antiquarian gentlemen who have for years been collecting materials for a biography of that truly great man. The parties at Denbigh who are described in the author's former work as descendants of William Myddelton the Poet, now set up the apparently substantiated claim of being descended from Sir William Myddelton, son of Sir Hugh, (see page 133 of this work,) notwithstanding, some contend that they have descended from Robert Myddelton, uncle of the said Sir Hugh Myddelton, Bart.

It is hoped the additional notices of Sir Richard Clough, and Catherine of Berain, will be equally interesting, especially to those who have read " *The Life and Times of Sir Thomas Gresham.*"

Some curious additional memorials of Robert Earl of Leicester, will also be found in this volume.

The subsequent pages also contain the first sketch of the real history of Abergele and Isdulas ever published.

With respect to the translation of the Latin documents, it is to be hoped that their full *purport* has been given. Some few terms should, perhaps, have been more fully explained, as " *purprestura.*" *Du Canges* has the following note upon this word :—*Purprestura.* (*Vox Fori Anglice,* porprendere—invadere, aliquid sua manu capere.) Dicitur Purprestura, vel propestura proprie ; quando aliquid super Dominum regem injuste occupatur, ut in dominicis Regiis, vel in viis publicis obstructis, vel in aquis publicis traversis à recto cursu , vel quando aliquis in civitate super regium plateam ædifi-

cando occupaverit; et generaliter quoties aliquid fit ad nocumentum
regii tenementi vel regiæ viæ vel civitatis, placitum inde ad
coronam Domini regis pertinet. Purpresturæ tres sunt; contra
regem, contra dominum capitalem, contra vicinum vel non dominum.
In *Tomlins' Law Dictionary*, we have, " Pourpresture, from the
French pourpris, conseptum, an enclosure. Anything done to the
nuisance or hurt of the king's demesnes or the highways, &c., by
enclosure or building, endeavouring to make that private which
ought to be public."

The original documents are full of " fearful contractions," and
abound in barbarous " law Latin" terms, derived from the Norman French, Saxon, and Welsh; which are sometimes difficult to
interpret. Thus "*forisfactura*," derived naturally from *foris*, the
outside, and *factura*, the *making of a thing*, signified in the conventional slang of mediæval lawyers, a *forfeiture;* and no doubt De
Beckele used it in this sense, so that at page 3 of this work, "lands
lying round in the same township," should have been "*forfeited*
lands," &c. Also, at page 5, " *attachments*," or customs of the manor, &c., should have been " *easements*," &c., mutual convenience
of neighbours, &c., " *aisiamentum*," not *attachiamentum*, being, no
doubt, the word intended.   " *Bercarium* " signified a sheepfold or
sheepcot; but " *barcarium*," (from the Welsh *barcty*, or *barcdy*,
barkty,) a bark-shed, tan-house, &c.   *Morceta, marceta, marcheta*,
from the Welsh *merchetta*, now to attach one's self to a female,
to marry, in the following pages signifies a fine paid to the lord
on the marriage of a tenant's daughter. *Letherwite, lederwite,
lairwite*, was a fine paid for a child born before marriage, or on
conviction of bastardy.—*Nativus*, fem. *nativa*, a native, convention-
ally, *a bondman, bondwoman*.—See Chap. II. *Heywite*, a custom
paid for permission to make and repair hedges, fences, dikes, &c.

" *Owrai Gowydd* " is translated the " *Warbler's Ode*," at page
91, but *Owri* signified a lament for the dead—

> " Ar ei fedd bu *owri* fawr,"

A wild cry of loud lamentation, like the " Scotch Coranich," or
" Irish Howl," a custom which is still preserved in the East.

The matter being totally foreign to the compositor, especially the
Latin and Welsh parts, the author has to regret the appearance of

a few typographical inaccuracies ; but, fortunately, they involve no serious error of fact, and will be readily detected as errata, by the intelligent reader, who will rectify them thus :—

Adgyweiriad y Wasg.

Tudalen 92, Sain' Sior *dros* i ynys yŵ. Dynion dec, *da* yn i tŷ, *dan* wybren, &c. Downus bryd, &c. Byrrion, *dynion* dianael. Huno a gais hen a *gwann.* Is sylvaen *y* bresswylva.—94, Marged gwraic *briod.*—95, Eurwas *o* brid urddas bro. Ei anedigaeth-wlad. 173, Gŵydd heli, gwŷdd a *hoelion.*—176, Eissiau yn hwy oes yn hon. *Ddyn* wiwdraul, i ddwyn adref.—181, *Oes* wart clau, &c. I'w frodyr *ddoe* bu frwydr ddydd. Gowaeth dug (*a duke*) waith diogan. 182, Oes naf Iessu i nefoedd.—191, *Gwlen.* 193, suwgr. Mwnai ym mewn, &c. Ni bu lân *neb,* &c. Tri bys y llew, &c., an " eight syllable " couplet.—200, *dan* dy wregys—dy *gnawd.* Oes *gwayw* aruthr, &c.—nis *byrrheuir.* 201, Ni wnai *ddyn* yn Wynedd, &c. Mae'n oleu yma'n *y* wlad, er marw llew mawr a lleuad.

Corrections of the press.—Page 62, Edwardi *Primi.*—71, Burgesses. — 75, Caervallen, Plas-trowbridge, Abergele. — 79, Henry VIII., not III.—96, Of a tongue so requisite, &c.—97, *expedition.*— 100, Llwynfrith-Magon, the woody hill of berries, woodwardreth. 129, Groes and Llwydiarth.—206, *celibacy, hospitiis.*

The author respectfully and gratefully acknowledges the kind aid of several learned and antiquarian gentlemen, among whom are, the Rev. A. B. Clough, B.D., Rector of Braunston; the Rev. C. W. Heaton, B.D., of Jesus College, Oxford; the Rev. E. W. Heaton, Vicar of Bettws-yn-Rhos ; the Rev. J. Meredith, Vicar of Abergele ; the late William Owen, Esq., of Tanygirt, Denbigh ; Ignatius Williams, Esq., of the Grove, Denbigh; Richard Peake, Esq., of Chepstow; Richard Williams, Esq., Town-clerk of Denbigh ; Mr Evans, schoolmaster, Abergele; and Miss Angharad Lloyd, of Rhyl ; Mr J. D. Jones, schoolmaster, Llanrhaiadr ; and others, for copies of inscriptions, &c.

To the Rev. A. B. Clough, and those who so readily and liberally responded to his appeal, for the pecuniary means of defraying the greater part of the expense of procuring copies of the records from which this volume is principally compiled, the author owes a double debt of gratitude, particularly, since this kind aid came at a time when he was surrounded by troubles and difficulties which would otherwise have been insurmountable.

In conclusion, the author regrets the fact that De Beckele's survey of Uchaled and Uchdulas, could not be given in this volume, for two cogent reasons, viz., that the book must then have very far exceeded the present price; and, secondly, that his applications for information from that quarter, in almost every case, were futile or unanswered.

In bringing a work of this nature through the press, many questions will arise which mere acquaintance with the topography of the region cannot determine, and which none but the resident antiquary can answer.

Two long Chapters on the parochial history and public charities of Denbigh have also been omitted. These *might*, indeed, be published in a separate form, with a map of the town and parish, at about one shilling per copy, were there any encouragement to undertake the task. The very same Chapters were left out of the former work to reduce the price of printing.

The only return for his labours which the author can with certainty expect must be the simple gratification of knowing that he has done more to bring to light and perpetuate the history of Denbigh than any other writer ever did, or can do hereafter. He may also humbly say that, whatever may be the imperfections of this volume, it has been to him a long laborious task to assort this ponderous luggage-train of historical *Facts*.

The long delay of four years, in the publication of this volume, arose wholly from circumstances over which the author had no control. The means and life to complete the history of the whole County of Denbigh are in the gift of Heaven.

THE RECORDS

OF

DENBIGH AND ITS LORDSHIP.

CHAPTER I.

THE LORDSHIP OF DENBIGH FIFTY YEARS AFTER THE CONQUEST
OF WALES—ITS EXTENT, VALUATION, TENANTRY, AND CUSTOMS—
THE MANORS OF YSTRAD AND KILFORD. A.D. MCCLXXXIV—
MCCCXXXIV.

[*Chiefly translated from the "Extenta Castri et Honoris de
Denbeigh, facta per Hugonem de Beckele, et per recognitionem
tenentium singularum villatarum, anno regni Regis Edwardi
Tertii (post Conquestum) octavo." A.D.* 1334.]

MORE than five hundred years have elapsed since Hugh de
Beckele, or Bockele, drew up his survey of the Castle and Lordship
of Denbigh, in the Latin tongue, the substance of which is now,
for the first time, given to the world. The original M.S. is
preserved in the British Museum. Of the author nothing further
is known than what appears to be evident from the document
itself; viz.:—that he was an Englishman, and no doubt the same
personage as Hugh de Bockele" (the old form of *e* being easily
confounded with *o* in deciphering manuscript), who is mentioned
as a landowner in the township of "Arquedelok" (*Archwedlog*), in
the parish of Llansannan. There is still a farm in the vicinity
called *Plas Bwcle*, or Buckley Hall. He must have been a person
of consequence—of such classical education as the age afforded—
and probably reputed for professional skill; but so utterly ignorant

B

of the right orthography and pronunciation of Welsh names as to
make it a matter of regret to the antiquarian enquirer, it being
often difficult, and in some cases impossible to say what places are
meant. The M.S. contains one hundred and sixty closely-written
folios, "full of contractions." There are evident remains of two
more sheets of parchment; but there is a memorandum in a hand
of the seventeenth, or latter part of the sixteenth century to the
effect that the book then contained "foure skore leaves and no
more." The last leaf is numbered 80. A portion of the survey
relating to Uchdulas is thus lost.

The compiler of these Records occasionally compares De
Beckele's survey with extracts from the Postmortem Inquisition
of the Estates of Henry de Lacy, Earl of Lincoln and Lord of
Denbigh, who died in A.D. 1310—M.S. dated A.D. 1311, preserved
in the Tower of London, and published in a subsequent part of this
work; and with the original charter, in Norman French, granted
by De Lacy to the first English burgesses of Denbigh, and still
preserved amongst the archives of that ancient town, a translation
of which has been given in the author's former work; with a
curious and interesting document, copied in a subsequent part of
the present work, being an indenture of the sixth year of Queen
Elizabeth, made between Robert, Earl of Leicester and Lord of
Denbigh—of immortal notoriety—and the tenants of this lordship.
Also, with various title-deeds, &c., of the sixteenth and seventeenth
centuries, and with the author's personal knowledge of the
district and territory.

Of the Divisions of the Lordship.—In the first place, it should
be understood that the Honour of Denbigh contains two cantreds
(hundreds) and a half; namely, the Hundred of "Ros" *(Rhôs)*,
which comprehends two commotes *(wapentakes)*, to wit, the Commote of "Istulas" *(Isdulas)*, and the Commote of "Ughdulas,"
(Uchdulas or *Uwchdulas)* : also, the Hundred of "Rowaynok"
(Rhyfoniog), which likewise contains two commotes; that is to say,
the Commote of "Ishalet" *(Isaled)*, and the Commote of
"Ughalet" *(Uchaled* or *Uwchaled)*. Likewise, half another
hundred "ceded" in one commote, called the Commote of
"Kayneerth" *(Cynmeirch*, commonly *Cinmerch)*. Whence the

survey is first made of the Commote of "Keymergh" *(the same)*, because "that is properly English," (that is, peculiarly so by settlement at that time,) and afterwards of the Commote of "Ishalet;" thirdly, of the Commote of "Ughalet;" fourthly, of the Commote of "Istulas;" and, in the fifth and last place, of the Commote of "Ughdulas."

THE COMMOTE OF KAYMERGH.

Of the order of the Survey.—It is to be understood that the prince (the ancient Welsh sovereign) had nothing appertaining to the lordship in this commote, but the manor of "Astret Oweyn" *(Ystrad Owain)*, the wastes of "Kernyneuet" *(Oernyfed,* otherwise *Oernoved)*, and "Bisshopeswalle * Berebowe" *(unknown)*, and "Havodlum" *(Havodlóm)*, with the wilds of "Askaerwen" *(Iscaerwen)*, and "Coidraghan," † and "Segrot" *(Segroit, Segruit, Segrwyd,* or *Isegrwyd)* Park, &c., the particulars of which will appear hereafter. But after the Conquest of Wales, the Lord Henry de Lacy, Earl of Lincoln, made for himself the manor of "Kylforn" (still called in Welsh *Cilffwrn,* but in English *Kilford)*, of lands lying round in the same township, and of a part of a certain township in the commote of "Ishalet," called "Astret Canon;" and of those lands which had not been formed around, in the township of "Kylforn," the said Earl made exchanges with the tenants, &c., so that he appropriated to himself the whole township of "Kylforn," for the aforesaid manor. Hence the survey follows, first of the manor of "Astret Oweyn," afterwards of the manor of "Kylforn," then of every township of that commote in detail, and lastly of the wastes and wilds aforementioned, that is, of every place in the order it should come.

Of the Perch.—It is first of all to be observed, that the afore-mentioned Earl made the perch of this lordship to contain twenty-one feet of his peculiar foot, which perch does not contain,

---

* Possibly, so called from some very ancient ruins described at the end of this chapter.

† The author was told that there is a wood which formerly went by the name of *Coed Rhychan, Coed-yr-ychen,* or *Coed-Ychan,* as *Llanychan;* but his search for it proved futile. There are dense woods still left about Postyn.

according to the "assize" (standard measure) of the king of England, more than eighteen feet and a half, and one inch ; and by that perch the content of the lands, woods, and commons, and all that was to be measured, has been taken in this survey.

THE MANOR OF ASTRET OWEYN.

Of the Capital Messuage.—And there is a manor, of which the capital messuage contains one acre, one rood and a half, sixteen perches, in which are two granges, one . . . one "bercarium," and one house for domestics, and also one "sheepcot;" whereof the attachments of the houses and court (*curarium*) are worth forty pence per annum. There is neither dovecot nor garden, but there are two crofts inclosed round the manor, which contain four acres, three roods, four perches ; whose herbage is worth six shillings and four-pence per annum, value per acre sixteen pence. There is also one "clogh" (*clough*), adjoining the manor, which contains one acre, one and a half rood, three perches, of dense brushwood ; the profit of which, if apportioned, might be worth eight-pence per annum.—The total value of the capital messuage, with the crofts containing seven and a half acres, twenty-three perches, ten shillings and four-pence.

Arable Land.—And there are belonging to the lordship, of arable land, not divided into more than one farm, but which might well be made into three, two hundred and fifteen and a half acres, and thirty-five perches ; worth eight pounds, six shillings, and four pence per annum ; whereof one hundred and thirty-four and a half acres, and thirty-three perches, are valued at ten-pence ; and four score acres, and two perches, at eight-pence per acre. There are also of old marshlands which have been included with the rest of the arable holdings, on account of their poorness, but lie for pasture, fifty-one acres and a half, and two perches, with one "bouk" (*balk*) by the mill ; which are valued at twenty-five shillings and nine-pence per annum ; price per acre, six-pence.— The total acreage of arable land, together with fresh-marsh, two hundred and forty-seven acres, and thirty-seven perches ; whose value per annum is estimated at nine pounds, twelve shillings.

Meadow-land of the Lordship.—And there are in the same

manor (in the lord's right), six acres and twenty-five perches of meadow-lands, which are worth sixteen shillings, and nine-pence, three farthings a year; price per acre, eighteen pence. Whereof there are in the "Holmes," with one small parcel on the north side of the river Ystrad (*ripæ de Astret*), near the above mill, eight acres and a half, and thirty-four perches; in several parcels in the "Middelfeld" (*Middlefield*), and between the "Estfeld" (*Eastfield*) and the "Middelfeld," one acre, one rood and a half, and thirteen perches; and in one parcel by the "Grenewey" (*Greenway*), opposite to the gate of the manor, one acre and eight perches.—The total acreage of meadow-lands in the lord's right, eleven acres and twenty-five perches; which are worth sixteen shillings, and nine-pence, three farthings per annum.

Pasture.—And there are two plots of inclosed pasture, which contain ten acres and a half, and thirty-five perches, worth seven shillings and one penny three farthings per annum; price per acre, eight-pence. There are also in certain little parcels between the Plain and the Long Clough, on each side, one acre, and three roods and a half, and ten perches, of poor pasture, worth altogether six-pence a year.—Total acreage of pasture, twelve acres and a half, and twenty-five perches, worth seven shillings, and seven-pence, three farthings per annum.

Rented Land.—And there are two free tenants * who hold in the lordship four acres, and a half, and thirty perches, at will; and render yearly, at two terms, that is to say, at the Pentecost and Michaelmas, nine shillings and eight-pence; at each term, four shillings and ten-pence, ;—namely, Walter de Bonde, who holds two acres and a half and thirty perches, rendering six shillings and eight-pence. And he holds one acre, with one house built thereon, rendering yearly three shillings.—Total shown, nine shillings and eight-pence.

Perquisites of the Court.—Also, through the enquiry of the court, as to the attachments (or customs of the manor), what they make by reapers yearly, these are estimated to be worth, one year with another, three shillings and four-pence. Amount shown; the

* There must be some "clerical error" here, since only one tenant is named, and one acre is not accounted for, although Bonde is made to pay the whole amount of rent for both holdings.

total value of the manor of Ystrad Owain annually, according to
the estimation made, eleven pounds, nineteen shillings, and nine-
pence half-penny.

THE MANOR OF KYLFORN.

Of the Capital Messuage.—And there is a capital messuage,
whose site contains seven acres, one rood and a half, and seven
perches, on which are two granges, one cow-house, one chamber
for the bailiff, and one dilapidated bake-house. Whereof the
attachments of the houses are worth ten shillings a year. And
there is one ruinous dovecot, which is worth three-shillings and
four-pence per annum.—The total value of the capital messuage,
with the dovecot, thirteen shillings, and four-pence per annum.

Arable Land.—And there are, in the lord's right, of arable
land converted into three farms (*in tres seisonas*), two hundred
and thirty-nine acres, two roods and a half, and seven perches;
which are worth annually eleven pounds, nineteen shillings, and
one penny half-penny; the price of each acre, one more and
another less, twelve pence. Whereof there are in the first
apportionment, viz. :—in the "Whytfeld" (*Whitfield* or *White-
field*), in two "furlongs," thirty-five acres, three roods and a half,
and fifteen perches; in cultivation near "Castelmed" (*Castle-mead*
or *meadow*), in three "furlongs," thirty-one acres, one rood, and
eight perches. In the second division (*seisona*), namely, in the
eastern plain (*campo occidentali;* Welsh, *maes*), which is between
the Church of "Thlanvargheth" (*Llanvarshell,* or *St. Marcellus*,
commonly called *Whitchurch*), and the "Culurehaye," twenty-five
acres, three roods and a half, and three perches. In the western
plain, under the manor-house, thirty-three acres, three roods and a
half, and twelve perches; and in the "Culurehaye," * twelve acres,
and one rood and a half. Also in the third holding, viz. :—in "Manenafeld" (qy. *Maen-Eva-field?*), fifty-six acres and a half, thirty-
eight perches; eight acres and twenty-six perches of poor marsh
in the same plain, which on account of their poorness are of no

---

* Query,—Whether the name be corrupted from *colluo, colluere* (Latin), to
rinse, wash, scour, &c., and "hay" (Saxon), a meadow?

value, except for pasture; besides four acres, one rood, and ten perches, below the same plain. And in "Rigwallefeld," forty-four acres and a half, and thirty-one perches; besides four acres and a half, and twenty-eight perches, in the same place, lying low, which on account of their wetness, are "ordained" for meadow, as appears below. The total content of arable lands, two hundred and thirty-nine acres, three roods and a half, and seven perches; worth nine pounds, nineteen shillings, and ten-pence half-penny a year.

Old Meadow-lands.—There are also in the manor of Kilford, one hundred and seventy-five acres, and eight perches, of old meadow-lands, which are worth nineteen pounds, and twelve pence, one farthing per annum; whereof thirty acres, three roods and a half, and ten perches, are in the "Castelmed;" price per acre, three shillings. Also, in "Troghmede" (*Trough-mead*), with two adjoining plots, fourteen acres, twenty perches. In a certain "place" between the "Castelmede" and Mapkelfeld" (qy. *Maple-field ?*), five acres and ten perches. In one "place" in the eastern plain, between the arable land, thirty perches. In "Maenenafeld," four acres, one rood, and ten perches. In "Rigwalle," with the "Stubbyng" (from *stub, stubble,* and *ing,* a *meadow*), forty-four acres and a half. In the "Newnyng" thirty-five acres and a half, and seven perches; besides five acres, one rood, and fifteen perches, of old marsh in the same place, which are accounted for below. In the "Calf-pasture" thirty-nine acres, besides five acres, thirty-four perches; of old marsh below the same meadow, &c. And in Dobbefeld le Ladde " (*the deep wet field of the water course, or fall of the river*), one acre, and one rood and a half; price per acre (some more and some less) two shillings.

New.—There are also in several plots of low wet arable lands, which are in many places found full of alders, together with several " places " of marsh, which from the present time are intended for grubbing up alders, and for meadow lands, (to be made thereof,) sixty-five acres, one rood and a half; worth, as they are now, sixty-five shillings, and four-pence half-penny; price per acre, twelve pence. And if so converted into meadow-land, it will be worth eighteen pence per acre, some more and some less; whereby the sum of not more than twenty-two shillings and seven-pence farthing

might be made.   Whereof there are four acres and a half, and
twenty-eight perches, of marsh in "Ryngwallefeld" (qy. if a corruption of *Cae'rhenwal*, old wall field, or *ring wall*, as *ring fence*) ;
in the "Newnynge" (pro. *Newning*, from the Saxon *ing*, a meadow
or grass field), five acres, one rood, and fifteen perches, of old
marsh ; in the "Calfpasture," five acres and thirty perches of old
marsh ; in the field called "Jonefeld le Rede" twenty-three acres
and twenty-nine perches old marsh ; in the field called "Dobbefeld
le Ladde," fifteen acres, three roods, and twelve perches ; and in
certain a "place" of old pasture adjoining the barns, which is
called "Kermed," eleven acres, and twenty-six perches.

Total acreage of new and old meadow-land, two hundred and
forty acres, one rood and a half, and eight perches ; which are
worth twenty-two pounds, six shillings, and four-pence three
farthings per annum.

Dry Pasture.—There are also belonging to the lordship, one
hundred and thirty-five acres, and seven perches, of dry pasture
land, worth six pounds, fifteen shillings, and one farthing a year ;
average price, twelve pence per acre.   Whereof seventy-six acres,
one rood and a half, and eight perches, are in the "Coupasture"
(*Cow-pasture*) ; in a certain "place" between the "Oldebrok"
(*Oldbrook* *) and the "Newnyng meadow," which used to be
arable land, but is now laid down for cattle pasture, eighteen acres
and a half, and thirty-two perches ; in certain old plots of pasture,
on both sides of the "Oldebrok," four acres, one rood, thirteen
perches ; in various little pieces in "Manenafeld," together with
old bogs, eight acres, twenty-six perches ; in the "Horsekerre"
(*Horse-acre*), seven acres, six perches, of dry pasture ; in the
"Koukerre" (*Cow-acre*), half an acre, and fifteen perches, of dry
pasture ; and in the "Wetekerre" (*Wheat-acre*), nineteen acres,
eighteen perches, of dry pasture.

Low-lying Pastures.— There are also one hundred and thirteen
acres, one rood, and eight perches, of deep marsh, overgrown with
alders—a low-lying, swampy pasture ; worth seventy-five shillings,
and sixpence, three farthings per annum ; price per acre, eight-

---

* There is a farm, a mill, and hamlet or village, near Whitchurch, called
Brookhouse—a small municipal suburb of Denbigh.

pence, more or less. Whereof thirty-two acres, and thirty-nine
perches, are in the "Horsekerre;" thirty-six acres, three roods,
three perches, in the "Coukerre;" and forty-four acres, one rood,
six perches, in the "Wetekerre."

Total acreage of all descriptions of pasture, two hundred and
forty-eight acres, one rood, fifteen perches; worth ten pounds, ten
shillings, and sixpence half-penny a year.

*Lands of the Lordship rented at will.—(Bayton, Grenolf,
Romworth, Peek, Danney, and Moston, tenants.)* And there are
in the lordship of the aforesaid manor, in the hands of several
tenants who hold at will, forty-nine acres, three roods, and thirteen
perches. Whereof "Richard de Bayton" holds four acres and a
half of land, rendering for each acre twelve-pence, at the "terms" of
"Pentecost and St. Michael" (Whitsuntide and Michaelmas), in
equal portions. Adam Grenolf holds for one acre, and one rood, a
certain plot of land, called "Tapelacre" (qy. pro. *Table-acre*, a flat,
somewhat elevated flat?), which contains one acre, one rood and a
half, and four perches, "rendering" (paying) for the acre twelve-
pence, at those terms (seasons). The same Adam holds one plot
near the "Cloyd" (pro. *Cluid* or *Clwyd*), for four acres, which
contains four acres, one rood, and thirteen perches; paying for each
acre eighteen-pence, at those seasons. And John de Romworth
and Richard del Peek hold near the "Cloyd" a certain plot of
land for twelve acres, which contains twelve acres, and twenty-
eight perches; paying for each acre eighteen-pence, at the said
seasons. And Alexander Danney holds there one plot of land for
seven acres, which contains eight acres, one rood, and seven
perches; paying for each acre eighteen-pence, at the said seasons.
The same Alexander holds from the honour in a part of "Astret
Canon," a certain parcel of land for six acres, which contains six
acres, three roods, and twelve perches; paying for each acre, twelve-
pence, at the aforesaid seasons. And Radulphus Grenolf holds of
the same honour one parcel of land for two acres, which contains
two acres, and ten perches, paying by the acre twelve-pence, at
the same seasons. And John de Moston holds from the same
honour two parcels of land for six acres, which contain six acres,
one rood, twelve perches; paying by the acre twelve-pence.

C

Total acreage of rented lands, forty-nine acres, three roods, thirteen perches; which produce fifty-eight shillings and nine-pence per annum. And thereof ten shillings are allotted to Alexander Danney for his ox-land, appertaining to his "burgage" (or town house), under the walls of "Denbiegh," by the charter of the Lord William Monte Acute;* his oxgang being assigned to him elsewhere; because that land was lying as it were in the heart of the lordship of this manor.

So stands the amount (of the existing farms of land rented according to ancient custom), at forty-eight shillings, and nine-pence, beyond the allocation aforesaid. † And so, by admeasurement of extent, the real amount will be fifty-four shillings, and two-pence. And so also the yearly value may be made five shillings and five-pence more than at present.

Perquisites of the Court.—These are estimated to be worth, taking one year with another, thirteen shillings and four-pence.

And so the sum total of the yearly value of the manor of "Kilforn," arising from all sources, according to the estimation by survey, as now, is forty-eight pounds, twelve shillings, and two-pence half-penny.

CONCLUDING REMARKS.

Those who are strangers to the district will need the further information that—

"Ros," in some other old documents called "Roos," and "Ross," in Welsh *Rhôs*, signifies a table-land, an elevated tract, a mountain plain, a flat or gently undulated region, elevated above a neighbouring level, whether the latter be land or sea. The ancient Hundred of Rhôs comprehended, as will be seen by the map, that promontory which lies between the estuary of the Conway and the Bay of Abergele, and was bounded on the south by the region anciently called *Pervedd-wlad,* or the interior; and on the east by the Vale of Clwyd. Camden tells us, that Denbigh was anciently called *Caledfryn-yn-Rhôs,* or the "Rough (or rocky) Hill in Ross,"

---

* William Montacute, Lord of Denbigh, Earl of Sarum (Salisbury) and King of Man. See *A. & M. Denbigh,* p. 72.

† That is, over and above the indemnity paid to Danney.

but upon what authority does not appear. If it was ever so called, it must have been in some very early, not to say pre-historic or fabulous age. The survey of De Beckele goes to prove that it was not in Rhos, but in Rhyfoniog, at the time of the annexation of Wales to the crown of England. The commotes of Uchdulas and Isdulas, now styled "hundreds," take their name from the river Dulas (dark-blue), a considerable stream which falls into the sea about two miles westward of Abergele; *Uch* or *Uwch* signifying above, and *Is*, below—that river.

"Rowaynok," variously written "Reweiniog," "Rewynok," &c., now called by the Welsh "Rhyfoniog," corruptly for *Rhiwoniog, gwlad rhiwiau,* or *Rhiw-weunog,* signifying the hill country—the land of slopes and brows.

"Ughalet" and "Ishalet," take their appellations from the river Aled, an affluent of the "Elway" or Elwy. The Aled flows from a lake of that name, in the Hiraethog Hills. These two commotes are likewise judicially dignified, at present, with the title of hundreds. •

"Astret" and "Kilforn" lie in the Vale of Clwyd. Ystrad (pronounced as *Ustrad,* the *Y* as *u* in the pronoun *us*), is beautifully diversified with diluvial ridges, and richly wooded, especially around Ystrad Hall. (See A. & M. Denbigh, p. 265, 266.) The lower valley has ceased to be mostly a "fresh-marsh," subject to inundation from the sudden floods for which the Ystrad is remarkable. But Kilford is an unbroken flat. It sinks slightly towards the Clwyd, and the confluence of that river with the Ystrad. The lower lands being still inundated two or three times a year. On the whole, it is but "sparcely" wooded. A portion of the older buildings attached to the manor-house, were consumed (some years back) by fire. There are no antiquities within this manor, except such as are connected with that very old ecclesiastical edifice called Whitchurch, which is fully described in the author's former work, p. 342—366, where it appears that Pope Nicholas, in A.D. 1291, included this church in his taxation, and that one of the canonries of St. Asaph was then partially endowed with certain revenues from "Kilfurn." The tenants, a century back, claimed exemption from parochial rates and taxes, small tithes, Easter dues, &c. Cotton Hall, so called from the illustrious family of the *Cottons*, of Lleweni and Combermere Abbey, is a modern mansion adjoining Kilford.

Ystrad, however, boasts of a remarkable remnant of antiquity, marked upon the ordnance map, and mentioned by Leland and other old authors, which, being nearly concealed by a dense wood, evaded the research of years which the writer bestowed upon the antiquities of the neighbourhood. This is a tumulus which stands at the back of a farm-house called Llys, upon the edge of a deluvial ridge, on the right hand side of the old road to Llanrhaiadr, just before you reach the top of the hill going over Pont Ystrad. It is of considerable size, almost perfect, and has, I believe, never been explored, but is worthy of the antiquary's visit and examination. Leland (vol. v., p. 59) mentions the spot as "Llesquenllean" *(Llys-Gwenllian)*, or the court of Wenchal de Lacy, relict of John Lacy Earl of Lincoln. She was the daughter of Llewelyn the Great—not the last Llewelyn—sovereign Prince of Wales, and grand-daughter of John, King of England. She became a dowager, holding a life-interest in "three towns" or townships by Denbigh, which, on her demise, Edward I. gave to Reginald Gray, Lord of Ruthin, contrary to the letters patent previously granted to her nephew Prince David ap Griffith. The King, personally at Denbigh, on the 23rd of October, in the tenth year of his reign—before the final conquest of Wales—confirmed this grant to Lord Gray, together with the Castle of Ruthin, and the greater part of the Vale of Clwyd.

Henry de Lacy, grandson of John Lacy aforesaid, held Denbigh, nearly twenty-six years, during which time he was made chief commissioner for the reformation of the English courts of law, ambassador to the court of France, commander-in-chief of the expedition into Gascony, viceroy of Aquitain, and lord protector of the realm of England. He led the van against the Scots at the battle of Falkirk, and was placed "higher than all peers except the king's son" in the English parliament. Such was the man who "made for himself the manor of Kilford," and although much of his active life must have been spent in the senate and the camp, or at court, we can only pity his "hard service," for his country and his king, if he did not find occasional relief from the din of a restless world on the quiet banks of the Clwyd and Ystrad, and recreative sport in those deep and marshy retreats "thickly overgrown with alder," as well as in his proximate chase of Lleweny.

In the time of the Tudors, Ystrad was the patrimony or the residence of a branch of the Myddelton family. There is a will of "Robert Myddelton of Astratt," dated as early as the third year of Queen Mary. "John Myddelton of Astratt Farme," was uncle to the renowned Sir Hugh Myddelton, "alderman of London and Denbigh." A tomb at Llanrhaiadr bears the following inscription:—"HIC JACET CORPVS MARIE POWELL VXORIS ROBERT MYDDELTON DE ASTRAD, GENER: SEPVLTÆ XXIV MAII, AN: DOM: MDCXXIX.

"ROBERTVS MYDDELTON DE ASTRAD JACET HIC CVM SPONSA. IPSA OBIIT DIE ET ANNO SVPRA MEMORATIS:* IPSE TRANSIIT XXVIII DIE AVGVSTI AN: DOM: MDCLIII. ET AN: PEREGRINATIONIS SVÆ LXXXII. &c."

The male line thus became extinct, and the estate passed to the Maurices and Conways by marriage; and finally, by purchase, it has become the property of the present high-steward of the Lordship. The view of Denbigh from the grounds of the present manson is very picturesque, rich, and beautiful.

"*Bisshopeswalle Berebowe.*"—The author's expedition in search of this spot resulted in no satisfactory discovery, the "oldest inhabitants" being unable to afford him any information upon the subject. On the moor, between Nantglyn and Cerrig-y-druidion, stands a remarkable ruin, wearing the greyness of ages, and measuring one hundred paces by ninety, with an inner erection measuring forty paces by ten. From its quadrangular form, and correspondence with the cardinal points, it has, generally, been taken for the remains of a Roman station, and called *Hen Ddin-*

---

* Thus she died and was buried on the same day, which may be accounted for if we reflect that this was the first year of Charles I, when a great plague broke out in London and spread over several parts of the country. Welsh ladies did not then assume the surnames of their husbands, but went through life by their own patronymic.

bych, old or ancient Denbigh ; but the mountaineer who conducted the writer to the spot, told him that it was, according to common tradition, an ecclesiastical ruin, of a very early time, and that the inner walls, formed of large blocks of stone, some retaining their original position, others strewed about, were those of a church, which, as he observed, ran east and west ; and the outer enclosure the church-yard.   But the author objected that it had been surrounded by a fosse, and that there were evident remains of other internal erections, on the opposite or north side.   The intelligent mountaineer, however, maintained that this arose from its being a monastic settlement of a warlike age.   Can this be " Bisshopes-walle," and so called from some mitred recluse, who sought security here in times of pagan persecution, Roman, or Saxon incursions into the inhabited valleys and hospitable glens around ?   Here was a desert—a bleak barren waste, shut out of the world by surrounding hills, outskirted then by impenetrable woods, offering, one would think, no temptation to an invader, especially one from a southern clime, to select it as a military station, unless it were during a summer campaign.   It is scarcely possible to conceive a more desolate and dreary region.   There are no human habitations within miles of view, not a solitary stunted tree, or lonely storm-shorn bush, or patch of enclosed land ; nothing but blooming heather, limpid streams, and blue mountain lakes, with occasional mounds or turmuli scattered over the plateau.

CHAPTER II.

ANCIENT WELSH LAWS AND CUSTOMS—DE BECKELE'S SURVEY
CONTINUED—SEGRWYD—HAMLET OF CADER—SEGRWYD PARK—
CUSTOMS AND SERVICES OF TENANTS.

BEFORE we proceed further with the survey, it will be necessary
to explain the various terms, usages, and customs of feudal times ; as,

Amobyr, amobrage, which was a fee paid to the lord upon the
marriage of a female vassal, by the person subject to such payment,
as will further appear hereinafter.

Ebedew, obediew, abediw, obeduw, obiduw, (pro obitu ?) relief, a
fee paid by the heirs at law, on taking up the estate which had
relapsed, or fallen in, to the lord, by the death of a tenant.

Gwobyr Estyn, an investiture-fee, paid on taking office, &c., or
the emoluments of such office.

Gelds, the three fees or tributes above-named.

Tung, tvng, twng, or *tunc,* called likewise, "*Punt* twng," or tunc
pound, the proportion of tribute-money due from each free tenant
to the lord in default of providing the stipulated supplies in kind.
This ancient source of feudal revenue, upon the annexation of
Wales, vested in the English crown, and is still collected in some
parts of North Wales, under the name of tunc-rent. See *Ancient
Laws and Constitutions of Wales.*

The following is an old and sufficiently curious

TABLE OF RELIEFS.

Mayor and Chancellor	ccxl pence.
Mayor	cxx do.
Chancellor	cxx do.
Noble	cxx do.
An *Aillt,* or "thane," naturalized, and having a church	
upon his land	cxx do.
An *Alltud,* or foreigner	xxiv do.

A male cottier	..	..	..	..	..	xvi pence.
Female ditto	..	..	..	..	..	xvi do.
Officers of the palace	..	..	..	..	..	cxx do.

* *N.B.—Except steward, chief-groom, chief-falconer, chief-huntsman, and page of the chamber.*

Foreign traveller dying on the land	..	..	..	xxiv do.
Female ditto	..	..	..	..	..	xvi do.

* *N.B —Innate noble or gentleman to pay though not landed.*

Mackewe, maccwy, maccui, magwy, a youth, a page ; *pen-maccwy*, chief-page.

Gweision (neu westion) bychain. Every tenant under the princes of Wales was bound to present his son and heir to the sovereign, upon such son's attaining his fourteenth year, at which age he became independent of his father. These youths were under the superintendance of the chief lord of the royal household, and passed their time in perambulating the country, and marauding in the marches—in annoying appressive lords-marchers, and revenging real or imaginary wrongs committed upon subjects of their sovereign master. Giraldus particularly describes their manner of life. Archbishop Peckham, the ecclesiastical tool employed to subjugate the Welsh under the Norman and Papal yoke, advises, in a letter to Edward I., that this custom, and peculiar species of vassalage, should be totally abolished, on account of the irregularites committed by these youths—"*La maniere de rivre de wession bychen fait oublier de toute.*"

"*Coidarius*," coediwr, a woodman, a forester.

Raglot, rhaglod, the chief civil officer of a commote, the deputy of the sovereign prince.

Priodor, now signifying a free-born native, but then, as in this survey, a proprietor.

Ringuild, ringyll, the summoner of the court, the usher.

It should also be observed that the old Welsh measures had little or nothing in common with the present English standard measures, as will appear by comparing the following table :

ANCIENT WELSH LAND MEASURE.

Iau.								
30	1	Erw.						
120	4	1	Tyddyn.					
480	16	4	1	Rhandir.				
1920	64	16	4	1	Gafael.			
7680	256	64	16	4	1	Tref.		
30720	1024	256	64	16	4	1	Maenol.	
384000	12800	3200	800	200	50	12½	1	Cwmmwd.
768000	25600	6400	1600	400	100	25	2	1 Cantref.

Thus, the *cantref* or *cantred*, hundred, was equal to 2 commotes, or 25 manors, or 100 townships, or 400 gavels, or 1,600 rhandiroedd, sharelands, or 6,400 tyddynod or farms, or 25,600 erwau, (often wrongly translated *acres*,) or 768,000 ieuau, yokes, of 7,680 Welsh square feet each. But the foot contained only 81 square inches. In like manner, the old Welsh mile was 2,275 English yards long, or more than 1¼ mile, according to the present statute measure.

The foregoing table must, however, be understood to refer merely to the original *statute* divisions. The terms *tyndyn*, a farm; *rhandir*, a portion-land; *gafael*, gavel; *tref*, township; *maenol* or *maenor*, a manor, &c., had ceased to signify any specific *quantities* of land long before the Conquest of Wales, and become expressive either of the kind of tenure, or of judicial, or popular and customary divisions of the territory, as De Beckele's survey must convince every observant reader. " *Wele*," *gwely*, translated *lectus*, a bed, signifies a heritage.

SEGROYT.

The township of Segroyt, with the hamlets of Cader and Pen-mankyng, together with a part of the hamlet of Cathus, in the time of the princes, before the Conquest, consisted of twenty-two gavels and a half, which were in the holding of natives; of which eleven gavels and a half came entire into the hands of the lord at the time of the Conquest, partly by reason of the tenants having died contrary to the peace (that is, fallen by the sword, or the hand of the executioner, in the last struggles for the liberty and independence of Wales); and partly by failure of those services which are detailed below, with the farms of land, &c. And eleven gavels still

D

remain in the holding of survivors, &c., of whose customary services the detail immediately appears below.

Natives.—Edeuet. ap Gron. ap Jor. *(Ednyfed ab Goronwy ab Iorwerth)*, Gron. ap Jor. Sayr *(Goronwy ab Iorwerth, saer,* carpenter), and Madoc ap Jor. Saer ; each of these holds one gavel.

Eignon ap Dynawet *(Einion ab Dunawd?)* Tudor ap Jor. and Gron. ap Willym *(Goronwy ab Gwilym)* ; each of these holds three perches of one gavel.

Gron. ap Eignon and Eignon his brother ; these two hold, one with another, three parts of one gavel.

Ken. ap Ithell *(Kenrick neu Cynrig ab Ithel)*, holds two parts of one gavel.

Yeuan ap Eignon ap David *(Ieuan ab Einion ab Dafydd)*, holds the third part of one gavel.

Eignon Vaghan *(Einion Fychan)*, Eignon ap Tuder, Tudor ap Jor. Saer, Jevan ap Hehillyn Ove *(Ifan ab Heilyn, ôf,* smith), Philip ap Ken., and Jevan Duy ap David *(Ifan Ddu ab Dafydd)* ; each of these holds half a gavel.

Gron. ap Heilyn Ove *(Goronwy ab Heilyn y gôf)*, Jevan ap Jor. Saer *(Ifan ab Iorwerth y saer)*, Eignon ap Madoc Grethe *(Einion ab Madoc Grydd, neu y crydd,* shoemaker) and David ap Tuder ap Jor.; each of these holds one gavel. And each of these eleven gavels pays twelve pence tung annually, at the feast of All Saints; and for provision for the prince's servants, two shillings and five pence, one farthing; that is to say, eight-pence one farthing at the Nativity of the Lord *(Christmas);* seven-pence at the season of Mid-Lent; seven-pence at the feast of the nativity of St. John the Baptist *(Midsummer)* ; and seven-pence at the feast of the Exaltation of the Holy Cross. And each gavel pays for provision for " *dextrarii et garcionum*" (jockeys and grooms, or for riding horses &c., *) thirteen-pence half-penny yearly ; eight-pence thereof at the nativity of St. John the Baptist, and five-pence half-penny at the Exaltation of the Holy Cross. And every gavel pays for one

* The laws of Wales provided that out of the twenty-five manors of each cantred, two *tyddynod* or farms, should be set apart for the horses and dogs of the prince. And that every township should pay sixty pence for the king's attendants.

grain of oats eight-pence yearly, at the time of Mid-Lent. And whoever may be holding these eleven gavels, whether they hold more or less, or whether the tenants be at the time many or few, they pay yearly, at the feast of the Exaltation of the Holy Cross, for . · . (*luctarii?*) *cum canibus* (competitors, or trainers with dogs ? *) one penny ; and for provision for the *penmackewe* (chief page) and weiss. baghen (the youths in attendance) one half-penny. And these so happen that the provision may be more or less as the native tenants of the soil may be more or fewer in number. Likewise, each of them renders at the Nativity of the Lord one penny for one hen. And the number of these hens accords with the greater or lesser ratio aforesaid. And each of them pays for provision for the raglots's horse four pence annually at the feast of the Exaltation of the Holy Cross; and for provision for stallions and grooms (in the Earl of Leicester's indenture called *Arian porthiant stalwyni*, provender-money for stallions), along with others, as appears in the particulars of this commote. And for three autumn works (three days' work in harvest), four pence half-penny at the feast of the Assumption of the Blessed Mary. And each of them pays for keeping in repair the houses of the manor of Ystrad one penny half-penny yearly at the feast of the Invention of the Holy Cross. And for repairing the mill and mill-dam at Ystrad three half-pence yearly, at the same season. And all these customs befall according to the greater or lesser ratio aforesaid. And whoever (of these tenants) makes a new hedge (or fence) round his corn (crop), or repairs old hedges, gives the lord one penny yearly at the feast of the Invention of the Holy Cross. And this custom happens to be more or less, as a greater number or fewer of them make or repair hedges. And these natives, in the same manner as all other natives of this commote, render to the lord yearly, twenty shillings, one with another, for releasing the office of reeve (or bailiff) to them, that they may be quit of the election of reeve, at the feast of the Exaltation of the Holy Cross. With those other customs that appear below among the common customs of this commote, &c.

* "Gweis y own," literally servants of the dogs. The master of the dogs was an honourable officer in the king's retinue.

The amount of tung form the whole township of "Segrot" annually at the term of All Saints is eleven shillings.

Amount of provision for the prince's household servants, at the seasons of

The Nativity of the Lord...............vij. *s.* 6*d.* ob. q.
Mid-Lent .... vj. *s.* v*d.*
The Nativity of St. John..................... vj. *s.* v*d.*
The Exaltation of the Holy Cross ... vj. *s.* v*d.*

So making annually ....xxvj. ix. ob. q.

That is, twenty six shillings, and ninepence, three farthings. Of the remaining customs, they are subjoined in the limit of the commote, with the like customs of all other natives of that commote, who are on the same conditions as these natives here, &c.

Distinquishment of Escheats.—And the "purpart" of the lord's escheats of the lands of natives in "Segrot," with its hamlets aforesaid, contains eight hundred and eighty-eight acres, one and a-half rood, eleven perches, of land and wood, and two hundred and seventyseven and a-half acres, seven perches of common. And of the other half of the hamlet of "Chatus," (otherwise written " *Cathus,*" now " *Casyth*") which is in the occupation of free tenants, that is to say, in the tenure of the "progeny" of " Wen Gogh" (*Gwên Goch*); of whose services the account is given below ; the eighth part appertains to the lord, and contains forty-three acres, three and a-half roods, of woodland and common. And thereof one hundred and sixty-seven acres, and thirty-two perches, are included under " Segroyt Park," the survey of which is given with the said park below.

And there further remain one thousand and forty two and a-half acres, twenty-six perches, which have been apportioned as shown immediately below. Here De Beckele subjoins a list of tenants who hold by relief, and paid every year in equal portions at Whitsuntide and Michaelmas.

	a. r. p . s. d . s. d.
Thomas Batemon (*Bateman*) . . .	xii, 0 x . 0 vj . . 6 0½
William de Bradeshagh (*Bradshaw*) .	iii. 0 0 . 0 x . . 2 6
Eignon ap Eden (*Einion ab Ednyfed*)	0. ij 0 . 0 viij . . 0 4
Juliana de Hallum ⎱	iv. 0 0 . 0 viij . . 2 8
Sibilla de Hallum ⎰	

Adam son of Robert Velyn (*Adda ab Rhobert Felyn*)	iv. 0 0 . 0	viij. .	2	8
Grono ap Heillyn Ove (*Goronwy*) ab *Heilin y gof*)	0 ij 0 . 0	vj. .	0	3
David ap Eignon Lloyd (*Dafydd ab Einion Lwyd*)	iv. 0 0 . 0	vj. .	2	0
Wenthlian wife of Eden. (*Gwenllian gwraig Ednyfed*)	i. ij 0 .		0	10
David ap Madoc (*Dafydd ap Madog*)	i. 0 0 .		0	6
Elias Englepeny (*Englepenny*) . .	iii. 0 0 .	vi. .	1	6
Thomas Pye	xii. 0 xxvj.		5	1

(Six acres thereof at 4d per acre, and the rest at 6d per acre.)

John de Moston called (*Mostyn*, in Wales)	viii. 0 0	vi. .	4	0
Henry son Roger le Coupere (*Cowper, or Cooper*)	iv ij. xxvii. 0	vi. .	2	4
Adam de Moston	vii. 0 0		4	0

(Whereof four acres were at six-pence per acre ; and the remaining three acres at eight-pence per acre.)

Robert de Hilton junior, holds three acres of a new apportionment close by "Kechlyforik" (*Cyffylliog, Gyffylliog*, that is, *y gell ffylliog*, the dark, shady, or gloomy wood), which was previously held by the community of the township, price sixpence per acre, &c. And the same Robert holds fifty acres of waste at " Keuynmayn" (*Cefn-maen*) price per acre six-pence paying, at the seasons aforesaid, twenty-five shillings.

Sum total of the farm-rents of " Segroyt"—at the season of Pentecost, thirty shillings and seven-pence farthing ; feast of St. Michael, thirty shillings and seven-pence farthing ; so making yearly sixty-one shillings and two-pence half-penny, for one hundred and twenty-eight acres, one and a-half roods, and three perches of land.

Of the Hamlets of " Cader Cathus and Penmonk," (otherwise Pennankyng, Pennanky, *Pennant-y-ci*), Thomas de Byrchensagh (*Burchinshaw*, that is, *Birchenshaw*,) holds, by charter, thirteen acres, one rood of land, paying annually for the whole (*in grosso*) at the seasons aforesaid seven shillings and nine-pence. Robert de Cattelowe (*Chatlow*) holds by relief five acres of land, at sixpence per acre, &c.

· Elias de Rommesbothem (*Ramsbotham*) holds, in the same manner, thirty eight acres of land ; whereof four acres are at eight-pence per acre; and the remaining thirty-four acres at four-pence per acre; rendering, at the same seasons, thirteen shillings and four-pence. And it is found, by measurement by the surveyors, that this land contains three acres, one rood, more than are set down in the rent-roll, every acre of which is worth four-pence more than what they have been let for, before the lord's council, &c.

Richard son of John de Romworch (sometimes *Ramworth*) holds in the same manner thirty-two acres of land, whereof thirty acres are at fourpence per acre, and the remaining two acres at two pence per acre; rendering every year, at the seasons aforesaid, ten shillings and four-pence. And it is found by the survey that that land contains thirteen acres, three roods, more than it stands for in the rental, which are worth three shillings and eleven-pence, per annum, price per acre four-pence. And it remains similarly, before the council, &c.

John son of Adam (the) *Miller* holds in the same manner six acres, of land, which the said Richard previously held, at six-pence per acre, &c., and it is found that that land contains one acre one rood, nineteen perches, more than it stands for in the rent-roll, of which every acre is worth sixpence a year. And so it remains until "discussed" before the lord's council, &c.

Madok Cunñok (*Madog Cynnog*) holds in "Pemaningy" (*Penmaen-y-ci*), nine acres of land, at sixpence per acre, &c.

John son of Adam Miller holds. in the same place, one acre of land, paying, at the seasons aforesaid, sixpence.

Richard del Birches (*Birches* vulgarly corrupted into *Burgess*, and confounded with *Birchenshaw*) and William de Groves (query whether of the "*Groes*," now a hamlet at a short distance), hold two acres of land, price per acre sixpence, &c. And the same parties hold two parcels of (inclosed) land, and waste, which until now they have held for seven shilling a year; and now they are measured by the surveyors, and it is found that they contain thirty-five acres, they are rented to the same (parties) from this time forth : viz., ten acres at sixpence per acre, and twenty five acres at four-pence per acre; rendering annually, at the aforesaid seasons, thirteen shillings and fourpence; to begin so to pay from the eighth year of King Edward (the Third, A.D. 1334). And so making an increase of six shillings and four-pence per annum.

Sum total of all the farms of the hamlets of " Cader and Pennan-kyngy,"

At Midsummer	. . .	xxviijs.	jd. ob.
Michaelmas	. . .	xxviijs.	jd, ob.

forty-six shillings and three pence, yearly, for one hundred and sixty-one acres, one rood, of land and waste.

NOTE.—And further by mensuration of extent, as appears in the above particulars, sixteen acres, one and a-half rood, nineteen perches, more of land are found, which if they were drawn out, might be let for five shillings, and five-pence, three farthings, per annum.

Herbage.—And there remain of the lord's portion, in the township of Segroyt, seven hundred and sixty-six and a half acres, and four perches, more of woodland and waste; for which the lord takes no yearly profit, excepting that the community of the township pay the lord annually for the herbage of their cattle, for the year, at the two seasons aforesaid, six shillings, and eight-pence. And yet, if they were divided, and drawn out by apportionment, every acre would, on an average, be worth yearly, two-pence at least. And so the apportionment (rental) might be made fifty-four shillings, and five-pence, per annum more than at present.

Total for leyland, annually, six shillings, and eight-pence.

Recognition of Natives.—And there are four natives of the soil, who are not tenants, every one of whom pays the lord twelve-pence per annum, at the two aforesaid seasons, as a yearly recognition, so long as they hold no land; namely, Jor. Duy (*Iorwerth Ddu*), Atha ap Eignon Saer (*Adda ab Eignon y saer*), Heillyn ap Eignon Saer, and Eignon ap Guyon Dyonal; but this last tarries *without* upon the land of the Lord Roger de Grey (of Ruthin). Therefore, he is removed with his cattle, his effects, &c.

Amount of annual recognition, four (?) shillings, from three natives.

This is certainly curious, and looks like a remnant of the nomadic custom, reminding us of the days of the patriarchs.

And there was one park, formed of portions of two hamlets,

containing altogether, one thousand, sixty-six, and a half acres, five perches, which has been allotted, as appears immediately following :

William Curteis (*Curtis*) holds one hundred and twenty acres of the same park, in quit by the charter of the Lord William de Monte Acute, in feoff, &c., for which he used before to pay annually six pounds, and now he has the same rent-free in exchange for the hamlets of Penmayn and Lessemayn," (*Penmaen* and *Llysymaen*), the survey of which is made elsewhere. All the other tenants of the same park, hold by relief, from the time of the Earl of Lancaster.*

Richard de Crofton (sometimes *Grafton*) holds thirty-two acres of land, price per acre, twelve-pence, &c. And the same Richard holds three and a half roods, which have belonged to the lordship of "Astret;" paying annually, at the seasons aforesaid, twelve-pence.

Then follows a list of the tenants, all of whom pay at the rate of twelve-pence per acre; except the first named, who only pays six-pence per acre, annually.†

	A.	R.	P.		s.	d.
William Curteis	vii.	0	0	. .	3	6
Alexander Danney	v.	0	0	. .	5	0
Robert de Schipton (*Shipton*) . . .	ix.	ij.	0	. .	9	6
Alexander Hemmyng (*Hemming*) . . }						
Richard Chiry (*Chirry*) . . . . . }	vi.	ij.	0	. .	6	6
Adam filius Isoldæ	x.	0	0	. .	10	0
Thurstan de Mouston (*Mostyn*) . . .	x.	0	0	. .	10	0
Richard de Wevere (*Weaver*) . . .	vi.	iij.	xx	. .	7	10¼
John de Hoghton (*Houghton*) . . .	vii.	iij.	xx	. .	7	10¼
Also	xii.	0	0	. .	12	0
Richard Chiry	ii.	ij.	0	. .	2	6
Alexander Hemmyng	ii.	ij.	0	. .	2	6
Henry de Frodesham (*Frodsham*) . .	vi.	0	0	. .	6	0
John de Pontefract	ii.	0	0	. .	2	0

* Thomas Plantagenet, grandson of Henry III., executed as a rebel, in A.D. 1321-2, but canonized as a saint in 1389. He held Denbigh in right of his wife, the Lady Alice Lacy. See the Postmortem Inquisition.

† This cannot help being interesting to the antiquary, not only because it shows the smallness of ancient farms, compared with the broad acreages of the present day, and the astonishing change which has taken place in the value of land—from six-pence to so many pounds per acre; but likewise it serves to illustrate the historical fact that De Lacy, by confiscations and removals, succeeded in establishing an English colony in this part of Wales.

And, besides, the said John holds in the same place, ten acres of land, for which he used to pay ten shillings a year; and now he has these in quit by the charter of the lord, for one oxgang, appertaining to his burgage at "Dynebiegh."

Roger de Wyssbewell (*Wisbywell*) . .	iv.	ij.	xx.	. .	4	7½
William le Wayte (sometimes *Waite*) .	iv.	ij.	xx.	. .	4	7½
Henry de Cliderowe (*Clitheroe*) . . .	xl.	0	0	. .	40	0

But by measurement of extent (or survey) they are not found to be more than thirty-nine and a half acres, and half a rood; consequently, of right, he ought to be relieved of four-pence half-penny of his rent.

John de Rened	vi.	ij.	0	.	6	6
Adam de Birhenshagh (*Burchenshaw*) .	xxvi.	ij.	xxvii.	.	26	8
Margeria and Margareria, daughters of William Griffud (*Gruffydd*, *Griffith*)	xiv.	j.	xiij½.	.	14	4
Adam de Penket	vi.	0	0	.	6	0
Agneta de Welford (sometimes *Walford*)	iv.	0	0	.	4	0
Matilda, widow (qy. of *Welford?*) . .	vi.	ij.	0	.	6	6
William de Cader (of *Cader*) . . .	x.	0	0	.	10	0
Robert le Taillour (the *tailor*, hence *Taylor*)	x.	0	0	.	10	0
Thomas de Bromleye (*Bromley* and *Bramley*)	v.	j.	0	.	5	3
John de Cader	v.	j.	0	.	5	3
John, son of Henry de Billyng (*Billings*)	ix.	0	0	.	9	0
William de Brunleye (*Burnley*) . .	ii.	0	0	.	2	0
Robert del Grenes (query of the *Green* Denbigh?)	ii.	0	0	.	2	0
Radulphus son of Robert de Lacheford (that is, *Ralph Lachford*) . .	vii.	j.	0	.	7	3
Adam son of Robert le Taillour .	v.	0	0	.	5	0
Margery and Johanna daughters of Henry de Docworth (*Duckworth*) .	v.	0	0	.	5	0
Adam de Casteley (*Castley* or *Caseley*)	v.	0	0	.	5	0
Henry del Spen. (*Spen*, *Span*, *Spon* &c)	xiv.	0	0	.	14	0
William del Mos (*Moss*) . . .	xxi.	ij.	0	.	21	6
Henry le Cartewrught (the *Cartwright*).	vi.	0	0	.	6	0
Henry son of Roger (qy. Cartwright?)	viii.	0	0	.	8	0
Thomas de Hulton (mostly *Hilton*) .	xxxvii.	ij.	0	.	37	6
John le Walsh' (qy. the "Welshman"?)	x.	0	0	.	10	0
Adam Birchenshagh, junior . .	x.	0	0	.	10	0
Adam Mody (*Moody*) . . .	ix.	0	0	.	9	0
John le Flecch. (*Fletcher*) . .	vii.	0	0	.	7	0

E

Thomas de Staynford (mostly *Stanford*)	iv.	0	0	. .	4	0
Adam de Mostyn	x.	0	0	. .	10	0

And the same Adam hold ten acres (which used to rent at ten shillings), in quit by the charter of the lord, for his oxland appertaining to his town house under the walls.

Juliana and Isabella, daughters of Henry de Hallum	x.	0	0	. .	10	0
William *Russell*	x.	0	0	. .	10	0
William Basket (qy. *Bascet*, now *Basset?*)	xxi.	j. 0		. .	21	3
William de Docworth . .	xxviij.	0	0	. .	28	0
Hugh del *Lowe*	x.	0	0	∴	·	10	0
William Cocus (*Cox*) and John Bercare (*Barker?*)	ix.	ij. xx		. .	9	7½
Richard de Bullesburgh (*Billesborough*)	xii.	0	0	. .	12	0
Richard son of William *Cox*. . .	iii.	0	0	. .	3	0
William le Morteruakere (the *Mortarmaker?*).	vi.	0	0	. .	6	0
Richard son of William Morteruakere	i.	ij. xx		. .	1	7½

And no more, because one rood and a half of his land, for which the rent paid was four-pence half-penny, is destroyed by the lord's quarry.

Thomas le Morteruakere . . .	vi.	0	0	. .	6	0
John le *Chapman* . . .	x.	iij. 0		. .	10	9
Hugh Carect' (qy. carecti?) i.e. of the Morass, *Huw o'r Gors*). . .	iii.	0	0	. .	3	0
Richard del Mos (*Moss*) . . .	iv.	0	0	. .	4	0
Emma del Mos	iv.	j. 0		. .	4	3
Richard del Byrches . . .	xx.	0	0	. :	20	0
William de Byrches . . .	ii.	0	0	. .	2	0
Robert Casteleye . . .	vii.	ij. 0		. .	7	6
Robert de Wyberlye (*Wyberley, Weverley*)	iv.	0	0	. .	4	0
William del Grenes . . .	xxiii.	0	0	, .	23	0
Richard atte Beche (*at Beck*) .	vi.	0	0	. .	6	0
Thomas le Schepherde (the *Shepherd*)	x.	0	0	. .	10	0
Robert de Hulton, senior .	xxxix.	ij. 0		. .	39	6
William le Peyntour (the *Painter*) .	iv.	0	0	. .	4	0
Thomas Bateman . . .	xxx.	0	0	. .	30	0
Henry Teleman (*Telman*) . .	vi.	0	0	. .	6	0
Richard son of Henry de Segroyt .	viii.	0	0	. .	8	0
John son of William (qy. De Segroyt?)	vi.	0	0	. .	6	0
Thomas Pye	vi.	0	0	. .	8	6
Henry le Deyesone (*Dyson* or *Tyson*)	viii.	0	0	. .	8	0

Henry de *Yoxhale*	vi.	0	0	. .	6 0
Alan de Bradsagh (*Bradshaw*) . .	ix.	0	0	. .	9 0
Robert son of William le *Carter* . .	ii.	0	0	. .	2 0
Henry de Cliderowe, (*Clitheroe*) at 8d.	iv.	0	0	. .	2 8
Henry *Gryme* (*Graeme*) at 12d. . .	ii.	0	0	. .	2 0
John de Lonnesdale (*Lonsdale*), and					
Thomas de Bonnesdale (*Bonsdale*), at 8d.	iv.	0	0	. .	2 8
John de Paas (*Pass, Pace*), at 12d. .	iii.	0	0	. .	3 0
Roger de Warton (*Warton* or *War-*					
burton), at 12d.	iv.	0	0	. .	4 0
Ditto ditto at 8d. .	ii.	0	0	. .	1 4
William de Warton at 12d. .	ii.	0	0	.	} 3 10¼
Ditto at 10d. .	ii.	j.	0	.	
William le Barbour (the *Barber*) at 8d.	ii.	0	0	. .	1 4
William le *Carpenter*, at 12d. . .	lxxx. iij.	0	£4		0 9

And, besides this, the same *Adam* * holds ten acres, for which he used to pay ten shillings a year. Now he is quit of all rent by the lord's charter, for his ox-land appertaining to his burgage of "Dynbiegh," under the walls.

John le Clerc (the *clerk, clarke, clare*) v 0 0 . . 5 0

Total—Farm rents of Segrwyd Park—
  At Whitsuntide . xxijli. viijs. viijd. q.
  At Michaelmas . xxijli. viijs. viijd. q.

So making annually xlivli. xvijs. ivd. ob.

For nine hundred and five acres, one rood and a half, and half a perch of land.

And there is no more farmed land in Segroyt Park (*de firma acrarum Parci de Segroyte*), since one hundred and fifty acres, which used to produce seven pounds, ten shillings, annually, have been ceded to different tenants in quit, by the written deed of the lord, as appears in the particulars above; and one rood and a half, which used to rent at four-pence half-penny a year, has been destroyed by the lord's quarry.

De Beckele here adds a note of the fact that the tenants afore-named occupied ten acres, three roods, four perches and a half, more than they were charged for, and that that land might be made to

* There must be a clerical error here. Query,—Whether it should have been the same *William*, or if the person intended before was Adam *son* of William le Carpenter, &c. ?

pay seven shillings and two-pence a year, reckoning it to be worth
eight-pence per acre.—"*Et sic supersunt de Parco de Segroyt,
x acræ, iij rodæ, iiij perticatæ dimidia, quæ omnino cedunt
avauntagio mensurationis tenentium supradictorum, quæ si extractæ
fuerint valerent per annum vij s. ij d., precium acræ viij d.*"

TOWNSHIP OF GARTHHENNOUGH.

Distinguishment of Escheats.—The township of "Gathhennouth"
(or "Garthenough" and "Garthennuch," according to the present
Welsh orthography, *Garthynwch*, now called *Garth*), which
contains three hundred and sixty-seven acres and a half, and ten
perches, was in the time of the princes in the holding of free
tenants. And thence five parts fell into the hand of the lord as
escheat, at the time of the Conquest of Wales, by reason of the
tenants thereon dying contrary to the peace; and the sixth part
which remained in the tenure of the progeny of "Gruffudd ap
Mereduth," fell to the lord by way of exchange, insomuch as the
Lord Henry de Lacy, late Earl of "Lyncolne" and Lord of
"Dynebiegh," first, after the Conquest, made exchange with the
said family, and allotted to them so much land in the "vill of
Gartherewyt" (*Gartherwyd*, now called *Caserwyd* for *Garthserwyd*), as their portion in Garthennogh" contained. And that
portion here contained forty-one acres, one rood, and one perch and
a half. And so the township of Garthennogh exists entirely (is
wholly) in the hands of the lord, and is apportioned as appears
immediately below.

Farms (or acreages) of Garthennogh.—David Loyt (*Lloyd*)
holds at will, one acre, and one rood; price per acre, six-pence;
rendering seven-pence half-penny, at Whitsuntide and Michaelmas,
in equal portions.

Roger de Warton holds by relief, ten acres and a half of land,
price per acre, ten-pence; rendering at the aforesaid seasons eight
shillings and nine-pence.

Henry de Cartewrught holds this year eleven acres of land, which
were David ap Cadug.'s (*Cadwogan's*) property, and half an acre
which belonged to Jevan ap Yevan (*Ifan ab Ieuan*), rendering
yearly, at the aforesaid seasons, nine shillings and seven-pence.

Madok ap Ll. Vaghan holds seven acres and a half of land; price per acre, ten-pence; paying at the aforesaid seasons six shillings and three-pence. And the same Madok holds half an acre, eighteen perches, of poor wood and waste, discovered by the survey, &c., [*quæ reperiuntur de incremento per mensurationem extentæ*], and let to him by measurement, to begin with the eighth year [of Edward III], and he pays six-pence a year at the aforesaid seasons.

Eden ap Jor. held four acres and a half of poor land, for which he paid three shillings and nine-pence per annum, at the aforesaid seasons. And now that land is in the hands of the lord by defect of tenancy.

Cadugan ap Eden' holds three acres of land; price ten-pence per acre, rendering at the aforesaid seasons two shillings and six-pence. The same Cadugan holds, of a new apportionment by survey, in the eighth year [of Edward III], half an acre and eighteen perches of waste, and pays at the aforesaid seasons, six-pence. And he begins to pay at the feast of St. Michael, in the eighth year [of the said king's reign].

Henry son of Roger, and Roger de Warton, hold two acres of land, price ten-pence, rendering at the aforesaid seasons twenty-pence.

Robert de Hulton has taken from the survey two acres of poor woodland and waste upon the confines of Segroit, and near his land of "Gechlyreder" [Gechlyreger, *Gellilygaer*, cranberry wood, now *Leger*], price per acre, sixpence; rendering at the aforesaid seasons, twelve-pence. And he commences paying at Michaelmas, in the [aforesaid] eighth year.

Total acreages of Garthhennough, at the seasons of

Pentecost	.	.	xvijs.	vjd.	ob.	q.
St. Michael's	.	.	xvijs.	vjd.	ob.	q.

So annually xxxvs. jd. ob.

[that is thirty-five shillings and three half-pence,] for forty-three acres, one rood, and sixteen perches of land, including the late increase.

Acreage of "Oakenewood."—[*Oakenwood*, but qy. *Coed Accas*, or *Coedcorniworch ?*] Roger de Warton holds in the "Oakenewood" thirteen acres in herbage, and takes nothing from the wood [timber], rendering annually, for the whole, three shillings and four-pence at the seasons aforementioned. This, they say, he holds by relief.

Robert de Hulton [of *Halton* or *Hilton,*) and Roger de Warton hold, in the same manner, thirteen acres, rendering at the aforesaid seasons three shillings and four-pence.

William le Peyntour [*the painter*], holds there at will thirty-four acres in herbage, for which he takes nothing [no profit] of the wood rendering at the aforesaid seasons six shillings and one penny.

Gregory de Wirhale [*of Wirral*], holds there, in the same manner, two acres, rendering at the aforesaid seasons, six-pence. And thirty acres more will be found in the Okenewode by measurement, which are released to Adam Birchenshagh [saving the oak to the lord, if it please the lord, &c.], rendering annually at the afore-mentioned seasons ten shillings. And he begins to pay, if it please the lord, in the ninth year of king Edward (A.D. 1335).

Total, farms of Okenewode, with the "new increase," in season, eleven shillings and eight-pence, and eleven shillings and eight-pence. So making annually twenty-three shillings and four-pence, for four score and two acres of land and wood,—

xxiiis. ivd.

[at Whitsuntide and Michaelmas].

And there are, of the township of "Garthhennogh," two hundred and forty-two acres, and fourteen perches of land, wood, and waste, included in Segroit Park, which are apportioned with the rest of Segroit Park above, &c.

CONCLUDING REMARKS.

Segrwyd Park, at the present day, is confined to the richly wooded, and romantic domain round Segrwyd Hall, the residence of the dowager Mrs. Mostyn. After the battle of Blackheath, Henry VII gave this demesne to Robert Dolben, as it appears from the *Harl. M.S.S., No.* 1971, *folio* 121, *Brit. Museum,* where it is said that he had "for his service at Blackheath; and his voyage to Exeter, with two noblemen, upon his *one* cost, with horses, a grant of certayne lands in Segroyt." There is also a passport granted to his son David, who was in the service of Henry VIII, of which the following is a copy:

"Bee it knowne to a . . maner of Sherriffes, Bayles, Counstables, and to all other the Kinge's officers, Gretinge, That I, Sir Jo : Wallope, Kt., and Highe Marschall of this Kinges towne of Calles [*Calais*], and Marches of the same, Doe license thys bearer, David Dolbyn, by thys his Passporte. Wherffore, I desire you and ev'ry of you to suffer him to passe and repasse, without any interrucion or lett to the contrarie, into the Realme of Englande. Written att Calles the first daye of Maye . . .

"SR JO : WALLOPE."

His grandson, Robert Dolbyn, "Recorder and Steward of the Lordship of Denbighland, under Sir Tho : Salusbury, married Marslye da : to Tho : Salusbury, of Denbighe," by whom he had "Robert Wyn Dolbyn, of Denbighe," who married "Janne da : to Owen ap Reignalt of Llinllygwy, Com: Cærn., by whom he had several children; as, David Dolben, Doctor-in-Divinitie, Bisshop of Bangor ; Henry Dolben, of Denbighe, mercer, married to Elizabeth Gethin, da : to Robert Gethin, of Kernioge; Ffoulk Dolben married to Margt. da : to Th : ap Harry ap Holl : ap Kend ; ; Owen and Rich : dyed S. P. ; Katherine wife of Piers Hughes, of Disart ; Emme, wife of Piers Lloyd of Rydudordd (*Rhydorddwy Fawr*, near Rhyl]; John Dolbyn, of Denbighe, who married Alles, da : to Rich : Mid'elton, of Denbighe, &c., by whom he had William Dolbyn, Doctor of Divinitie, &c. ; William of Denbighe, High Sherriff, 1663, mar : to Jane, da : to Edw : Holland of Conway, *
* * Foxhold [*Foxhall, Denbigh*], by whom he had John Dolbyn of Segroite, Com : Denb : * who mar : Jane, da : of Jo : Thellwalle of Bathaverne, or Place Coch, whose sonne John Dolben, of Segroite, mar : mar : Mary Jo : Parry of Wrixham ; and his sister Jane married Sir Jeffrey Shakerley," of Gwersyllt.

The Segroit estate was sequestered by Cromwell. The male line of the Dolbens became extinct in the time of Queen Anne, and by the marriage of the heiress, the patrimony passed to the Mostyns, in whose family it still remains. The last proprietor, Captain Mostyn, R.N., became allied to the Townshends of Trevalyn.

* Lieutenant Colonel in King Charles's army, during the Civil War.

CHAPTER III.

DE BECKELE'S SURVEY CONTINUED—THE REMAINING PORTION
OF THE WAPENTAKE OF CINMERCH—THE TOWNSHIPS OF PRION,
CERNYVED, POSTYN, SCEIBION, BACHYMBYD, LLWYN, LLEWESOG,
BRYNLLUARTH, CASERWYD, CLICEDIG, KILFORD, AND YSTRAD
OWAIN.—RENTAL AND CUSTOMS.

TOWNSHIP OF PEREYON.

THE township of "Pereyon" (*Prion*) which contains one thousand,
two hundred, and eight acres and a half, twenty-five perches, of
wood and waste, was, in the time of the princes, entirely in the
holding of natives, in eight gavels, and the third part of one
(other) gavel. And thereof there devolved about one entire
gavel into the hands of the lord, by reason of deaths contrary
to the peace (that is, by confiscations, consequent upon the late
war in Wales, and convictions arising therefrom), the particulars
of which are given below with the escheated farms. And seven
gavels, and the third part of one gavel (more) remain as yet in the
hands of living tenants, the particulars of whose tenure and services
are given below :—

David Lyot (*pro. Loyt, Lloyd*), and
David ap Yevan ; each of whom holds the third of one gavel.
Cadugan ap Eignon holds two parts of one gavel.
Madoc ap Yevan holds the half of one gavel.
David ap Gron. Vaghan, and
Madoc ap Wyon (*Gwïon*), each of whom holds three parts of one
    gavel.

Jevan ap David.	David Vaghan.
David ap Lauwargh (*Llywarch*).	Jor. Gogh (*Iorwerth Goch*).
Gron. ap Heillyn.	Jor. Goryth (*Grydd*).
Eign. (*Einion*) ap David.	Lanwarth (*Llywarch*) ap David.
Eign. ap Ithel.	Cadugan ap David.
David ap Eignon.	Gron. ap Madoc.
Jevan ap Eignon.	Gron. Voil ap Eignon.
Jevan ap Madoc.	Madoc ap Eignon.

    Each of these holds the fourth part of one gavel.

And for every one of these gavels, and the third part of one gavel, they pay twelve pence of tung; all together performing the same services as one of the gavels of Segroit above; and it matters not who may be holding thereof, he is upon the same conditions, in all things, as one of the natives of Segroit above, whether they be few or many.

Amount of Tung from Pereyon annually, at the feast of All Saints, seven shillings and four pence.

Amount of provision for the prince's servants at Christmas, five shillings and one half-penny.

At Mid-Lent, four shillings and three pence one farthing, and the third part of a farthing.

At the Nativity of St. John the Baptist (Midsummer, called in Welsh, *Gwyl Ifan yn yr haf*) four shillings and three pence, one farthing, and the third-part of a farthing.

At the feast of the Exaltation of the Holy Cross, four shillings and three-pence, one farthing, and the third-part of a farthing.

So making annually seventeen shillings, and ten pence, one half-penny. That is, besides their tunc-rent.

De Beckele here propounds a question for the escheators, with the view of settling a dispute which seems to have been raised by the tenants, that if the aforesaid natives were entitled to a share proportionate with the amount of their tunc-rent, as common, in the woods, wastes, and lands, one with another, then the proportion of each gavel would be four score and eleven acres, one rood and a half, six perches, of " scrubland" (uncleared wood), and fifty-three acres and a half, and half a rood, of common ; and as much woodland, and waste be escheated to the lord as should appertain to one gavel. Nevertheless, according to the common assertion, neither these natives, nor any others of this commote, have part of the common-wood, or waste, except as common of pasture for their own animals and needful beasts by permission of the lord's foresters. It appears that the tenants had become dissatisfied, and the case was referred to the lord's council or court, as our author says, " *Ipsi tamen nativi hoc non concedunt, super quo considerandum est inter concilium domini.*"

Our author proceeds to enumerate the tenants :—

John la Stalemynne (qy. *Sion y'Stalwyn*, John of the Stallion? that

F

is, the groom,) holds four acres of land, at the same price (six pence), rendering at the aforesaid seasons, two shillings.

Madoc ap Yevan, for half an acre, four pence.

Richard Honeydrope, *(Honeydrop,)* for twenty acres, ten shillings.

David Horsyn, *(Horson,)* for half an acre, six pence.

Gregory de Wirhale, for one rood and a half, two pence.

Adam Michel, for one acre, six pence.

John de Groves, for one acre, six pence.

Cadugan ap Eignon holds *(de purprestura sibi de novo arentata anno Edwardi Regis octavo)* half an acre, nine perches, paying at the seasons aforesaid, three pence.

Cadugan ap David Voil *(the Bald)* holds, of a similar inclosure let to him from the aforesaid year (8 *Edward III*) sixty-nine perches, rendering two pence. Yevan ap Madoc Gogh holds, of inclosure let to him from the same year, twenty perches for one penny.

Total—farms of Pereyon, at the seasons of

Whitsuntide	viijs.	.	vjd.
Michaelmas	viijs.	.	vjd.
So, annually	xvijs.	.	0d.

For thirty-three acres, one rood and a half, and eighteen perches of land.

Herbage.—And so there remain, of the escheated portion of the aforementioned gavel, according to a just proportion, one hundred and eleven and a half acres, eight perches, of woodland, and waste, of which the lord takes no annual profit, excepting that the whole township pays yearly for the herbage of the said "purpart," six shillings, at two seasons. And yet if they had been separated and drawn out, every acre, for apportionment, would have been worth, on an average, four pence a year, at least. And so the rental might be made twenty-one shillings and ten pence halfpenny more than at present.

Total for herbage, yearly, vjs.

HAMLET OF BRENBACLE.

Distinguishment of Escheats.—The hamlet of Brenbacle *(Brynbagle, Brynbagl, Brynbagyl)* which contains four hundred and twenty-seven and a half acres, is said to have at one time belonged to the aforesaid township of Pereyon, and is wholly an escheat of the lord. And in the time of the Earl of Lancaster the said hamlet was released to eight tenants (to be held in ley) who afterwards built (on) the said hamlet, and converted one hundred and sixty acres thereof into arable land, contrary to the letter of the said lease, &c. Ten tenants now rent the same in eight holdings, rendering annually, at Whitsuntide and Michaelmas, sixty shillings, for four hundred and twenty-seven and a half acres of land and waste.

Note.—And that hamlet is at the lord's will, because the *Earl of Lancaster,* who so re-leased the said hamlet to them, had no power except during his own life-time; and because the aforesaid tenants have turned the said hamlet to tillage, contrary to the stipulation of the lease. For reasons which appear in the " Concluding Remarks" of this chapter, the original must be given.—"*Et est illa hamella ad voluntatem domini, eo quod* COMES LANCASTRIÆ, *qui dictam hamellam eis sic dimisit, non habuit potestatem, &c., nisi pro tempore suo; et quia prædicti tenentes dictam hamellam manuoperaverunt contra formam dimissionis, &c.*" And two hundred acres thereof are worth one hundred shillings per annum, price per acre six-pence. And two hundred and twenty-seven and a half acres, which are poor waste, are worth, in herbage, with the other land, six shillings and eight-pence, a year, at least. And so the said hamlet might let at thirty-six shillings and eight pence more than at present.

TOWNSHIP OF KERVYNEVET.

The township of Kerveynevet, *(Kernoved, Cernyfed,)* which was formerly a wilderness, (a forest brake, *boscus vastus,*) from the time of the princes, is a newly made township, apportioned (inclosed) from the time of the *Earl of Lancaster,*who first let the same, and contains six hundred and thirty-six and a half acres, thirty-two perches. And insomuch as the lord and his council had been given to understand that the tenants of the same township had inclosed for themselves, more of the common than had been let, (arrented,) it was ordered that the surveyors and escheators should proceed to the said " vill," and examine the inclosures so made by the said tenants. This resulted in the measurement of each holding separately, as appears below, for De Beckele adds, "*Cum ibidem, accesserent, et de hujus purpresturis inquisierint, non reperierint, qui eis certas metas hujus purpresturæ monstrare scriverint propter quod ipsi per demonstrationem ipsorum tenentium ad hoc juratorum tenuras cujuslibet tenentis per se mensurare fecerunt, et mensuram tunc repertam irrotulare fecerunt prout subsequitur.*"

And the tenants say that they pay for every acre they hold, in the said "vill" six-pence a year.

	A.	R.	P.		s.	d.
Simon de Whitacre	v.	0	xxxiv	...	2	7¼
Adam de Whitacre	ix.	0	j	...	4	6
William de Rommesbothum . . .	xxi.	ij.	xiv	...	10	9½
The same	vii.	0	xxiij	...	3	6¾
Richard le Turner *(the turner)* . .	vii.	0	xxij	...	3	1
John le Turner	xlii.	iij.	xxxij	...	21	5½
Simon le Turner	xii.	0	xxxiv	...	6	1¼
The same	xi.	iij.	xxvij	...	5	11½
Roger del Holyn	iv.	0	jv	...	2	0
Robert, son of Simon le Turner . .	ii.	ij.	xxxj	...	1	4
The same	xix.	j.	xxxij	...	9	8½
Roger del Peek	xi.	0	xvj	...	5	6¼
Robert, son of John le Turner . .	iii.	j.	xxxiv	...	1	8½
Thomas le Turner	vii.	0	xxx	...	3	8
The same	xv.	0	viij	...	7	6¼
Thomas le Hore	xvi.	0	xxxix	...	8	9¼
The same, and Robt. son of Sim. le Turner	vii.	0	xxiv	...	3	6¾
William Lathum (in five holdings) .	xvii.	ij.	xxiij½	...	8	9¼
The same, and William de Brandavesholm	ix.	j.	vij	...	4	7¾
Eignon Drankes	lii.	0	vij	...	26	0
Elias de Holond *(Holland)* . . .	xlviii.	ij.	ix	...	24	3¼
Henry del Spen	iv.	ii.	xxxiii	...	1	10
William de Dukworth	xiv.	0	0	...	7	0
William Mody	viij.	0	0	...	4	0
Margaret de Rommesbotham . . .	xi.	ii.	ix	...	5	9½
Hugh del Hales	xv.	0	xv	...	7	6½
Alexander le Hore	v.	0	xxiv	...	2	7½

Besides William de Rommesbotham, and Simon de Whitacre, who hold xxiiA. iijR. xvjP. (late in the occupation of Richard le Turner) for which they pay eleven shillings and five pence per annum.

The rest are native Welsh: in all, thirty tenants; who pay, for thirty-six farms, ten pounds, seven shillings, and seven pence, one farthing yearly; for four hundred and fifteen and a half acres, and thirty-six perches of land.

There are also two hundred and twenty acres, three and a half roods, sixteen perches, of waste, the herbage of which is common to all the tenants, and for which they pay fifteen shillings, yearly in season.

Marghthenbouk.—And there is a certain wood there called Marghthenbouk* which contains four score and three acres, and twenty perches, in which the said tenants have their animals by permission, &c.   And the ground occupied by the wood is of no value, because it overhangs lofty precipitous steeps *(pendet in altis collibus.)* And all the above-named tenants claim common of pasture there, in respect of the above-mentioned ley.

And there is also another wood there nearly laid waste (cleared) which is called Le Bedowe, *(y Bedw,* in the vicinity of *Penbedw,)* and it is capable of being inclosed, because the aforesaid tenants claim common there, for the above reason, &c., and this unjustly. And the same wood contains four score and fourteen acres, seven perches, from which the lord has no profit; and yet every acre would be worth, for apportionment, six-pence a year at least.   And then the increase might be made forty-seven shillings more than at present.

Escaerwen.—And the lord has a wood there inclosed (in a ring fence) called Escarwen, *(Iscaerwen,* and *Esgairwen,)* which is close upon the boundaries of Karnyvenet *(Cernyfed, Carnyfed,* qy. *Carn-Ednyfed?)*   And it contains two hundred and one and a half acres, ten perches, from which the lord takes no yearly profit, neither can he take anything without the waste, *(nec capere potest absque vasto)* but along with the waste.   And if the herbage (that is, of the open portion) thereof were fenced out, it would be worth six shillings and eight pence per annum.   Nevertheless, all the tenants of Karnyvenet claim common of pasture there in consideration of the aforesaid fifteen shillings which they pay for grass.   And it does not come into the "total" (amount) of the survey until it is discussed before the lord's council, whether this community ought or ought not to have it.

* The name intended would seem to be *Marchenbwll,* which was, probably, situated somewhere about *Difwys,* in the deep ravines south of *Moel-y-boeed.*

Bishopeswall.—There is, also, there a certain waste called Bisshopeswalle, which contains one thousand, one hundred and twenty-
seven acres, three and a half roods—with the hamlet of Berebowe and
Havotlum adjoining—the pasture of which is sold yearly to the
community for twenty shillings. And yet if it should be apportioned,
every acre would be worth one penny yearly at least. And so the
apportionment would be made seventy-three shillings and nine pence,
three farthings, per annum. And if the lord thought proper to occupy the said pasture with his own animals, then he might sustain
(maintain) there eight bulls, and one hundred and four score and
twelve cows, in winter as well as in summer, and have sufficient fod-
der in the same waste for the sustenance of the said animals in
winter.

The pasture and herding of these cattle, De Beckele estimates at
eight pence per head for the year.

Total value of Bisshopeswall, one year with another, twenty
shillings.

TOWNSHIP OF POSTU.

Proceeding with an abridgement of the " Extenta,"* we come to
the township of Postu (now called *Postyn*) which is said to contain
one thousand and ten acres, three roods, and ten perches, of land,
wood, and waste, in the tenure of natives. Postu, with Kolforn and
Kywedyk (*Kilford* and *Cliciedig*, properly *Cilcedig*) in the time of
the princes, consisted of twenty-three gavels, each of which, if evenly
proportioned, would have fifty-three acres, and three perches; of
which eleven gavels, and a half, and the third part of a gavel, all in
the township of Postyn, remain in the holding of " living tenants,"
(natives still in possession,) comprehending six hundred and twenty-
seven acres, one rood, two perches of land, wood, and waste, &c. And
twenty-one gavels, and the sixth part of a gavel, in the said three
townships, have fallen, as escheats, into the hands of the lord. Eight
natives hold one gavel each, and five others hold each half a gavel.
Three other (Welsh) tenants hold portions of two other gavels.
Each of these gavels pays seven pence one farthing tung yearly at
the feast of All Saints. And each tenant performs all other services

* Made expressly for this work by Mr J. Birtt, of the Chapter-house, Westminster.

in the same manner as those of Segroit. Total amount of tung from the township of Postu, seven shillings, and one penny three farthings per annum; total amount of provision for the prince's servants, twenty-eight shillings, and ten pence, three farthings yearly.

The part escheated to the lord contains three hundred and eighty-three acres, one rood and a half, and eight perches; of which six tenants, hold thirty-eight acres, one rood and a half, ten perches, paying, altogether, twenty shillings per annum. The only English name among them is that of John de Swynemore.

And there remain in Postu three hundred and forty-four acres, three roods, thirty-eight perches, of woodland and waste, of which the lord takes no annual profit, except five shillings for the year's herbage. But a portion of the underwood might be cut every year, and so produce four pounds, three shillings, and eleven pence half-penny.

And there is a wood there called Coydragheyn, which occupies one hundred and fifty-eight acres, one rood and a half, whereof the lord takes (receives) no yearly profit, by reason of the thickness (density) of the great oaks there, and because all the tenants of Postu claim common of pasture there, in consideration of the five shillings aforesaid.

TOWNSHIP OF SKEYBEON.

The township of Skeybeon (*Sceibion, Ysceibion, Ysgeibion*) contains eight hundred and forty-seven acres of land, wood, and waste, and is entirely an escheat of the lord. Probably, all the native tenants " died contrary to the peace," and hence this township became principally an English settlement. Here follows the list of tenants:—

Yevan ap Yevan Siewe.
Hugh de Spen.
Eignon Ove.
William Mody, and
Marg. his wife.
Elias de Plesynton.
Stephen del Grene.
John del Spen.
Ralph de Wode.
Richard de Paunton (*Panton*).

William le Taillour.
Robert de Postu.
Richard be Hale.
Henry de Plesynton.
Henry Cosyn.
Jor. son of Wm. le Cartwright.
Thomas de Oweleye.
Ken. Loyt.
Robert de Lacheford.
Lawargh Gogh.

Henry de Bolde.
Robert de Chaddesleye.
Jevan Goth (*Ifan Goch*).
Jor. Vagh.
John Pygot.   [*Hurt ?*).
David Hurt (qy. *Hurst*, or *Dafydd*
Yockin Duy.
John de Swynmor.   [*farry ?*)
Eignon de Botuarre (qy. of *Bod-*
Henry de Sutton.
William le Cartwright.
John le Rode.
Robert the Miller.
Alan le Rede.
Adam Wildyng.
William Staleworthman.
David Siewe.

Robt. son of Wm. le Serjaunt.
Richard del Spen.
William de Plesynton.
Mad. le Taillour.
Adam de Eccleston.
Katherine Spilloponne.
Henry de Yoxhale.
David le Taillour.
Richard le Turnur.
Eignon Heen (*Einion Hên*).
David ap Edene. Weyn.
Yockyn, Groom of the Foresters.
Roger le Haiward (*Hayward*).
Reginald de Hale.
Robert de Hale.
Eden. Ove.
John del Spen.

Avisia, Agnes, and Anabella, } daughters of Robt. de Eccleston.

These hold (collectively) six Tuthyns (*tyddynod*), one " place," and two hundred and seventy-seven acres, ten perches of land ; for which they pay nineteen pounds, three shillings, and eight pence, one farthing, per annum.

And there are there one hundred and sixty-nine acres, three and a half roods, ten perches, of land and wood, for which the lord takes no yearly profit, but the aforesaid tenants claim common of pasture there for all their beasts.

And there is a water-mill there rendering annually twenty shillings ; but formerly it produced forty shillings.

TOWNSHIP OF MAGHENBET.

The township of Maghhenbet (*Bachymbyd*) contains eight hundred and forty acres, three roods and a half, of land, wood, and waste, in the holding of free tenants. Thereof Ralph ap Meredith and Jeuaf ap Meredith held the third-part of the township, which third part fell " entire" to the lord, as so much escheat, because all the tenants rose contrary to the peace in two wars.* And the sixth-

* We are left uninformed to what " two wars " De Beckele alludes. Could they be the insurrection of Madoc (ap Llewelyn) in 1294, and the revolt of Sir Griffith Lloyd in 1322? or the commotions of Edward the Second's reign—the rebellion of Thomas Plantagent, then Lord of Denbigh ?

part of the same township was in the tenure of the descendants of
" Gruff ap Meryd." (*Griffith ap Meredith, Gruffydd ab Meredydd*)
And thereof one-half fell to the lord as escheat, by reason of the
aforesaid insurrections.

Thirty-seven tenants, all of whom, except " Robert Griffuth,"
who holds just one acre and a quarter, appear to be English: including five Spens, seven Suttons, two Hales, ten Plesyntons, five
Boldes, two Peeks, and one of each of the following names, Haiward,
Wode, Staleworthman, Chadeleye, Le Mercer, and Lonnesdale, who
hold four hundred and forty-eight acres, one rood and a half, of land;
nineteen acres, ten perches, of meadow; and two " places;" rendering
eighteen pounds and three pence, three farthings, annually in season.

And there are there also sixty-two acres of land and wood of
which the lord takes no profit, &c.

And there is a certain water-mill there rendering thirty-four
shillings and four pence annually in season.

Total rental of Bachymbyd, xix*li.* xiij*s.* vij*d. ob. q.*
That is £19 13s. 7¼d. per annum.

TOWNSHIP OF THLOEN.

The township of Thloen (*Llwyn*) contains one hundred and
thirty-seven acres, three and a half roods, twelve perches, of wood
and waste. And in the time of the princes it was wholly in the
tenure of the family of Owen Goch; but the eighth part of the same
township fell to the lord as an escheat, by reason of the tenants
having died contrary to the peace; and that eighth part is held in
heritage by William de Swynmor, (in virtue of a charter from the
Earl,) whose services are fully detailed among (those of) the tenants
who hold by military service in the township of Lowenny, in the
commote of Isalet, &c.

TOWNSHIP OF LAVASSOK.

The township of Lauassok (*Llewesog, Llawesog,* having outskirts,
probably so called from its woody glen and ravines, forming the
outskirts of the ancient forest of Postyn) contains four hundred
and seventy-eight acres, three and a half roods of land, wood, and
waste. The whole township was, in the time of the princes, held by
free and native tenants: but the greater part has fallen to the lord
as escheat, by reason of the tenants having died contrary to the

G

peace. Three remaining natives render eight-pence yearly as tung, and perform the same services as those of Segroyt. Total amount of provision for the prince's servants :—

Twenty-one pence,
Three farthings,
Half a farthing, and
The fourth part of a farthing

Yearly, at Christmas, Mid-Lent, Midsummer, and the Exaltation of the Holy Cross.

Margaret, daughter of John de Kylford, Thomas de Billyng, Robert Gruffuth, John Pygot, John his son, John de Swynmor, Robert de Kilford, Adam, son of Michael, and John del Grene, together, hold two hundred and twenty-four and a half acres, and thirty-five perches of land; besides fifty-nine acres, one rood, six perches of waste, &c. for which they render seven pounds, twelve shillings, and one penny yearly in season.

And there are there forty-five acres and eleven perches of (inclosed) land; and twenty-six acres, three roods, five and a half perches, of common from which the lord takes no yearly profit, but the whole is left to the advantage of the tenants.

And John de Wyberlee, Jor. ap Lewell, (*Iorwerth ab Llewelyn,*) and Cadug' Bucton, hold a water-mill there, with the mill of Segroyt, rendering for the same nine pounds annually in season.

And Jor. ap Lewell, pays twelve shillings yearly for having a water-course to his mill at Brenthluer.

TOWNSHIP OF BRENTHLUER.

And the township of Brenthluer (*Brynlluarth*), which contains two hundred and twenty-two and a half acres, is in the holding of two free tenants, one of whom holds only fifteen acres. These render twenty pence tung yearly, and perform other small services, like the rest of the free tenants of the commote.

And there is one water-mill there held free by Jorwerth ap Llewelyn.

TOWNSHIP OF GARESHEREWYT.

The township of Garesherewyt (*Garthserwyd*, now *Caserwyd*, erroneously *Caeserwyd*) contains one hundred and fifty-eight acres of wood and waste, held by free native tenants. This township is described by De Beckele as existing in five divisions, and a third part of those divisions (three-fifths) is held by the family of Audoen Goth (*Addwyn Goch*). The portions of this township which have fallen into the lord's hands as escheat, are two houses built upon the common-ground, which are let at two pence per annum; and thirty-six acres, one rood and a half, of wood and waste of which the lord takes no annual profit, except twenty pence for the year's herbage.

TOWNSHIP OF LUGHHERN.

The township of Lughhern (Leghherne, *Llechyrne*, *Llechyrnau*, now called *Llech* and *Talyrne*) contains one hundred and forty-five acres, and one rood, of wood and waste. Out of the five divisions of the same township, the third part is in the tenure of the progeny of Audoen Gogh. Sixty-seven acres and one rood of land, fallen into the lord's hands as escheat, are held by Robert del Grenes, Adam de Penketh, John de Macclesfeld, Agnes de Welleford, John Pygot, John de Swynemor, John de Reved, William de Cader, and William de Brymleye, who render fifty-seven shillings and nine pence, three farthings, annually in season. And there are inclosed in the Park of Segroyt two acres and a half, and thirty-two perches, belonging to this township. There are also ten acres, three roods, of waste, of which the lord takes no profit, but the tenants have that advantage.

TOWNSHIP OF KILKEDYOK.

The township of Kilkedyk (*Cilcedig*, corruptly *Cliciedig*) contains one hundred and twenty-eight acres, twelve perches, of land; and is fallen wholly to the lord as escheat, &c., of which ninety-two acres, and three roods, are held by William and John de Swynmor, by charter from the Earl of Lincoln, in entail, for service as guards of the castle, &c. as appears in detail, among the tenants who hold by military service, in the vill of Loweny, in the wapentake of Issalet.

Thomas de Billynge and John de Swynemor hold twenty-seven acres of land, rendering annually in season, fourteen shillings, and ten pence.

And there are nine acres, one rood, twelve perches, of land; of which the lord takes no yearly profit, but it is all to the advantage of the tenants.

TOWNSHIP OF KYLFORN.

The township of Kylforn (*Kilford*) contains six hundred and seventeen acres, one rood, seventeen perches, of land, wood, and waste; out of which the lord has a manor containing five hundred and seventy eight acres, one rood, seventeen perches. The remainder is held by Ralph de Grenolf, and Adam de Grenolf, who render thirty-six shillings and eight pence annually in season, for thirty-nine acres of land.

TOWNSHIP OF ASTRET OWENE.

The township of Astrett Oweyne (*Ystrad Owain*) was always in demesne, as a manor; besides a cottage, with two crofts, held by bond tenants who did diverse services to the prince. Total customs of native bondmen, eighteen pence yearly in season. Madoc Kannok held formerly a messuage here, but now he has an allowance of waste, rendering for the same eight pence per annum. And Ithell le Coupere (*the cooper*), also held formerly a messuage here, &c.

Here follows an account of the families of native freemen of this commote, and their services, viz.—

Gavael Owen Goch.

1 Mad. ap Lewelin Vaghan   4 Ririd and Madoc, his brothers.
2 Lewellin and Eden. his brothers.   5 Eignon ap Kerewet.
3 Cadug. ap Owen Vaghan.   6 Gruff. Eden. & Tudor his brothers.

Gavael Griff. ap Meredith.

Mad. Vaghan ap Mad. ap Grono, and
Lewellin, his brother.

Gavael Grono ap Morgan.

Jor. ap Egn. ap Jor. ap Egnon Loyd.
David ap Eden. his brother.
David ap Mad. Goz. (*Goch*)
Jevan his brother.

Gavael Ithel Pengwern.

David Loid ap Jor. ap Jevan.
Jevan Vaghan ap Jevan ap Mad.

Amount of provision for the prince's attendants, &c., from the free tenants :—

Thirty-six shillings.
One halfpenny, and
Two parts of one farthing,

And they render five pence annually for building houses.

GENERALITIES.

Common Customs.—Every free tenant, not having an under-tenant, pays for provision for dog-trainers, (*pro pastu luctrarii cum canibus*) and for provision for the penmackewe, and waisson bagheyn, three halfpence annually; but a free tenant having an under-tenant is quit thereof. And this custom is worth eight shillings and three halfpence per annum, taking one year with another. And each bond tenant shall render for the same (custom) three halfpence. All tenants pay the lord for provision for stallions and grooms, and this amounts to six shillings and eight pence yearly. And for provision for two " satellites "* two pence per day, or find them sufficient food and drink. This custom is worth sixty shillings and eight pence annually, and is collected from all the tenants, including those of the bishop, according to their chattels, and should be paid at the Pentecost and the feast of St. Michael.

If a married tenant dies intestate the lord has half his goods ; excepting of corn, which goes to the raglot. If unmarried, the lord takes all, saving the rights of the raglot and the church.

The son of a free tenant gives ten shillings to the lord, as relief, to have his father's land, upon the death of the latter. Descendants in the third degree pay twenty shillings : beyond that degree they have it only at the lord's will, at a valuation. Daughters of free tenants, convicted of wantonness or adultery (*super transgressione luxuriæ vel adulterii*) pay ten shillings ; wives to give ten shillings (*pro morceto*). If they have it not, their nearest relatives are to pay. The son of a bond tenant to pay five shillings for relief; other descendants, to the third degree, ten shillings. Daughters and wives of bond tenants to pay five shillings when convicted upon charges of unchastity. Bees or honey found in the lord's wood to belong to the lord; if in that of tenants to belong to those tenants ; and so also in the case of sparrow-hawks.

The office of *raglot* of the commote is worth sixty-two shillings per annum ; *ringuild*, fifty shillings ; *judge*, twenty-three shillings and four pence ; *forester*, sixty shillings ; *serjeant-of-the-peace*, and satellite, thirty-two shillings ; " *advocar*." twenty shillings ; *amobr*.

---

* Serjeants-at-mace, rather than yeomen of the guard.

four pounds, per annum. Total, sixteen pounds, seven shillings, and four pence.

Forests.—The lord has the forests; but the tenants have house-bote and haybote by view of the foresters (see *Ancient and modern Denbigh*, page 307.) The fall-wood and dead-wood are estimated at twenty shillings per annum; pleas and perquisites of the forest-court at sixty-six shillings and eight pence; customs of the bond tenants for brushwood to repair their hedges, at two shillings yearly. Total, four pounds, eight shillings, and eight pence, taking one year with another.

Perquisites of (other) courts, reliefs, fines, and escheats from both English and Welsh tenants, thirteen pounds, six shillings, and eight pence; besides other small items.

Total annual value of the commote of Caymerch:—£243 14s. 7¼d. and the fourth part of a farthing. And it might be increased by £23 12s. 11¼d. yearly.

CONCLUDING REMARKS.

Upon reference to the Postmortem Inquisition of De Lacy, in a subsequent part of this work, the reader must be struck with astonishment to find this commote tripled in value, in the short space of twenty-three years—from £80 5s. 3½d. per annum, to £243 4s. 7¾d. This arose, probably from numerous escheats, or confiscations, consequent upon the rebellion of Thomas Planta-genet. From the crown (virtually) these passed to Montacute, now (1334) lord of Denbigh.

The foregoing survey will enable us to trace, upon the ordnance map, the limits of the ancient commote of Cinmerch, with consider-able accuracy. On the north and west, it was bounded by the river Ystrad or Lliwen, except near the confluence of that stream with the Clwyd, where De Lacy, in making for himself the manor of Kil-ford, made a diversion from the original and natural boundary, inclosing certain portions of land on the north side, in the immediate neighbourhood of Brookhouse, Whitchurch, Kilford, and Cotton Hall. On the east, we have the Clwyd for a short distance, and the course of the Clywedog for a considerable way, until we turn, at Pontuchel, up the branch coming down from Gyffylliog; thence up another branch-stream to Nant Niwlyg, in the moorland, near the source of the Clwyd. Here, for some half a mile, we have no natural boundary; until we come to a small stream emptying itself into the Alwen, a little below the ancient camp of Caerddunod. Thence, proceeding up the Alwen, for some way, we turn northward up a mountain-stream called the Brennig, and an eastern branch called Bechan. From this water-course, there is, for a few hundred yards, no natural boundary-line, until we come again to the source of the Lliwen; having made a circuit of more than thirty miles. Thus, the whole commote is nearly surrounded by the aforementioned streams, and is well watered throughout.

Perhaps, no tract of country is more diversified in its physical and geological features, considering its extent. From the elevated desert of Hiraethog in the south-west, we come down to a cultivated undulating region, with picturesque glens and woodlands, dipping into the fertile and famous Vale of the Clwyd, towards the east and north-east. The geology of the district is equally interesting. The new and old red sandstone, the limestone, and clay-slate formations seem here to be almost blended together, and it is believed that a coal-field exists under Segroit Park. Beautiful specimens of agate, jasper, and chalcedony are found in the rocks above Llanrhaiadr. There is a cave near Prion, which is several hundred feet long, and very lofty, terminating, so far as human ingress can penetrate, in a natural chamber of a circular form, the diameter of which is about twenty feet. From this point the passage is so narrow that it is impossible to make any further progress. The descent is steep and unpleasant, owing to a stream of water which appears in various places. The same stream, as is believed, pursues a subterranean course of some two miles, and emerges in an ancient bath, called St. Dyfnog's Well, near Llanrhaiadr Church. This " holy well" was celebrated in popish ages for the alleged miraculous efficacy of its waters. Nor have miracles ceased at Llanrhaiadr in Methodist times. Towards the close of the last century, a female of the name of Mrs Anne Parry, who was the first person in this neighbourhood to open her door to itinerant preachers, and to keep a Sunday school at her house, died and was interred here. " Forty-three years after her decease, on the occasion of her son's burial in the same tomb, her coffin was opened, and the body of this excellent woman was found to be in a perfect state of preservation, undecayed in the slightest degree, and her countenance bearing the hues of living health. The very flowers which had been strewed upon her body, it is said, were as fresh in colour, and as fragrant in odour, as when they were first plucked from their native boughs. The body of this lady was exhumed about three years afterwards (1841), and was in the same state of preservation." See *Roscoe's Wanderings in North Wales, Davis' Handbook to the Vale of Clwyd*, and the numerous Methodist and other Welsh publications aud papers of the time. The story is certainly " marvellous," more especially since the miracle extends to the preservation of the flowers, shroud, and timber of the coffin, though imbedded in soil.

The church is a white-washed edifice, with a low square tower, half hidden in a wood. But internally it possesses much to interest the archæologist and ecclesiologist. The date of the great eastern window, of the north aisle, and the tradition connected therewith, have been the subject of antiquarian debate. The painting, which fills it, is a genealogical tree, representing the lineage of the Messiah, springing from the Root of Jesse, including all the kings of the House of David. It is in a fine state of preservation, and the pencillings are masterly; with this drawback, that the figures are so stunted in stature, (from au absurd whim common among the later mediæval painters,) as to give the whole group a grotesque effect, which is utterly at variance with the artistic taste of the present age. The date is,

" m.ccccxxxiii.".—1533.*

On the corresponding window in the south aisle,

" m.ccccbiii."—1508.

On a carving, 1597.

According to tradition the " Jesse window" was twice " piously" preserved from demolition : the first time, at the dissolution of Basingwerk Abbey, when it was purchased with the offerings of pilgrims to St. Dyfnog's Well, and placed here ; and the second time,

* In 1854, the Rev. H. Longueville Jones, an excellent antiquary, pointed out to the members of the Archæological Society, an earlier date and inscription, nearly effaced, which stated that the glass was inserted by a rector of the parish.

AND ITS LORDSHIP. 49

on the outburst of Cromwell's Rebellion, when, to save it from the fanatical fury of the Roundheads, the glass was taken out, placed in the almonry-chest, (a primitive coffer, of rather formidable strength and size, being formed of the trunk of an oak-tree, squared with the axe, and hollowed out with the chisel and adze,) and secretly buried in a neighbouring wood, where it was discovered after the Restoration, and refitted into its legitimate place.

There are some fine modern monuments in this church, and many sepulchral inscriptions around, relating to various families of distinction, besides the Myddeltons, to whom we have already made allusion; as the Lloyds of Pentre Llech, Llwyn, and Rossa; as,

```
+-------------------------------------------------+
|    JOHANNIS LLOYDE DE PENTRE GENERO              |
|                                                 |
| S  PVLVERIS. IN. LECTO. JACEO. MODO.         S  |
| P  MOXQ. RESVRGAM. CHRISTE. VIGORE.          E  |
| V  TVO. CARNE. VIDERE. DEVM. JAM. TER-       P  |
| R  RENVS. ERAM. MOD. .. SVM. CÆLESTIS.       V  |
| O  IESV. MORTVVS. AC. VIVVS. SVM. MAN-       L  |
| C  EOQ. TVVS. A. ME. DISCE. MORI. LECTOR:    T  |
|       QVO. VIDERE. POSSIS. MORS. FVIT.       I  |
| T     EN. MI. HODIE. CRAS. TIBI. FORSAN.        |
| E          ERIT. HIC. JACET. CORPVS.         D  |
| C     EDWARD. LLOYD DE LLECH.                E  |
| A  GENOVI. MORTEM. OBIIT. . . . . 1665.      C  |
| H                                            I  |
|       TERTIO DECEMBRIS ANNO DOM. 1650.       M  |
|                                              O  |
+-------------------------------------------------+
```

David Lloyd of Llwyn died in 1671, &c. Also, "*Hic jacet corpus Johannis Lloyd de Rossa, et Annæ Vxoris sva Thomas*, &c., 1678 and 1697." In an outhouse at Rossa, there is a date with armorial bearings, and the initials H. K.: C. K. 1650. At Llanrhaiadr, is the tomb of Edward Wynne, of Ystrad, esquire; (son of Maurice Wynne, of Gwydir, Esquire, by Catherine of Beren;) who had four sons and seven daughters. He died the 20th of Oct. 1640. His son, Capt. Wnyne, was slain at the siege of Denbigh, in 1646, and buried here with military honours.

The following exhibits the " pride of ancestry :"—

Here Lyeth the Body of
JOHN AP ROBERT of PORT:
AP DAVID AP GRIFFITH AP DAVID
VAVCHAN AP BLETHYN AP GRIFFITH
AP MEREDITH AP JERWORTH AP

H

LLEWELYN AP JERWORTH AP HEILYN
AP COWRYD AP CADVAN AP ALAWGWR
AP CADELL
KING OF POWIS,
who departed this life the 20th day of March,
in the year of our Lord God
1642, and of his age 95.

As reminiscences of popish times and evidences of the Reformation, and the utilitarian age that followed, the rood-screen has been
removed to the west end of the church, and built up into the present
gallery, or organ-loft, and the stoup used up as one of the coping-
stones of the churchyard wall.   There is an hospital adjoining the
churchyard for aged poor; and other charitable endowments are
connected with this extensive parish, a part of which is comprehended within the " Liberties" of the ancient borough of Denbigh; a
rivulet called *Aberham*, or *Aber Ham*, on the road to Denbigh, forming the boundary-line.

Here the late Venerable and excellent Archdeacon Newcome,
author of the *Memoirs of Gabriel Goodman, Sketches of the Histories
of Denbigh and Ruthin, &c.*, spent the evening of his days.

A neat little district church, in the early English style, and dedicated to St. James the Apostle, has lately been built at Prion, from
the design of Richard Lloyd Williams, Esq., of Denbigh, upon
land given by J. Parry Jones, Esq., then Mayor.   It is a substantial
building in perfect keeping with the natural features of the landscape.

Llanrhaiadr had, from time immemorial, belonged to the diocese
of Bangor, when, after the demise of the late Bishop Bethell, it was
transferred to the see of St. Asaph.

In *Brown Willis's Survey of the Diocese of Bangor*, we find the
following notices of Llanrhaiadr :

A quotation (as from *Pope Nicholas's Taxation*,) shewing that this
church belonged to Bangor in A.D. 1291, and was then worth six
marks and a half yearly.   " *Taxatio Bonorum Spirit. et Temp. in
Dice. Bangor. Anno* 1291.   *Ecclesia de Llanrhaidr* vjm. *et dimid.*"
(p. 200.)

" Thomas Cheryton, Bp. of Bangor, in (A. D.) 1441. procured
the restitution of Llanrayader Rectory to the Chapter of Bangor."
The patent is printed in the *Appendix*—"Llanrayader in Kinmersh."

" *Summa Valorum, &c. Episcopatus Bangoriens. facta in Anno
26 Hen : VIII.—*1534.—*Denbigh Land, Manerium de Llanrayder et Kenmerch valet ad firmam, per annum, cum pertinentiis. & sic
dimittiiur Henrico Salisbury, Generoso,* ivli. vis. 0d.

" *Reprisalia.—Feoda Willhemi Salesbury, Seneschalli, in Llanrhaidr & Kinmerch, per annum,* xiijs. ivd."—13s.

At page 272, " Names of all the Churches and Chapels in the
Diocese of Bangor * * * * *

" *Llanrhaidr.* Rectory sinecure. Tythes settled on the Bishop-
rick. *Fanum prope vel ad cataractam aquarum.*

Rhaiadr (rhaiadyr, but generally pronounced with the last *r*
silent, as *rhaiad,* and *Llanrhaiad,*) signifies a cataract; hence
cataract-church, from a cascade or fall on the passing torrent.

In *Bishop Merick's Return* of this diocese, in A. D. 1561, we
have the names of all the Parsons and Vicars within the diocese, and

" D (Dominus) Hugh Davies, alias Johns, Prist. Vicar of Llanrayder [Llanrhaidr-Yngheinmerch] forsaid, and kepeth house."
(p. 268.)

" Llanrhayador-in-Kinnerch," occurs in an Act 1 James 2, (A.D.
1685,) for the Repair of the Cathedral Church of Bangor." (p.291.)

Ysceibion and Bachymbyd are in the parish of Llanynys. Bachymbyd was formerly one of the numerous seats and " wide estates"
of the Salusburies, (*see Ancient and Modern Denbigh, p.* 166, 213,
230.) Llewesog, which once belonged to the same illustrious family,
stands on the verge of an ornamental lake imbosomed in a deep
woody glen.

Dispute.

In conclusion, it should be remarked that upon the appearance of
the author's former work, he was favoured with numberless commu-
nications from archæologists, in Wales and England, both in the
shape of commendations and criticisms. Two or three antiquarian
gentlemen, of most respectable standing, gave expression, privately
and publicly, to their doubts as to the correctness of the statement
that Henry de Lacy was succeeded in this lordship by Thomas
Plantagenet, Earl of Lancaster. They enquired of certain copyists
at the Record Office, and examined the postmortem inquisition
of the estates of the Earl of Lancaster, and not finding in that

document any mention of Denbigh, they were convinced that this was an historical error into which the author had fallen, in following Camden and others.   Consequently, in a paper upon Denbigh Castle, &c., read before " the Architectural, Archæological, and Historical Society of Chester, and published in the Journal of that body, for 1856, and afterwards in a separate pamphlet, we find— " Henry de Lacy &c., is said to have been succeeded, in 1310, by Thomas Plantagenet, Earl of Lancaster, but it appears doubtful whether Denbigh ever passed into the possession of the Earls of Lancaster ; and it is suggested that this supposition has arisen either from a miswriting or misreading of the Earldom of *Lincoln*, abbreviated as both titles constantly were in the Latin deeds, into *Lincr.* and *Lancr.*, with a contracting mark over the words." This objection De Beckele has, in the foregoing pages, set for ever at rest.

But the most remarkable fact is the decay and extinction of the " English Colony of Caymerch." The social revolutions of five centuries have not left of it " a wreck behind." The only surnames associated with reminiscences of its departed existence, which came down to times within our recollection, were *Wilding, Peake, Burchenshaw*, and one or two " doubtfuls"; and these are no longer borne by any residents of the commote. The *Peakes* are noticed elsewhere. The *Burchenshaws* spread to Isaled, where they have just the vestige of " a local habitation and a name." But ages have passed since they ceased to be " English." The most illustrious member of this family was John Burchenshaw, Abbot of Chester at the close of the fifteenth century. Brown Willis takes him to be a native of Wales, from the fact of his name appearing upon the great bell at Conway ; and the following Welsh ode written three hundred and fifty years ago, proves him to have been a Welshman, conversant with the old British tongue, and well versed in Welsh poetical lore. He was appointed, by the Pope, Abbot of St. Werburgh, on the 4th day of October, 1493. He is said to have been opulent, generous, and high-minded ; whilst his history proves him to have been no less ambitious. Indeed, his panegyrist describes his deportment and bearing as that of a " prelate and pontiff ;" his hospitality and profuseness excelling the bountifulness of a hundred barons, famous for his affability and benignity ; talent, learning, and erudition ; excelling as a linguist, classical scholar, and divine. He was chaplain to Henry VII., and the allusion to St. Saviour's points, probably, to a previous connection with the celebrated Monastery of Bermondsey ; and he may have held canonries at Durham and Bath; and ecclesiastical manors or preferments in Anglesea and at Dwygyfylchi. He built the great western porch of Chester Cathedral, which he intended to flank with corresponding towers, the foundation-stone of one of which he actually laid in 1508. The poet speaks of his buildings. Some attribute to him the hall of the manor of Ince; and he "beautified" the manor-house of Saughton. These, probably were his " castell-dai," castellated houses " kept by his sword and bow." In the sixth year of Henry VIII., he obtained a royal license to convert to parks (for the chase) one thousand acres of land in Huntingdonshire and at Cheveley and Saughton ; and, at the same time, a charter granting to him freedom of chase over all his lands in the county of Chester that did not form a part of the king's forests. In 1511, when one Thomas Smith was mayor of Chester, a bitter contention broke out between the citizens and the Abbot, and Thomas Highhill and Thomas Marshull were appointed to act successively in his stead. This quarrel lasted for years, but Burchenshaw was restored to his abbacy about the year 1530, and is supposed to have held it until his death, which took place in 1537. It would appear that he assumed something like archiepiscopal dignity, for in 1516, a commission was issued from Rome authorizing Thomas (Cardinal) of York to hear and decide the dispute between Geoffrey, bishop of Litchfield, and John Burchenshagh, Abbot of Chester, touching the right of wearing the mitre and pall, and of carrying the crosier.

AWDYL MOLIANT I SION ABBAD CAERLLEON.

Vn tad yn abbad wynebwr—grassvs
A groesses Sain' Saviwr ;
Y gwaed o'r gwin geidw'r gwr,[1]
Jessv'n evrbyrth Sain' Werbwr.[2]

Sain' Werbwr ?—pwy'r gwr piav'r goron—avr
Y' Nvram[3] nev Vaddon,[4]
A chadw braint kwvaint kyvion
Ar gledd a saeth ?—Arglwydd Sion.[5]

1 An allusion to transubtantiation. 2 St. Werburgh's. 3 Durham. 4 Bath.

Sion—gwr val l'ysievyn gwyrdd,
A wyr ein ffydd ar jawn ffordd ;
Vrddas vydd ar ddewis vardd
I abbad Kaer wybod kerdd.

Wynebwr o jawn wybod
A 'dnebydd *Duw* yn abbad :
Ni roed 'i ras ar dy wrid,
Sion, heb wyneb Sain' Bened.[6]

Sain' Bened, Berned,[7] gyda'r Barnwr—mawr,
Mab Mair, vo dy nerthwr :
Ar dy Dduw'r wyd weddïwr,
A Duw a'th wnaeth dithav'n wr.

Oesswr, kedrannwr kydrïeni—maer
Môn a'r Ddwygyfylchi ;[8]
Arvon a'i chyffion, y chwi
Y' nhir y Brenin Harri.[9]

Gwr gweddi Harri hiroes—a'i siaplen,
Sy aplaf i ddwyn kroes ;[10]
Gwr a ynnill gair vnoes,
Gwr ni chyll gair yn ych oes.

Oes dvr ac avr pvr gorav pery—rhai'n
Ar yr hwnn a'i dyly ;
Jessv 'n hyn oes no hynny
Gwneled d'oes i gynnal ty.

Ty dy glych yn wych a wnai—yn gavell,
Yn gyvoeth, ac ossai ;
A chadw gwledd modd y gweddai,
A chadw 'ch tir a chodi 'ch tai.

T'ai, tir, ni threissir, na'th ras—er beilchion
Ni cheir bylchv d'vrddas ;
Gwynn yw d'enw gan a dinas,
Ni bytho gwynn neb o'th gas.

Yn gwynn dy vyw ynn dyveinwyr—kavell
Kwfaint ac Eglwysswyr ;
Vn nid gwell, enaid y gwyr,
Neithr pab neb athro pybyr.

Pybyr nerthwr   Pob llawenydd
Pob dierthwr,[11]   Hyd Vilienydd,[12]
Pab aberthwr,   Pob awenydd,
   Pawb a borthed.   Pawb a aned.

5 Lord of those manors above. 6 St. Bennet, founder of the Benedictines. 7 St. Bernard, founder of the Cistercians. 8 Carnarvonshire. 9 Henry VII. 10 Than Geoffrey of Litchfield. 11 Stranger. 12 Maelienith, South Wales.

Pan ganassant,
Y traethassant
Jaith y passant,[13]
   A'th happvsed.

Mawr y'm noddaist
Y'm gwahoddaist,
Maeth a roddaist
   Ym a thrwydded.

Ar bysc eigiav
O vôr greigiav,
Ac ar seigiav,
   Ym gwressoged.

Ac avr lestri
Ar ffenestri,
A'r ryvestri[14]
   Avr a vwstried.[15]

A mil am wys
I'r vro ar vrys
A droes i'r llys
   A'i drws ar lled.

Am yn llessv
A'n kynnhessv
Y'th beirch Jessv
   A'th barchvssed.

Angel ffeiriav[16]
Vchel greiriav[17]
A gar geiriav
   Y gwr gwared.

Yn kanolic
Ffydd Gatholic,
Y Nadolic,
   Yn dy weled.

Ni ddarparwn,
Ac ni charwn
O'r kann barwn
   Wr kynn bvred.

Ni rydd, ni roes,
Nid yw, nid oes,
Ni bu'n yr oes
   Neb enw a red.

Ar vinteiav
O'r gwindeiav,
O'r kann rriav
   Wr kynn rrywied.

Am dy roddion
Aeth gormoddion
Ymadroddion
   Am dy rwydded.

A'th ddaioni,
Heb ddiglloni,
A'th haelioni,
   A'th lawened.

Ac yn orav
Dy gydghorav,
A'th ragorav
   Wythryw giried.[18]

Ar gallineb,
Heb erwineb,
A'th ddoethineb—
   Awr dda 'th aned.

Ar wyr koethion,
Y cyvoethion,
Vwchben doethion
   Y'ch bendithied.

Ar holl ieithiav
Y taleithiav
Gwnewch od weithiav,
   Gan y'ch doethed.

Ar Rvveinwyr,[19]
A darlleinwyr,
A'r dyveinwyr,[20]
   Avr dy vonedd.

Yn ail Siarom[21]
Y darparom
Enw a garom
   Yn agored.

Vn vodd yn vab,
Vn bwyll yn bab,
I'th bair sythvab
   Harri Seithfed.

Vn Dvw yn d'oes,
Ar hwnn a'i rroes
Ynnill y groes
   Wrth wynn holl gred.

Wrth gyflenwi
Kaer o'th henwi—
Kyvion d'enwi,
   Kefn y dwned.

13 Peasant. 14 Revestiary. 15 Mustered. 16 Feriæ, holidays. 17 Relics.
18 Bounty. 19 Latinists. 20 Divines. 21 St. Jerome.

Yn berffeiddiaf,   Mynych mae yno
Yn sancteiddiaf,   Ordr Vair dra vo ;
Abbadeiddiaf,   Mal bro Sain' Bevno
     Y'ch bedyddied.   Nev Sain' Bened.

Yn breladaidd,   Aed ystod Jestin,[22]
Offeiriadaidd,   Aeth i farn i'th vin,
Jaith abbadaid,   Awstin parth gwerin
     I'th wyboded.   Pyrth agored.

Mae 'ch tir, mae 'ch tyrav,   Aeth y dref i'th dras,
Mal braint Kaint yn cav,   A thabl avr i'th blas,
Mannav gwinllannav ;   A thi ydyw gras
     Mae 'n gynn llowned.   A thad y gred.

                TUDUR ALED A'I KANT.

This ode, a masterly composition so far as rhyme and harmony (*cynghanedd*) are concerned, was first published by the editor of this work in 1857, in a local journal. It is an excellent picture of the sentiments and manners of the age. It is needless to say that our poet's prediction that his patron should, through the influence of king Henry VII., be raised to the pontificate, was never fulfilled.

The Church of Llanynys, situated on the other side of the Clywedog, stands on what may be called a peninsula—upon a perfectly level, but well-cultivated and richly-wooded plain, almost surrounded by the Clwyd and Clywedog rivers. The Welsh word *ynys* was formerly used to denote a peninsula (now called *gorynys*) as well as an Island, as " Ynys Tudno ;" or as Leland tells us, " *Llaneinys* is not all in Kynmarth, but part in Deffryn Cluid. It is caullid *Llaneineis* by cause the Chirch is set betwix the Rivers Cluid and Cluedoc, as in an Isle."—Vol. v. p. 57. The church, which is said to be dedicated to St. Sæm, is a double-aisled structure, devoid of a tower, except a lantern turret for two bells, and the internal design has been utterly *ruined* by a barbarous admixture of Grecian with Gothic architecture. This " improvement" was introduced some time in the last century, before the revival of " the masonic art." In vain we look around for ancient epitaphs ; that in memory of " Morris Cadwaladr, of Bachymbyd, buried the 7th day Nov. 1687," has been copied for the author as the oldest. Indeed, it is a very remarkable fact that nowhere do we find such memorials dating before the Reformation.

                22 Justinian.

CHAPTER IV.

"CASTRUM DE DYNBIEGH."

AND the Lord William de Monte Acute holds the Castle of Denbigh, which is situated in the commote of Issalet. And that is not
surveyed by reason of the greatness of its charges,* (*Et quod non
extenditur propter magnam ejus reprisam.*") And he holds that
castle, with the honour, from the Lord the King *in capite.*

Parks and Pools, &c.—And there is a large inclosed park there,
which comprehends two hundred three score and four acres, of land
and wood, reckoning by the perch of eighteen and a half feet of assize. And another park called the Galghull, *(Galch-hill,* lime-hill,)
which is likewise inclosed, and contains, by the same standard
measure, three score and two acres. Also, another large inclosed park,
which contains four hundred two score and two acres, of land and
wood, called Moillewyk *(Moelewig.)* And the underwood, if cut
down, might be worth eleven pounds, eight shillings, yearly. And
the herbage there is worth twenty-one pounds, six shillings, per
annum. In all, thirty-two pounds, fourteen shillings. Charges
(deducted) ten pounds, ten shillings; so (making) the clear annual
value twenty-two pounds, four shillings. And there is a manor
there, near the Castle, the site of which contains sixty-four perches.
And there is a dovecot there, and two great fish-ponds there which
are not surveyed, (" *Et sunt ibi duo magna vivaria quæ non exten-*

---

* " REPRISA.—*Deductio ex proventibus alicujus prædii, pro solvendis pensita-
tionibus, quibus obnoxium esse potest. quacunque ex causa. . . Salva reprisa ultra
rationibiles reprisas.*"—*Du Cange.*

What these *charges* were, in the case of Denbigh Castle, we are not told ; probably, the keep of so many archers, men-at-arms, &c. So in the *Postmort. Inquis.
Hen. de Laci,* we are told that it was of no value beyond its charges.

I

duntur, &c.") besides arable lands, and (grass) fields, worth, in all, six pounds, seven shillings, and one halfpenny, per annum.

		£	s.	d.
Total.—Parks, 768 acres,	. . .	22	14	0
Manor and farm, &c.	. .	6	7	0½
So, making annually	. .	29	1	0½

" BURGUS DE DYNBIEGH."

And there is the burgh (borough) of D'nbiegh *within* the walls, together with the market town *(villa mercatoria,* the suburban mart) *without* the walls. And the burgesses of the town within the walls hold of the lord by foeffment *(ad feodum firmam,* in other words, by feudal tenure) the whole of the aforesaid burgh, and the whole of the said vill, with the advantages (privileges, or profits) arising therefrom, *(cum omnibus exitibus)* rendering yearly to the lord twenty pounds for the same: that is to say, one half thereof at the Pentecost, and the other moiety at the feast of St. Michael.

" *Capella de Dynbiegh.*"—And they find one chaplain to celebrate Divine service in the Chapel of Dynbiegh, within the walls, (St. Hilary's) for the lord, his predecessors and successors in perpetuity. The erection and reparation of this chapel, as appears hereafter, devolved upon the free and native tenantry of Taldrach, from the time of the sovereign princes of Wales; as well as to build and repair, for the prince, a hall, a chamber, a wardrobe, domestic offices, &c., at Dynbiegh; and to construct and keep in repair the fences there round the court of the prince.

Denbigh, in the time of the princes consisted (originally) of two gavels; the first, called in Welsh, according to De Beckele, " Gavell Rethe;" *(Gafael Rhydd,)* the other " Gavell Kaythe" *(Gafael Caeth.)* Gavell Rethe was so called because it was free; and the other Gavell Kaythe, because it was not free; (" *fuit de vilioribus and de pluribus servitutibus quam prima gavella;)* the tenantry being subject to more and viler services.

Gavell Rethe was afterwards subdivided into six gavels, viz:—

Gavel Waspatrik

A moiety of which is held by Ithell ap Grono Loyd, Jevan, and Eden, his brothers, who render for *ardreth* (rent) two shillings, and six pence per annum.

David ap Bleth' Sæer *(D. ab Bleddyn y Saer)* holds the third part of another moiety in Tyrpryd, rendering for the same ten pence per annum.

Jevan ap David, Jor' and David, his brothers, have an eighth part of the same half gavel, rendering for the same three pence, three farthings, yearly.

Mad. ap Ken' Voyle holds a twelfth part, at the rent of two pence, one halfpenny, per annum.

A fourth part of the same gavel, minus a twelfth part, is a pure escheat of the lord, and is arrented with the rest of the escheats.

Gavell Seynyon.

Jevan ap Ithel, pannour, *(y pannwr,* the fuller,) and Eignon, his brother, hold a moiety of Gavell Seynyon, rendering for the same two shillings and six pence yearly.

Jevan ap David, Tuder and Jevan Duy, his brothers, hold two parts of another moiety of the same gavel, rendering twenty pence for the same, yearly.

Jevan ap Mad' Goz, Eignon and Jevan, his brothers, pay ten-pence yearly for a third part of the same gravel ; and

Jevan ap Mad' Creche (qy. *Crydd* or *Crach* ?) and David his brother, render ten-pence yearly for a third part of the same; but they say they have nothing from it.

Gavell Osbern.

John de Wyberleye holds the whole of this gravel *(quæ est jus Eignon ap Ith' ap Gron ;)* which is the right of Einion ab Ithel ab Goronwy, (but held by Wyberley) because the said Einion is "impotent," (labouring under disability, *quia dictus Eignon est impotens),* at the rent of five shillings per annum.

Gavell Iskethlin

Has fallen altogether into the hands of the lord, because Eignon ap Kendale ap Gron., who is the right heir to the same, is "impotent."—Rent, five shillings per annum.

Gavell Gwynnot.

Atha *(Adda,* Adam) ap Madok ap Gwynnot *(Gwynnod),* Eignon and Jevan, his brothers, hold a moiety of this gavel—Rent, two shillings and sixpence per annum. The other moiety is arrented along with the acreages.

Gavell Gwassane.

Jevan ap Mad. ap Gwassane, Grono ap Eignon ap Mad., and Gwên his brothers, hold four parts of this gavel, &c., rendering four shillings yearly. They also hold one eru *(erw)* of the fifth part thereof, at a rent of ten pence per annum. Also Jevan ap Mad. ap Gwassane holds one eru thereof at ten pence per annum.

So the whole of these six gavels now render twenty-two shillings, and ten pence, one farthing, yearly in season, for "ardreth." And the tenants give ten shillings for relief and amobrage, like other free tenants of the commote.

Of the three gavels into which Gavell Caithe has been subdivided—

Gavell Vernath.

Eignon Lloid ap Eignon ap Yonas holds the third part of the moiety of Gavell Vernath, at the rent of twelve pence per annum. Mad. ap Eign. ap Yonas holds another third part *(treian)* at the same rent. The other third part, which Gronou Bondus ap Eignon ap Yonas (once) held, has come into the hands of the lord.

Gavell Cadug' ap Ken'.

One half of this gavel, and the sixth part of the other moiety, which Mad. ap. Cad. ap Ken. (once) held for seven shillings per annum; together with the five (remaining) parts of the other moiety, which Gron. ap Cadug. held, for five shillings per annum, have come entirely into the hands of the lord.

Gavell Ithel Wolewen.

Cadug. ap Eign. ap Ithel holds the third part of this gavel, for four shillings per annum. Jevan ap Mad. ap Cad. ap. Ithel (once) held a moiety thereof, at six shillings, and eight pence, per annum. It afterwards came into the lord's hands, and was demised to Henry Moder Soule, but is again in the hands of the lord. A sixth part thereof is in Denbigh (town), and is an escheat, &c.

And all the heirs of the three (last-mentioned) gavels, give two shillings for relief, or "amobrage," and do no other services, as they say.

And be it known that the whole "vill" of Denbigh, which was formerly in the hands of the tenants of the two original gavels, came into the hands of the Earl of Lincoln, partly by escheat and partly by exchange. And it contains in the whole, eight hundred and eighteen acres, and three roods of land, wood, and waste.

Acreages of Denbigh.—And nine tenants hold forty-one and a half acres, eighteen perches of land, rendering for the same thirty-six shillings and five pence, at Hocktide and Michaelmas; yearly, in equal portions; namely,

	A.	R.	P.		s.	d.
Hugh de Hulton	viii	0	0	...	5	8
Thomas Pygot	iv	iij	xx	...	3	4
Ditto, and Alice his wife	x	0	0	...	10	0
Henry del Spen	i	0	0	...	0	8
Richard de Rossyndale	ii	i	0	...	1	6
Juliana and Isabella daughters of Henry } de Hallum . . . . }	i	2	0	...	1	6
John Bost (qy. *Sion Bost*, John the Postman?)	iv	0	0	...	4	0
Thurstan de Orell	ix	0	0	...	9	0

John Bost also holds one curtilege, with its appurtenances, and one clough, containing three roods, eighteen perches, for nine-pence per annum.

And there is a mill there broken down by the flood, in lease to William Waleys with that of Astret Oweyn; so nothing is rendered there.

Total annual value of the vill of Denbigh, with the manor, &c., £56 6s. 6¾d.

CONCLUDING REMARKS.

The reader should, perhaps, be reminded that De Beckele does not enumerate the burgesses of Denbigh, who held burgages, curtilages, and oxgangs of land, by charter from the Earl of Lincoln and his successors. These numbered six score, in A. D. 1310, and it is certain that they were more numerous by this time. Nor can the reader have any correct conception of the extent of the English settlement until we have gone over Lleweny, and the surrounding townships, in their order.

In the present chapter, De Beckele has completely refuted the supposition that Denbigh derives its name and origin from De Lacy, its first lord after the Conquest of Wales. Had it been so, it is absurd to suppose that, writing his *Extenta* just twenty-four years after the demise of the (now) alleged founder, he could have been ignorant of that fact, and have described the place as existing, under the name of " Dynbiegh," (which could be nothing else but the Welsh *Dinbych*, in its old orthographical form *Dynbeich)* from the

times of the princes of Wales—times immemorial—and a place
where the prince had a court, hall, chapel, apartments, wardrobe,
&c. It is incredible that this matter-of-fact man, who is correct
in his statements to the smallest fraction of a farthing, could have
penned a fiction purporting to be a "survey" upon oath, when his
noble employer might have found hundreds of living witnesses to
disprove it. And that De Lacy could have "first given it the
name *Denbigh*, after *Deneby*, a manor which he possessed in Yorkshire," is as improbable, the former being written "*Dynebieghe*" in
his Charter, (*A. & M. Denbigh*, p. 301,) and "*Dynebegh*" in the
Inquisition given hereafter. Indeed, that is impossible; unless it
can be proved that he was in possession of this "honour" before
the actual Conquest of Wales and fall of "the Last Llewelyn."
This is evident from the following quotations, made for the author
by W. Wynne Foulkes, esq., barrister-at-law, historic secretary of
the Chester Archæological Society, from *Ayloff's Calendar of
Welsh and Scotch Rolls*, p. 82 : the marginal notes by Ignatius
Williams, esq., of Denbigh, or by the author.

ROTULUS WALLIÆ, ANNO 10 EDWARDI PRIMA.

1 Deputed to convey the excommunication of the Welsh princes and people ?

" *De conductu (occasione guerræ) pro fratre
Johanne le Waleys,*[1] *transmissio ab archiepiscopo
Cantuar' ad exequendem officium spirituale in
Wallia.—Apud Dynbey, 25 Octobris.*" (1282.)

2 Convoying provisions for the army in Wales.

" *De protectione et conductu pro quibusdem in
ducendo victualia ad exercitum*[2] *Wallia.—ut
supra.*"

3 Ruthin Castle, the Vale of Clwyd, &c. confirmed to Reginald Grey.

" *Castrum de Rutthin, et Cantredum de Des-
frencloyt, et terra Wenchelianæ de Lascy, con-
firmata Reginaldo de Grey,*[3] *per manum Regis.
—Apud Dinby, 23 Octobris.*

4 Parson of Bunbury, Cheshire, called Bonnebur. — Pope Nich. Tax.

" *De protectione pro David persona Ecclesiæ
de Bonbir, &c.*[4] *—ut supra.*"

5 Peter de Monte forte was employed in the Welsh Wars.

" *Quod Nicholaus de Monte-forte*[5] *is obsequio
regis, non ponatur in assisis juratis, seu
recognitionibus aliquibus.—Apud Dinbey, 26
Octobris.*"

"*Abbas et conventus de Basingwerk habent protectionem, dum tamen non concomitent cum Walensibus rebellibus,*[6] *&c.*"

"*Johannis Bonquer in ducendo victualia ad exercitum Walliæ, ut supra.*"

Membrana 1.

"*De Rogero Extraneo*[7] *(morieats Rogero de Mortuo-mari) constituto capitaneo in munitionibus Abbi Monasterii Oswaldestre, et Montes Gomeri.—Apud Dynbegh, 30 Octobris.*"

Membrana 5, dorso.

"*De capiendo manum regis castra et terris Rogeri de Mortuo-mari*[8] *senioris, defuncti, in Wallia et Marchia.—Apud Dynbey, 29 Octobris.*"

"*De levando curiale subsidium in civitate Hereford, promissum ratione expeditionis Walliæ, Apud Dynbey, 28 Octobris.*"

Quod Rogerus,[9] *filius Rogeri de Mortuo-mari, faciet ea quæ Rogerus Extraneus capitaneus munitionum in partibus Walliæ, dicet ex parte regis.—Apud Dynbych,*[10] *31 Octobris.*

Membrana 1.

De protectione et conductu pro William de la Chambre[11] *et Ricardo de Bannfeld, &c., in ducendo victualia ad exercitum Walliæ.—Apud Denbegh, 3 Novembris.*

Here we find the king personally at Denbigh, before the Conquest, directing the movements of his army, and conducting other affairs of his kingdom. Nevertheless, all who have written upon the history of Wales, tell us that after the death of Llewelyn, which took place on the 11th day of the following December, the Welsh nobles met at Denbigh, and proclaimed David ap Griffith their prince. Was Edward occupying or merely besieging Denbigh in October and November? If in possession of the place, it seems very incredible that David could have "summoned the Welsh chieftains to meet him at Denbigh" in December, or afterwards. (See *Warrington's History of Wales, Lond. Edit.* (1788), *p.* 485. *Hanes Cymru, p.* 730. *Prydnawngwaith y Cymry, p.* 129, and others.)

---

6 See Brown Willis's App. St. Asaph.

7 Roger le Strang Baron of Ellesmere.

8 The Baron Mortimer, of Wigmore.

9 Baron Mortimer of Chirk.

10 The unmistakable Welsh name "Dinbych."

11 See notice of Chambres hereafter.

CHAPTER V.

LEAVING De Beckele for a while, we turn to certain facts and events in the municipal and parliamentary history of this ancient borough, which are not narrated in " *Ancient & Modern Denbigh*." Since the passing of the Municipal Reform Act, the office of recorder, or judge of the borough sessions, has been vacant, although it was not actually annulled by that statute, and may be again revived. The " governing charter" 14 Charles II, provides that Denbigh might for ever thereafter " have one honest and discreet man, who should be called the Recorder of the said Borough," and also that " one court of record should be held on Friday, in every second week, throughout the year, for all pleas, actions, suits, and demands of all sorts of transgressions, by force and arms, or otherwise, done, &c.; and of all manner of debts, accounts, bargains, frauds, detaining of deeds, writings, and muniments ; taking away and detaining of beasts, cattle, or goods ; and all contracts, whatsoever, &c." But the office of recorder of the borough had been in existence for many generations previous to the reign of Charles, probably since the second year of Richard II., A.D. 1378. Recorders of the Lordship, commonly called "recorders of Denbigh," existed from Norman times, long before " Rhys ap Llewelyn Chwith, of Chwibren, assassinated Dean Pemberton, the recorder of Denbigh."

In the reign of Elizabeth, John Panton, Esq., " designer," of New Foxhall, in the vicinity of the town, (the " ivy-mantled" ruin of which forms so fine a subject for the pencil,) held this office, and whilst he sat in parliament for the borough, his brother, Foulk Panton, acted as deputy recorder. His name appears at the foot of the following curious old table of

"Efees.

Lymited and appoynted for the Recorder, alowed by ye Ald'men, & balifs, and other the Capitall Burgs., of the Borow and towne of

Denbigh xxviij° Die maij, A° Rne. * * Elizabethe ec. xliiij—1602.

Imprimis, for the entrie of eu'y acçon. (action) vndre } ijd.
the some of Cᵉ & for eu'y varant of atturney . }

Itm.—for eu'y declaraçon in all acçons. of a Deapt } ijd.
vndre xls. . . . . }

Itm.—for eu'y warant of atturney . . . . ijd.

Itm.—for eu'y answere, Replic. & Joininge to issue } ijd.
vndre xls. . . . . }

Itm.—for the etrie of eu'y acçon. of a Cᵉ (£100) . . xijd.

Itm.—for th'entrie of declaroçon, answere Replic. }
Re . . . gder & surre . . . gder in all acçons. of xls. } iiijd.
and aboue, vnder the some of Cᴸ . . . . . }

Itm.—for eu'y pleadinge in acçons. of Cᴸ . . . . . xijd.

Itm.—for th'entre of acçons. of Repl. . . . . . . ijd.

Itm.—for eu'y pleding in acçon. of Replevie . . . . . xijd.

Itm.—for th'entrie of acçons of trespasse & trespasse } ijd.
vpon and deteynve . . . . }

Itm.—for Declaraçon, Answere, Replicaçon & Re . . gder } iiijd.
vndre the some of Cᴸ . . . . }

Itm.—for eu'y pleadinge of Cᴸ . . . . xijd.

Itm.—for eu'y Judgeme't or Verdict of eu'y acçon. . . vjd.

Itm.—for eu'y writt of execuçon . . . . iiijd.

Mᵈ.—that the xxviijth day of May 1602 ffowlk Panton, Deputie Recorder, for & in the name of his brother John Panton, gent., nowe Recorder of this towne & lib'ties of Denbigh, that he shall and will make or cause to be made all the estreats of the towne court at his owne cost & charges, & deliu'e the same frely to the Balys, for the tyme beinge, to th'end they may leavy the same, to the townes use, and to remitt all form' accompts & demand for making of any estreats heretofor,

By me, ffoulk Panton.

It would appear from the following "minute" that Sir Hugh Myddelton afterwards held the office of recorder :—

" At a Councell held in the Councell Chamber, within the Shire Hall of Denbigh, the second day of Julie 1660.

" Wee &c. doe hereby vnanimously ellect and choose Sᵗ· John Salusburie, Barronett, one of the capitall Burgesses of this Towne, to be Recorder of the said Towne. To hold the saide office for his liefe & to receive and enioy all fees, regards, p'fitt, & advantages thereto belonging, and to execute the same office or place dureing the terme of his liefe, by himselfe, or his sufficient deputie or deputies, assignee or assignees; yealding, and payeing, doeing, & p'formeing such &

K

the same, or the like, rents, duties, and service yearelie dureing the
said terme vnto the said Aldermen, Bayliefes, burgesses, and theire
successors ; at such dayes, tymes, and places as heretofore were by
any grante made by the late Aldermen, Bayliefes, & Burgesses of
Denbigh vnto Sr Hugh Myddelton, Barronet; & Sr Richard
Wynne, knight & Barronet, or either of them yealded, or paied,
done, or p'formed & served.

" And wee doe hereby order that A graunte of the said office
shall be made vnto the said Sr John Salusburie according to this
our ellection & shall be sealed by & with the comon seale of this
Towne. And this our order shall be a sufficient warrant for fixing
the said seale to the said graunte."

This appointment was confirmed by his Majesty King Charles II.
in the usual form—" We appoint, make, & and constitute our well-
beloved Sir John Salisbury, Baronet, &c. Recorder of our Borough
of Denbigh, &c. Witness ourself, &c. at Westminster, this 14th
day of May, in the 14th year of our Reign.—1661.

                              CARL. REX."

No writer seems to have noticed that Sir Hugh Myddelton was
recorder of Denbigh, as well as alderman, and M.P. Indeed, from
the frequent entries made, in his own handwriting, in the " *Corporation Book*," the worthy baronet might have been the actual
town-clerk at the time, such was the deep and active interest he
took in the welfare of his native town.

Among the corporate muniments the author found several
original letters from Sir Hugh Myddelton, of one of which the following is a copy :—

" Lovinge Coosins and ffrinds.—Vnderstanding of my Coosin
Panton (yor Recorders) death, I thought good, owt of care & good
respecte, and well-wyshinge to all the whole Towne, to recom'end
vnto you this berer (my coosin Hughe Parrey) to be yor Recorder,
whoe I ame verely p'swaydyd will geve you good contente in dys-
charginge the place honestlie and svfficientlye, p'testinge I wyshe
y^t asmutche for yor good as for his, soe well I ame p'swaydid of
his Jntegritie towards the Towne. I shall not neade write more of
the man, beinge soe well knowen vnto you all. I haue herde
of some exaxtione of fees wch I wyshe maie bee reformed for the

generall good of the Towne, yet soe as the place may bee sufficient
for a man of worthie sorte. I doupt not of yo' care and warynes in
yowr choyse, yet my love hath bynn and shalbe (God willinge)
suche to yo' towne as I cannot chowse but wt° yow my oppinyon
wch I leave to yo' good consideraçon, and what yow shall doe for
the berer I shall take as donn to myselfe. Soe wth very harty
com'endaçons to yow all, I shall eve' remaine

Yor. lovinge

"London,   Coosin & ffrinde

   13th of   HUGH MYDDELTON."

    M'che 1618."

From the following communication, written the next year, it
would not appear that Hugh Parry was successful in his application.
The office, no doubt, devolved upon (Sir) Hugh Myddelton himself.

" Lovinge Coosins & ffrinds.—Vnderstandinge, by a good ffrinde
of myne, that one was an ernest sutor for a lease in reversion of the
Littel Pk. (*Little Park.*) I did presently repaire to his highnes
counsell, (whoe I founde verye honorable) and acquainted them
with the state of the cause, and howmutche yt concerned all the
Towne, whearvp° It pleased them to enter an order, and to direct
theare lrs. The lre. & coppis therof I sende yow herwth, for wch I
I paied xxv sts., wyshinge yow with all convenient spead to w^{tr} the
said lre., prainge and desiringe all ther paines therin for the dys-
patche of the survey & speady returne of ther certyfycatt, accordinge
to the tyme lymytted. Iff all cannot be thear, yow mvst gett
three at least that donne ; then mvst yow make choyse of one, or
twoe, of the sufficientest and honestest men amongest yow, gevinge
them ffull & absolute authoritie to come vpp to followe the cause,
and to compownde for the newe lease, ether by Jmprovinge the rent,
or fyne, as shall seeme best to that honorable boorde, bringinge wth
them the olde lease in beinge, and all orders and notes tovtchinge
that cause. I thinke Coosin Hugh Parry (being hier) will doe
well for one, & so save mutch charge of horse & man ; wch I leave
to yo' better Judgment. I have spoken wth Coosin Mutton,
whoe I fynde verye willinge to do yow anie service hee cann, and
soe I hope of all the rest. Yow are to consider well of this cause,
howe mutch it concerneth yow and all the Towne, & take heed of

preventions wch is to be avoydid by gevinge ffull power to them
that shall deale for yow, that they maie conclude withowt delaie for
the lease, consultinge & debatinge it well with all the contents,
wch wilbee best for the Towne, to deale by fyne, or to rayse the
rent, wch in my oppinyon is the esiest waie for the poorer sort,
wch are most to be respected and wilbee most regarded by his highnes
Comysson" I write yow of straindge certyficats wch have byn dd.
(delivered?) his highnes Counsell towtchinge the cause. I leave
that to o^r meetinge, and them to God, whoe are the actors, hopinge
they wilbe of better mynde hereafter towards the poore towne.
Soe wyshinge yow all the same I desire to myself, and happy suc-
cesse for yor lease wch is mainlye aymed att, wth my verye hartie
comendaçons, comitt yow all to God.—London, this 21st of ffeb-
ru'ie, 1619.—Slepe not in this busenese.

Digon yn ymel dygall
Men Mayr? hanner gair i gall.

Yo^r assured Lovinge Coosin & ffrind

" To the right wo^{shy}   HUGH MYDDELTON."
  My assured good ffrinds & Coosins
   The Aldermen & bayliffes
     Comon Counsell & Burgeses of
      the Towne of Denbighe—These &c."

In 1634, Edward Williams, gentleman, (afterwards of Pont-y-
Gwyddyl?) was deputy-recorder. In 1648, Sir Richard Wynne,
knight and baronet, was the recorder. Sir Richard Wynne, of
Gwydir, and Sir John Salusbury were aldermen, in 1665; and in
1675, John Clough, gentleman, was elected capital burgess, or common-councilman, in place of Sir Richard Wynne, of Gwydir,
deceased. On a monumental tablet at Whitchurch, it is stated
that Thomas Shaw, gentleman, who died in 1717, was for many
years Recorder of the Lordship and Town of Denbigh. In 1750,
Richard Myddelton, Esq. held the same office. William Simon,
gentleman, was deputy-recorder, in 1773. Since then we have the
following elections of recorders—

    1794, Sept. 29th, Richard Myddelton Biddulph, Esq.
      Chirk Castle.
    1796, Sept. 29th, the Rev. R Myddelton, D.D.
    1802, Sept. 29th, Robt. Myddelton Biddulph, Esq. in
      place of Dr. Myddelton, resigned.

1814, Sept. 14th, the Rev. Dr. Myddelton, again.
1815. Dec. 9th, the Rev. Edward Chambres Chambres, of
Llysmeirchion, in place of Dr. Myddelton, deceased.
1817, Feb. 17th, John Wynne Griffith, Esq., of Garn.

After the decease of the last-named gentleman, there was a con-
test for the office, between his son, Geo. Griffith, Esq., and the late
John Heaton, Esq. The former was appointed by the letters
patent of his late Majesty King William 4th, in the usual form.

It is evident, that the recorder, or his deputy, formerly kept the
corporate records, as the name itself implies. Foulk Panton did so.
In 1613, William Merton had the freedom of the borough presented
to him in consideration of his keeping the minutes, or recording the
proceedings, of the town council—in a word, acting as the town-
clerk. The following year, Henry Thomas performed the same
duties. 1617, "Richard Evance, sonne of John-ap-Edward-ap-
Jeuan of the Mould in fflintshire was towne clerk." In the time of
the Commonwealth, John Roberts held this office, and he was succeeded by John Lloyd of Wickwer, who did much to restore the
municipal records.* John Hosier was appointed town clerk by a
patent of King George II., given at St. James' the 12th day of
March, 1740. He was, in 1766, succeeded by Thomas Williams,
who was in office one year, and was succeeded by William Simon,
who died in 1803. Then John Copner Williams, Esq., who resigned
in 1813; and Samuel Edwardes, Esq., who acted for twenty-two
years : were succeeded by the present town clerk, Richard Williams,
Esq., in 1835. Some of the earlier, pro tem., town clerks, as William
Merton, mercer, were not attorneys-at-law, others were eminent
in the profession, as John Lloyd of Wickwer.

---

* In 1683, George Lloyd was appointed in place of John Lloyd of Wickwer,
who acted as deputy-alderman for the year. John Lloyd of Rossa was made town
clerk in 1684, and Thomas Shaw in 1692.

CHAPTER VI.

It appears, from *Bateson's Chronological Register*, that the privilege of returning a representative to Parliament was first granted
to this borough about the year 1536,* or the 27th Henry VIII.
The following year, according to *Lewis's Topographical Dictionary*,
Ruthin and Holt were made contributory boroughs; but the corporate records of Denbigh make no mention of their being included
in the representation earlier than the year 1680, when a dispute
arose, and some legal proceedings were pending, between the
boroughs of Denbigh and Ruthin, " touching the right of returning
a burgess to parliament."† It is supposed that Sir John Salusbury,
who was alderman of Denbigh in 1678, was returned to the parliament called in 1679; and again, the following year, he contested
the representation of the borough, and was returned in opposition
to Edward Brereton, Esq., who, according to Bateson, petitioned
against Sir John's return. In 1690, William Williams, Esq., petitioned against the return of Edward Brereton, Esq.; and again, in
1701, Thomas Cotton, Esq. petitioned against the same candidate's
return. But Bateson's *list* of representatives begins only with the
first parliament after the union of England and Scotland—1707;
Brown Willis's (*Notitia Parl.*) gives the returns for this borough
from A.D. 1542 down to 1658-9. Thus these two authorities leave
" a hiatus" or blank of nearly half a century. The author is indebted for the following list, the most correct ever published, and

---

* The new Parliament met on 4th of February, and sat forty days, and then
stood prorogued to the 15th April, 1539.

† " The House of Commons resolved, on the 7th of February, 1743, ' That
the right of election of a burgess to serve in parliament for the borough of Denbigh is in the burgesses, inhabitants of the boroughs of Denbigh, Ruthyn, and
Holt respectively.' "—*Laws of Election, by a Gentleman of the Inner Temple*, 1768.
The Reform Act has added the town of Wrexham.

the only one which approaches to completeness, to the researches of the Rev. A. B. Clough, B.D., Braunston ; and Ignatius Williams, Esq., of the Grove, near Denbigh.

Parl. Met. A. D.   **33 *Henry VIII.***

1542,* Richard Myddelton—father of Sir Hugh Myddelton, Sir Thomas, Lord Mayor of London, &c.

1 *Edward VI.*

Nov. 4, 1547, Simon Thelwall, of Plasward.

Mar. 1, 1553, Re-elected.—Recommended, or nominated, by the king's council.

1 *Mary.*

Oct. 5, 1553, Simon Thelwall, gent., re-elected.

April 11, 1554, John Salesbury, Esq.—returned twice within the same year.

2 & 3 *Phillip & Mary.*

1555, John Evans, gent.

1557, Re-elected.

Reign of Elizabeth.

Jan. 25, 1558, John Evans, gent.—sometimes called John ap Evan
1559.   or Ivan ; and the family " Evance," or Evans, (*A. & M. Denbigh, p.* 105, 112, 250, & 310.)

Jan. 12, 1563, Humphrey Lloyd, Esq.† (*A. & M. Denbigh, p.* 181, 186 & 344.)

April 12, 1571, Simon Thelwall, gent.

1572, Richard Candish, alias Cavendish. He was returned in opposition to Henry Dynne, the Earl of Leicesters' nominee, (*A. & M. Denbigh, p.* 98.)

1585, Re-elected.

1586, Robert Wrote, Esq.

* It met again, on the 23rd of Nov., 1545. It is possible, therefore, that Richd. Myddelton represented the borough, as its first member, from 1536 to 1547.

† " Robert Lloyd of Denbigh, gent. father of Humphrey Lloyd, Esq. M.P., the celebrated antiquary, &c. married Joan daughter of Lewis Pigott, of Denbigh ; but had no legitimate issue: his natural son, Humphrey Lloyd, obtained from William Harvey, clarencieux king-at-arms, a grant by which he was enabled to bear the Rosindale arms, differenced by a border gules, and for his crest a lion passant, also gules. The colours of the shield were likewise transposed.

1588, John Turbridge, Esq.

Feb. 19, 1592, Simon Thelwall, gent.

Oct. 24, 1597, John Panton, gent.--Recorder of Denbigh.

   „ 27, 1601, Re-elected, (*A. & M. Denbigh*, p. 105, 114, 186 & 312.) But, unless he unseated Thelwall, of which there is no evidence, he could not have sat for Denbigh, in 1592, as has been stated by Pennant and others.

Reign of James I.

Mar. 19, 1603, Hugh Myddelton, Esq.

   1604. 1614, Re-elected. This year he brought the New River to London.

      1620, Re-elected.

      1623, Re-elected as Sir Hugh Myddelton, Bart.

      1625, Re-elected as Sir Hugh Myddelton, knight & baronet.

Reign of Charles I.

      1625, Re-elected.

      1628, Re-elected.

April 13, 1640, John Salusbury, Esq. jun.

Nov. 3, 1640, Simon Thelwall, Esq. jun.—He sat in the long Parliament. (*A. & M. Denbigh.* p. 110.)

Time of the Commonwealth.

Jan. 30, 1658, John Manley, Esq. Brynyffynnon.

Reign of Charles II.

April 25, 1660, Sir John Carter, (*A. & M. Denbigh*, p. 243 & 250.)

May 8, 1661, Sir John Salusbury.

Jan. 23, 1678, Re-elected.*

Mar. 21, 1681, Re-elected.

Reign of James II.

May 19, 1685, Sir John Trevor, Master of the Rolls and Speaker of the House of Commons. He was a man of considerable learning and talent, and one of the most influential "tories" in the kingdom; and although guilty of political corrupt practices, he was a benefactor to the

He appears to have been elected without opposition:—" 10o Apr Anne R. R. Jacobi secd. eo. pro Sr Jon Trevor, knight, was

---

* A Parliament was also called in 1679, which met on the 6th of March. Another parliament met on the 21st Oct. 1680, in each of which Sir John Salusbury is supposed to have sat.

sworne burgesse of this Twne, and Burrough by ye consent of ye Aldermen, Bayliffes, and Cappital Burgesses of the s^d Towne gratis, & tooke the oathes of allegiance and supremacie. The s^d S^r Joⁿ Trevor was elected then Burgesse, to serve in parliam^t for this Towne — who meet 19o May, 1685." — *Corporation Books.*

town of Denbigh. He was the principal founder of the Grammar School, and gave some benefactions to the corporation in trust for the poor. (*A. & M. Denbigh, p.* 275 *and* 297.) It appears that he was returned for the county in 1681, when Richard Middelton, Esq. petitioned against his return.

*Jan. 22, 1689, Edward Brereton, Esq.

Reign of William III. and Mary II.

May 20, 1690, Re-elected, in opposition to William Williams, Esq. son of Sir Wm. Williams, Speaker of the House of Commons.

Reign of William III.

Nov. 22, 1695, Edward Brereton, Esq.

Dec. 9, 1698, Re-elected.

Dec. 30, 1701, Re-elected in opposition to " Thomas Cotton."

Reign of Queen Anne.

Oct. 20, 1702, Edward Brereton, Esq.

Oct. 25, 1705, William Robinson, Esq.

Oct. 23, 1707, Sat again—after the Union with Scotland. He was, therefore, the first that sat for this borough in " the Parliament of Great Britain."

Nov. 18, 1708, Sir William Williams, bart., Plasyward.

Nov. 25, 1710, John Roberts, Esq. Bavod-y-bwch, (*A. & M. Denbigh, p.* 205.)

Dec. 11, 1713, John Wynne, Esq. of Melai.

Reign of George I.

Mar. 17, 1715, John Roberts, Havod-y-bwch, Esq.

Oct. 9, 1722, Robt. Myddelton, Esq. Chirk Castle.

Reign of George II.

June 27, 1727, Robt. Myddelton, Esq. re-elected.—Died, new writ ordered, 1733.

1733, John Myddelton, Esq. Chirk Castle.

Jan. 17, 1734, Re-elected.

---

* Writs for calling this parliament were issued on the 28th Nov. 1688, the houses to meet on the 15th Jan. 1689. The king fled on the 23rd Dec. 1688.

L

Dec. 4,   1741, John Wynne, Esq. of Melai.

Nov. 10, 1747, Rich⁴· Myddelton, Esq. Recorder of the borough,
                high-steward of Bromfield and Yale, and Lord-
                lieutenant of the county.

May 31,   1754, Re-elected.

Reign of George III.

Nov. 25, 1762, Rich⁴· Myddelton, Esq. re-elected, Chirk Castle.

May 10,   1768, Re-elected.

Jan. 13,   1774, Re-elected.

Oct. 31,   1780, Re-elected.

May 18,   1784, Re-elected.   Made Steward of the Chiltern Hun-
                dreds, in 1786.

           1786, Richard Myddelton, Esq. jun. son of late member.

Nov. 26, 1790, Re-elected.

Oct. 6,   1796, Re-elected.   Died, and new writ issued.

Nov. 2,   1797, Thomas Tyrwhitt Jones, Esq. Carreghova.

Jan. 22,   1801, Re-elected.   Sat in the first " Imperial Parliament"
                after the Union of Ireland.

Nov. 16, 1802, The Hon. Frederick West—uncle to the Earl of
                Delawar.

Dec. 19, 1806, Robt. Myddelton Biddulph, Esq. Chirk Castle.

June 26, 1807, Re-elected.

Nov. 24, 1812, Viscount Kirkwall, father of the Earl of Orkney.

June ... 1818, John Wynne Griffith Esq., Garn.

Reign of George IV.

April 27, 1820, John Wynne Griffith, Esq. re-elected.

Nov. 14, 1820, Double return—Frederick Richard West, Esq. Ru-
                thin Castle, and Joseph Ablett, Esq., Llanbedr
                Hall.

           1827, Frederick Richard West, Esq.

Reign of William IV.

Oct. 26, 1830, Robert Myddelton Biddulph, Esq. Chirk Castle.

June 14, 1831, Robert Myddelton Biddulph, Esq. Chirk Castle.

Jan. 30,   1833, John Madocks, Esq. Glanywern.

Feb. 9,   1835, Wilson Jones, Esq. Hartsheath.

Reign of Queen Victoria.

           1837, Wilson Jones, Esq. re-elected.

1842, Townshend Mainwaring, Esq.

1848, Frederick Richard West, Esq., Ruthin Castle.

1852, Re-elected.

1857, Townshend Mainwaring, Esq.

1859, Re-elected.

Notes on some of the M. P.'s for the Boroughs.

Nov.4, 1547, Simon Thelwall.

This Family came into the Vale in the service of Lord Grey de Ruthyn, from Thelwall, in Cheshire, about the middle of the 14th century. The original John Thelwall married Felia dau^{r.} and heir of Walter Cook, alias Ward, of Plasyward, from whence they branched off to Bathafern, Plas Coch, Blaen Ial and Llanbedr.

1588, John Turbridge, Esq.

This probably was one of the family of Caervllaen and Plastowbridge, n^{r.} Ruthin, of whom we have the following account from a monument in Ruthin Church :—" Here lieth the body of Robert Tourbridge, of Caervallen, Esqre. Son & heire of John, son & heire of Robert, son & heire of Robert Tourbridge, Esqre. Baron of Exchequere and Surveyor of North Wales, who married Ann Dau^{r.} of Samuel Mostyn of Calcote, Esqre. by whom he had issue Ann, his only Dau^{r.} & heire. He died ye 20 of July, A.D. 1679, in ye 55th year of his age."

Nov. 1, 1708, Sir Wm. Wms. Bart. Plasyward.

The Estate of Plasyward he obtained by marriage in 1680, with Jane Dau^{r.} and heir of Edw. Son of the Simon Thelwall, M.P. in 1640, and it is now inherited by his lineal descendant, Sir Watkin Williams Wynn, M.P. for the county.

Nov. 25, 1710, John Roberts, Esqr. Havod-y-bwch.

He married Susan Dau^{r.} of Wm. Parry, of Llwyn Inn, (Ynn) descended from Bishop Parry, Godfrey Goodman, and the Hollands, of Hendre-fawr, Abergale.

Dec. 11, 1713, John Wynne, Esqre. of Melai.

He was only Son of Wm. Wynne, and Mary, Dau^{r.} and Heir of Hugh Lloyd, of Segroit ; and he married Sydney,

Dau[r.] of Sir Wm. Williams, of Llanforda, and their Dau[r.]
and heir Jane was married to Sir John Wynn, of Bodvean,
Bart. grandfather to the present Lord Newborough, who
has inherited Melai from them. On his monument at
Llanfairtalhaiarn, it is recorded that " He served his
Country faithfully, both at home and in Parliament—he
was well esteemed and beloved by all his neighbours, being
a Person of good natural and improved parts, and exceedingly courteous, just, and hospitable. He died May 29,
1718, in the 50th year of his age."

Nov. 2, 1797, Thomas Tyrwhitt Jones, Esq[r.] Carreghova.
    Descended from " the honourable and ancient House" of
    Tyrwhitts, Knights of Kettilby, Co. Linc.   The elder
    branch of which assumed the surname of their Cousin Sir
    Thos. Jones, of Stanley Hall.

1802, Hon. Fred. West, Uncle to the Lord of Delawar, married
    Maria, second Dau[r.] and co-heir of Rich[d.] Myddelton,
    Esq[r.] of Chirk Castle.

1806, R. M. Biddulph, of the Ledbury branch of the ancient family
    of Biddulph Hall, Co. Stafford,—married Charlotte eldest
    Dau[r.] and co-heir of Rich[d.] Myddelton, Esq[rs.] of Chirk
    Castle.

1835, Wilson Jones. His ancesters resided at Cefn Coch, n[r.] Ru-
    thin, from the time of L[d.] Grey de Ruthyn.   They pur-
    chased Gelligynan, in 1730, and Hartsheath 1836.

1842, T. Mainwaring, (A. & M. Denbigh, p. 329,) of Marchwiel Hall,
    a younger Son of the Family of Bramborough Co. Cest.
    and Oteley Park, Co. Salop, married Anna Maria, eldest
    Dau[r] and co-heir of J. L. Salusbury, Esq[r.] of Galltfaenan.

Alderman Sir Hugh Myddelton, bart., M.P.

Having, in the former work, given a sketch of the life of this
worthy and eminent native, little need be added here. He was
about thirty-four years a member of the town council, counting
from the date of Elizabeth's charter to his decease; although it is
probable that he was a capital burgess before that charter was
obtained; and the many entries in the corporation books, in his
own hand-writing, prove that he personally attended to his muni-

cipal duties, while his (preserved) letters prove that he had the welfare of his native town closely and deeply at heart, amid his other multiferous engagements. He was a person of most active and industrious habits, as well as most enterprising, persevering, and indefatigable. The following communication preserved among our corporate muniments will "bear out" and illustrate those exemplary traits in his character which we are endeavouring to delineate. It is addressed to the corporate authorities, and the general body of burgesses, and has evidently a reference to the borough election of 1614, when he was returned to parliament, as the representative of his native town, the second time.

"Lovinge Coosins & ffrinds,

I have receved yor l're, and the confirmaçoue of yo^t waraunte for, wch as for yo^{r}forme^r kiudnesse in grauntinge I, oute againe hartelie to thanke yow all, wyshinge, wth all my harte, that in th^e office, or by anie other my travell and Indevo^{m}, yt laie in my power to doe the Towne good, In gen'all, or anie of you or yo^{m} in p'ticuler; p'testinge that yf I weare assured anie man ment asmutche good to the Towne as I doe, and would gaine noe more by the place *then* I wyll I woulde vp^s the least request fro' yow surrender the place againe with thankes.

Conc'nynge yor petetion to my Lo: President, I referr yo^w to Coosin Parrey's l're, aswell for my travell as what was doun therin. Ther was noe tyme lost for the effectinge what yo^w desired, and yf things fall not owt as shalbe fittinge and resonable, write me therof, and I will (God p'mittinge) travell them againe.

My Lo: Secretary had lent X^s. wh^{ch} Coosin Mathew repaid Coosin Parrey. Some money was saved in that busenesse.—And soe, wth my very harty comendaçons to yo^w all, in hast comitt yo^w all to God.—London, this 10th Maie, 1614.

Yo^r assured lovinge Coosin & ffrinde

HUGH MYDDELTON."

The next communication that we shall now give appears to be a reply respecting a legacy left to the poor of Denbigh, which had not been paid by the executors of the donor, and is the more interesting from the fact of its having been written just upon the completion of the New River. The sign of the possessive case is given within parenthesis to assist the sense ; it does not appear in the original.

    " Lovinge Coosins and ffrinds,

        I have received yo[r] letter by this berer, my Coosin Oliver Lloyd, yo[r] Baylyfe: thervpo[n] I went to Longe Lane to Mr. Ffludd('s) howse, John Roberts, (my late servant's) executo[r], who hath p'mysed mee this next Somer (god p'mittinge to be at Denbighe, wher hee will pay yo[w] the *tenne powends*, acquaintinge mee with many sutes w[ch] nowe are against hym for his brother('s) dette ; of w[ch] hee *most* see some ende, before hee canne paie my legasis. Nothwithstandinge, I will aske counsell, and be advysed what may be don, for the recov'rie therof in the maine tyme : and be assured yf hee lyve (notwithstandinge thes delaies) I will have yt of hym (god p'mittinge).

    Noe Burgis of Denbighe shalbe more forward & willinge then myself to ffurther any good for the Towne, and I take yt very frindlie that yo[w] will Jmploye me in any busenese that may tende to the publicke or privatt good of that Towne, and I sorrowe to thinke that I cann doe no more good for yo[w].

This berer hath spoken wth ffludd, and cann well advertyse yo[w] of the case as now it standeth.

I thanke you all for yor well wyshinge to my greate worke, nowe (I thanke God) well effected & p'formed, which made mee all this tyme neclect some good dutie towards the Towne (Denbigh) wh[ch] I shall more fully p'forme as God shall enable mee, vnto whose most blessed p'pection, with my hertie commendaçons, I comytt yo[w] all, and shall soe rest

              Your assured lovinge Coosin & ffrinde,

Lon: 3rd ffebru'y, 1613.   HUGH MYDDELTON."

CHAPTER VII.

COUNTY ELECTIONS—MEMBERS OF PARLIAMENT FOR DENBIGH-
SHIRE.

By an Act* of Henry VIII. the County of Denbigh was em-
powered to send one Knight to Parliament; the Reform Act (1832)
gave it two representatives. The following are all the Returns
now found on record:—

A.D.   *Reign of Henry III.*

1542, John Salusbury, (qy. Esquire?)—*Note.*—The name is va-
      riously spelt, Salebury, Salesbury, Salisbury, Salusbury,
      &c. In a Survey of Denbigh Castle, made in this reign,
      we find " John Salusbury, the Elder, Esquire, Chamber-
      lain of Denbigh." He was the first High-Sheriff of the
      county. (See *List* in the present work, also *A. and M.
      Denbigh, p.* 91.)

                Reign of Edward VI.

1547, John Salesbury, re-elected.

1552, Robert Puleston (qy. " of Bersham, Esquire?")

                Reign of Mary I.

1553, (Sir) John Salesbury, Knt.

1554, Re-elected twice in the course of this year.

1555, Edward . . . . the obliterated surname was probably
      Aylmer, or Almer, of Almer, or Pant Yockin, Esquire.

1557, Return lost.

                Reign of Elizabeth.

1558, Robert ap Hugh, (of Creuddyn, Esq.) High Sheriff in 1562.

1563, Simon Thelwall (of Plasward, Esq.)

---

* This statute is made to be of the 27th, 34th, and 37th year of this king's
reign in different authors.
    The Principality of Wales returned twelve Members to Parliament out of each
of the North and South Provinces, as early as 15th Ed. II., but how chosen is
uncertain, nor were there after any returns till the time of Hen. VIII., nor does
there appear any complaint of undue elections till 1681, when Richard Myddelton, Esq. petitioned against Sir John Trevor.

1571, Robert Puleston (of Bersham, Esq.)

1572, William Aylmer (Esq.)

1585, Evan Lloyd de Yale (Esq.)

1586, Richard Salesbury de Rug (Esq.)

1588, John Edwards de Chirk (Esq.)

1592, Roger Puleston (Esq.)—*Note.*—Brown Willis is not quite correct as to the assembling of this parliament. He states that it met upon the 19th of November, 1592, whereas it was not summoned until the 19th of February, 1593.

1597, (Sir) John Salesbury, Knt.

1601. Re-elected.

Reign of James I.

1603, Peter Mutton (Esq.) Afterwards Sir Peter Mutton, Knight, Chief-Justice of North Wales, &c. See *A. and M. Denbigh, p.* 218.

1614, (Sir) John Trevor, Knt.

1620, (Sir) John Trevor, jun. Knt.

1623, Eubulus Thelwall (Esq.)

1625, Thomas Myddelton (Esq.)

1625, Eubulus Thelwall (Esq)

Reign Charles I.

1625, Eubulus Thelwall.

1640, (Sir) Thomas Salisbury, Bart.

1640, (Sir) Thomas Myddelton, Knt.

The Commonwealth.

1653, Only six members returned for the whole of Wales.

1654, Col. Simon Thelwall. Col. John Carter.

1656, Col. John Jones. Col. John Carter.

1658-9, (Sir) John Carter, of Kinmel, Knt.

Reign of Charles II.

1660, Sir Thomas Myddelton, (of Chirk.)

1661, Re-elected, and also for the parliament of 1678, and of 1681, the fourth and last in this reign.

Reign of James II.

1661, Sir John Trevor.—*Note.*—This parliament, in 1665, sat at Oxford, whilst the plague raged in London.

1685, Sir R. Myddelton.

Reign of William and Mary.

1688, Sir Richard Myddelton. Also for the parliament of 1690; and of 1695, and 1701, under *William* alone.

Reign of Anne.

1702, Sir Richard Myddelton, Bart. Also for the parliaments of 1705, 1708, 1710, 1713, and 1715.

1707.—*Parliament of Great Britain.*

Reign of George I.

1715, Sir R. Myddelton. Re-elected. Died, new writ May 12th, 1716.

1716, Watkin Williams Wynn, (Esq.) Wynnstay, *vice* Myddelton, deceased. Also for the parliament of 1722. Robert Myddelton, Esq., petitioner.

Reign of George II.

1727, Watkin Williams Wynn (Esq.)

1734, Sir Watkin Williams Wynn, Bart.

And having, on the death of his father, accepted the Stewardship of Bromfield and Yale, he was re-elected in 1740. He also sat in the parliament of 1741.—John Myddelton, Esq., not duly elected.

1749, Sir Lynch Salusbury Cotton, Bart., Lleweni,* *vice* Wynn deceased. New writ issued Nov. 16, 1749. Also for the parliament of 1754.

Reign of George III.

1761-2, Sir Lynch Salusbury Cotton, Bart. Also for the parliament elected in 1768.

1774, Sir Watkin W. Wynne, Bart., Lord Lieutenant of the counties of Merioneth and Denbigh. Also for the parliaments of 1780, and 1784. Died, new writ Aug. 6, 1789.

1789, Robert Watkin Wynn, of Plasnewydd, Henllan, and Garthmeilio, *vice* Sir W. W. Wynne, deceased.

1790, Robert Watkin Wynn, Esq.

1796, Sir Watkin Williams Wynn, Bart. Also for the parliaments of 1796, 1801, 1802, 1806, 1807, 1812, and 1818.

Reign of George IV.

1820, Sir Watkin W. Wynn, Bart. And for the parliament of 1826.

---

* Receiver General of the King's quit rents in North Wales.

M

Reign of William IV.

1830, Sir Watkin W. Wynn, Bart. Also for the parliament of 1831.

Under the Reform Act.

1832, Sir Watkin W. Wynn, Bart. R. Myddelton Biddulph, Esq.

1835, Sir Watkin W. Wynn, Bart. The Hon. William Bagot.

Reign of Queen Victoria.

1837, Sir W. W. Wynn, Bart. The Hon. William Bagot.

1840, The Hon. H. Cholmondley, *vice* Sir W. Williams Wynn, deceased.

1841, Sir Watkin Wynn, Bart. The Hon. W. Bagot.

1845, Sir W. W. Wynn, Bart., re-elected, having been made Steward of Bromfield and Yale.

1848, Sir W. W. Wynn, Bart. The Hon. W. Bagot.

1852, Sir W. W. Wynn, Bart. Col. R. M. Biddulph.

1857, Re-elected.   Re-elected.

1859, Re-elected.   Re-elected.

The return for 1536 is lost. See " *Willis' Notitia Parl.*"; also a little book called, " *An exact List of all the Places and all the Members, &c.*"—" *Smith's Parliaments of England,*" and *Bateson's Chronological Register, &c.*"

CHAPTER VIII.

WALES was first divided into shires about 32 Henry VIII. The present County of Denbigh was formed by attaching to the ancient territory of "Denbighland" certain portions of the old princedom of Powys; and the following is the only complete List of its High Sheriffs that has ever been published.

[*From a curious Welsh M.S. (about A.D.* 1597) *found at Gwaenynog, in the last stage of decay, and for which the author is indebted to the memory of the late Capt. Myddelton. The use of capital letters and points was apparently unknown to the writer.*]

"*llyma afv o siryddion yn sir ddinbech er pan aeth Kymrv yn dir siroedd.*" *

Sion salbri siambl'en.
syr sion salbri
syr sion pilstwn
sion pilstwn tir mon.
sion owain
Robert salbri or rvc
sionn edwart or wavnn
Kadwalad, am morvs
Robert wyn i fab
doctor elis prys
sion llwyd o ial
william moston
edwart almor
Robert massi
ffowc lloid
tomas bylet
doctor elis prys
edwart almor
Robert pilston
Robert ffletsier
tomas ap morvs
Robert ap hiiw
ssieffre holant
sion wiliams
edwart conwy
hiiw pilstwnn
ffowc lloid
jeiij lloid o ial
doctor elis prys

Robert pilstwn
edwart almor
ssimwnt ffelwal
doctor elis prys
Robert win ap kadwaladr
syr sion salbri
edwart sions
sion wyn ap wiliam
pirs holant
tomas ab morvs
jeiij lloid ab Re.
owain brvwton
edwart hiiws
jeiij lloid o ial
pirs owain
hari pari
wiliam wyn o lanfair
wiliam almor
owain briiton
edwart evton
edwart ffelwal
powel o hosle
ffowc lloid
hari jeiij lloid
gr. wyn
tomas wyn ap ric.
dd. holant
syr Robert salbri or rriic
tervyn.

* That is, being interpreted, "Here are such as have been sheriffs in Denbighshire, since Wales became a land of shires."

[*From a List of High Sheriffs for the County of Denbigh since such officers were first appointed for North Wales, to* 1828; *existing at Denbigh in M.S.*]

Reign of Henry VIII.

1541, John Salusbury, Chamberlain of Denbigh, Esq.
1542, Sir John Salusbury of Lleweny, Knight.
1543, Sir John Puleston, of Bersham, Knight.
1544, John Puleston, of Sir Mon, Esq.
1545, John Owen, of Abergeley, Esq.
1546, Roger Salusbury, of Bachymbyd (or Rug), Esq.

Reign of Edward VI.

1547, John Edwards, of Chirk, Esq.
1548, Cadwalader Maurice, of Foylas, Esq.
1549, Robert Wynne ap Cadwalader, of Foylas, Esq.
1550, Ellis Price, of Plas Yolyn, Doctor,
1551, John Lloyd, of Yale, Esq.
1552, William Mostyn, of Maes Glas, Esq.

Reign of Mary.

1553, Robert Massey, of Maesmynnan, Esq.
1554, Edward Almer, of Almer, Esq.
1555, Foulk Lloyd, of Henllan, Esq.
1556, Thomas Bellot, of Burton, Esq.
1557, Ellis Price, of Plas Yolyn, Doctor.

Reign of Elizabeth,

1558, Edward Almer, of Pant Yokin, Esq.
1559, Robert Puleston, of Bersham, Esq.
1560, Robert Fletcher, of Llanfair Dyffyd Clwyd, Esq.
1561, Thomas Morris, of Ruthin, Esq.
1562, Robert ap Hugh, of Creiddin, Esq.
1563 Jeffry Holland, of Eglwysfach, Esq.
1564, John Thomas ap William, of Glan-Conway, Esq.
1565, Edward Conway, of Bryn-Eithin, Esq.
1566, Hugh Puleston, of Bersham, Esq.
1567, Foulk Lloyd, of Henllan, Esq.
1568, Evan Lloyd, of Yale, Esq.
1569, Ellis Price, of Plas Yolyn, Esq.
1570, Robert Puleston, of Bersham, Esq.
1571, Edward Almer, of Pant Yokin, Esq.
1572, Simon Thelwall, of Plasyward, Esq.
1573, Ellis Price, of Foylas, Doctor.
1574, Robert Wynne, ap Cadwaladar, of Foylas, Esq.
1575, Sir John Salusbury, of Lleweny, Knight.
1576, Edward Jones, of Cadwgan, Esq.
1577, John Wynn ap William, of Meley, Esq.
1578, Pierce Holland, of Abergele, Esq.
1579, Thomas Maurice, of Ruthin, Esq.

1580, John Price, of Derwen, Esq.
1581, Owen Brereton, of Borras, Esq.
1582, Edward Hughes, of Holt, Esq.
1583, Evan Lloyd, of Yale, Esq.
1584, Pierce Owen, of Abergeley, Esq.
1585, Henry Parry, of Maes Plas, Esq.
1586, William Wynne, of Meley, Esq.
1587, Thomas Almer, of Pant Yokin, Esq.
1588, Owen Brereton, of Borras, Esq.
1589, Edward Eyton, of Wat Stay, Esq.
1590, Edward Thelwal, of Plas y Ward, Esq.
1591, Thomas Powell, of Horseley, Esq.
1592, Foulk Lloyd, of Henllan, Esq.
1593, Henry ap Evan Lloyd, of Havodunos, Esq.
1594, Griffith Wynne, of Llanrwst, Esq.
1595, Thomas Wynne ap Richard of Llanrwst, Esq.
1596, David Holland, of Kinmel, Esq.
1597, Sir Robert Salusbury, of Bachymbyd, Knt.
1598, Edward Brereton, of Borras, Esq. *
—— Robert Sontley, of Sontley, Esq.
1599, Thomas Price, of Spytty, Esq.
1600, William Myddelton, of Gwaenynog, Esq.
1601, Owen Vaughan, of Llwydiard, Esq.
1602, David Holland, of Abergeley, Esq.

Reign of James I.

1603, Edward Eyton, of Wat Stay, Esq,
1604, John Lloyd, of Vaynol Rug, Esq.
1605, Cadwalader Wynne, of Voylas, Esq.
1606, Sir John Wynne, of Gwydir, Knight.
1607, Evan Meredith, of Glan Tannat, Esq.
1608, Morgan Broughton, of Marchwiel, Esq.
1609, Hugh Gwyn Griffith, of Berth Ddu, Esq.
1610, Sir Richard Trevor, of Trevalyn, Bart.
1611, Robert Sontley, of Sontley, Esq.
1612, Simon Thelwal, of Plas y Ward, Esq.
1613, Thomas Goodman, of Plas Uchaf, Llanfair Dyff. Clwyd, Esq.
1614, William Wynne, of Meley, Esq.
1615, Richard Williams, of Ruthin, Esq.
1616, Thomas Powell, of Horseley, Esq.
1617, Thomas Needham, of Clocaenog, Esq.
1618, Robert Wynne, of Berth Ddu, Esq.
1619, Foulk Myddelton, of Llansilin, Esq.
1620, William Vaughan, of Eyton, Esq.
1621, Hugh Meredith, of Wrexham, Esq.
1622, Sir Edward Trevor, of Bryn Kinallt, Knight.

* Edward Brereton, dying before his year was expired, was succeeded by Robert Sontley, of Sontley, Esq.

1623, Foulk Lloyd, of Henllan, Esq.
1624, Thomas Price Wynne, of Geeler, Esq.
1625, Sir Richard Grosvenor, of Eyton, Knight.

Reign of Charles I.

1626, George Bostock, of Holt, Esq.
1627, Edward Price, of Llwyn Ynn, Esq.
1628, Sir Henry Salusbury, of Lleweny, Knight.
1629, Edward Meredith, of Stansty, Esq.
1630, William Robinson, of Gwersyllt, Esq.
1631, Robert Wynne, of Voylas, Esq.
1632, William Dolben, of Denbigh, Esq.
1633, John Parry, of Plas yn Rhal, Esq.
1634, Roger Holland, of Abergeley, Esq.
1635, Hugh Lloyd Rosindale, of Denbigh, Esq.
1636, Hugh Lloyd, of Foxhall, Esq.
1637, William Wynne, of Meley, Esq.
1638, Edward Maurice, of Glan Cynlleth, Esq.
1639, Sir Thomas Powell, of Horseley, Bart.
1640, Richard Langford, of Allington, Esq.
1641, John Vaughan, of Henllan, Esq.
1642, John Bellot, of Moreton, Esq.
1643, John Thelwall, of Plas Coch, Esq.
1644, Sir Evan Lloyd, of Yale, Bart.
1645, Ditto   ditto
1646, Ditto   ditto
1647, John Kynaston, of Ruabon, Esq.
1648, Robert Sontley, of Sontley, Esq.

Time of the Commonwealth.—Usurpation of Cromwell.

1649, Thomas Ravenscroft, of Pickhill, Esq.
1650, Richard Myddelton, of Llansilin, Esq.
1651, William Wynne, of Garthgynnan, Esq.
1652, Thomas Ball, of Burton, Esq.
1653, John Edwards, of Chirk, Esq.
1654, William Edwards, of Eyton, Esq
1655, John Jeffreys, of Acton, Esq.
1656, Sir Owen Wynne, of Gwydir, Bart.
1657, Sir Thomas Powell, of Horseley, Bart.
1658, Robert Price, of Geeler, Esq.
1659, Edward Vaughan, of Llwydiart, Esq.

Reign of Charles II.

1660, Edward Vaughan, of Lwydiart, Esq.
1661, Charles Salusbury, of Bachymbyd, Esq.
1662, Watkin Kyffin, of Glascoed, Esq.
1663, Roger Puleston, of Emrall, Esq.
1664, Robert Wynne, of Voylas, Esq.
1665, Sir John Carter, of Kinmel, Knight.
1666, Charles Goodman, of Glanhespin, Esq.

1667, Morris Gethin, of Kernioge, Esq.
1668, William Parry, of Llwyn Ynn, Esq.
1669, Hugh Lloyd, of Foxhall, Esq.
1670, Edward Thelwall, of Plas y Ward, Esq.
1671, Mytton Davies, of Llannerch, Esq.
1672, John Thelwall, of Plas Coch, Esq.
1673, Edward Morris, of Lloran, Esq.
1674, Sir John Wynne, of Watstay, Bart.
1675, John Lloyd, of Gwyrch, Esq.
1676, David Morris, of Penybont, Esq.
1677, John Langford, of Allington, Esq.
1678, Edward Brereton, of Borras, Esq.
1679, Hedd Lloyd, of Havodunos, Esq.
1680, Thomas Holland, of Teirdan, Esq.
1681, William Edwards, of Chirk, Esq.
1682, Joshua Edisbury, of Erthig, Esq.
1683, Griffith Jeffreys, of Acton, Esq.
1684, Thomas Powell, of Horseley, Esq.
1685, Robert Griffith, of Brymbo, Esq.

Reign of James II.

1686, William Ravenscroft, of Pickhill, Esq.
1687, Robert Davies, of Llannerch, Esq.
1688, Sir Richard Myddelton, of Chirk Castle, Bart.

Reign of William and Mary.

1689, Roger Mostyn, of Brymbo, Esq.
1690, William Robinson, of Gwersyllt, Esq.
1691, Thomas Wynne, of Dyffryn Aled, Esq.
1692, Simón Thelwall, of Llanbedr Hall, Esq.
1693, David Williams, of Ty Newydd, Llansilin, Esq.
1694, Humphrey Kynaston, of Bryn Gwyn, Esq.
1695, David Parry, of Llwyn Ynn, Esq.
1696, William Williams, of Plas y Ward, Esq.
1697, John Hill, of Sontley, Esq.
1698, Sir Edward Broughton, of Marchwiel, Bart.
1699, Thomas Jones, of Carreghova, Esq.
1700, Sir Nathaniel Curson, of Coedmarchen, Bart.
1701, John Lloyd, of Brynlluarth, Esq.

Reign of Queen Anne.

1702, Eubule Thelwall, of Nantclwyd, Esq.
1703, Maurice Jones, of Plas Newydd, Esq. *
——— Thomas Roberts, of Llanrhydd, Esq.
1704, Elihu Yale, of Plas Gronow, Esq.
1705, John Roberts, of Havod-y-bwch, Esq.
1706, Henry Vaughan, of Dinarth, Esq.

* Maurice Jones dying before his year was expired, was succeeded by Thos. Roberts, of Llanrhydd, Esq.

1707, Thomas Holland, of Teirdant, Esq.
1708, David Lloyd, of Bodnant, Esq.
1709, John Wynne, of Garthmeilio, Esq.
1710, Ambrose Thelwall, of Plas Coch, Esq.
1711, Edward Wynne, of Llannefydd, Esq.
1712, John Wynne, of Meley, Esq.
1713, John Chambres, of Plas Chambres, Esq.

Reign of George I.

1714, Sir Thomas Cotton, of Leweny, Bart.
1715, John Williams, of Plas Issa, of Llennefydd, Esq.
1716, William Carter, of Kinmel, Esq.
1717, John Lloyd, of Trevor, Esq.
1718, John Jones, of Llwyn Ynn, Esq.
1719, Eubule Lloyd, of Pen-y-lan, Esq.
1720, John Lloyd, of Fox Hall, Esq.
1721, Thomas Price, of Glynn, Esq.
1722, Henry Roberts, of Rhydonnen, Esq.
1723, Thomas Hughes, of Penbedw, Esq.
1724, John Puleston, of Havod-y-wern, Esq.
1725, Henry Powell, of Glan-y-wern, Esq.
1726, Edward Salusbury, of Galltfaenan, Esq.
1727, Humphrey Brereton, of Borras, Esq.

Reign of George II.

1728, William Wynne, of Rhos, Esq.
1729, Maurice Wynne, of Llwyn, Esq.
1730, Robert Morris of Astrad, Esq.
1731, Thomas Salusbury, of Erbistock, Esq.
1732, Robert Ellis, Groes-newydd, Esq.
1733, Robert Price, of Bathavarn Park, Esq.
1734, Richard Williams, of Penbedw, Esq.
1735, Humphrey Parry, of Pwllhalog, Esq.
1736, Edward Lloyd, of Plumamog, Esq.
1737, Edward Williams, of Pont-y-Gwyddel, Esq.
1738, John Jones, of Squinnant, Esq.
1739, Cawley Humberston Cawley, of Gwersyllt, Esq.
1740, John Williams, of Plas Ucha', Esq.
1741, William Myddelton, of Plas Turbridge, Esq.
1742, John Edwards, of Gallt-y-Celyn, Esq.
1743, Aquila Wyke, of Marchwiel, Esq.
1744, Edward Jones, of Ddol, Esq.
1745, Robert Davies, of Llannerch, Esq.
1746, Thomas Lloyd, of Fox Hall, Esq.
1747, R. Williams, Pwll-y-Crochon, Esq.
1748, Robert Wynne, of Garthmeilio, Esq.
1749, John Mostyn, of Segroit, Esq.
1750, Thomas Jones, of Llantisilio, Esq.
1751, John Holland, of Tyrdan, Esq.

1752, John Jones, of Llwyn-ynn, Esq.
1753, Kenrick Eyton, of Eyton, Esq.
1754, Edward Maddocks, of Fron-yw, Esq.
1755, Watkin Wynne, of Voylas, Esq.
1756, Maurice Jones, of Gelligynnan, Esq.
1757, John Lloyd, of Havodunos, Esq.
1758, Robert Wynne, of Dyffryn Aled, Esq.
1759, Hugh Clough, of Glanywern, Esq.
1760, Griffith Speed, of Wrexham, Esq.

Reign of George III,

1761, Pierce Wynne, of Llanychan, Esq.
1762, Simon Thelwall, of Blaen Yale, Esq.
1763, Robert Wynne, of Henllan, Esq.
1764, William Dymock, of Wrexham, Esq.
1765, Thomas Kyffin, of Maenan, Esq.
1766, Evan Vaughan Lloyd, of Bodidris, Esq.
1767, John Davies, of Llannerch, Esq.
1768, Edward Lloyd, of Trevor, Esq.
1769, Robert Wynne, of Garthewin, Esq.
1770, Richard Price Thelwall, of Bathavarn Park, Esq.
1771, John Vaughan, of Groes, Esq.
1772, Peter Davies, of the Grove, Esq.
1773, Edward Lloyd, of Royden Hall, Esq.*
—— Sir Edward Lloyd, of Pengwern, Bart.
1774, William Jones, of Wrexham Vechan, Esq.
1775, Richard Parry, of Llanrhaiadr, Esq.
1776, John Humberston Cawley, of Gwersyllt, Esq.
1777, Robert Foulkes, of Gwerneigron, Esq.
1778, John Foulkes, of Erriviatt, Esq.
1779, David Roberts, of Kinmel, Esq.
1780, William Thomas, of Bryncaredig, Esq.
1781, The Hon. Thomas Fitzmaurice, of Lleweny.
1782, Sir Thomas Jones, of Carreghova, Bart.†
—— Richard Clough, of Glanywern, Esq.
1783, Charles Goodwin, of Burton, Esq.
1784, John Ellis, of Eyton, Esq.
1785, John Twigge, of Borras, Esq.
1786, Phillip Yorke, of Erthig, Esq.
1787, Sir Foster Cunliffe, of Acton, Bart.
1788, Richard Wilding, of Llanrhaiadr Hall, Esq.
1789, Charles Brown, of Marchwiel Hall, Esq.
1790, Edward Lloyd, of Ceven, Esq.
1791, John Jones, of Cefn Coch, Esq.
1792, Thomas Jones, Llantysilio Hall, Esq.

* Edward Lloyd, of Royden Hall, dying before his year was expired, was succeeded by Sir Edward Lloyd, of Pengwern, Bart.

† Sir Thomas Jones dying before his year was expired, was succeeded by Richard Clough, of Glanywern, Esq.

N

1793, Edward Eyton, of Eton Hall, Esq.
1794, Bryan Cooke, of Havod-y-wern, Esq.
1795, John Wynne, Gerwin Fawr, Esq.
1796, John Hughes, of Horseley Hall, Esq.
1797, Robert Hesketh, of Gwrych, Esq.
1798, John Jones, of Penybryn, Ruabon, Esq.
1799, John Wilkinson, of Brymbo Hall, Esq.
1800, John Lloyd Wynne, of Coed Coch, Esq.
1801, John Meredith Mostyn, of Segroit, Esq.
1802, Daniel Leo, of Llannerch Paik, Esq.
1803, Henry Ellis Boates, of Rose Hill, Esq.
1804, Robert William Wynne, of Garthewin, Esq.
1805, Samuel Riley, of Marchwiel Hall, Esq.
1806, Richard Jones, Belan Place, Ruabon.
1807, Simon Yorke, of Erthig, Esq.
1808, Richard Harry Kenrick, of Nantclwyd, Esq.
1809, Joseph Ablett, of Llanbedr Hall, Esq.
1810, Richard Lloyd, of Bronheulog, Esq.
1811, John Wynne, of Garthmeilio, Esq.
1812, William Edwards, of Hendre House, Esq.
1813, Thomas Marrall Griffiths, of Wrexham, Esq.
1814, Edward Rowland, of Gardden, Lodge Esq.
1815, Charles Wynne Griffith Wynne, of Voylas, Esq.
1816, Edward Edwards, of Cerrig-llwydion, Esq.
1817, Pierce Wynne Yorke, of Dyrffyn Aled, Esq.
1818, Edward Lloyd, of Berth, near Ruthin, Esq.
1819, John Chambers Jones, of Bryneisteddfod, Esq.
1820, John Lloyd Salusbury, of Galltfaenan, Esq.

Reign of George IV.

1821, John Madockes, of Fronyw, Esq.
1822, Samuel Newton, of Pickhill, Esq.
1823, Sir David Erskine, of Pwll-y-Crochon, Bart.
1824, Richard Myddelton Lloyd, of Wrexham, Esq.
1825, William Egerton, of Gresford Lodge, Esq.
1826, Thomas Fitzburgh, of Plas Power, Esq.
1827, John Price, of Plas-coch, Llanychan, Esq.
1828, Lloyd Hesketh Bamford Hesketh, of Gwyrch Castle, Esq.

[*From Joseph Peers, Esq., Clerk of the Peace, for the County.*]
1829, William Lloyd, of Bryn Estyn, Esq.

Reign of William IV.

1830, Job Hanmer, of Bodnod, Esq.
1831, Wilson Jones, of Gelligynnan, Esq.
1832, Edward Lloyd, of Cefn, Esq.
1833, William Parry Yale, of Plas yn Yale, Esq.
1834, Francis Richard Price, of Bryn-y-pys, Esq.
1835, Sir Robert Henry Cunliffe, of Acton, Bart.
1836, John Robin, of Tan-y-graig, Esq.

Reign of Queen Victoria.

1837, John Heaton, of Plas Heaton, Esq.
1838, Samuel Sandbach, of Hafodunos, Esq.
1839, Sir John Williams, of Bodlewyddan, Bart.
1840, Townshend Mainwaring, of Marchwiel Hall, Esq.
1841, Colonel Boates, of Rosehill.
1842, Colonel Molineaux Williams, Penbedw.
1843, John Townshend, of Trevallyn, Esq.
1844, Henry Warter Meredith, of Pentre-bychan, Esq.
1845, Charles Wynne, of Garthmeilio, Esq.
1846, Brownlow Wynne Wynne, of Garthewin, Esq.
1847, R. Lloyd Edwards, of Nanhoran, Esq.
1848, Simon Yorke, of Erthig, Esq,
1849, Thomas Griffith, of Trevallyn Hall, Esq.
1850, John Burton, of Minera Hall, Esq.
1851, Thomas Hughes, of Ystrad Hall, Esq.
1852, Francis James Hughes, of Acton House, Esq.
1853, Pierce Wynne Yorke, of Dyffryn Aled, Esq.
1854, Richard Jones, of Bellan Place; Ruabon, Esq.
1855, Henry Robertson Sandbach, of Hafodunos, Esq.
1856, John Jesse, of Llanbedr Hall, Esq.
1857, John Edward Madocks, of Glanywern, Esq.
1858, John Jocelyn Ffoulkes, of Eriviatt, Esq.
1859, Thomas Lloyd Fitzhugh, of Plas Power, Esq.
1860, James Hardcastle, of Penylan, Ruabon, Esq.

CONCLUDING REMARKS.

A brief notice of each of the foregoing Members of Parliament for the County, and High Sheriffs, or even of the family to which each belonged, would of itself fill a volume ; so that we can only afford here a passing observation with respect to two or three of the more ancient or remarkable families and characters.

The chief aim of this treatise is to pourtray, not in fictious imagery, but in real characters, the social history of Wales during the past five hundred years. The "RECORDS OF DENBIGH AND ITS LORDSHIP" are but a part and parcel of the general history of those times. And nothing throws more light upon the dim page of Welsh annals, after the subjugation of the Principality to the rule of England, and before the rise of modern Welsh literature, than the effusions of the bards of the sixteenth and seventeenth centuries. But, unfortunately, many of those curious and matchless "rhymes" have either fallen a prey to accident, or are to be found only in musty

MSS., in old baronial libraries, closed, as it were, from the perusal of
the Welsh reader and historiographer. Among the present author's
antiquarian gleanings, in the historical town and neighbourhood of
Denbigh, are some of these fragmental gems of Welsh mediæval
poetry, which cast a sort of archæological lustre upon the domestic
annals of those " unlettered ages"; and since they illustrate the religious sentiments, and depict the social condition and manners of
" our great sires," they claim a page in the " Records of Denbigh
and its Lordship," as the following, which was written about four
hundred years ago, though never before published.

I.

"Hawdd vyd heddyw i vwydau : hawddamawr y wledd vawr vau.
A'r lle rroir i'r llu ar hynt : a'r ddeuddyn a'i rrydd iddynt.
Sion Edwart os hwnn ydyw ; Sain' Sior drws i ynys yw.
Heulwen haf hael Wenhwyvar : a hyn vo'r ddeuddyn na'r dd'ar.
Kriadog karai wowdydd : *Vreichvras* wr i'r verch vry sydd.
A thegau uwch Porthwgonn : a llaes yw'r vantell i honn.
Dynion tec dan yn i ty : da'n wybren Dwywaen obry.
Downus b Cryd ynys Brydain : drysau'r hael a droes i'rrain.
Dau'n kostiaw dan y kastell : dan Dduw ni chaid annedd well.
Ddinas y Klawdd ynys y Kler : a Rruvain y rrai over.
Mann rrydd mwnai a rroddion : mae dwy swydd ym o dai Sion ;
Maer uwch aelwyd merch Elis : a mab maeth yma mhob mis.
Vy lle'r wyl ni phallai'n un : vy llety vu oll atun.
Fy nau dâl vy nodau ynt : vy ergyd oedd vwrw gwawd iddynt.
Noter gwyr yn i tair gwart : nid oes nod ond Sion Edwart.
Ef a gaiff o vwa gwawd : vy ergydion tra vo'r geudawd.
Eiddil yw llu i ddal llys : wrth enaid yr wyth ynys.
Byrrion, ddynion dianael : byr wrth hwn, mab Jorwerth hael.
Enaid i'r gwann ydyw'r gwr : arth y kaid wrth hokedwr.
Allt serth i williaid yw Sion : goriwared i'r gwirion.
Wrth wyr o lys, Arthur lân : y lluniwyd i holl anian.
Gwr moesawl yw grymus wedd : gwnn ar hwnnw gann rrinwedd.
Gwr kadarn goreu keidwad : gwaed Ywain Glynn i gadw'n gwlad.
Syrr Wiliam sy ryolw'r : Sion gyda'r Goron yw'r gwr.
Llaw'r Waun yn llywio'r ynys : llaw arall ar holl wyr y llys.
Yn rhaid y baedd rhodio bu : yn Lloegr ninnau'n llewygu.
Duw a'r saint a'r troes ef : o'r vrwydr ef a'i wyr adref.
Wrth wyn naw kannyn a'i kar : a gwyn hevyd Gwenhwyvar.
Ofnus vyth vu'r vynnwes vau : er's deuvis hyd nos Diviau.
A Threvor, neithwyr aviach : a Swydd y Waun sydd yw iach.
Huno a gais hen a gwaun : hun wellwell o hynn allan.
Hun y gwaed honno a gaf : hiraeth hagr hwyr i'th ddygaf.

GUTO'R GLYNN."

II.

KOWYDD MOLIANT SION LLWYD, YSGWEIER, O JAL.

(High Sheriff, A. D. 1551.)

" Y Llwyd arial, llew dewrwych : y llu beirdd a gâr lle bych.
Sion ofn i'th gasseion wyd : Swydd ddrud i suddo'r ydwyd.
Aer wyd, llew euraid llawen : o Dudur Llwyd, waed Jeirll hen.
Dwc oll rediad a gallu : Davydd Llwyd i veiddiaw llu.
A thra da, wrth roi dyall : ydyw'r llin o'r Llwyd i'r llall.
Wyrion haelion a eurwyd : Ynyr hen, un o'r rrain wyd.
Sion dy gyffion da gaffael : sy winwydd hen Sandde hael.
Da uchod dy iachoedd : o du'r taid, Sion Edwart oedd.
Mur gwlad a'i mowrglod ydwyd : maen growndwal yn Jal ynn wyd.
I drin, neu daro annial : a llu doech, y Llwyd o Jal.
Llu ich ol dan ych llaw'ch hun : lle'r aethoch a holl *Ruthun.*
Ystor tec ystiwart wyd : ysta sad ustus ydwyd.
Gwych wyd wr ac awch dewredd : os gwych vu (H)ector vraisk wedd.
Wyd irlan lain nod eurloyw : os glan Absalom wisk loyw.
Hael wr wyd hylaw deiriaith : os hael vu Nudd sylvaen jaith.
Mewn pur wlad maen perl ydwyd : mewn aur yn Llanarmon wyd.
Dy dwr lle'r ydwyd eirwir : dy lys Sion a dal y *sir.*
Llys Katrin, lle sy gytraul : Llanrrayadr oll un*rryw draul.*
Ag yw rrann, ail eigr hi : yr aeth tir ei thad *HARRI.*
Hi yw rhyw rwydd-deb y rhawc : barwnes *SALBRI* enwawc.
A gwawr o vric goleuryw : Kloddaith, un dec haelddoeth yw.
Llin hyd seth lle nodais sydd : llin Einion berllan winwydd.
Llwyn îr yn llawn o aeron ; Llywarch hael lle'r â'r iach hon.
Grawnwin vu'r tec rieni : gwawr hael yn dwyn gair y *rhi.*
Oes glaerloer mor ddisgleirliw ? oes gwraic well i scweier gwiw ?
Oes o'n iaith mor rymus neb : a chwi Sion barchus wyneb ?
Priviaist ymhob rryw avael ; priviad corff provedic hael.
Kadw'r wlad, i kadrwal ydwyd : Kai hir Sion mewn kuras wyd.
Er traws y gwr wtresswin : neu er y balch ni roi binn.
'I'wr nod val teyrn ydwyd : tad y gwir tawedoc wyd.
*Dr*wy dewi yn dra duwiol : dy rann ni edi ar ol.
*Ll*ew brau wyd, a llaw eb rus : llariaidd hael a chellweirus.
*Gai m*awr val i'th gymerwyd : ymraich Jâl a Cheinmyrch wyd.
Ni bu, nid adwaen neb ail : nid oeda veirddion d'adail.
*De*win grassol yw d'wyneb : dy dai'n Jâl nid oedai neb.
Dy lys lle kaid alussen : dy dwr sy Moâidris wenn.
Yn d'adail dyn Duw ydwyd : yn dy gaer vaen digrif wyd.
Yno down i windai Jal : yno kawn enwoc kynnal.
* * * drwy lawenydd : A chychwi Sion chwechoes hydd.

SIMWNT VYCHAN yn 1560."

The *Italics* show where the original is torn or illegible. But our poet's hero dies, and a scrap of his masterly elegy remains :—

III.

Gwal dew vur galed a vai : gwnn achos ae gwannychai.
Ent'raw o dwyll—nid tra da : Js sylvaen bresswylva.
O chilia uwch heolydd : y marn rrai y mur a'n rrydd.
Mal yr aeth mae wylaw'r wyl : mur Jal wenn, mawr wal annwyl.
Wyrion Ynyr un wanec : o Jal dir oedd y wal dec.
Maen growndwal am Ynyr : oedd Sion Llwyd urddas hen Llyr.

* * * *

Dyrras oedd val kwymp derwen : dorri sail Bodidris wenn.
Yno deiliaid yn dolef : wedy 'r Llwyd, heb dorri llef.
Y dydd oer o'i dai ydd aeth : i'r ddwywlad yr oedd alaeth.
Bro Jal yn wir brawlawn oedd : bro Glwyd un berygl ydoedd.
Lle'r äi bu uwch llawr y bedd : llu Sion, gwyr llys, yn gorwedd.
Llu tec iawn i llety gynt : llu du wedy'r Llwyd ydynt.
Llu trist lle mae llety 'r tras : Llannrrayadr val llu'n Rroias.
Os gloes oer dasc wylaw sydd : yn mro Dyfnoc mae'r defnydd.
Aml yw och brudd am walch brau : yn Rruthun oer yw hithau.
Od aeth, bid adwyth a bar : y stiwart mewn ais dayar.

* * * *

Trwkio ennyd ty'r kynnal : torri nen y twr yn Jal.
Troi llif amgylch teiau'r Llwyd : troi yn brudd Gatrin o'r breuddwyd.
Lloer Harri Salbri os aeth : lle'r el a ddwc llwyr alaeth.

* * * * * *

Aer a gyrraedd ragorion : a dywys Jal wedy Sion,
Ynnill yw'r Llwyd yn lle'r llall : eurllew dewr yw'r Llwyd arall.
(H)ector Jal a gwayw Troelys : yw Jevan Llwyd yn y llys.
Jal a gair yw ol i gyd : Jal o'i goval a gyvyd.
Annwyl o vewn Jal yw vo. * * *

Along with the old list of High Sheriffs, there is a curious fragment of a pedigree in a different hand, which is amusing.

(Original.)	(Translation.)
. . . . gr. ap madoc gloddaeth oedd fam ritsiart ap howel ap Jeiij vychan, a mam hari salbri, a'i chwiorydd undad unfam, sef yw chwiorydd hynny :—	The . . . . . of Griffith son of Madoc Gloddaeth was the mother of Richard son of Howel son of Jeuan Vychan, and the mother of Henry Salusbury and his sisters of the same father and same mother, that is, to those sisters :—
elsbeth afv wraic briod i bris or hob, a chwedi hynny a elwid arglwyddes pilstwn, o achos pyriodi ar ratsier pilstwn marchoc.	Elizabeth who was the wedded wife to Price of Hope, and afterwards called Lady Puleston by reason of marrying Sir Roger Puleston, knight.
marged gwraic æriod Robert ap gr ap Re ap howel o ddinamael.	Margaret the wedded wife of Robert son of Griffith son of Rees son of Howel of Dinmel.

sioned gwraic briod howel ap sion ap ithel vychan o ysgeivioc ynnhegaingl.

Janet the wedded wife of Howel son of John son of Ithel Vychan of Esceiviog in Englefield.

Anes gwraic briod sion ap gr ap lln, ap kwlkyn o chwaen ynghwmwd llivon ymonn.

Agnes the wedded wife of John son of Griffith son of Llewelyn son of Hulkin of Chwaen in the neighbourhood of Llivon, in Anglesea.

lowri, gwraic briod wiliam ap wiliam ap gr ap Robin gywhillan.

Laura the wedded wife of William son of William son of Griffith son of Robin Cochwillan.

Katrin gwraic briod hiiw ap sion ap madoc ap howel o fodfel yn llyn. a chwedi bynny hi abriodes pirs ap gr. ap dd. ap ithel fychan, kwnstabyl rruddlan a sersiant farmys.

Catherine the wedded wife of Hugh son of John son of Madoc son of Howel of Bodvel in Lleyn (Carn.) and afterwards she married Pierce son of Griffith son of David son of Ithel Vychan, Constable of Rhuddlan, and Sergeant Vermys.

tervyn.

conclusion.

Nor can we omit another beautiful effusion in praise of Eyon of Watstay, ancestor of the present worthy baronet of Wynnstay, as the mansion is now known.

IV.

KOWYDD I WILIAM EYTON, O RIWABON.

Eurwn gerdd o rann y gwir : i lew eurdorch Maelordir.
Awn—a gwaed enwoc ydyw—at Nudd—Wiliam Eutyn yw.
Ysta eurwalch ystyriwn : ystor holl Varsdir yw hwnn.
Argae ydyw ar gedyrn : o godiad derchaviad chwyrn.
Ysgwieirwalch braisk eurwy : a gyrraedd vod mewn gradd vwy.
Yn *Syrr*, darogenais hynn : y noter mab Sion Eutyn.
Mae yw balf val mab Elen : yspail Sion ap Elis hen.
Gwiwglod o haedd brigowglin : Griffri dec a roe ffrwd win.
Da haelwaed hen sy'n dal tir : dyledawc waed Elidir. [lin aeth.
Kydwaed Pilstwn, barc odiaeth : *Kaofle (Calverley)* 'n un cyva
Brans eurddail a gynnail gwyr : bric Einion ber ac Ynyr.
Da deiliad pleidwad Wiliam : * * *
I vreuder a'i vawr odiaeth : val i ryw dros Vaelor aeth.
Mynn air Rolant ! mae'n *riwliaw* : Mastr Wiliam ddinam a ddaw.
Mae i lan gorff ymlaen gwyr : Maelorydd mal ryw eryr.
Mae son nid am sy annewr : mal am ddec am Wiliam ddewr.
A mwy son am sy unair : i wraic ddoeth rywiog air.
A dinam son am dani : Marsia hael y Mers yw hi.
Meistres Ann, ba vann heb vod : mawl i hon em loyw bynod?
* * *
Llyma lin Kwchwillan lys : Llin enwoc llanwai ynys.
Eurwas brid urddas bro : tu Einion yw plaid honno.

Tu Salbri draw yn euraw'n iaith: treigleiddwæd trwy ryw Gloddaith.
Iach dec a chayad ogylch: iach Ann ni cheir chwyn o'i chylch.
Oes i wr is awyr iach: wraic weddaidd rywiogeiddiach?
Na gwr gwell oll gwir gall wedd: no gwr Ann am enwoc rinwedd.
Dan nef nid adwaen ovwy: dau yn un hael dôn a hwy.
Na dau yn rroi i da'n rhad: yn i goror un gariad.
Mal y kaf a mael kyvan: alw am gerdd William ac Ann.
Os doeth diwagvost ieithydd: os hael, pand Wiliam y sydd.
Os ty rrydd vydd ac a vu: Band ty William ben-teulu.
Ni cheuir ty, ni char twyll: Nudd Rriwabon ddewrbwyll.
Af yw lys, i vawl a wnn: Wyl Vair ato hael Vryttwn.
Llawer bendith y llywydd: y llew Siou o vewn llys hydd.
Llyna rad Duw'n llenwi'r tai: llwyddiant a ddaw lle'r haeddai.
Pill Maelor pell y molwn: y llaw hael sydd i'r llew hwn.
Llaw Nudd a urddodd lle'n iaith: llaw William velly uniaith.
Llaw Vair rrac pallu a'i eryr: llaw Dduw ai llwyddo a'i wyr.

SIMWNT VYCHAN."

Sir Richard Trevor, who was High Sheriff in 1610, erected at Gresford a remarkable monument for his father, with the following inscription :—

" SION TREVOR TREVALYN YSGWIER, Y 19 O DAD I DAD O DVDVR TREVOR, A FV FARW YN LHVNDAIN YMIS MEHEVIN 1589, EI ESGYRN EF EI VAB AI AER S^{R.} RICHARD TREVOR A BARODD EI MVDO IR FEDDROD HONN I ORPHWYS GIDAI HENAFIAID, FAL WRTH YMADO A'R BYD I DVMVNODD. BLYNYDDOEDD EI IEINCKTID A DROS-FWRIODD EF YN RHYVELOEDD FRAINCK DANN VRENIN HENRY 8. EI GANOL-FYD A GYFOESODD EF YN YMDAITH DIERTH-WLEDYDD. EI DDIWEDD-OES A GARTREFFODD EF YN LLYWOD-RAEH A GWASANAETH EI ANEDIGAEH-WLAD. EF A BRIODODD MARY MERCH GEORGE BRIDGES, YSCWIER ; AC A FV IDDO O HONI BVMP O VEIBION A DWY O VERCHED. SEF I S^{R.} RICHARD TREVOR MARCHOC DEPVTY-LIF'ENANT Y SIR HONN, YR HWN A BRIODODD KATRIN MERCH ROESIER PVLESTON O EMRAL YSCWIER, FAB S^{R.} EDWARD PVLESTON, MARCHOG. 2. SION TREVOR YSCWIER, GOLYGWR AR LYNGES ARDDERCHAWG Y VRENHINES, YR HWN A BRIODODD MAR-GED MERCH HVW TREVANIAN, CARIHAYS YNGHERNYW YSCWIER, VAB S^{R.} HVW TREVANIAN, MARCHOC 3 RONDL TREVOR, A FV FARW YN CYFAGOS AROL EI DAD 4 SACKVIL TREVOR, CAPTEN YN AWRYW O LONGAV'R VRENHINES 5 THOMAS TREVOR, MYFYRIWR Y CYF-RAITH : 6 WINIFFRED, A BRIODFS EDWARD PVLESTON O ALYNTON YSCWIER T. AC ERMIN A BRIODES ROBERT LLOID O HERSEDD YSCWIER."

The above are fine specimens of mediæval Welsh, and as such, very interesting to the student, a tongue so requisite to the British antiquary and historian.   Indeed, the author presumes that the " original " must be so well understood by the general reader, that were it possible to give " fair and just" *translations* of such poems, they would neither be appreciated, nor conduce anything to the study of Welsh archæology, and so defeat one great "end" of the present work. But to give the mere English reader some idea of the interesting nature of these poetical remains, we will take, as a specimen, poem No. I., which comes from the highly talented and humorous pen of *Guto'r Glynn*, a chief-bard, who flourished from A.D. 1430 to 1480. The lines are in celebration of a great banquet, given by a Welsh chieftain, an ancestor to the High Sheriff of 1547, upon his return home with his clan, consisting of nine hundred armed men, from an expidition into England, and a battle connected with the Wars of the Roses. The event must have taken place some time between A.D. 1467 and 1472. The " *boar*, at whose need they marched," must mean Edward IV. The disloyalty of the chieftain's household bard, seen in an epithet so disrespectful of majesty, leads us to suspect the real hollowness of the " lord's " allegiance, which turned, no doubt, upon the oscillating policy of the time. The scene of festal mirth is the hero's court, in the wild glen of the Ceiriog, which is described as " the citadel of minstrels, and the Rome of revellers," (alluding to the carnivals of " the Eternal City,") where they were always loaded with money and other gifts ; the bard humorously describing himself as a functionary there, in the two-fold capacity . of " mayor of the hearth" and monthly nursling of the chieftain's hospitable lady ; the host being spoken of as King Arthur, at his table, and the hostess as Queen Winiver ; whilst the former is also compared with " Caractacus of the Strong Arm"—one in whose veins the patriotic blood of Owen Glendower flowed for the defence of his country. His honours at court and influence with the king, are described as great. The lines which we may render—

> " And from the metric bow
> To him my rhymes are shot
> While gut remains,"

must be a pun, having at the same time for its purport that he would never cease to " string" the praises of a hero so " largely" hospitable, whilst his appetite for the viands lasted ; no one else being allowed to occupy his seat upon festival days. The anxiety felt for the lives of the chieftain and his brave followers, during the past two months' campaign, is beautifully contrasted with the soft

o

slumbers into which the rejoicings of their native glen sink upon their safe return, which our poet, as a good Papist, attributes to the interposition of " God and the *Saints*."

In the same old M.S. we have the names of the principal *airs* played by the minstrels of that time, and the names of the composers :—" henwey y prif gainkie, a henwey neb a wnaeth bob vn :"—

1.—" Ourai gowydd" (which we may perhaps interpret as, *The Warbler's Ode*,) by KADWGAN.

2.—" Kas gan dinker," *The Tinker's Dislike*, (probably so called because it was difficult for a " tinker," or inferior musician to play,) by KYHELYN.

3.—" Kas gan grythor," *The Fiddler's Dislike*, (probably a piece more suitable for the harp than the violin,) by KADWGAN.

4.—" Dillin efaa" *(Eva)*, *Eve's Fashion*, by KYHELYN.

5.—" Krechwen veinir," *The Maiden's Laughter*, by KADWGAN.

6.—" Organ levkv" *(Leuci)*. *Lucy's Organ*, by KYHELYN.

7.--" Llonen hafar," which we may, perhaps, interpret, *Light, Easy, and Free ;* or *The Merry Slattern*, by KADWGAN.

8.—" Y gowefthas," *The Party*, or *Picnic*, by KYHELIN.

9.—" Awen wrli," *The Reeling Muse*, (evidently implying a waltz or quadrille,) by KADWGAN.

10.—" Afel y fawd," *(Gafael y fawd,)* *The Thumb-Note*, (probably the same as " Synwyr y Fawd,") *The Random*.

11.—" Awen olevdydd," *The Daylight Muse*, (perhaps so called because played at the " wind-up" of the ball at dawn,) by KADWGAN.

12.—" Eos wrli," The Nightingale Reel, a dancing or ball tune, no doubt, by KYHELYN.

" Oerloes (probably *irlas*) goeden," *The Young Green Tree — The Sappling*, by KADWGAN.

13.—" Kaink nest berwyn," *Nesta of Berwyn's Air*, by KYHELYN.
" Koc wenllian," *Wenchal's Cuckoo*, by KADWGAN.

14.—" Y gaink hir i *Kyhelyn*," *The Long Air*, by KYHELYN.

15.—" Y gaink fer i *Kyhelyn*," *The Short Air*, by KYHELYN.

16.—" Kaink y krythor dv," *The Black Fiddler's Air*.

Thus, Cadogan and Kyhelin were the great composers of Wales, four hundred years back, and how many of their airs or musical compositions, have come down to the present time, presents an interesting problem for the solution of the musical antiquary.

CHAPTER IX.

THE POSTMORTEM INQUISITION OF THE ESTATES OF HENRY DE LACY, EARL OF LINCOLN—FROM THE EVIDENCE TAKEN BEFORE THE COURT AT DENBIGH, AT MIDSUMMER, A.D. 1311.

[*The following is copied from a document of great interest to the antiquary and historian, as the earliest known valuation of the Lordship of Denbigh. Having for ages lain in the Tower, it was lately removed to the new Record Office. The want of suitable type has compelled the printer to use apostrophes and periods for the contractions with which the M.S. abounds.*]

"*Among the Records deposited in the Public Record Office, London, to wit, Inquisition 4, Edward II., No. 51, it is thus contained :—*

DYNEBEGH.

' Inquis. de terr. & ten. de quibz. Henr. de Lacy Comes Linc. fuit seisit. in d'nico suo ut de feodo die quo obiit. vidlt. quantu' terre idem Henr. tenuit de d'no Rege in capite & quantu' de aliis. Et p. qd. s'viciu'. Et quantu' terre & ten. illa valeant p. annu' in o'ibz. exit. Et quis p'pinquior heres ej' sit & cuj' etatis fca. cora. Eschaetore apd. Dynebegh die D'nica p'xia ante festu' Sci. Petri in Cathedra anno r. R. Edwardi quarto : p. scrm : Thome de . . . . unfrete[a] Ade de Swynemor[b] Lewelini ap Yorverth Madoc. ap Gronou Griff' ap Rees[c] Keneverd Loyd Yorev'th Duy Yorev'th . . . . Tudir . . . arwet Ken' Loyd & Jevan ap Ithel, Iur. qui p. scrm. suu' qd. p'd'cs Henr' Com Linc' tenuit in d'nico suo ut de feodo die q° obiit priam de Roes & de Row . . . . . & Com'otu de Caymergh' cum cast'° de Dynebegh' de d'no Rege in capite p. s'viciu' militare. Et castrum ibidem nichel valet p. annu' ult* reprisas & alit' valeret p. annu' decem libr. Et sunt ibidem iiij[xx]. acr. terre arrabiles in d'nico que valent p. annu' iiij.*li*. p'c. acre xij.*d*. Et sunt ibidem tres parce[d] quor. unus parc' valet p. annu' x.*li*. & alius valet p. annu' x. (*xvi?*) marc' & t'cius parcus valet p. annu' cent' sol. Et est ibidem q°ddam molendinu' aquaticu'[e] qd. val. p. annu' iiij.*li*. Et est ibidem q°ddam columbar' qd. val. p. annu' iiij.*s*. & piscar' val. p. annu' ibide' iiij.*s*. Et est ibidem queda' villa m'catoria in qua sunt vj[xx]. Burgag' que reddent p. annu' xl.*s*. quodlibz. eor. iiij.*d*. & tolnet. ej'dem ville val.

(*a*) Thomas du Pontefract or Pomfrete, one of the first burgesses resident within the walls of Denbigh. (*b*) Also second on the first list of burgesses. (*c*) Witness to first charter of incorporation. The rest also tenants. (*d*) The Castle, Galch-Hill, Garthysnodiog or Crest Parks. (*e*) The origin of the present old King's Mills.

p. annu' lx.*s.* Et est ibidem queda' feria die Sce. Elene[f] annuatim
& val. p. annu' lx.*s.* Et est ibede' de redditu assis. libor. tenenciu'
Anglicor forincec' xl.*s.* viij.*d.* Et dicu't qd. plita. & p'quisit' Cur.
val, p. annu' iiij.*d.*

Sm* xliiij.li. ij.s. (iiijd. omission.)

Et dicu't qd. idem Com. habuit ibidem de redditu assi'o

Asstret libor. tenociu' Anglicor. viij.<i>li.</i> & est ibidem quidam parcus
Owyn. qui vocat' Segru't cuj p'ficuu' val. p annu' lx.*s.* Et est ibid.
Cliffarne qddam Molend. aquat. qd. val p. annu' xl.*s.* vj.*d.* Sm* xiij.
Lanasset. <i>li.</i> vi.*d.* Id. Com. h'uit ibide' de redditu assiso. libor. ten
Kilkedy. xx.*s.* Idem h'uit apd. Lannasset de redditu assio. libor.
ten xxx.*s.* & est ibide' unu' Molend' aq*tic' & val. p. annu'
Cathus xx.*s.* iiij.*s.* Idem h'uit apd. Kilkedy de redd. ass'io libor.
Cader. ten. viij.*s.* iiij.*d.*

Idem h'uit ibide' lxviij.s. de redd. assio libor. ten. & est
ibidem medietas cuj' da' Molend. aq*tic' qd. val. p. annu'
xx.*s.* Id'm h'uit ibide' de. r. ass'io libor. ten. lxvj.*s.* v.*d.*

Sm* xi.li. xiij.s. j.d.
. . . . . . (effaced—ij.li. xix.s. viijd.)

Mahenbeth. Idm. Comes h'uit ibide' iiij. acr' terre arrabil' in d'nico
que val. p. annu' xx.<i>li.</i> p.c acr' xij.*d.* & sunt ibide' xvj.
Skybion. acr. p*ti. que val. p. annu' xxiiij. sol. p'c acr. xvj.*d.* & est
......Ilford. ibide' qddam. columbar' qd. val. p. annu' iiij.*s.*
......Cano.
Sm* xxi.li viij.s.

Id'm Comes h'uit. ibidem de r. ass'io libor. ten. xl.<i>li.</i> &
Lewenny. ibide' q°ddam Molend. aq*tic' qd. val. p. annu' xx.*s.* iiij.*d.*
Et est ibidem . . . . parcu' cuj. p'ffciu' val. p. annu' xx.*s.*
Sm* xlij.li. iiij.d.

...enynan. Idm. h'uit ibidem de r. assio. libor Anglic' xx.*s.* iiij.*d.*
Henthlan. Et est ibidem unu' Molend. qd. val. p. annu' x.*s.*
Sm* xxx.s. iiij.d.

Bramskip. Idm. h'uit ibidem de r. assi'o libor. ten. Anglic xxxiij.*s.*
W...annok. iiij.*d.* . . . . . xxxiij.*s.* iiij.*d.*
Wenanok Idm. h'uit de r. assi'o libor. ten. anglic' x.<i>li.</i> xiij.*s.* iiij.*d.*
Wynt.' Et est ibidem q°ddam. Molend. aq*tic. qd. val. p. annu. xl.*s.*
Talabrini <div align="center">Sm* xij.<i>li.</i> xiij.<i>s.</i> iiij.<i>d.</i></div>
Bodenestan. Idem h'uit de r. ass'io libor. ten. Anglic' x.<i>li.</i> Et est
ibidem qddam. Molend. qd. val. p. annu' xx.*s.* Et dic'ut
qd. p'lita & p'quisit' Cur. Anglor. val. p. annu' xl.*s.* Et
o'mes isti p'dci redd. solvi debent 'd festa Aplor. Phi. &
Jacobi & Sci. mi'chis . . . .
Sm* xiij.li.

Et dicu't qd. p'dcs. Comes h'uit apud Caymerth de r.
Caymerth. ass'io libor. ten. Wallens' xx.li. viij.*d.* o' ad festa Natal.
Dni. Aplor. . . . . . Sci. Petri & Oim. Scor. equis

(*f*) Qy. whether St. *Blere* for Hilary, the patron Saint of Denbigh-within-
the-Walls, whose Chapel still stands as the principal place of worship—or Holy
Cross Fair?

* It is almost certain that this was Berain.

porcoibz. Et de r. assi'o nativor. Wallens' ibid'm. lxiij.*.
iiij.d. ad eosde. t'minos . . . . ad eosde'
t'minos & est ibide' q°dam consuetudo que vocat' Amobr'
qve val. p. annu' xl.*. pli'ta & p'quisit. Cur. Wallens' . . .
    Sm* xxxj.*li*. iiij.*. ob. (*xvili. omitted.*)
Idm huit ibidem de r. assi'o libor. ten. Wallens' xx.*li*.
ad quatuor p'dcos t'os & r. assi'o natior. ibide' lx. . . ad Uthalet.
eosde' t'ios Et . . . . . . p. advocacoibz ad eosde'
t'ios Et sunt ibide' duo Molend. ad feodi firma' dimissa
p. v. m*rc. p. annu' ad eosde' t'ios Et su't ibidem. . .
. . . . custuma que vocat' Amobr'. Et est ibid. q°da'
custuma que vocat' Tung' tam de libis. ten. q°m de villanis
q° val. p. annu' l . . *. ad eosd. . . . . . . plita &
p'quisita Cur. ibide' val. p. annu' x.*li*.
    Sm* xlv.*li*. vj.*. viij.*d*. (*vi*.li. *x.s. omitted*)
Id'm h'uit in Roweynok de r. assi'o tam libor. ten, q°m Roweynok.
villanor. xv.*li*. ad p'd'cos iiij. ti'os equis p'coibz. Et de advocac'oibz. xx.*. ad eosd. . . . . Id'm h'uit lx.*. tam
de lib'is q°m de nativis p. quada' custuma que vocat' Tung'
ad eosde' t'ios & p. custuma que vocat' . . . . . .
t'ios. Et dicu't qd. pli'ta & p'quis. Cur. ibide' valent p.
annu' viij.*li*.
    Sm* xx. . . . li. (*rectius xxvi*.li.)
Idm. Comes h'uit in p'ria de Roos in Com'oto de Istulas Com'ot. de
in villa de Dynrobin vj*xx* acr. terre arrabil' in d'nico que Istulas.
val. p. annu' vj. marc' p'o . . . . . acr' viij.*d*. Et est in
d'co Com'oto de r. assi'o libor. ten. Wallens' lx.*. ad festa.
Aplor. Phi' & Jacobi S'ci Petri ad vincla' & Oim. Scor'
equis porc'oibz. solvend. Et est ibide' q°da' custuma que
vocat' Tung' que val. p. annu' xlvj.*. viij.*d*. Et est una alia
custuma que v. . . . . Porthian que val. p. annu' xl.*. ad
festa Natal' D'ni solvend. Id'm h'uit apd. Kilmeyl de r.
ass'io libor. t . . ide' xl.*. Et de . . . . ejusdem ville vj.*.
Id'm h'uit in Kilmeyl de r. assi'o libor. ten. xxx.*. Id'm
h'uit in Kilkydok de r. assi'o libor. ten. x. . . *. (*xxs.?*) Id'm
. . . . in Dynorbyn Vacham de r. assi'o libor. ten. viij.*.
Id'm h'uit in Meymoc de r. assi'o libor. ten. xiiij.*. Et de
pastura in eadem villa (*vi.s.?*) . . . . Id'm h'uit in Boderhen-
wyn de r. assi'o libor. ten. xvj.*. Id'm h'uit in Hendregeda
de r. assi'o libor. ten. xx.*. It'm de pastura . . . . ville
iiij.*. Id'm h'uit in Abergel' de r. assi'o libor. ten. xl.*.
Et de pastur. viij.*. Id'm h'uit in Dynhengren de r. assi'o
x.*. Et de pastura' iiij.*. Id'm h'uit in Brunssant de r.
assi'o libor. ten xiij.*. Id'm h'uit in Seritor de r. assi'o libor. ten. xx.*. Id'm h'uit in Massawith de r. assi'o libor.
ten. xx.*. vj.*d*. Id'm h'uit in Tulgard de r. assi'o libor. ten.
v*. ij.*d*. (*qy. iij*.d.?) Id'm h'uit in Garthewynt de r. assi'o
libor. ten. vi.*. viij.*d*. Id'm h'uit in Toronoth de r. assi'o
libor. ten. xx.*. iij.*d*. Id'm h'uit Kilkewyn de r. assi'o libor.

ten. xx.*s.* viij.*d.* ob. Id'm h'uit in Bod . . . . . minori de r. assi'o libor. ten. viij.*s.* ob. Id'm h'uit de r. assi'o duor. Molend. in eode' Com'oto x.*li* ob. Et de redditu Nativor. ej'dem Com. xxvj.*s.* viij.*d.* Et de quada' custuma q. vocat' Amobr' ej'dem Com'oti lx.*s.* Et de advocacoibz. ej'de' Como'ti xx.*s.* viij.*d.* Item dicu't qd. p'lita & p'quis' Cur. ibidem valent p. annu' x.libr.

Sm^a liij.li. xiiij.s. v.d. ob.

Com'ot. de Ughdulas. I'dm. h'uit in Com'oto de Ughdulas in p'ria de Roos de r. assi'so tam libor. ten. q^am nativor xvij.*li.* viij.*d. (xviij.)* Et est ibidem defirma acr. de r. assi'o xvj. m^arc'. Et om'es isti reddit^e custume solvi debent ad festa Aplor. Phi' & Jacobi. Ad vincla' Sci. Petre Oim Scor. & Natal. D'ni Id'm h'uit. de r. assi'o Molend. xxviij.*s.* Et est ididem queda' custuma que voca^r Amobr' que val. p. annu' lx.*s.* Et de advocac'oibz xx.s. Et solvi debent ad t'ios p'd'cos equis porcoi'bz. Id'm dicu't qd. p'lita & p'quis Cur' val. p. annu' viij.*li.*

Sm^a xlj.li. ij.s.

Id'm h'uit q^adam villa M'cator' que voca^r Abergelen in qua sunt xx^{ti.} iiij^{or.} Burgens' qui xxiiij^{or} Burgag' tenent & reddunt p. annu' v.*s.* iij.*d.* Et iidem tenent forinc' ten. p. quibz. reddunt p. annu' viij. li. Et solvi debent ad festa Pentecost' & Sci. Mi'chs. Et est ibidem de r. assi'o cuj'- dam Molend xxx.s. ad t'ios p'dcos. Et tolnet' ibidem valz. p. annu' xxx.s. sic t^adit^r ad firma' solvend' ad eosdem t'ios. Et est ibide' queda' feria que val. p. annu' xxviij.*s.* iiij.*d.* ob . solvend' t'is p'deis. Id'm Comes h'uit ibide' advocac'om cuj'dam eccl'ie qui vocat^r Kikedok' que valz. p. annn' x. m^arc. Et dicu't qd. p'lita & p'quis Cur. valent ibide' p. annu' lx *s.* Et dicu't qd. Alesia filia d'ce Henr' de Lacy. Comitis Linc. ux' d'ne Thome Com' Lancastr' est p'pinquior h'es & fuit etatis xx.^{ti.}ix. annor. die Natal D'ni ultimo p^rt'to, In cuj' rei testimoniu' p'd'ci Iur. huic Inquis' sigilla sua apposueru't

Sm^a xv.li. xiij.s. viij.d. (viiid.?) ob.

. . . . quidam Herwardus dns. de Deminel. qui tenet unu' feod milit' in Comoto' de Roos & valz. cu' acciderit xx.*li.*

Feod. Milit. Et h'uit advocac'om eccl'ie de Kikedok & valz. p. annu' x. m^arc.

Sm^a toci' ccclxxvij.li. xx.d. ob.'

(Translation, by the Author of this work.)
DENBIGH.

"An inquisition touching the lands and tenements of which Henry de Lacy, Earl of Lincoln was in possession in his lordship, by feoffment, on the day that he died; to wit, how much land the same Henry held of the lord the king, in chief, and how much otherwise. And for what services; and how much those lands and tenements are worth yearly altogether, *(in omnibus excitibus,* in all things arising therefrom.) And who may be his nearest heir, and whose age being shown, before the escheator at Denbigh, (on the Lord's Day next before the feast of St. Peter,) in the chair, in the fourth year of King Edward II., upon the oath of Thomas de Pontefract, Adam de Swinemor, Llewelyn ap Iorworth, Madoc ap Gronow, Griffith ap Rees, Kenevert Lloyd, Yorwerth Duy, *(Ddu)* Yorwerth . . . . . . Tuder . . . . arwet, Ken. Lloyd, and Ivan ap Ithel, jurors who say upon their oath that the said Henry held in right of his lordship as by covenant (in feoff.) on the day that he died, the territory of Rhôs and Rhyfoniog, and the commote of Cinmerch, with the Castle of Denbigh, of the lord the king in chief, for military service. And the castle there is of no yearly value, beyond its charges, *(ultra reprisas,)* and otherwise it would be worth, annually, ten pounds. And there are four score acres of arable land there belonging to the Lordship, which are worth four pounds per annum, price twelve pence per acre. And there are three parks there, of which one park is worth ten pounds per annum; and another worth sixteen marks per annum, and the third park is worth one hundred shillings per annum.

The King's Mills.—And there is a certain water mill there, which is worth four pounds per annum. And there is a certain dovecot there, which is worth four shillings a year, and a fish pond there, worth four shillings per annum.

Denbigh Town.—And there is a certain market town there, in which are six score burgesses, and they render forty shillings per annum, each of them four pence; and the tolls of the same town are worth sixty shillings per annum. And there is there a certain fair upon the day of St. "Elere" (Hilary) annually, and it is worth sixty shillings per annum. And there is there from the rent-charge of free English tenants around *(forinsecus,* from without) forty shillings and eight pence. And they say that the government fees and perquisites of the court are worth four pence per annum.[*] Total, forty-four pounds, two shillings and four pence.

Ystrad Owain.—And they say the same Earl had there from the rents of free English tenants, eight pounds.

Segrwyd.—And there is there a certain park, which is called "Segruit," whose profit is worth forty shillings per annum. And there is there a certain water mill, worth forty shillings and six pence per annum, Total, thirteen pounds, and six pence.

[*] This is not, however, reckoned in summing up the total. Perhaps this four pence was allowed to some officer, or keeper of the court.

Kilford.—The same Earl had there from the rent-charge of free tenants, twenty shillings.

Llewesog.—Also the Earl had at "Lauuassok," from the rents of free tenants, thirty shillings. And there is there one water mill, and it is worth twenty shillings and four pence, per annum.

Cilcedig, or Cliccedig.—He had also at Cilcedig, from the rents of free tenants, eight shillings and four pence.

Casyth or Cathus, y Felin Hen-Cader.—The same (Earl) had there sixty-eight shillings from the rents of free tenants. And there is at the same place the moiety of a certain water mill, worth twenty shillings per annum. And he had there, from the rents of free tenants, sixty-six shillings and five pence. Total, eleven pounds, thirteen shillings, and one penny.

Bachymbyd, effaced, *ij.li. xix.s. viij.d.*

Ysceibion, Llwyn (?) and Kilford.—The same Earl had there four hundred acres of arable land, belonging to the lordship, which are worth twenty pounds per annum, price per acre, twelve pence. And there are at the same place, sixteen acres of meadow land, which are worth twenty-four shillings per annum, price per acre, sixteen pence. And there is a certain dovecot there, which is worth four shillings per annum. Total twenty-one pounds, eight shillings.

Ystrad Canon.—And the same Earl had there, from the rents of free tenants, forty pounds. And there is a certain water mill there, which is worth twenty shillings and four pence, per annum. (With *Lleweni.*)—And there is a park there, whose profit is worth twenty shillings per annum. Total, forty-two pounds and four pence.

Galltfaenan, Henllan, "Bremship."—The same Earl had there, from the rents of free English tenants, twenty shillings and four pence. And there is one mill there, which is worth ten shillings per annum. Total, thirty shillings and four pence.

Gwaenyuog, Gwaenynog, Wyntus.—And the same (Earl) had, from the rents of free English tenants there, thirty-three shillings, and four pence. Total, thirty-three shillings, and four pence.

Berain ?—And the same (Earl) had, from the rents of free English tenants, ten pounds, thirteen shillings, and four pence per annum. And there is there a certain water mill, which is worth forty shillings per annum. Total, twelve pounds, thirteen shillings and four pence.

Talybryn, Bodysgaw.—He had also from the rents of free English tenants, ten pounds. And there is there a certain water mill, which is worth twenty shillings per annum. And they say that the fees and perquisites of the English court, are worth forty shillings per annum. And all ought to pay the aforesaid rents at the feasts of the Apostles St. Philip and St. James, and Michaelmas, ... (the rest is effaced, but there can be no doubt that it was *equis portionibus,* in equal proportions. Total, thirteen pounds.

Cinmerch.

And they say that the said Earl had in Cinmerch, from the rents

AND ITS LORDSHIP. 105

of free Welsh tenants, twenty pounds, and eight pence halfpenny, at the feasts of Christmas, of the Apostles . . . . . (names lost) St. Peter, and All Saints, in equal portions. And from the rent-charges of Welsh natives there, sixty-three shillings and four pence at the same seasons . . . . (effaced, but there is little doubt that it was to the effect that he had the profit of a custom called *tung*,) at the same seasons. And there is there a certain custom called Amober, which is worth forty shillings per annum. The fees and perquisites of the Welsh court* . . . . *(effaced)* Total, thirty-one pounds, four shillings, and one halfpenny.

Uchaled.

And he had there, from the rents of free Welsh tenants, twenty pounds, at the four aforesaid seasons, and from the rent-charges of natives there, forty . . . . . . at the same seasons. And . . . . by advocations at the same seasons. And there are two mills there, held on lease for five marks per annum, at the same seasons. And there are at the place† . . . . a custom which is called Amober. And there is a custom which is called *tung*, as well from free tenants as from villains (bondmen or serfs) which is worth fifty shillings per annum, at the same . . . . (seasons, no doubt.) And the fees and perquisites of the court there, are worth ten pounds per annum. Total, forty-five pounds, six shillings, and eight pence.

Rhyfoniog.

And he had in " Rhiweunog" (Rhiwoniog) from the rents of free tenants, as well as of " villains," fifteen pounds, at the aforesaid terms, in equal portions. And from advocations twenty shillings, at the same . . . . (seasons, no doubt.) And he had forty shillings, from free tenants as well as natives, by a certain custom which is called *tung*, at the said seasons. And by the custom called . . . . . (amober?) . . . . at the same seasons. And they say that the fees and perquisites of the court there are worth eight pounds per annum. Total, twenty-six pounds.

Commote of Isdulas.

The same Earl had in the territory of Rhôs, in the Commote of Isdulas, in the township of Dinorben, six score acres of arable land in the Lordship, which are worth six marks per annum, price . . . eight pence per acre. And there is belonging to the Lordship in the commote, from the rents of free Welsh tenants, sixty shillings, to be paid at the feasts of the Apostles St. Philip and St. James, St. Peter ad Vincula, and All Saints, in equal portions. And there is a certain custom there, called tung, which is worth forty-six shillings, and eight pence, per annum. And there is another custom which is called porthiant, worth forty shillings per annum, to be paid at the feast of the Nativity of the Lord *(Christmas.)*

* These, with the tung, must have amounted to six pounds.
† This, with the rents and advocations, amounted to six pounds, ten shillings.

P

Kinmel.—And he had at Kinmel, from the rents of free tenants there, forty shillings. And from the . . . . of the same township six shillings. The same Earl had in Kinmel, from the rents of free tenants, thirty shillings.

Cegidog or Cilcedog.—The same (Earl) had in Cegidog (St. George), from the rents of free tenants, twenty-six shillings.

Dinorben Bach.—And he had in Dinorben Fechan, from the rents of free tenants, eight shillings.

Meivod.—And he had at Meivod, from the rents of free tenants, fourteen shillings, and from the pasture in the same township . . .

Bodyrhenwyn.—And he had in Bodyrhenwyn, from the rents of free tenants, sixteen shillings; (qy. *Bodrochwyn,* or *Bodoryn ?*)

Hendregyda.—And he had in Hendregyda, from the rents of free tenants, twenty shillings. Also from the pasture . . . . of township, four shillings.

Abergele.—And he had at Abergele, from the rents of free tenants, forty shillings. And from pasture, eight shillings.

Dinhengron.—And he had in Dinhengron, from the rents of free tenants, ten shillings. And from pasture, four shillings.

Brynsant.—And he had in Brynsaint, from the rents of free tenants, thirteen shillings. (Place *unknown.*)

Serïor.—And he had in Serïor, from the rents of free tenants, twenty shillings.

Maesegwick.—And he had in Maesegwick, from the rents of free tenants, twenty shillings and six pence.

Tylgarth.—And he had in Tylgarth, from the rents of free tenants, five shillings, and three pence.

Garthewin.—And he had in Garthewin, from the rents of free tenants, six shillings, and eight pence.

Trovarth.—And he had in Trovarth, from the rents of free tenants, twenty shillings, and three pence.

Kilkennin.—And he had at Kilkennin, from the rents of free tenants, twenty shillings, and eight pence.

Bodlemmon.—And he had at Bodlemmon, from the rents of free tenants, eight shillings, and one halfpenny. And he had from the rents of two mills in the same commote, ten pounds and one halfpenny. And from the rents of the natives of the same commote, twenty-six shillings, and eight pence. And from a certain custom, which is called Amober, in the same commote, forty shillings. And from Advocations in the same commote, twenty shillings and eight pence. And they say that the fees and perquisites of the court there are worth ten pounds per annum. Total, fifty-three pounds, fourteen shillings, and five pence halfpenny.—(But perhaps *Bodrochwyn Bach ?*)

Uchdulas.—And the same (Earl) had in the commote of Uchdulas in the territory, from the rents, as well of free tenants as of natives, forty-eight (?) pounds, and eight pence. And there is there from the rents of certain farms of land, sixteen marks. And should pay those rents by custom at the feast of the Apostles Philip and James, St. Peter and Vincula, All Saints, and Christmas. And he had from the rent of a mill, twenty-eight shillings. And there is a certain custom there called amober, which is worth forty shillings per annum : and from advocations twenty shillings. And they should pay at the aforesaid seasons, in equal portions. And also they say that the fees and perquisites of the court are worth eight pounds per annum. Total, forty-one pounds, two shillings.

ABERGELE.

The same (Earl) had a certain market town, which is called Abergele, in which are twenty-four burgesses, who hold twenty-four burgages, and pay five shillings and three pence. And the same (burgesses) hold tenements around the town, for which they render eight pounds per annum. And they should pay at the feasts of Pentecost and St. Michael (Michaelmas). And there is there from the rent of a certain mill, thirty shillings at the aforesaid seasons. And the tolls there are worth thirty shillings per annum. So the whole is said to be payable by agreement, at the same seasons. And there is a certain fair there, which is worth twenty-eight shillings, and four pence halfpenny, payable at the aforesaid seasons. The same Earl had there the advowson of a certain church, which is called Cegidog (St. George) which is worth ten marks per annum. And they say that the fees and perquisites of the court there, are worth forty shillings per annum.

And they say that the Lady Alice, daughter of Henry de Lacy, Earl of Lincoln, wife of Thomas Earl of Lancaster, is the nearest heir, and her age was twenty-nine years, upon Christmas Day last aforesaid.

In testimony whereof the aforesaid Jurors to this inquisition affix their seals.

And there is a certain Herward, Lord of Dinmel, (Dinmael,) who holds a military feodary, the value of which comes to twenty pounds.

And he had the advowson of the Church of Cegidog, and its value is ten marks per annum. Sum total, three hundred and seventy-seven pounds, and twenty pence, halfpenny.

Summary.	£	s.	d.
Denbigh, parks, mill, town tolls, &c., ...	44	2	4
Ystrad, Segrwyd, park and mill, ...	13	0	6
Llewesog, with mill ; Cilcedig, Cassyth, Cader,&c.	11	13	1
Ysceibion, Llwyn ? Kilford, ...	21	8	0
Lleweni, Ystrad (Canon)	42	0	4
Galltfaenan, Henllan, &c.	1	10	4
Gwaenynog	1	13	4
. . . . .(Berain) . : . . .	12	13	4
Talybryn, Bodyscaw, ...	13	0	0
Cinmerch	31	4	0½
Uchaled	45	6	8

		£	s.	d.
Rhyfoniog, or Isaled, ...	.	26	0	0
Isdulas, ...	.	53	14	5½
Uchdulas	.	41	2	0
Abergele, tolls, fairs, mill, &c. . . .	.	15	13	7¼

£374 2 0¼

The total in Survey . . £377 1 8½
Total above £374 2 0¼

Bachymbyd, the value effaced in manuscript, . . 2 19 8

Total, as per survey corrected, . . . £377 1 8½

Thus De Lacy's revenue, from Welsh freemen, natives, and bondmen, who were subject to the payment of the various customs described above, amounted to £197 7s. 1d. annually; and £179 14s. 9¼d. from the free English colony, spreading, more or less densely and compactly, from Denbigh, as a nucleus, over the surrounding parishes—down the Vale of Clwyd, and up the Western hills—with the smaller out-lying English settlement at Abergele, as described hereafter.

CHAPTER X.

In the 12th Chapter, page 98, of the author's former work, a quotation is given from Pennant, stating that the tenants made the Earl of Leicester a present of £2,000, at his first entrance into the lordship. And further, that he raised the old rents of £250 a year to £800 or £900. Some time back, whilst the author was examining a great number of old documents, kindly shown to him by the late Robert Myddelton, Esq., at Gwaenynog, he accidentally fell upon the very " deed " of agreement made between the Earl and his tenants—a most interesting document, highly characteristic of the notorious royal favourite's rapacity and hypocrisy. Here it is—

" Apud Denbigh in Northwalia xxvj.
Die Septembris, Anno Reginæ,
Elizabethe, &c., sexto."*

" Whereas by reasone of the yearely revenue of the Seignory or Lordshippe of Denbighe, whereof the Right hon'able the Lorde Robert Dudley, Knight of the most noble order of the Garter, one of the Queenes mats. P'vie Councell, and m' of her highenes horses, is rightfull honor and hath estate, of inheritance in fee simple, being presently in great decaye, wch hath heretofore, in ancient time, bene answered vnto the Lords & owne^{rs} of the said seignorie or Lordship yearly of a greater some then is p'sently answered over and besides demayne landes, Parkes, fforests, chases, woodes, wasts and co'mons, ffishings, ffowlings, wards, mariadges and Reliefes, with all other Rialties, in the manuall occupation of the owners and Lords of the said Seignory and Lordship, for their best vse, Comoditie, and profite, wch owght to bee issuinge, and yearely payable out of and by such porçons of landes w^{th}n the said Lordship, as the nowe tenants of the said Lordshipp doe occupie at this p'ent albee it they nowe p'tende to have the same parcells of landes of inheritance, by the Stewards grauntes of the said Seignory discharged from the said rents nowe decayed as by the records of the p'misses evidently appeareth, ffurthermore, by the Colome of a Charter which the said tenants and inhabitants seeme to have of the graunt of the Late King henry the vij^{th.} as they do pretend, alleaging them thereby to be discharged of divers customable rents, duties, and seruices hereafter memçoed,

At Denbigh, in North Wales, on the 27th day of September, in the sixth year of Queen Elizabeth,—1563.

Dowbting the valitite thereof in Lawe, wch are comonly called by the names of *amb^r woodwarderth, forestwoorth, p. pastu, forestarij,* als. *arian woodward,* vel *arian brestai,* aut *arian,* pro pastur. *frith lech deniel, kavod elwy, Egyrchyd, pennant, llwyufrits magou,* et *bonds de Denmell,* als. voce *arian tervyn Dimaell, arian porva,* vel *arian manerij* voce *gwaithllys,* de construçoe omor, et als. voc. *treth gaer* de *kolch de pastur Stalion,* et *gartois* als. voc. *porthiant stalwynd,* de *pastur lucrar. cm. canibus, qu de molend.* de *pastur. eg Raglog,* et de *pastur. S^r . . nts pach,* als voc. *kylch enkys,* vel *arian de pastur pennarlion,* et *gwestion bychain,* et de aduocat. als. voc. *arderk et denar.* als. voc. *arian arderk,* wch should amount vnto the some of two hundreth forty poundes and above. And whereas also a greate part and quantity of the Lords Comons are inclosed, incroched, and converted to the privat occupaçon, comoditie, and profite of divers the tenants and inhabitants of the said Lordshipp without lisence, or any maner of Rent to his L. answered. Therefore, for reformaçon thereof to the end the said Seignorie and Lordshipp with the possessions, Land, and Rent, Rialaties, and interest of the same, aswell one the behalfe of the said Lord Robert as of the particuler tenants and occupiers of the same, may be reduced and brought to a certain perfection accordingly. The lord Robert greatly desiringe not only certentie thereof but also the favourable entreatie and great increase of the tenants dwelling within the Lordshipp, and also for the Zeale and care wch he hath of his said tenants, is wel contented and pleased not only to remitt a greate part of the said decayes, but utterly for ever to release and discharge them of all the said straits, costomes, and exactions, and mynding also to forbeare rigour of Lawe to bee co'menced againts the said tenants, and for performancie thereof his Lordshipp his hon'able good will and carefulnes of them hath favourably sent by his Comission, and authorised, nominated, and appointed his trvstie servants and frindes, John Dudley, William Glasvor, Thomas Reese, Esquiers, and to every of them to survey, viwe, and travaile the same by all such lawfull and favourable meanes, as for reformaçon of the p'misses appointeth, wch now be in execution accordingly. The Reu'end father in God Thomas Bushopp of St Assaphen,* ordinary of the same place, Sr John Salesbury, knight,† Ellis Pryce, doctor of Lawe, and Robert wyn ap Cad^{lr.} Esquier, and all other the tenants and inhabitants of the said Seignorie and Lordshipp, with one whole minde and assent, humblie submittinge themselves to a reasonable conformitie and reformaçon of the same, by the travaile and labour of the said Reverend father, Sr John Salesbury, Ellis pryce, and Robert wyn ap Cadd^r, who be authorized by, and appointed by Comission of all the said tenants, to travail in the p'misses, have most instantly desired and prayed the said John Dudley, and others the Comissioners of the said L. Robert, to accept

* Dr. Thomas Davies consecrated May 26th, 1561. Died Michaelmas, 1573; interred as some say at Abergele.

† Intereed at Whitchurch.—See *Ancient and Modern Denbigh,* p. 1, 164, 165, 344, and 345.

and Receive for the vse and behoof of the said L. Robert, not only their faithfull and most assured harts and goodwills, but also their Duties, services, and powers vnto his hono' most redy and vnfaynedly offered at his honors Co'mandment and appointment in all lawfull respects, the Duties and alleagence, vnto the Queenes Heighnes, her graces heirs and Successors, Kings and Queenes of England, alwayes reservede. And for the accomplishment of the p'misses the said sutors and peti'ço'rs, by the said attrneys,* factors, and travailers, have most hartely desired and requested the said John Dudley and others the comissioners aforesaid, one the behalfe and for the vse of the said L. Robert, to accept and take by these p'ntes, they for them and their heires and executors doe now freelie give and graunt vnto the said L. Robert, and his heires, not only the some of *ona Thow-sande Poundes* to be paied in maner and forme followinge. That is to say in the vigill of St. Andrewe nowe next to come, five hundreth pounds; the twentieth daye of m'ch then next ensuinge an other fyve hundreth Poundes in full payment of the same thowsande poundes for the release and discharge of the said chargeable Rents and bond-aiges and welsh customes and services imagined to be discharged by the aforesaid persons. But also freelie give and graunt, for them and theire heires, one yearlie Rent of three hundreth thirtie and three pounds, sixe shillings and eight pence to be received vpon the lands and tenements wᶜʰ the said tenants have and claim to have as their inheritance within the said Seignory or Lordshipp ; savinge such as hould by speciall Charters and doe pay the ould and accustomed rents reserved vpon the same ; euery tenant to pay his particuler parte and and porçon yearely at the feasts of thanunçiaçon of our Ladie and St. Michaell tharchangell for ever, from the feast of St. Mi-chaell tharchangell next cominge, and to continew the same payment yearely vnto the said L. Robert and his heires for ever, after and by a rate wᶜʰ amongst theme selves, with the assistance of the L. stewards or Comissioners aforesaid, or any of them shallbe reduced and appointed over and besides the yearely Rents alredie payed ; and wᶜʰ is now in yearely revenue and charge within the said Seignorie and Lordshipp. And other the Reliefes, services, and Roialties. And for the better performance of the same Rents partlie revived vnto the said L. Robert, and his heires, the atturneys and factors, one the behalf and for the said tenants have, hartely desired that vpon the said Rates for particuler payment thereof, It would please the said L. Robert to accept and take the same to be reserved chargeable and issuinge out of the particuler p'cells of the p'misses in their seu'all occupaçons, by such seuerall writings as by such Councell learned, wᶜʰ the said L. Robert and the said atturneys for the said tenants and inhabitance shall nominate and appointe, shalbe devised and advised. The said tenants by their said attorneys and them-selves personally by these pa'ties do promise one their partes to p'forme the same, all which suits, petiçons and requests ; And also the offers, gifts and graunts before mençoed, The said Comissioners

---

* Ellis Pryce, doctor of laws, and Robert Wynn ap Cadwaladr.

one the behalf of the said L. Robert havinge hearde, and pondering
deeply the consideraçons & circunstances thereof, not only for thaug-
mentaçon of the honor of the said L. Robert within their sircuite in
this behalf but also for the great benefit, wealth, and comoditie of
the said tenants, wch they greately desire to be encreased, and chiefly
in accomplishment of the will and pleasure of the said L. Robert, according to the greate trust in them reposed for the alteraçon of such
bondages and extremities which the said tenants p'sently stande in
danger of and to remove from them and their assignes hereafter such
bondages, feeblenes of estate, scruplenes, and doubtes as are mani-
festly obiected against their dissents and inheritance of the said
landes in euery of their possessions which they now claime to have
by inheritance before recited. And most of all for the performance
of their better goodwills and services vnto his honor, to be firmely
obliged and assured for ever, vpon deliberat consideraçon and
good advisement have agreede and assented one the behalfe, and for
the said L. Robert and in his Lordshipps name to accept receive and
take for his Lordships vse the said offers, gifts, and grauntes, before
mençoed. And also the said Comissioners, in behalfe and for the
said L. Robert, and in his Lordshipps name doe promise that vpon
a particular booke or verdict to bee made and yealded vpp by the
verdict of the Juries now sworne for the surveing of the premisses or
sóme other Sufficient Jurye within the said Lordshipp vnto the said
Steward or vnto the said Comissioners of every tenants lands and
po'ssions within the said Lordshipp, wch they have by title or colour
of any estate of inheritance, and whereof they bee now in po'ssion accordingly to gether with such incroachments and incroached landes
as they and every of them have made vpon that pretended estate of
inheritance. That the said L. Robert shall make vnto every tenant
soe to be named and mençoned in the said booke or verdict soe good,
sure, and perfeict conveiance in the Lawe, in ffee simple, as the Councell learned to be appointed as is before recited shalbe devised and
advised, with a reasonable Comon of Pasture as by the said Charter
is graunted and given reserving vnto the said L. Robert and his heires
and assignes such Rents in every of the said assurances as the booke
of verdict shall expresse, soe that in the whole the same Rents doe
and will amount yearlie of revival vnto the some of three hundreth
thirtie an three poundes sixe shillings and eight pence p. ann. over
and above the yearely rents and p'misses now answered and payed.
And that the Seignories and services of the said tenants and other
the reservaçons Roialties, suits of Court, and service before mençoed
for the vse of the said L. Robert and his heires. And soe that the
demeasne landes, the Parkes of moelewig, Snodiock, Castell parke,
and Postyn parke, fforests, Com'ons, woods, water-pooles, fishings,
and all other lands, called escheate lands, and other hereditaments
whatsoever which nowe bee in lease or haue bene in lease since the
first daye of the Raigne of the Late king Henry the vijth, and therby
possessed or enioyed be not touched or intermedled. And the said
Com'issioners aforesaid in the behalfe and for the said L. Robert

doe also promise that euery bondeman, villain, bondewoman, and wifes, nowe beinge within the same Seignorie and theire sequells shall have, at his or their reasonable request and suite to bee made vnto the said Lorde Robert or the said Comissioners, a sufficient manuçon or discharge of their bonde for them and their sequells for ever; without any fine or some of money to be payed thereforr, other then their contributions for their partes vpon the rates before recited. Jn witnesse of the faithful, true, and vnfayned performance of all and si'gular the p'misses and euery part before mençoed to bee well and truly performed observed and kept, aswell the said Comissioners, one the behalfe and for the said L. Robert, haue to the one parte of this writinge indented put to their seales and subscribed their names : As also the said atturneys and factors, one the behalfe and for the said tenants and inhabitants, haue putto their seales and subscribed their names the said sixe & twentieth daye of September in the sixt yeare of the Reigne of our said souereigne Lady Elizabeth by the Grace of God of Englande, ffrance, and Irelande, Queene defender of the faith, etc."

The reader will perceive that although Pennant is correct as to a gift being made, and the raising of the rents, these facts have been exaggerated very greatly ; the gift being only one thousand pounds, instead of two thousand ; while the augmentation of rent could not have been much more than one half the amount laid down by Pennant.

CHAPTER XI.

(Lansdowne MS. No. 62, f. 218,—Brit. Museum.)

Righte honorable and my good L., my dewtie moste humbly remembred. Maye it please yo' good L. to be advertyzed that sythence the delyverye of the laste bookes for Denbighe unto yo' L. Ther is come to my hands a p'fecte survaye of the tearme lands and demeasnes tantum wthin everie severall co'mott, wch booke, so soone as god shall make me hable to attende yo' E. I will delyver unto yo' L. In the meane tyme I have thoughte good to advertyze yo' L. that the number of acres as they ar su'med upp in this survaye doo amounte unto vj^m DCC lxvij acres besydes DCCC or a thowzande acres more wch weare founde by Inquisiçon to be deteyned from my L. of Leicester not longe before his L. deathe, for wch the ten'nts entered into coveunte by Indentur wch his L. to paye unto him xij^cli, (£1200.)

Theise tearme lands wyll yelde xx^{tie} yeares p'chase at the leaste, exceptе it be some smale quantetye wch is of late ymproved to an extreame racte rente. And a greate deale of money wyll be made thereof towards the purchase of y' Lordshipp' (if hir Matie please to depte wth the inherytance thereof to the p'ticuler ten'nts thereof) and yet the rente nowe answered maye be reserved uppon their charters, and soe the yeerlye valew styll holden on foott. But my good L. I wishe not that anye p'te of the demeasnes nor these terme lands wch adjoyne to the castell shold be severed from the howse, for it weare pyttye so to dysmember a Seignorye of so greate state, mauredd *(mawreddy)*, precincte, and jurisdicçon.

I humblye prase yo' good L. to favor and remember my suyte made unto yo' h. towchinge my office an the reaste, wherin my good La. and Mris the Cowntes of Leicester hathe sundry tymes entreated yo' honorable favor, for the wch hir La. wyll be beholdinge and my selfe in all dewtie greatlie bownden to yo' good L. doo moste humblie take my leave of yo' E.

Lynclones Jnne 24 Aug. 1590.

Yo' good L. readie at co'maundem^t

W. SPARKE.

COM. DENBIGHE.—*Parcell. terrar. et possessionu. Robti. nup. Comitis Leicestr. ac quond'm p'cell. terrar. et possessionu. nup. Comit. Marchie.*

Qre' what was ye old rents of assise, what was ye new rents made by ye Erl. of Licest^r. •	*Redd. assie' libor. tenentiu' infra bur-gum et villam de Denbighe* . . vj.^{li.} iiij.*s.*

Dominiu' de Denbighe val. in.

Nota.—o^{l.} ye rent is xx.^{l.} ret. for Kilforn p'ke claymed by Th. Salisbury.

A Court called ye town Court.

A Court baro' and lete for ye lord.

Redd. assie' libor. tenentiu' infra burgum et villam de Denbighe . . vj.^{li.} iiij.*s.*
Redd. assie' libor. tenentiu' infra comotum de Kymmerche . . . . cxxj.*li.*
Redd. assie' libor. tenentiu' infra co'motum de Issallett . . . . . ccviiij.^{li.}
Redd. assie' infra sep'ales co'motos de Istulas. Uchalett. et Uchdulas libor. tenentum' ib'm . . cccxiiij.*li.* iii.*s.* viij.*d.*
Redd. terrar. dnicaliu' dimiss. tenen' ib'm ad termin' annor. & ad volunta' tem ac aliar. terrar. ad termin' annor. dimissor. . . . . cxl.*li.* ^xvij.*s.*
Perquisit. Cur. infra villam et dniu' de Denbieghe co'ibz annis . . . . xx.*li.*

DCCC.X.^{li.} iij.*s.* viij.*d.* (a)

whereof

(*Thus.*)—To be deducted for Tho. Manneryngg annuetie who marryed M'garet o' of ye heares of Edw. bullar, yf the chardge be good in lawe–xxvj^{li.} xiij.*s.* iiij.*d.*

More for the rente of Penmen and Llysvayen recovered from the Lordeshipp by hir Matie the laste tearme . . . . . v^{li.}

for y^t this was not p'cell of ye manor of Denbighe.

Et sic

Remanet Clare . . . DCC.iiij.^{xx.} xviij.*li.* x.*s.* iiij.*d.* (b)

Towardes the supplye of the said valewe deducted owt of the totall.

1.—It is to be considered that the escheated landes in the chardge of thexcheator of the said Lordeshippe (as I ame enformed) weare never accompted for in the chardge of the . . . . of the revenew afforesaid, but only in the p'ticaler accompte of the said Excheator.

Tho. Challoner of Denbigh ye escheator xv li.

The valewe of the escheated lands (beinge settled) wyll well be worthe xv^{li.} p' annum. Moste p'te of theise landes wyll be concealed except the said escheator be well looked into, for my selfe haue hadd thexamynaçon of the badd practyze allreadie used by the said Escheator & others to conceale the said lands, besydes it is thoughte ye moste p'te of the arrerag's of the sayd lands wyll fall owt to be in thexcheators hands.

2.—Also the proffytts of the ffaiers and marketts wthin the said towne of Denbighe in toll and stallage beeinge at the leaste worthe xx^{li.} p' annu'. The said towne have allwaies receyved the same, xxli. Qr. for a q. warra'to. but I colde never see that they hadd warrant eyther by wordes of their charter or otherwise to receyve the same.

• The marginal notes and the memoranda at the end are in Lord Burleigh's handwriting, and not always clear.

And if they hadd it by force of their charter, yet nowe their charter is overthrowen by judgemᵗ⁻ in a Quo warranto and so cleerlye the proffitts of the said faiers and m'ketts in hir Maᵗⁱᵉ⁻

3.—Also ther was founde by verditt in my Lorde of Leicesters lyefe tyme, diverse tearme lands concealed by diverse of the free- holders for wᶜʰ the ten'nts by composiçon shold have *lands concealed xij.li.* payed my L. xij.ᶜˡⁱ⁻ In consideraçon whereof my L. was to have passed to the ten'nts the feesymple of the said landes. But before anye estate made unto them, or before the money paid by them, Therle (c) dyed, and so theise lands maye be disposed towards the supplye of the said valewe dedueted.

4.—*Memorand.* that the advowson of the p'sonage of Denbighe is in her Maᵗⁱ gyfte (as I ame enformed) And is end'wed of a viccar, wᶜʰ, as I ame also enformed, is of the presentaçon of the Bysshopp. what they ar in valewe I knowe not.(d)

5.—*Memorand.* also yᵗ the p'ke of Gorsnodiocke p'cell of the said demeasnes was stored wᵗʰ deere in my L. lyefe tyme and at the tyme of his deathe and the ten'nt thereof bownde to keepe a nomber of deere certen over & above his rente.

6.—*Nota,* yᵗ I have not sett downe the officers fees amongeste the rents and chardges resolute & payable owt of the sayde mannor, for that the said officers hadd no patents or other securitye thereof but at wyll, and also for that moste of the said officers & fees maye well be removed & deducted if the Lordeshipp, come to hir Maᵗˢ⁻ *Tho. Sarisbury* hands. ffor fyrste whear the offycer of Receyver had a *receiver,* fee of xiijˡⁱ⁻ vjˢ⁻ viijᵈ⁻ p' annu' the said Lordeshipp maye *xiijli. vje. viijd.* nowe be in the receipte of hir Maᵗˢ⁻ Receyver of North Wales & so the said fee saved. Nexte thexcheator, who had vˡⁱ⁻ fee *Tho. Challyner* p' annu' maye be dischardged and that place supplyed by *Escbetr. vli.* his Maᵗˢ⁻ excheatoʳ of the Shier or eles by the Bayliffs of the Lordeshipp of Denbighe, and so hir Maᵗⁱᵉ⁻ shall be beaste *D. Ellis Stewd.* awnswered of all casuall proffytts growing by the said *iiijli.* offyce. The lyke corse for other unnecessarie offycers. *to ballyn xli.* Nota, that the fee of the Stewarde was iiijˡⁱ⁻ p' annu', and *pater Moyce ap Tho.* the fees of the bayliffe in all not above xˡⁱ⁻

W. SPARKE.

The Q Matʸ is to pay to yᵉ Mʳchants
interest for yᵉ first yer j.*m.* vjᶜ   befor yᵉ xˣ of Dece'ber vij.*li.*
        2 yer j.*m.* vjᶜ   befor yᵉ last of March vij.*li.*
        di yer viij.ᶜ *l.*   befor yᵉ last of October vij.*li.*

Parks wᵗʰ the L of De'bigh.
        Gorsnodyoke p'ke wᵗ deare, out
            of les, (e) yᵉ herbage is let for   xˡⁱ
    Castell p'ke disp'ked and lett   & Moyelewycke p'ke fro' yer
to yer . . lˡⁱ⁻   in les to   Hutte is
                                    xxˡⁱ⁻

        Killthorn . . . xxˡⁱ⁻ ⎫
                        xxˡⁱ⁻ ⎬ o
                        lxˡⁱ⁻ ⎭

Midleto' shuld pay to y⁰ m'cha'ts viij.*m.* ⎫
The Q. Ma*ᵗʸ* to pay . . . . x.*m.* ⎬ xviij.*m.* inde.
⎭
              iij.*m.* befo' y⁰ e'd of hill. term. and
              ij.*m.* befor' y⁰ end of Ester. and
              iij.*m.* mich'
(f) X.*ᴹ·*   iij.*m.* at o' lad. day ⎫
              iij.*m.* befor' Trinit. term ⎬ Towards
              iiij.*m.* befor' ⎭ this if it
x.*m.* inde ij.*m.* viij.*c.*   be viij.*c.* there
remayneth vij.*m.* ij.*c.*   will be ij.*m.* at
                           o' Lad. daye.
            and for arr. of a co'posit. viij.*c.*
So must be p*ᵈ·* viij.*m.* & vij.*m.* ... xv.*m.*

(Endorsed)   Aug* 1590.
               Denbighe,
      A p'ticuler of the yeerly valewe of Denbighe.
for viij yers, vij*ᵐ·* iiij*ᶜ·* xlij*ˡⁱ·* j*ˢ·* iiij*ᵈ·* *(g)*
  for 9   rend j*ᵐ·* ij*ᶜ·* xxiiij*ˡⁱ·* xij*ˢ·*

Remembraunces toching Denbigh cawse.

When her Ma*ᵗⁱᵉ* hath signed her part of the Indentur, the same
Saleab. & Co'. to be kept by my L. Tresorer, untill Mr. Salisburies and
way to sign ther p't. Mr Conwaie have sealed and knowledged their parte of
those Indentures, and sealed a band of m.m*ˡⁱ·* to p'forme the cove-
n'nts and then to passe the seale.
That this bonde upon a new bonde to be taken by the Co'missioners
A bo'd of ij.m. of those parties and other sufficient sureties such and in
such so'me as the L. Th'rer shall allowe of to her Ma*ⁱᵉ* use, for
the p'formaunce of the coven'nts, and retorned into thexcheq',
this bonde of m.m*ˡⁱ·* to be redelyvered.
That yt maie please my L. Th'rer to consider of fytt Co'mission's to
Comissonars, deale in this cause, first to survaie the demeane & terme
lands, then to apporçon the rent of ccxxx*ˡⁱ·* yerelie uppon the demeane and terme lands, according to the Indentures, and such
averplus as shall fall out more then that, if anie be, ratably uppon
eche ten'nt of that lande.
Then to assesse what fine eache ten'nt shall paie for his demeane &
Assess. of terme landes, so as in the whole yt maie amount unto
fynes, viij.m.*li.* for the same.
Then that those Co'missioners certifie into the excheq' w*ᵗʰ* expediçon
Certificat of ye the survaie w*ᵗʰ* the rates for the fines and rents of
Co, into ye Checqr, everie severall tenement, uppon everie several ten'nt.
Then the L. Th'rer to sett downe the time of payment for those
Ye tymes of fynes, and to geve ordes for the assuraunce to be geven
payment of ye fynes, y⁰ to her Ma*ᵗⁱᵉ* for those severall fynes, occording to those
times.

And theruppon the leases to passe.

                               J. POPHAM.

(*Endorsed.*)   To the Righte Honorable
                    my good Lorde the L. Tresorer
                         of England.
   A Survay of y° terme lands & demesnes of Denbigh.
                     Aug*· 1590.
         Remembrances towching Denbigh cause.
                     Aug*· 1590.

   (*a*) £810 3s. 8d.   (*b*) £778 10s. 4d.   (*c*) The Earl.   (*d*) In
the former work, (*A. & M. Denbigh, p.* 351,) is a Latin charter,
transcribed from *Brown Willis,* purporting to be a grant of the
advowson of Denbigh to the See of St. Asaph, in A. D. 1313, by
Philip Mortimer, Earl of March : but since, the author's attention
has been called, by two antiquarian correspondents, to the fact that
no such person as *Philip,* Earl of March, (2 Edward II.) ever
existed.   (*e*) Lease.   (*f*) £10,000.   (*g*) £7,442 1s. 4d.

CHAPTER XII.

ORIGINAL CHARTER, IN NORMAN FRENCH, PRESERVED AMONGST
THE RECORDS OF THE CORPORATION OF DENBIGH.—ANTE A.D. 1290.

*(For a Translation and history, &c. of this Charter, see A. & M.
Denbigh, p. 301–309. It is interesting also as a fine "legal" specimen of the language spoken at the Court of England in Norman times. The words contracted in the original are given in
extenso by the transcriber, Albert Way, Esq., F.A.S. In the first
word, the initial H has been here supplied, a space appearing ob-
viously left for a rubricated or illuminated initial, which may have
become effaced by time.)*

[H]ENRI de Lacy, Counte de Nicole, Conestable de Cestre, Seignur de Roos et de Rowynioke, A toux ceux qui cest escrit verrount
ou orront, salutz. Sachiez nous avoir done et graunte, et par ceste
notre presente chartre conferme, a Williame du Pountfreit deux
burgages en la ville de Dynebieghe dedenz les murs, et deux curtilages en Dynebieghe dehors les murs, et deux bovees de terre od
les apurtenaunces en Lewenny. A Adam de Swynemore un burgage
en Dynebieghe dedenz les murs, et un curtilage en Dynebieghe
dehors les murs, et un bovee de terre od les apurtenaunces en
Astret Canon. A Richard de Sheresworthe un burgage en Dynebieghe dedenz les murs, et un curtilage en Dynebieghe dehors les
murs, et une bovee de terre od les apurtenaunces en Lewenny. A
Williame Pedeleure un burgage en Dynebieghe dedenz les murs et
un curtilage en Dynebieghe dehors les murs, et une bovee de terre
od les apurtenaunces en Lewenny. A Adam del Banke deux burgages en Dynebieghe dedenz les murs, et deux curtilages en
Dynebieghe dehors les murs, et deux curtilages en Dynebieghe dehors les murs, et deux bovees de terre od les apurtenances
en Lewenny. A Johan de Westmerland un burgage en Dynebieghe
dedenz les murs, et un curtilage en Dynebieghe dehors les murs, et
une bovee de terre od les apurtenaunces en Lewenny. A Thomas
de Hultone un burgage en Dynebieghe dedenz les murs, et un curtilage od les apurtenaunces en Dynebieghe dehors les murs. A
meisme celui Thomas un burgage en Dynebieghe dedenz les murs,
et un curtilage en Dynebieghe dehors les murs, et une bovee de terre
od les apurtenaunces en Lewenny. A Adam de Castelford deux
Burgages en Dynebieghe dedenz les murs, et deux curtilages
en Dynebieghe dehors les murs, et une bovee de terre od les

apurtenaunces en Lewenny. A Williame le palefraymon un burgage en Dynebieghe dedenz les murs, et un curtilage en Dyne- bieghe dehors les murs, et une bovee de terre od les apurtenaunces en Kilfur. A Pieres le fitz Robert le clerke un burgage en Dyne- bieghe dedenz les murs, et un curtilage en Dynebieghe dehors les murs, et une bovee de terre od les apurtenaunces en Lewenny. A Richard de Bernesleghe un burgage en Dynebieghe dedenz les murs, et un curtilage en Dynebieghe dehors les murs, et une bovee de terre od les apurtenaunces en Astret Canon. A Thomas Pye un burgage en Dynebieghe dedenz les murs, et un curtilage en Dynebieghe de- hors les murs, et une bovee de terre od les apurtenaunces en Lewen- ny. A Anable de Blakeburne un burgage en Dynebieghe dedenz les murs, et un curtilage en Dynebieghe dehors les murs, et une bovee de terre od les apurtenaunces en Lewenny. A Johan de Swynemore un burgage en Dynebieghe dedenz les murs, et un cur- tilage en Dynebieghe dehors les murs, et une bovee de terre od les apurtenaunces en Astret canon. A Wautier le fuitz Egline un bur- gage en Dynebieghe dedenz les murs, et un curtilage en Dynebieghe dehors les murs, et une bovee de terre od les apurtenaunces en Astret Canon. A Johan de Adelingtone un burgage en Dynebieghe dedenz les murs, et un curtilage en Dynebieghe dehors les murs, et une bovee de terre od les apurtenaunces en Lewenny. A Robert fe fitz Thomas du Pountfreit un burgage en Dynebieghe dedenz les murs, et un curtilage en Dynebieghe od les apurtenaunces dehors les murs. A Williame de Stayneburne un burgage en Dynebieghe dedenz les murs, et un curtilage en Dynebieghe dehors les murs, et une bovee de terre od les apurtenaunces en Lewenny. A Alisaundre de Donecastre un burgage en Dynebieghe dedenz les murs, et un curtilage en Dyne- bieghe dehors les murs, et une bovee de terre od las apurtenaunces en Lewenny. A Agneyse la fille Richard de Hickelinge un burgage en Dynebieghe dedenz les murs, et un curtilage en Dynebieghe de- hors les murs, et une bovee de terre od les apurtenaunces en Lewenny. A Thomas le fuitz Thomas du Pountfreit un burgage en Dynebieghe dedenz les murs, et un curtilage en Dynebieghe de- hors les murs, et une bovee de terre od ies apurtenaunces en Lew- enny. A Johan le fuitz Roger le Qieu un burgage en Dynebieghe dedenz les murs, et un curtilage en Dynebieghe dehors les murs, et une bovee de terre od les apurtenannces en Lewenny. A Henri le Clerke un burgage en Dynebieghe dedenz les murs, et un curtilage en Dynebieghe dehors les murs, et une bovee de terre od les apurte- naunces en Lewenny. A Johan de Wilbreley un burgage Dyne- bieghe dedenz les murs, et un curtilage en Dynebieghe dehors les murs, et une bovee de terre od les apurtenaunces en Lewenny. A Pieres le Taillour un burgage en Dynebieghe dedenz les murs, et un curtilage en Dynebieghe dehors les murs. et une bovee de terre od les apurtenaunces en Lewenny. A Henri du Wyce un burgage en Dynebieghe dedenz les murs, et un curtilage en Dynebieghe dehors les murs, et une bovee de terre od les apurtenaunces en Astret Canon. A Johan de Symundeston un burgage en Dynebieghe dedenz les

murs, et un curtilage en Dynebieghe dehors les murs, et une bovee
de terre od les apurtenances en Wickewere.   A Johan de Mostone
un burgage en Dynebieghe dedenz les murs, et un curtilage en
Dynebieghe dehors les murs, et une bovee de terre od les apurtenances en Lewenny.   A mesme celui Johan un burgage od les
apurtenances en Dynebieghe dedenz les murs.   A Thomas del Peke
un burgage en Dynebieghe dedenz les murs, et un curtilage od les
apurtenaunces en Dynebieghe dehors les murs.   A Williame Baskete un burgage en Dynebieghe dedenz les murs, et un curtilage en ·
Dynebieghe dehors les murs, od les apurtenaunces.   A Williame le
fuitz Griffri un burgage en Dynebieghe dedenz les murs, et un curtilage od les apurtenaunces dehors les murs.   A Adam de Cathertone
un burgage en Dynebieghe dedenz les murs, et un curtilage od les
apurtenances dehors les murs.   A Alayn de Brereleghe un burgage
en Dynebieghe dedenz les murs, et un curtilage od les apurtenaunces
en Dynebieghe dehors les murs.   A Johan de Rosse un burgage en
Dynebieghe dedenz les murs, et un curtilage od les apurtenaunces
en Dynebieghe dehors les murs.   A sire Williame de la Montaigne,
(Montaigue?) persone, deux burgages en Dynebieghe dedenz les
murs, et deux curtilages od les apurtenaunces en Dynebieghe dehors
les murs.   A meisme celui sire Williame un burgage od les apurtenaunces en Dynebiegh dedenz les murs.   A Richard de Dokeworthe
un burgage en Dynebieghe dedenz les murs, et un curtilage en Dynebieghe dehors les murs, et une bovee de terre od les apurtenances en
Astret Canon.   A Robert de Ecclesale un burgage en Dynebieghe
dedenz les murs, et un curtilage en Dynebieghe dehors les murs, et
une bovee de terre od les apurtenaunces en Astret Canon.   A Raufe
del Peke un burgage en Dynebieghe dedens les murs, et un curtilage
od les apurtenaunces en Dynebieghe dehors les murs.   A Richard
Pygote un burgage en Dynebieghe dedenz les murs, et un curtilage
en Dynebieghe dehors les murs, et une bovee de terre od les apurtenaunces en Beringe.   A Robert de Chirche une bovee de terre od
les apurtenaunces en Lewenny, et a les treis fillies Eynnon de Lodelowe une bovee de terre od les apurtenances en Lewenny.   A avoir
et a tenir a eaux et a lour heirs, et a lour assignez Engleys de-
morauntz en lavauntdite ville de Dynebieghe dedenz les murs, de
nous et de noz heirs par les condicions soutzescrites.   Cest assavoir
que chescun des avaunditz Burgeis, Williame du Pountfreit, Adam
de Swynemore, Richard de Sheresworthe, Williame Pedeleure Adam
del Banke, Johan de Westmerlond, Thomas de Hultone, Adam de
Castelford, Williame le Palefreimon, Pieres le fitz Robert le Clerke,
Richard de Bernesleghe, Thomas Pye, Anable de Blakeburne, Johan
de Swynemore, Walter le fitz Egline, Johan de Adelingtone, Robert
le fuitz Thomas du Pountfreit, Williame de Stayneburne, Alisaundre
de Donecastre, Agneyse la fille Richard de Hickelinge, Thomas le
fitz Thomas du Pountfreit, Johan le fuitz Roger le Qieu, Henri le
Clerke, Johan de Wilberle, Pieres le Taillour, Henri del Wyce, Johan
de Symundestone, Johan de Mostone, Thomas del Peke, Williame
Baskete, William le fuitz Griffri Adam de Cathertone, Alayn de

R

Brereleghe, Johan de Rosse, Sire William de la Montaigne, persone,
Richard de Dokeworthe, Robert de Ecclesale, Raufe del Peke, et
Richard Pygote, et les heirs ou les assignez de chescun de eaux
Engleys, troverount un homme defensable en lavaundite ville de
Dynebieghe dedenz les murs a la garde et al defens de lavaundite
ville de Dynebieghe, pur chescun Burgage et curtilage avauntnomez.
Et ceaux qui tienent fors que bovees soulement ferront les services
qa bovees apendent.   Et rendaunt a nous et a noz heirs par an,
chescun des Burgeys avauntnomez et les heirs de chescun de eaux,
ou les assignez de chescun de eaux Engleis avaunditz, un dener a
Noel en noun de Housgable pur chescun des Burgages et curtilages
avaunditz.   Hors pris Sire Williame de la Mountaigne person, qui
paera a Noel avauntnome, pur les Burgages et curtilages avaunditz,
cesze deners, Johan de Mostone a meisme le terme pur un Burgage
qatre deners, Richard de Dokeworthe a meisme le terme pur un
Burgage et un curtilage dusze deners, Robert de Ecclesale a meisme
le terme pur un Burgage et un curtilage dousze deners, et Raufe del
Peke a meisme le terme pur un Burgage et un curtilage deux soudz.
Et ensement rendaunt a nous et a noz heyrs chescun de eaux
avauntditz qui bovees tienent, et les heirs de chescun de eaux et les
assignez Engleis de chescun de eaux avauntditz, pur chescune des
bovees avauntdites severaument, qaraunte deners par an, Cest assavoir vint deners a la feste de Pentecouste, et vint deners a la feste
Seynt Michiel, horspris Richard de Shoresworth, Adam de Kendale,
Johan de Westmerlaund, Johan de Adelingtone, Wautier le fitz
Engline, Henri le Clerce, Robert de Ecclessale, et Henri del Wyce,
les quieux rendront a nous et a noz heirs chescun par sey les deners
de housgable avauntnomez par an taunt come il vyvent, et apres
lour decesser lour heirs ou lour assignez et les heirs de lour heyrs, et
les heyrs de lour assignez Engleis, chescun par sei rendront a nous
et a noz heirs par an, pur chescune bovee avauntdite, qaraunte deners
a les termes avauntditz, et ja du maynz pur les Burgages et les
curtilages les deners de housgable avauntnomez al terme avauntdit.
Et ensement fait assavoir qe les heirs et les assignez, et les heyrs de
lour assignez Engleis de trestoux les Burgeis avauntaomez rendrount a nous et a noz heirs le primier an apres la morte lour
auncestres, pur les Burgages et pur les curtilages nn dener en noun
de Reliefe.   Et les heirs et les assignez, et les heirs des assignez, de
toux ceux qui bovees tienent, rendront a nous et a noz heirs le
primier an apres la morte lour auncestres pur chesune bovee qaraunte
deners en noun de Reliefe.   Hors pris ceo qe les heirs et les assignez
de le avauntdit Sire Williame, et les heyrs de ses assignez, rendront
a nous et a noz heirs le primer an apres la morte lour auncestres pur
les Burgage et curtilage cesze deners en noun de Reliefe; les heirs
et les assignez Johan de Mostone rendront a nous et a noz heira le
primer an apres la morte lour auncestres pur son Burgage quatre
deners en noun de Reliefe; les heirs et les assignez Richard de
Dokeworthe rendront a nous et a noz heirs le primer an apres la
morte lour auncestres pur les Burgage et curtilage dusze deners en

noun de Reliefe ; es heirs et les assignez Robert de Ecclessale rendrount a nous et a noz heirs le primer an apres la morte lour auncestres pur les avauntditz burgage et curtilage dusze deners en noun
de Reliefe, et les heirs et les assignz Raufe del Peke rendrount a
nous et a noz heirs le primer an apres la morte lour auncestres
pur son Burgage et son curtilage deux soudz en noun de Reliefe.
Et si'nul des avauntdites Burgeys ou ses heirs ou ses assignez
ovauntditz faille ou faillent de garder et defendre par lui ou par
homme defensable la dite ville de Dynebieghe sicome est avauntdit,
bien lirra a nous et a noz heirs,et a ceaux qui serrount seignurs du
chastel de Dynebieghe, chescun Burgage et curtilage et bovee de
terre avauntditz en noz mayns [ou] en lour mayns seisir et retenir,
par la ou le servise desus dit ne soit pas pleynement fait, issi qe si
ceaux qui faillent del avauntdit servise, ou certein homme defensable
pur eaux ne veigne ou ne veignent dedenz lan et le jour al dit servise
faire, et assietz faire de les arerages del dit servise qarere sount, de-
meurgent les Burgages curtilages et bovees de terre od les apurtenances a nous et a noz heirs, de faire ent notre volente a toux jours.
Et estre ceo nous avoms graunte pur nous et pur noz heyrs qe noz
Burgeis avauntditz, et lour heirs et lour assignez avauntditz, eyent
housbote, et haybote en le boys quest appele Cardelewenny, cest
assavoir du chemin qui va de Denebieghe au pount Griffyn jusques
a Elewey, par vewe de noz forestiers. Et estre ceo nous avoms
graunte a les avauntditz Burgeis et a lour heirs et a lour assignez
avauntditz la commune de pasture a lour propres bestes levauntz et
couchauntz en meisme la ville de Dynebeighe, od fraunke entre et
issue en lavauntdit boys issi qe eaux en temps vuerte communent od
les autres fraunks hommes de Lewenny apres bledz et feyns em-
portez. Et nous voloms et grauntoms pur nous et pur noz heirs qe
chescun Burgeis qui tient burgage en lavaundite ville de Dynebieghe
dedenz les murs eyt ses porcs fraunks de paunage en lavauntdit boys
en temps de paunage, cest assavoir de la feste seynt Michiel usque
la feste seint Martin, et si pluis de porcs eyent, paent come les autres
du pays fount. Sauve a nous et a noz heirs notre foreste, notre
garenne, et totes les choses que a foreste et a garrenne apendent, et
tote manere de oyseaux qui autres oyseaux pernent. Et toux les
Burgeis manauntz en la ville de Dynebieghe dedenz les murs et lour
heirs et lour assignez avauntditz moudrount lour bledz et lour brees
a noz molins de Dynebieghe et de Astret al vintisme vassel. Et
toux les avauntditz burgeis et lour heirs et lour assignez avauntditz
qui naverount propre furne, furniront a notre commun furne dedenz
meisme la ville. Estre ceo nous avoms graunte a les avauntditz
Burgeis, et a lour heirs, et a lour assignez avauntditz, qils soyent
fraunks de Tolune et de estalage par totes noz terres de Gales et
D'Engleterre. Et qils eyent les attachementz de lour burgeis dedenz
la ville, ensemblement od la garde de la prison dedenz la ville, sauve
a nous et a noz heirs les pledz, les amerciementz, les Raunçouns, et
le Juyse, et totes les choses qa Juyse apendent. Et nous et noz
heirs les avauntditz Burgages, curtilages, Bovees de terre od les

apurtenaunces, communes, et paunages, et totes les autres fraunchises
avauntdites, a les avauntditz Burgeys, Williame, Adam, Richard,
Williame, Adam, Johan, Thomas, Adam, Williame, Pieres, Richard,
Thomas, Anable, Johan, Wautier, Johan, Robert, Williame,
Alisaundre, Agneyse, Thomas, Johan, Henri, Pieres, Henri, Johan,
Johan, Thomas, Williame, Williame, Adam, Alayn, Johan, Sire
William, Richard, Robert, Raufe, Richard, Robert, et les treis fillies
Eynnon de Lodelowe, et a lour heirs et a lour assignez avauntditz,
warauntiroms et par lavauntdite servise defendroms autaunt avaunt
come notre seignur le Roy Dengleterre et ses heyrs nous warauntiront
noz terres en Gales.   En tesmoigne de quieux choses a la partie de
cest escrit cyrograffe demoraunte vers les ditz Burgeys et lour heirs
et lour assignez avauntditz avoms fait mettre notre seal, et lautre
partie demoraunte vers nous et vers nos heirs, les avauntditz Burgeis pur eaux et pur lour heirs unt mys lour seals.   A ceaux
tesmoignes, Monsire Johan Grey, Sire Johan Dargentyn, Sire
Robert de Shirlaund, Chivalers; Sire Williame de Nony, Thomas de
Fissheburne, Sire William la persone de Dynebieghe, Robert de
Bynecestre, William de Caldecotes, Gron. vacch'n, Griffr' ap Rees,
et autres.   [L.S.]

[*The seal, now much damaged, is appended by two laces of silk; one
red, the other green, forming a plaited cord of four strands; the
impression is on hard white wax.   OBVERSE.—The mounted figure
of Henry de Lacy, the inscription lost, but from other impressions
of his seal it appears to have been—" S' Henrici de Laci Comitis
Lincolnie et Constabvlar' Cestr'."   On the REVERSE, is an impression
of the SECRETUM, on bright red wax imbedded in the white—SIGIL-
LVM SECRETI.*]

A List of Charters granted to the Borough of Denbigh by various
Sovereigns.—From the evidence of the Parliamentary Commissioners.

18	Edward I.	......	28 August,	... A.D. ...	1290.
6	Edward III.	......	27 October,	... „ ...	1333.
2	Richard II.	......	22 February,	... „ ...	1378-9.
2	Richard III.	......	10 December,	... „ ...	1485.
1	Henry VII.	......	27 March,	... „ ...	1485-6.
22	Henry VIII.	......	20 November,	... „ ...	1531.
5	Edward VI.	......	25 April,	... „ ...	1552.
39	Elizabeth	......	20 June,	... „ ...	1597.
14	Charles II.	......	14 May, .	... „ ...	1662.

Several of these are in a fine state of preservation.   They are
beautiful specimens of ancient penmanship, and the last is illuminated with a much admired miniature portrait of the king.—An
abridgement of the " governing charter" is given in *A. & M. Denbigh,* p. 119—125.

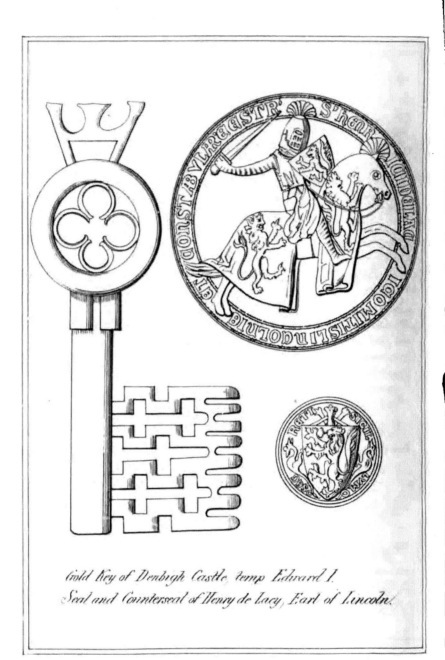

Gold Key of Denbigh Castle, temp Edward I.
Seal and Counterseal of Henry de Lacy, Earl of Lincoln.

CHAPTER XIII.

CORPORATE RECORDS CONTINUED—MUNICIPAL ELECTIONS—
CAPITAL BURGESSES OR COMMON–COUNCILMEN—ALDERMEN (WHO
HAD THE AUTHORITY OF CHIEF-MAGISTRATES OR MAYORS)—
BAILIFFS OR BOROUGH SHERIFFS—EMINENT PERSONAGES AND
FAMILIES IN DENBIGH AND NORTH WALES—MEMORABLE EVENTS,
ETC.

THE loss of the *first* volume of the Corporate Registers, has buried in oblivion the names of the capital burgesses of Denbigh during the long period of three hundred years. The "Second Book" commences with A.D.1596-7. The new council elected under the charter then granted (39 Elizabeth) appears in the author's former work, (*A. & M. Denbigh, p.* 105,) and the list of aldermen and bailiffs (*at pages* 111 *and* 112, *in that vol.*) is complete down to A.D. 1651, so that neither needs repetition here. We, therefore proceed with the long-promised completion of the " Municipal History "—to the passing of the " Corporations' Reform Act," or rather to the end of Corporation Book II.

Election.	*Common-Councilmen.*	*Instead of.*
1600	John Smythe, *vice*	No record.
1602-3	Robert Knowsley, *vice*	Unknown.

These two probably succeeded John Mershe and William Knowles, of whose deaths we have no account.

1603, June 27, Robert Salusbury, Bache-
    graig, *vice*........................... Alderman Hugh Clough, dead.
       (See " *Life and Times of Sir Thomas Gresham.*")
1603, June 27, John Richard Clough,⎫
    Aldman. & Jno. Matthewe, gent.⎭ No record *vice* whom.
1604, Jan. 3, Robert Salusbury, son of
    George Salusbury, *vice* .... Alderman Piers Lloyd, deceased.
1605, Feb. 24, John ap Llewelyn, *vice* Humphrey Doulben, deceased.
1605, Oct. 22, Ffoulke Salusbury, son of
    Robert Salusbury, gent. *vice* ...... John Chambres, deceased.
1606, Sept. 29, John Latham, gent. *vice* Thos. Lloyd Rosindale, deceased.
1606, Dec. 5, Edward Salusbury, *vice*... Hugh Hughes, deceased.

The latter was treasurer for the Corporation for nine years.

1607, Dec. 21, John Salusbury, *vice* ... Alderman Robt. Salusbury, dead.
1611, Sept. 16, Ffoulke Panton, (see
      p 65,) *vice* .... Humffrey Clough, deceased.
1612, Sept. 25, Anthony Mathewe,
      linendraper, *vice* .... Hugh Piggott, deceased.

Lloyd of Wickwer.—John Lloyd, of Wickwern, Esq., sworn
burgess in 1611.

MEM.—*Mysterious burial of Sir John Salusbury.*—" Uppon
Fridaye, being the xxivth daie of July, about ten of the clocke in
y* morning, Syr John Salusbrie of Lleweni, in y* County of Denbigh, Knt., ffather of Mr Henrie Salusburie of Beraine, grandson
to Catrin Heiress of Beraine , ... who maried y* daughter of
Syr Thomas Myddelton of Chirk Castle, knight, died att his House
of Lleweni, and as reporte(d) was buried that night. *Mem.*—Be
itt further remembered, that upon Sondaie the fourthe daye of
October, 1612, the Funerall of y* saide Syr John Salsbury was celebrated.—*MS. Diary of Piers Roberts of Bron-hwylva, Registrar of
St. Asaph, began* 1572."—According to *Collin's Baronetage*, (Edit.
1720,) " Sir John the Strong died in 1613." But here it is evident
that this must involve an anachronism or confusion of persons.
" Syr John y Bodiau," the modern Sampson of popular legend, was
born in the time of Henry VII., was a page of the court of Henry
VIII., and died about 20 Elizabeth. See *Salusbury Poems*, at the
close of chapter on Lleweny.

William Myddelton, the Poet, was still living, (not dead ante
1603, *A. & M. Denbigh, p.* 161,) as is proved by the will of his
brother, Robert Myddelton, of London, merchant, who leaves him a
legacy of £50 ; besides his bequests to the Guilds of Mercers, Smiths,
Weavers, Glovers, Corvisors, &c., at Denbigh.

1613, April 15, ffrancis Twyston, *vice*... Richard Clough, deceased.

This ffrancis Twyston appears to have been a leading member of
the Company of Mercers, and was the Alderman Twyston of 1620.
See notice of the Cloughs at the end of this chapter.

In De Beckle's time, Peter de Twysilton, was a tenant of the township of
Bodeiliog, in the vicinity of Denbigh—probably from the reign of Edward I.
And for upwards of 500 years we find the name, *Twiston, Twyston, Twisdon,
Twisleton,* &c. connected with the military, municipal, and parochial history of
Denbigh. The late Lieut. Twiston, son of John Twiston, Esq., mayor of Den-
bigh, deceased, was the last male representative of this very old family.—" A.D.
1618, upon the thirde of Julye, one Jane ffirst wieff of ffrancis Twiston, mercer,
havinge XI children (livinge at the time of her decease) was burried, and Mr
Evan Morrys, vicar of Llanevydd, made a funerall sermon."—*P. Roberts' Diary.*

1613 William Barker, *vice* .... John Pryse, *alias* Price, *alias* ap
.   Rees, resigned.

Pryse was a master smith—and an enterprising member of the
Company of Hammermen—but his state became so " decayed," and

so involved in troubles and debts, that he was " no longer able to mayntayne the state and dignitie of a cappitall burgesse."

1613 William Merton, mercer, *vice* ... John Drihurst, gent., deceased.

See notice of the Dryhursts in a subsequent page.

The Pantons of Henllan.—xvth of May, 1613, Hugh Panton second sonne to Syr Thomas Panton, clerke, sworn burgess a Evan Panton, sonne of William Panton of Henllan, gentleman."—Old Panton Hall, in the town of Denbigh, was in the parish of Henllan ; as well as New Fox Hall.

1613, May 15th, Oliver Lloyd, gent. *vice* Robert Lathom, deceased.

" Lathom Fields," near the town, still retain the name. In an old " Cess Book," they are rated with " Payne's Fields near Paradise."—Weavers, mercers, drapers, &c., "assized," with the iron standard yard.

" *Mem.* 1614.—Upon Wednesday, the 1st Feb., 1614, ffoulke Lewys & Elsbeth vch morgan, his wieff were clandestingly married at Denbighe, in yᵉ House of Edward Davydd the Serjiant at mace of yᵉ saide towne."—*P. Roberts' Diary.*

" 1615, *Mem.*—Upon Saturday, in yᵉ morning of the xxij of Julye, Hugh Pennant, (Brother of Mr Pierce Pennant of Bychdan,) Esq., dyed, being hurt & wounded upon the Head by one Pierce Hughes, upon the mondaie before."—*Ibid.*

These were lawless times, and open acts of atrocity were common.

Many wealthy and emiment citizens of London were then proud of the honour of being also freemen of the ancient borough of Denbigh, as " Robert Myd'elton, cittizen & martchant of London ; Humffrey Hall, citisen, & marchant of London ; Leonard Myd'elton, cittizen & dier of London ; Benjamin Charke of London, William Myd'elton, of London, gouldsmyth ; John Roberts of London, cutler ; Richard Drihurst of London, haberdasher ; Robert Newell, cittizen & marchant tayler of London ; John Lewis, cittizen & gouldsmyth of London ; Evan Griffith, cittizen & embroyderer of London ; Edward Pritchard, cittizen & marchant of London ; Arbellin Holland, gent., sonne & heire to Hugh Holland of London, gent.; Moris Lloyd of London, marchant tailer."

1617, Michaelmas, Hugh Drihurst, son of
  John Drihurst, *vice*..................Alderman Robert Salusbury, dead.

This Robert Salusbury was murdered on the bench, as is said, in the Town Hall, in Denbigh.

1617 Richard Doulben, son of
  Humphrey Doulben, *vice* .... John Latham, gentleman.
1618, July 22, William Clough, gentle-
  man, *vice* .... Alderman William Mereton.

" 1618, *Mem.*—20 Aprill apud fflint, the daie & yeare above

named, y* Right Honble. W^m. L^d. Crompton, Lord President of y*
King's marches of Wales, came in Person to view and see the
Country, & his trained Souldiers ; beinge in the Assise week there;
and soe to Denbighe the nexte weeke followinge."—*P. Roberts' Diary*.

1618, xxvi*th* Oct., John Lloyd obtains his freedom gratis, upon
the petition of the Right honourable William, Lord Crompton,
Earl of Northampton, &c.—*Corporate Records.*

1618 John Lloyd, gentleman, *vice*...... Unknown.
1618 Thomas Eves, gentleman, *vice* ... Unknown.
1619, May 21, John Lloyd, of Wick-
    wer, gent. *vice* .... Richard Lloyd, deceased.
1619, Sept. 23, John Davies, " sonne
    & eayre" to David Lloyd, ap Evan,
    gent. *vice* ...., Richard Doulben, deceased.
1619 Reynauld Rutter, gent. *vice* ...... Alderman William Barker, dead.

Wynne of Eyarth—" xvj*th* Oct. 1619, Thomas Wynne of Eyarth, in the county
of Denbigh, gent.. servant in lyvery to the Right Wor^ll Syr Thomas Chamberlayne, Knight, chief justice of Chester, &c., sworn burgess of Denbigh."

1620, March 17, Ffoulk Lloyd, gent. *vice* Timothie Barker, deceased.
1620 William Davies, *vice* .... Unknown.
1621, May 17, Rowland Barker, *vice*... Charles Myddelton, deceased.

" 1621, *Mem.*—up' Tuesdaie in Easter weeke, beinge the 3rd daie
of Aprill, Charles Myddelton, late of the Castle of Denbighe (Brother of Syr Thomas Myddelton, Alderman, of London,) was burried
in Eglwys Wen, neere Denbighe. He lefft & bequeathed divers
Legacies to charitable uses."—*P. Roberts' Diary*. Charles Myddelton succeeded his father, Richard Myddelton, as governor of
Denbigh Castle, and his will (made in 1620) is a proof of " filial
piety" and devotion, and of the absence of another Christian virtue.
He bequeaths five pounds to be laid out on land, to produce five
shillings yearly, to keep in repair the tomb of his father in the
south porch of Whitchurch. And if it should not require that outlay every year, the money was to be deposited in the church chest.
He leaves five pounds for the purchase of a silver communion-cup
(still in common use) for the " Chappel of St. Hillary," with the
inscription, " *Carolus Myddelton, Burgensis Villa de Denbighe, in
Honorem Deo me fieri fecit.*" Also forty shillings for the repair of
the church, and forty shillings for four funeral sermons to be preached
at Whitchurch in the course of the two years following his death.
And also sixty pounds for the poor, to be invested upon security
deposited among the archives of the town, the interest to be distri-
buted to the poor yearly at Christmas. He also left " provision"
for his " reputed children," by his concubine, Margaret uch Thomas,
alias Salter. He speaks of his (natural) sons Charles and Hugh ;
his daughter Ann, who was married to John Chambers, and William
his son, whom he appoints his residuary legatee, hoping he would
not be compelled to give up his " occupation."

1621, May 17, William Doulben, mercer,
vice ... . Oliver Lloyd, deceased.
1621 Nov. 20, Harry Thomas, gent. vice Henry Rutter, gent. deceased.
1622, June 13, Hugh Lloyd Rosindale, vice Alderman Anthony Mathewe,
deceased.

Alderman Mathewe left his plate to the corporation for the use
of the poor.*

1623, May 27. Ffoulke Salusbury, jun.
linendraper, vice .... John Mathewe, deceased.
1623, Aug. 14, Richard Drihurst, mercer,
vice .... Ffoulke Salusbury, deceased.
1623 Nov. 20, Robt. Salusbury, sonne
of Robt. Salusbury, doctor-at-
Lawe vice .... Richard Price, deceased.

In 1619, (xxiij. Sept.) Robt. Salusbury, esqr., was sworne burgess
over "a potell of wyne," as "sonne of Robt. Salusbury, esqr., doctor
of divynitie."—There was another Richard Price, holding a seat in
the council in 1625, as "bayliffe," or borough sheriff, of whose
election there is no record.

The Vaughans, of Groves and Llwydiarth, often figure in the local
annals of those times.—Capt. Thomas Vaughan, brother to the
Right Hon'ble Lorde Vaughan, sworne burgesse, xxi Oct. 1623, &c.

1625.—(*Rex.*) MEM.—Upon mondaie the iiij. daie of Aprill, our
noble Prince Charles was (after the deathe of our late soverigne
K. James, King of Engl : ffrance, and Irelande, (who dyed upon or
about the 27th of March laste, as is reported) proclaimed king
in the Towne of Denbighe by the Aldermen."—*P. Roberts' Diary.*

..... At midsummer, Piers Thomas slew his brother, Edward
ap Thomas ap John &c., with a bill-hooke, at Denbighe.

1626.—*John Lloyd ap Thomas* (Alderman) is supposed to be the
same person as "John Lloyd," who was elected capital burgess in
1618, and to be described as "ap Thomas" to distinguish him

---

* *The Mathewes of Lleweny.*—The notice of the family of *Mathewes* which ap-
peared in the Author's former work, chiefly from *Burke's Landed Gentry*, has
called forth some private criticism, especially from the friendly scrutinizing pen
of Joseph Morris, Esq., of Shrewsbury, who argues that they were in no way connected with the Mathews of Llandaf, as stated by Burke; but we have no space
in this work to open the question. Let it suffice that the Author here cancels his
"endorsement" of the note, (*A. & M. Denbigh, p.* 113, 114) and has been scru-
pulously cautious, in the present work, not to draw a fraction upon the credit of
Burke's Landed Gentry, or upon his own "speculations." Others have maintained that the Mathews of Denbigh could have been no more than tenants at
Lleweny; and it has been suggested that, since some of them are described as
"of the Forge," they were the first to erect iron-works at Bodfary, as the
Mathews of Llandaff were the *patriarchal* iron-masters of South Wales; a
coincidence which would lead to the inference that they were originally of the
same connection. This, however, is mere conjecture, not historical fact.

S

from his namesake Mr. Bailiff Lloyd of that year, who was "of Wickwer."

Dolben of Segrwyd.—xij. Die Augusti, 1626, David Doulben, doctor-in-divinitie, one of the sonnes of Robt. Doulben, of this towne, gent., sworne burgesse, &c.

1629, Jan. 11, William Myddelton, *vice* Hugh Parry, deceased.
1629, May 3, Richard Doulben, linen-
    draper *vice*........................ John Llewelyn, deceased.
1630, Nov. 22, John Doulben, gentle-
    man, *vice* .... Ffoulke Myddelton, Esq. deceased.

Ffoulkes Erriviatt. — Piers ffoulkes, gent. sworn burgesses, Sept. 5th, 1630.

1631, Aug. 30, Harry Salusbury, *vice* Hugh Dryhurst, deceased
1631, Aug. 30, John Eves, gent, *vice* Ffoulke Panton, deceased.
1631, Oct. 18, Rich. Lloyd, *vice* ...... Bailiff Rich. Evance, deceased.

We have no record of Evance's admission into the council.

1631,*Dec. 1, Hugh Lloyd of Foxhall,
    Esquire, *vice*...................... Sir Hugh Myddleton, deceased.

Sir Hugh Myddelton, if not the greatest, was certainly one of the best and most eminent men ever connected with the history of London and Denbigh. But will the world believe the fact that Denbigh has proved itself so unworthy of the honour of being the birth-place of this great and good man, and so ungrateful for all his services, that it has never raised the smallest "memorial" of him—in stone or metal, on glass or canvass! True it is that his claim to immortality needs no such perishable memorials to ensure its perpetuation, but Denbigh does to preserve the repute of being the place of his nativity. He was, at least, thirty-four years an active member of the council; alderman, recorder, and M.P. for the borough, successively.

Lloyd of Berthlwyd.—Sir Edward Lloyd of "Berth Lloyd," k^{nt}, Sir Thomas Salusbury, Baronet, Sir John Maynard, K.B., William Roberts, D.D., Cup-almoner to the King, &c. sworn burgesses, Sept. 10th, 1632.

1633, Feb. 18, Sir Thomas Salusbury,
    Baronet, *vice*...................... Reinald Rutter, deceased.

---

* *The Wynnes of Nantglyn.*—[MEM.] 1631.—Upon mondaie the vi^{th} of ffeb'ry Robert Wyn, gent. (sonn & Heire of ffowk Wyn, gent. sonn & Heyre of Robert Wyn ap Meredydd ap Tudor, all deceased) and one Jane Lhwyd, eldest dau: of Hugh Lhwyd, Esqr. nowe one of the Aldermen of Denbighe, were married in ye Chappel of St. Hillary, in Denbighe, by Thomas Barker vicar of Denbighe, and by force of a Licence unto hym directed by Dr. Griffith, Chancellor of Lhanelwy, (St. Asaph) "in ye presence of William Dolben, Esqr. nowe High Sheriff of ye Co: Denbighe, Piers Lhwyd of Llanynys, and divers others, to (the) number of C.C." (200) "parsons or more."—*P. Roberts' Diary.*

1633, *Thomas Salusbury* bailiff this year, alderman in 1638, no further record.

1634, June 9, Edmund Vaughan, Esq.
vice .... John Davies, gent. deceased.

Wynnes of Ystrad.—" Edward Wynn, of Estrad, sworne burgesse xxxi. Martii, 1634," &c.
Thelwall of Plasward.—Symon Thellwall of Plas Ward, Esq. sworn burgess 31st March, 1634.
The Mostyns of Mostyn.—In 1635, Robert Mostyn, esquire, sonne of S[r.] Roger Mostyn, Kt. was sworn burgess.
1634.—[MEM.] Upon sondaie y[e] 8th of June, Thomas Salusburie, sonne & heire of Syr Thomas Salusburie, B[rt.] (sonne of Syr Harrye S., Bart., sonne of Syr John S. all deceased), was borne, & xtened [Christened] upon the xxix[th.]

1634, March 6, Edward Williams, deputy-recorder *vice* .... Edmund Vaughan, deceased.
1634, March 6, John Roberts, Bailiff, gentleman. *vice* .... Richard Clough, imprisoned.
1634 Same day, Mathew Salusbury, Esq.
vice .... Richard Price, imprisoned.
1634 Same day, Thomas Shaw, skinner,
vice .... John Lloyd, imprisoned.
1634, March 29, John Myddelton, Esq.
vice.................................. Robert Knowsley, deceased.

Knowsley was thirty-seven years in the council.
Mostyn of Talacre.—Sir Robt. Mostyn, knt. and John Salusbury, of Bachegraig, steward of Denbigh, made burgesses, 7th July, 1635.

1636, May 1, Robert Ffoulkes, mercer,
vice .... William Clough, imprisoned.
1636 Same day, John Evans *vice*......... Richard Doulben, disfranchised.
1636 July 10, John Madocke, gent.
vice .... Hugh Lloyd Rosindale, deceased.

It is a singular fact that four members of the council were lying in prison at the same time, and were " displaced," having discontinued their attendance owing to long imprisonment, and troubles. Most probably they were incarcerated upon political charges, although the troubles of the reign of Charles had not yet well commenced.

1638, July 19, John Vaughan, gent.
vice .... John Myddelton, deceased.
1638, Aug. 1, John Salusbury of Bachegraig, Esq. *vice*.................... (no record.)

The Salusburies of Leadbrook.—Thomas Salusbury, the younger of Leadbrook, was sworn burgess of Denbigh, in A. D. 1638.

1639, Sep. 21, John Wynn, Esq. *vice*... (no record.)
1640, Sep. 26, William Chambres, gent.
vice .... William Myddelton, deceased.

1640 Same day, Foulke Jones,gent. *vice* William Dolben, disfranchised.

"An Act entered January 28, 1639. [*Memorand.*] Whereas Wm. Dolben hath divers ways misbehaved himself towards the officers, councell & Towne of Denbighe, as hath bein made apparant before vs hereunto subscribed, and whereas att this tyme and euer since . . . . (1639.) he has stood endited for a common carretor, it is by our g'rall consent thought fit that he be removed from being any longer of the councell of the saide Towne, or reputed as a capitall burgess."   *Signed*, Jo. Salusbury.

Aldermen, Ffoulke Salusbury, Robert Ffoulkes.—*Bailiffs*,

King Charles had, in the first year of his reign, granted Dolben free pardon for all manner of political offences and crimes that man could be guilty of, within the realm of England.—See *A. & M. Denbigh, p.* 207.

Mem.—Sir Thomas Salusbury, Bart., was alderman in 1634, 1635, 1636, 1637, again elected in 1839.

1641, March 15, Robert Parry, gent.
     vice .... Thomas Dryhurst, deceased.

Thomas Dryhurst was forty-four years a member of the Town Council.

Thomas Vaughan, gent. was *Bailiff* this year, but we have no account of his election as town-councillor.

1642. [MEM.]—"The Countie of Denbigh presented his Matie (King Charles) a petition for protection ag^t the orders & ordinances of Parliament, & gave the King a compleate Regim^t of Volunteers, and £1000."

1643, Sep. 24, John Hughes, tanner, *vice* Sir Thomas Salusbury, Bart.
                                             deceased.

Sir Thomas Salusbury, Bart., was alderman in 1634, 1635, 1636, 1637, and was again elected at Michaelmas, 1639.

Denbigh Castle fortified and garrisoned for the King.

1643, Sept. 24, John Jones, mercer,
     bailiff, *vice* .... Unknown
1644. Thomas Taylor, borough sheriff
     vice .... (unknown)

The Williamses of Estymcolwyn.—In 1644, "John Williams of Ystyncolwyn, in the Com. of Montgomery, Esquier, was sworn burgess."

The Lloyds of Llech.—Also "Peter Lloyd of Llech in the Com. of Denbigh, gent. And Henry Salusbury, sonne of Paule Salusbury M^r of Arts, Rector of Lowell in Oxfordshire."

1645.—The Parliamentarians, under General Mytton, lay siege to Denbigh Castle in April this year : market held at the Elm Tree, near the Abbey. Sept. 25, the King comes to Denbigh, attended by Sir Francis Gamull, Mayor of Chester, Alderman Cowper, and others, and takes up his apartments in the tower still called the "King's Tower." He holds a general review of his troops on the 27th, at Geffylliog'(page 21.) Cromwell's camp was at Whitchurch, or the White Church in the Fields by Denbigh, during the summer, but towards the end of autumn the rebel infantry took up their quarters in the suburbs of the town, outside the walls, and the cavalry in the country houses and farms around.—Thomas Taylor and Matthew Salusbury were elected *aldermen*, and Foulk Salusbury and John Hughes, *bailiffs*, at the usual Michaelmas municipal election. — The place was straitly besieged, and in October there was a great battle at Denbigh, when the royalists, (except those within the walls) were routed with considerable loss.—See *Great Siege, A. & M. Denbigh, p.* 208–238.

1646.—The usual municipal election was not held this year. The citadel surrenders at discretion, and the royalists evacuate Denbigh.

1647, June 18, Sir William Middelton,
  Baronet, Governor of Denbigh
  Castle, *vice* .... Hugh Lloyd of Foxhall, deceased.

We must, however, observe that something approaching to an anachronism seems at first sight to exhibit itself here, for Denbigh Castle was delivered up to General Mytton late in the autumn of 1646, and Colonel George Twistleton, was made a capital burgess at Michaelmas, 1648, being then governor of the fortress. He had been one of the commissioners appointed to treat for its surrender, and had distinguished himself at its siege; whilst not a syllable is before mentioned of this Sir William Myddelton. But we cannot doubt or contradict the corporate records and memoranda taken at the time. It would, therefore, appear that, on its surrender, the custody of the place was, in the first instance, given to Sir William Myddelton, probably through the influence of his relative, Sir Thomas Myddelton, whilst his paternal connection with Denbigh, and the respect in which the memory of his father was universally held, rendered his appointment to a post that had been so long and honourably filled by his grandfather very politic on the part of those who were newly installed in power *vi et armis*. But then it remains for us to account how he held the place but for so brief a period. His appointment proves him to have been a Parliamentarian, but most probably he carried his political views no further in that direction than those of his relative (Sir Thomas,) and like him was totally averse to the extinction of the regal power; and that as soon as he discovered the "ulterior ends" of the faction with whom he had been hitherto blindly acting, and that, perhaps, from pure religious and patriotic motives, he withdrew from them with disgust, disdaining to associate himself with such violent republicans and determined regicides. Consequently, that he either resigned the command of the fortress, or was displaced to make room for Colonel Twistleton, who was a thorough Cromwellite.

1648, Sep. 29, Col. George Twistleton,
    vice .... John Salusbury, deceased.

This must have been the John Salusbury who was elected capital
burgess in 1607, bailiff in 1608, 1614, 1622, and 1628, and alderman
in 1610, 1619, 1629 and 1637. For a John Salusbury was acting as
Twistleton's colleague in the aldermanic office in 1648, and John
Salusbury of Bachegraig was alive in 1657, when he resigned his
seat in favour of his son.
1649.   No record of any municipal election.—Colonel Twistleton
was " in full power," having not only the military command of the
castle and district, but absolute control over municipal affairs. The
downfal of monarchy and the spoliation of the church, seem to
have been the building up of Twistleton's fortune.—*Sale of
Church Lands by Cromwell.*—March 25, 1650, the mannours of
Landegla, Witherin, and Meliden, with other lordships, mannours,
and lands, sold to John Jones and George Twistleton, Esqrs. for
£3,797 : 00 : 00.—*M.S. of Thos. Rawlinson, Esq. of the Middle
Temple.*
At the Michaelmas election, John Jones and John Vaughan were
chosen aldermen.

1850 *Aldermen*, George Twistleton, and John Salusbury.
1651, Jan. 9, Thomas Shaw, tanner, *vice* Sir William Myddelton, deceased.
1651, Jan. 9, Rowland Price, tanner, *vice* William Salusbury, Esq.
1652 *Aldermen*, Ffoulke Salusbury, and John Madockes.—*Bailiffs*, Rich-
    ard Lloyd, and Humffrey Haward.
1653, Sep. 13, Thomas Salusbury, Bart.
    vice .... unknown. (See A.D. 1634.)

Humphrey Haward and John Madockes, "gentlemen," were in
the council in 1650.
Twistleton institutes an enquiry into the " Townes stocke of
moneys," which he finds " lying in danger of decaye ;" constitutes
Mr Bailiff Madockes receiver, with power to prosecute all defaulters,
and obtains a decree from Oliver Cromwell touching the public Chari-
ties. (*A. & M. Denbigh, p.* 245-7, where the date should be 13th
July, 1656. This was " Madockes of Bron-Yew."
Wynn of Melai.—Sworn burgess, Dec. 22, 1653.
There is no record of the election of aldermen, &c. this year.

1654 *Aldermen*, Sir John Salusbury, Bart., and John Madockes.—*Bai-
    liffs*, Ffoulke Salusburie, and Henrie Parrie.

From this date we have no record of the election of any new
alderman or bailiff for five years, although we have an account of
more than one hundred fresh burgesses, among whom we recognize
several Parliamentarians, as Colonel John Carter, Andrew Mills, who
desecrated the cathedral church of St. Asaph, and turned it unto a
cow-house and piggery. And David Richardson, of Gresford ;
William Sumner, Thomas Ball, of Burton, Esq., John Archer, gent. :

Thomas Ashton, Thomas Turrell, Esq., and Tymothy Tyrrell, of Okeley, Bucks, Esq. Gilbert Jackson, of Shotover, in the county of Oxford, gent., Col. Robt. Busbridge, Esq., William Carter of Beachampton, com. Bucks, gent. —1655.

The Stoddards of Denbigh.—The first of the name, on the burgess rolls, was sworn under the Commonwealth,—" William Stoddard sonne of William Stoddard, of Carnarvon."

1657, John Salusbury, the younger, of
Bachegraig, Esq *vice*............... John Salusbury, the elder, resigned

1658–9.—Alderman George Twistleton, " in full power,"—sole and absolute tribune.

A curious incident, arising out of official neglect had preserved the names of the bailiffs for that year, viz.—

1659 . . . . . Richard Dolben, mercer ; Robert Dolben, tanner. [MEMORAND.]—xxij. of January, 1600. " Richard Dolben, mercer, and Robert Dolben, tanner, beinge of late bayliffs w^{th}in this corporation, in whose custody the *maces* were, wch maces of silver coste . . . . . But forasmuch as the same were negligently loste. It is therefore ordered by th' aldermen and bailliffs, and counsaill, that the said Ric' & Robt. shall pay for the saide maces the so'me of xxxvij^{•} xv^{s.} apeace."

Cromwell had designated the mace "a child's bauble."

There is no record of 1660, further than the admission of common burgesses, among whom we find some of the *Lloyds of Llanynys, gentlemen ;* " Bernard *Price of Pullgwynn,* gentleman, servant to Sir Rich. Wynne, of Gwedir," Edward " *Thelwall of Place-y-Ward, Esq.*" *&c.*

It may be worth remarking that the list of aldermen and bailiffs drawn out, *in form,* by Mr. John Lloyd, of Wickwer, town-clerk, in the time of Charles II., is left *blank* from 1651 to 1661. Now, we might very naturally infer that no municipal election really took place during that time, and that our local legislators must have held a sort of Long Parliament, in miniature, for ten years. A further investigation, however, convinces us that this remarkable omission is solely owing to the " culpable or intentional neglect " of the then town-clerk, (a Mr. John Roberts,) who did not enter much of the proceedings of the republicans " in the corporation minute-book, but left them scattered in notes and pages," among his own papers. From these slips and scraps his successor had to supply as much as possible of the municipal history of past years.

From 1661 to 1669, the list of corporate officers is given in the former work, (p. 113.) and the names of all the members of the council, in the first-named year, from King Charles's charter. *See A. & M. Denbigh,* 121. Nearly one-half of the old council died off during the civil war, and the reign of the republican senate.

1660, Foulke Myddelton, Esq. *vice*... Colonel George Twistleton, disfranchised.

1661, John Myddelton, Esq. *vice*...... Unknown
1664, Sep. 29, Capt. John Salusbury, of
    Llewesog *vice* .... Harry Parry, gent. deceased.

Wynne of Coedcoch.—Hugh Wynne, tanner, the sonne of Piers Wyn, of Coedcoch, Esquire, sworn burgess in 1661. *Williams of Pont-y-Gwyddyl.*—John Williams, of Pont-y-Gwyddel, gent., sonne of Edward Williams, some time deputy-recorder of this town. 1668. *Salusbury of Rug.*—William Salusbury, of Ruyg, Esq, was burgess in 1661.
Lloyd of Penporchell.—See ostentatious letter from William Lloyd, of Penporchell, gent., to aldermen, &c., at the coronation of Charles II.—*A. & M. Denbigh, p.* 254.
The Cottons of Combermere Abboy.—Sir Robert Cotton, of Combermere, Knight, sworn burgess in 1665; but Charles Cotton, Esq. of Combermere was burgess of Denbigh in 1660.
The Davieses of Llannerch.—Mutton Davies, Esq., sworn this year.
Ashpool of Plas-Ashpool.—John Ashpoole, of Llandyrnog, gent. sworn burgess in 1665.
Hewit of Headley—Sir John Hewit, of Headley Hall, Bart., sworn burgess 4th July, 1665.
Mem. The following gentlemen, were at the Restoration, created knights of the Royal Oak (for) the county of Denbigh, the yearly value of of each one's estate being given:—Charles Salusburie, Esq. £1,300; Hurcall Thelwall, Esq., £600; Foulke Myddelton, Esq., £600; John Wynne, Esq., £600; Bevis Lloyd, Esq., £600; Sir Thomas Myddelton, Knt., of Chirk Castle, of Westminster afterwards (spent most of his estate,) £600; John Lloyd, Esq., £800.—*From Wotton's English Baronetage, Ed.* 1741.

1666, Aug. 30, Thomas Mathewes, gent.
    vice .... John Wynne, Esq. deceased.
1666 Sep. 19, Foulk Davis, apothecary.
    vice .... Thomas Mathewes, gent. deceased.

1665. Sir Richard Wynne, recorder of Denbigh, elected alderman.
In 1666, many persons of distinction were admitted burgesses, as John Windebank, Esq., sonne to Sr Francis Windebank, Secretarie of-State.
Humphreys of Oundles.—John Humphreys, of Oundles, gentlemen, in the countie of Montgy.
Grosvenor of Eaton.—Hugh Grosvenor, son of Sir Richard Grosvenor of " Eyton," in the county of Chester, &c.

1667, Aug. 4, Mutton Davies, Esq. *vice* Richard Hughes, gent. deceased.
1668, March 2, Roger Myddelton, gent
    vice .... Alderman John Clough, deceased.
1668 John Hughes, jun., gent. *vice*... John Hughes, sen. deceased.
1670, John Lloyd (of Wickwern) town-
    clerk, *vice*........................... John Jones, (the elder) deceased.
1670 Thomas Jones, mercer, *vice*........ Ffoulk Runcorn, deceased.

Lloyd of Cefn.—Edward Lloyd of Kefn, gent.—*Williams of Trelynniau,* " Peeter Williams, of Trelynnie in the county of fflint, gent., sworn burgesse in 1671."

1672, March 15, Richard Hughes, tan-
ner, *vice*......................... Robert Salusbury, deceased.
1672, Sept. 28, Thomas Twyston, tan-
ner, *vice*......................... John Salusbury, of Llewesog, deceased.

1671 *Aldermen,* John Myddelton, Ffoulke Davies.—*Bailiffs,* Hugh Lloyd, Thomas Jones.

Among the common burgesses sworn in 1671, we find " *Pennant of Bychtyn,* Piers Pennant of Bighton, Esq.; *Griffiths of Cwybir,* John Griffith of Cwybir, in the com. of fflint, gent.; *Salusbury of Bachegraig,* John Salusbury of Bachegraig, gent; *Parry of Pwllhalog,* Richard Parry, gent., son and heire app'nt of John Parry of Pwllalog, Esq. ; *Vaughan of Llech,* Owen Vaughan of Llech, gent. ; *Wynne of Voelas,* Cadwalader Wynne, Esq. of Voylas ; *Edwards of Llech,* Thomas Edwards of Llech, gent.; *Maysmor of Maysmor,* John Maesmor, gent."

1672 *Aldermen,* Edward Davies, John Hughes.—*Bailiffs,* Matthew Salusbury, Robert Salusbury:

Memorand.—" The sixteenth day of ffebr. *anno regni dm. regis Caroli se'di. Anglie ec. xxiiij°.* Ordered that Mathew Salusbury, gent., baylief of the sd. towne, doe find a sergeant-at-mace at or before next Co^{rt.} to be holden for the sd. towne, on payn of fiue pounds to be leavied of his goodes and cattell."

1673 *Aldermen,* Humffrey Haward, Thomas Roberts.—*Bailiffs,* John Salusbury, Thomas Twyston.
1674 *Aldermen,* Hugh Lloyd, John Salusbury.—*Bailiffs,* Rowland Pryce, Humfrey Evans.

There is no record of Humphrey Evans' previous election as towncouncillor. See A.D. 1682.

Among the common burgesses admitted in 1674, we find—*Wynne of Tower,* " Mr John Wynne, of the Tower, near the Mould." *Williams of Carwedvynydd,* Edward Williams, of Carwedvynydd, gent., sworn burgess. *Salusbury of Ystrad,* John Piers Salusbury, of Astad, gent. *Pennant of Bychtyn,* John Pennant, gent., son of David Pennant, of Bighton, Esq. deceased.

1675, Sept. 11, Owen Lloyd, mercer, *vice* Capt. Reynauld Rutter, deceased.
1675, same day, Robert Knowles, silver-
smith, *vice*......................... John Hughes, deceased.
1675, same day, Robt. Jones, corvisor,
vice......................... Richard Hughes, deceased.
1675, same day, John Clough, gent. *vice* Sir Richard Wynne, Bart., (of Gwydir,) deceased.

1675 *Aldermen,* Rowland Pryce, Thomas Jones.—*Bailiffs,* Owen Lloyd, Robert Knowles.

T

Common burgesses sworn in 1675—*Myddelton of Chirk Castle,* Sir Thomas Myddelton, Baronet, and his servant " Peeter ffoulkes, sonne of ffoulk ap Evan ap Hugh, of Abergeley." *Myddelton of Bodlith,* Richard Myddelton, Esq. *Llo d of Tyddyn or Farm,* Edward Lloyd, of Tythen, Esq. *Salusbury of Llewenny,* Thomas Salusbury, gent. *Lloyd of Gwrych,* John Lloyd of Gwrych, Esq., sworn January 24th.

1676, Sept. 29, the Right Worshipful Sir
Thomas Myddelton, Baronet, *vice* Humphrey Haward, gent. dead.
1676, same day, John Wynne. Esq, of
Melai, Steward of the Lordship,*vice* Mathew Salusbury, gent., dead.
1676, same day, Edward Chambres,
gentleman, *vice*......................... John Eves, gent., deceased.
1676, same day, John Salusbury, the
younger, Esquire, *vice* .... John Salusbury, the elder, dead.

1676 *Aldermen,* Sir John Salusbury, bart., Mutton Davies.—*Bailiffs,* John Clough, gent., Robert Jones.

1676 „ „ Peter Lloyd, *vice*.............. Ffoulk Salusbury, disfranchised.

1677, *Aldermen,* Sir Thomas Myddelton, bart.; John Myddelton, Esq.—*Bailiffs,* Thomas Roberts, Ffoulke Jones.

1677, Sept. 19, Peter Lloyd, *vice* ...... Ffoulke Salusbury, disfranchised.

Among the common burgesses sworn this year, were—*Pennant of Downing,* John Pennant of Downing, gent.

1678, *Aldermen,* John Wynne, of Melay, Esq., John Salusbury, of Bachegraig, Esq.—*Bailiffs,* Edward Davies, Edward Chambres.

1678.—Among the common burgesses sworn about this time, were—*Lloyd of Havodunos,* Hedd Lloyd, Esq., sheriff elect of the county of Denbigh, sworn burgess, Feb. 18th, 1678. *Price of Giler,* Robert Price, of Geeler, Esq. *Ravenscroft of Bretton,* Edd. Ravenscroft, of Bretton, Esq. *Wynne of Cesailgyfarch,* Robert Wynne, of Gesylgyfarch, Esq. *Lloyd of Croesyockyn,* Evan Lloyd, of Croesyockyn, gent. *Vaughan, of Bronheulog,* William Vaughan, of Bronheylog, Esq. *Vaughan of Caergai,* Edward Pugh, tanner, a grandchild of Rowland Van of Caergay, Esq. *Lloyd of Pentrehobyn,* Edward Lloyd, of Pentrehobyn, Esq. *Meredith of Pentrebychan,* Mr Hugh Meredith, of Pentrebychan. *Davies of Gwasanney,* Mr John Davies, of Gwasanney.
1679.—Among the common burgesses sworn this year, were—*Willoughby D'Ersby.*—"*Mem.*—xvj° Die Januarii, anno Dmi. 1679, a° regni dni regis Caroli 3d. Anglie ec. xxxj°· The right ho^ble· Robert Lord Willoughbye of Ersbie, sonne & heire app'ant of the right ho^ble The Earl of Lyndsay, Lord High Chamberleyn of England, was sworn burgess of this Towne. John ffarthing, a gentleman attending the said Lord. Morris Jones, of Llanroost, clre. vsher of y° school." John Griffith, of *Pengwern.* *Edwards of Rhual,* Thomas Edwards, of Rual, gentleman.

Wynne of Bodyscallen, Robert Wynne, of Bodyskallen, Esq. *Conway of Bodrhyddan,* " Sir John Conway, of Botruthan, Bart. *Lloyd of Plymmog,* Robert Lloyd, sonn of Nicholas Lloyd, of Plummog, gent." *Nanney of Nanney,* Griffith Nanney, of Nanney, in the county of Merioneth, Esq. *Hookes of Conway,* " Robert Hookes, of Conway, Esq., Sir John Davies, and Robert ap Richard of *Henllys,* &c."

1679, Dec. 12, Rees Jones, apothecary,
  vice............................ ...... Thomas Twiston, deceased.
  The same day, John Wynne of
  Coplenny, Esq., *vice* .... Robert Roberts, gent., deceased.

1679, *Aldermen,* Sir John Salusbury, Mutton Davies, Esq.—*Bailiffs,* John Salusbury, mercer, Owen Lloyd, mercer.

To a certain class of our readers a peculiar interest will attach itself to the name of Mr Bailiff Salusbury. It appears that he was one of the first individuals in this neighbourhood who held Presbyterian views. For a long time, he refused to abjure the *Solemn League and Covenant,* and several times ran out of town or otherwise absconded, when summoned to be " sworn in" as sheriff, on which account he was ordered to be fined for contempt of the Court of Convocation, which, finding him still untractable, at last took the following rather unceremonious and summary method of dealing with his conscientious scruples :—" fforasmuch as John Salusbury, mercer, one of the capital burgesses of the s^d· towne and borrough of Denbigh, hath been, on Mich'mas Day last past duely elected to be one of ye baylieffes of the s^d· town and burrough, for ye next ensueing yeare, & hath been legally, & duely, & tymely summoned to app^re here at this Corte holden this day, for to take his oath for ye due execuçòn of ye office of baylief; and hath not app'ed, but made contempt of this Co^rt· It is therefore ordered by this Courte that the s^d· John Salusbury for his s^d· default & contempt be, and hereby is fined in five pounds, which said five pounds are to be paid vpon sight of this order, or coppy thereof left at his dwelling by the Clr^e· of the peace, to ye hands of the aldermen, &c , within eight days now next ensueing, and in default thereof, to be displaced and disfranchised of being capitall burgesse of the s^d· town & burrough." It would, however, appear that he ultimately submitted, took the oaths required, and served his year.

The inhabitants were, at this time, burthened with several " leys and mizes" for "interteyning of ye judges, the manteyning of a p'oner in the gaole of the s^d· town, called Charles Mihan, and the support of the millisha." And the town council, by the exercise of their collective wisdom, and with the view of allaying public discontent, and saving their " cheese-parings" to purchase popularity, made the following prudent order :—" That ye bayliefes sell and dispose of such *pewter* as remayn in ye chest."* Their notions of

* The pewter scrvice used at corporation feasts,

municipal economy and public liberality were, however, not quite *so lofty* as those of " John Davies of henllan, carpenter, who was then sworne burgesse, and bestowed *a greate ladder* for y˘ servace of the Towne."

1680, *Aldermen*, Edward Chambres, Edward Davies, gent.—*Batliffs*, Hugh Lloyd, Rees Jones.

Among the common burgesses were sworn—" *Lloyd of Gwerclas*, Hugh Hughes Lloyd, of Gwerclas, Esq. *Whitley of Ashton*, Thomas Whitley, gent., son & heire appar˘ of Robert Whitley, of Ashton, in the county of fflint, Esq.; Thomas Whitley, Receiver Gen'all of Northwales. *Morgan of Golden Grove*, Edward Morgan, of Goldgreave, Esq."

1681.—Sir Hugh Myddelton, barronet, great grandchild of the first Sir Hugh; with *Minshulls*, of Stoke and Chester.

1681, *Aldermen*, John Wynne, of Copplenny, Esq., ffoulke Davies, gent. —*Bailiffs*, Robert Knowsley, Robert Jones, gent.

Copplenny is *Copoleuni*, the beacon-light eminence, an Ancient British or Roman signal station, by Newmarket, in Flintshire.

1682, Sept. 29, Thomas Davies, mercer,
     vice .... Humphrey Evans, resigned.

It is not recorded how long Humphrey Evans sat in the town-council; he was bailiff in 1673. He petitioned the corporate body in 1682, to release him from his municipal duties on the plea of his great age and infirmities. The council respectfully accepted his resignation, and tendered to him a grateful acknowledgment of his many services to the town and borough.

Aldermen, John Clough, Robert Knowles.—*Bailiffs*, Thomas Harpur, John Twiston.

There is no earlier record of Thomas Harpur, as common-councilman.

1683, Sept. 23, Thomas Evans, gentle-
     man, *vice* .... Hugh Lloyd, deceased.

Aldermen, Sir John Salusbury, Bart., John Myddelton, Esq.—*Bailiffs*, Thomas Davies, Robert Jones.

The signature of Sir John Salusbury, Bart., to the minutes proves his personal attendance in the town-council, but whilst he was in parliament, John Lloyd, Esq. (of Wickwer), sat as his deputy upon the bench at Denbigh.

1684, Aug. 15, Sir Richard Myddelton,
     Bart., *vice*............................ Alderman Sir John Salusbury, Bart deceased.
1684 Same day, John Foulkes, *vice* ... Sir Thos. Myddelton, bart. dead.
1684 Same day, John Shaw, *vice* ...... John Clough, late Alderman, deccasead.

Aldermen, John Lloyd, Owen Lloyd.—*Bailiffs*, John Twiston, Thomas Evans.

On the list of common burgesses, we have—*Ravenscroft of Pickhill*, " Thomas Ravenscroft, a Genevay marchant, second son of Thomas Ravenscroft of Pickhill, in County of fflint, Esq. *Wynne of Farm*, John Wynne of ffarme in the county of fflint, Esq."

1685, July 28. Robert Davies, of Llannerch, Esq. *vice* .... Mutton Davies, Esq., deceased.

Aldermen, Sir Richard Myddelton, Bart., John Myddelton, Esq.—*Bailiffs*, Rice Jones, Robert Knowles.

Among the common burgesses admitted, were—*Trevor of Brynkinallt*, Sir John Trevor, speaker of the House of Commons, &c. *Conway of Bodrhyddan*, Sir John Conway, of Botruthan, barrt. *Grosvenor of Eaton*, Captain Richard Grosvenor.

1686, Aug. 27, Hugh Lloyd, of Foxhall, Esq. *vice* .... No record.
1686, Sept. 18, Thomas Shaw, gentleman, *vice* ... . Thomas Shaw, the elder, dead.
Same day, Richard Jones, *vice* ... Unknown.
1686, Sept. 27, William Wynne, of Melai, Esq. .... No record.

Richard Jones is sometimes described as a *dyer*, and sometimes styled " gentleman," which may be accounted for on the supposition that he had *retired*. William Wynne was steward of the Lordship.

Aldermen, Robert Jones, Rice Jones.—*Bailiffs*, John ffoulkes, John Shaw.

These two aldermen, died sometime after their election, and Thomas Harpur and John Twiston, served for the remaining part of the year.

1687, Aug. 1, John Myddelton, of Gwaenynog, Esq. *vice* .... John Myddelton, Esq , deceased.
1687, Sept. 29, Thomas Myddelton, Esq. *vice* .... Edward Davies, deceased.

Aldermen, Robert Davies and William Wynne, Esquires.—*Bailiffs*, Thomas Shaw, Richard Jones.

Among the common burgesses, we have—*Conway of Rhydorddwy*, " John Conway, of Riddordduye," who paid the fee, and " two bowles of wyne."

1688, *Aldermen*, Thomas Myddelton, Esq., John ffoulkes, gent.—*Bailiffs*, Roger Myddelton, Robert Jones.

Among the common burgesses, we have—*Lloyd of Bodidris*, Sir Evan Lloyd, Bart.

1689 *Aldermen*, Ffoulke Lloyd, Esq., Thomas Davies, mercer.—*Bailiffs*, Thomas Shaw, gent., Richard Jones, dyer.

1690 *Aldermen*, Roger Myddelton, Esq., Ffoulke Davies, gent.—*Bailiffs*, Thomas Harpur, Robert Knowles.

1691, April 1, Sir John Wynne, of Wat-
    stay, knight and bart., *vice*......... John Wynne, of Melai, Esq.,dead.

This Sir John was grandson of the celebrated Sir John Wynne of Gwydir, author of " *The History of the Gwydir Family.*"   He was member of the town-council of Denbigh, twenty-eight years, and alderman in 1695.   He married Jane, daughter and heiress of Eyton Evans, of Watstay, Esq., re-built the mansion, enclosed the present extensive park, and planted the much and justly admired avenue of now gigantic trees, ascending from the village of Ruabon to the ornamental lake, fronting the manse, and changed the name to Wynnstay.   He has the credit of introducing into Wales a very improved system of horticulture.   He died at the advanced age of ninety-one, being then blind and childless. "Sir John," says Yorke, in his " *Royal Tribes of Wales*," " was a man of pleasure in his youth.   Late in life he made a visit to court—in the early days of Queen Anne—and meeting in the drawing-room, after many years' absence, his old Westminster school-fellow, the Apostolic Beveridge of St. Asaph, ' Ah, Sir John! Sir John,' says the good bishop to him, ' when I knew you first, the Devil was very great with you.' ' Yes, my Lord,' replied Sir John, ' I wish he was half so *great* with me now.' "   He left Wynnstay and other estates of great value, to his kinsman, Watkin Williams, of Llanvorda, afterwards called Sir Watkin Williams Wynn.   .

1691, April 1, Joshua Salusbury, mer-
    cer, *vice*............................ Ffoulke Davies, gent., deceased.
1691 Thomas Twyston, tanner, *vice* ... Robert Jones, deceased.

Thomas Twyston was Steward of the Company of Tanners ; and a silver cup of the company is still in the possession of his descendants at Denbigh.

1691, same day, Robert Price, corvisor,
    vice...................................... Thomas Harpur, deceased.
1691, Thomas Jones, ironmonger, *vice* Unknown.
Aldermen, Roger Myddelton, William Wynne, Esquires.—*Bailiffs*, Robert Knowles, Joshua Salusbury.

1692, Sept. 29, John Myddelton, dyer,
    vice.......... .... Ffoulk Lloyd, of Foxhall, dead.
1692 Thomas Roberts *vice* .... John Lloyd, of Rossa, deceased.
1692 Hugh Hughes, gent., *vice* .... Owen Lloyd, deceased.
Same year, John Twiston, tanner, *vice*... Unknown.

Aldermen, Thomas Shaw, Robert Knowles.—*Bailiffs*, Robert Price, Thomas Twiston.

1693, Aug. 11, Edward Brereton, of
    Borras, Esq. *vice* .... William Wynne, of Melai, Esq.,
                                        deceased.
Aldermen, Thomas Jones, Joshua Salusbury.—*Bailiffs*, John Twiston, John Myddelton, Esq.

1694, *Aldermen*, Robert Davies, Edward Chambres, Esquires.—*Bailiffs*, John Twiston, John Myddelton, Esq.

1695, *Aldermen*, Sir John Wynne, knight and baronet; John Myddelton, Esq.—*Bailiffs*, John Twiston, John Myddelton, dyer.

1696, Sept. 29, Foulke Davies, apothe-
    cary, *vice* ....Ffoulk Jones, gent., deceased.

Aldermen, Edward Brereton, Esq., Roger Myddelton.—*Bailiffs*, Robert Price, Thomas Twiston.

1697, *Aldermen*, Thomas Twiston, Robert Price.—*Bailiffs*, John Twiston, John Jones.

1698, *Aldermen*, John Twiston, John Jones.—*Bailiffs*, Thomas Jones, John Shaw.

1699, June 20, John Heaton, gentleman,
    vice................................... Hugh Hughes, deceased.
Same day, Robert Roberts, gent., *vice*... Richd. Jones, gent. deceased.

Aldermen, Roger Myddelton, John Shaw.—*Bailiffs*, John Myddelton, Thomas Roberts.

1700, Jan 22, Sir Robert Cotton, Knt.
    and Baronet *vice* .... Roger Myddelton, deceased.
Same day, Richard Heaton, gent., *vice* Robert Roberts, deceased.

Aldermen, John Myddelton, dyer; Thomas Roberts.—*Bailiffs*, Robert Knowles, Thomas Twiston.

1701 *Aldermen*, John Myddelton, Esq., Thomas Shaw.—*Bailiffs*, Richard Heaton, Robert Price.

1702 *Aldermen*, Richard Heaton, Robert Price.—*Bailiffs*, John Ffoulkes, John Jones.

1703 *Aldermen*, John Ffoulkes, John Jones.—*Bailiffs*, John Shaw, Thomas Twiston.

1704 *Aldermen*, John Shaw, Thomas Twiston.—*Bailiffs*, John Myddelton, Thomas Roberts.

1705, Sept. 29, John Chambres, Esq. *vice* Edward Chambres, Esq., dead.
Same day, John Chambres, gent., *vice* Thomas Davies, deceased.

Aldermen, John Myddelton, Thomas Roberts.—*Bailiffs*, John Jones, Robert Knowles.

Alderman Roberts is styled a gentleman. There were three others of the name; father, son, and grandson; who were butchers, graziers, and cattle-dealers: the first elected common-councilman in 1669, the second in 1719, and the third in 1730. At first sight, three "jolly butchers," attired in the robes of aldermen, cut a rather awkward figure among so many knights, baronets, and esquires. However, these three knights of the cleaver appear to have been respectable parties, who passed off as tribunes of the people—men not only capable of doing justice to a corporation dinner, but useful public officers, as is inferred from the fact of their having been several times re-elected. Nor ought we to forget that the distinction of *caste* was not then so nicely defined, or not so rigidly acted upon, as it is now. The standard of "respectability" stood several degrees below its present level. The model of the gentleman was not yet so carefully and delicately *fashioned* as to compel

the sons of " the lords of the soil " to abstain from all trades and
mechanical professions, or manufacturing and commercial pursuits.
Hence we find the sons of some of the oldest and most aristocratic
gentry in North Wales, numbered among the Denbigh tradesmen
of those days.   Our present Welsh notions of the dignity of gentle
birth are quite shocked at the mention of such vulgar occupations
as were, " in that rude age," adopted by men like John Lloyd, of
Denbigh, mercer, son of John Lloyd, Esq., of Wickwer and
Havodunos ; Hugh Wynne, of Denbigh, tanner, son of Piers
Wynne, Esq., of Coedcoch ; Edward Heaton, hatter, one of the old
Anglo-Cambrian family of that name, seated for ages at Lleweny
Green ; and a host of Salusburies, Myddeltons, Dolbens, Pantons,
&c., who followed the professions of skinners, glovers, mercers, dy-
ers, corvisors, &c.   But we are not to think that such men, reckoned
among the common-councillors, sheriffs, and aldermen, were mere
operatives, but manufacturers and masters of such trades and mys-
teries—men who staked their capital upon the encouragement of
useful and honest crafts, and by identifying their own interests
with those of their poorer brethren, contributed largely towards
supplying the million with their daily bread.   Indeed, such have
been the men to establish communities, to build cities, to incorpor-
ate municipalities, and to found families of more VIRTUOUS, and
consequently of more *noble* origin, than you could derive from a
thousand generations of ancestral *Nimrods.*   But to proceed—
     Great numbers enlist under the Duke of Marlborough, as ex-
pressed in a popular ballad of that day :—
          " Gwyn i fyd na fawn i'n g'lommen
            Ar ben clochdy *Pawl's* yn Llundain,
            I gael gweled pa sawl Cymro
            Sy'n gwas'naethu'r *Duke o' Marlbro.*"
Hence, within our own recollection, there was a common expression
in Wales—" Gone to Flanders," that is, gone and lost.
1707, Sept. 29, John Wynne, of Melai,
     Esq. *vice* .... John Shaw, deceased.
1708, Sept. 29, Mark Roberts, gent. *vice* Robert Knowles, deceased.
1710, Sept. 29, Robert Davies, of Llan-
     nerch. Esq. jun. *vice*.................. Robt. Davies, Esq. sen deceased.
1712 Sept. 29, Robt. Price, jun. tanner,
     vice .... John Jones, gent., deceased.
     For seven years, from 1705 to 1712, Robert Knowles, John
ffoulkes, Thomas Twiston, Richard Heaton, Robert Price, John
Myddelton, Thomas Roberts, and two gentlemen of the name of
John Jones, held alternately and successively the chief corporate
offices. In 1710 the initials of the aldermen's names were four *jays*:—
                    J. J.: J. J.
That is John Jones and John Jones ; but the name is so common
as to afford no safe clue to individual identity.   Probably the one
described as John Jones, innkeeper, was the bailiff of 1697, and was
not a capital burgess prior to that date.

1713, Sept. 19, Sir Thomas Cotton, Bart.
    vice .... Sir Robt. Cotton (the father) dead.
Same day, Roger Evans, mercer, *vice*... Alderman Thomas Roberts, dead.
Aldermen, John Jones, Robert Price, sen.—*Bailiffs*, Roger Evans, Robert
Price, jun.
1714, Sept. 19, John Myddelton, of .
    Gwaenynog, gentleman, *vice*...... Ffoulke Davies, deceased.
Aldermen, Robert Davies, Esq., John C. Chambres, Esq.—*Bailiffs*, John
Myddelton, gentleman ; Thomas Roberts.
The same day (Sept.29), Thomas Roberts
    was elected capital burgess, *vice*... Robt. Price, jun. deceased.

And for part of next year, Mark Roberts, gent., acted as deputy
(alderman) for John Wynne of Melai, Esq., whilst the latter sat in
Parliament for the borough.

1715 *Aldermen*, John Wynne, Robert Myddelton, Esquires.—*Bailiffs*,
David Williams, John Myddelton, dyer.

The two last were bailiffs in 1717, 1720, and 1721.

1716 *Aldermen*, John Chambres, Esq., Mark Roberts.—*Bailiffs*, John
Myddelton, Thomas Roberts.
1717, July 27, Sir Robert Salusbury
    Cotton, baronet. *vice* .... Sir Thomas Cotton,bart.,deceased.
Same day, John Davies, mercer, *vice*... John Wynne, of Goppa, Esq.
                                                    deceased.
1717, Sept. 29, Robert Myddelton, of
    Salop, Esq *vice* .... Sir Rich. Myddelton, bart.,dead.
Same day, David Williams, gent. *vice*... Thomas Shaw, gent., deceased.
Same day, John Knowles, glover, *vice*   John Twiston, tanner, deceased.
Aldermen, John Wynne, Esq., Robt. Myddelton, Esq.

Alderman John Wynne (of Melai), late M.P. for the borough,
died early in the spring of 1718, and was succeeded in the civic
office by John Myddelton, Esq., of Gwaenynog.

1718, Aug. 20, John Myddelton, of
    Chirk Castle, Esq. *vice* .... Alderman John Wynne, (of Me-
                                                    lai,) deceased.
Same day, Robert Jones, innkeeper,*vice* John Heaton, gent., deceased.
Same day, Robert Knowles, ironmonger,
    vice .... John Jones, innkeeper.
Same day, Wm. Knowles, glover, *vice*... John Myddelton, dyer, deceased.
Aldermen, John Myddelton, Esq., Roger Evans, mercer.—*Bailiffs*, John
Knowles, glover, Robert Knowles, ironmonger.
1718, Sept. 29, John Humphreys, gentle-
    man, *vice* .... Robt. Jones, innholder, deceased.

John Lloyd, gent., of Coedaccas, was elected common-councilman, some time this year.

1719, Sept. 29, John Lloyd, of Foxhall,
    Esq. *vice* .... Sir John Wynne Knt. and Bart.
                                                    deceased.

U

Same day, Edward Lloyd, Esq. of Love-
lane, *vice* .... Joshua Salusbury, mercer, dead.

Aldermen, John Knowles, Robert Knowles.—*Bailiffs,* Richard Heaton, John
Humphreys, gents.

1720 *Aldermen,* John Lloyd (of Foxhall), Esq., Edward Lloyd (of Plummog), Esq., whose town house was in Love-lane.

1720, Sept. 24, Robert Wynne, of Plas-
newydd, Esq. *vice* .... Thomas Evans, gent., deceased.

Same day, Thomas Lloyd, gent. *vice* ... Mark Roberts, deceased.

1721 The *Aldermen* for this year were—John Myddelton, of Chirk Castle,
Esq., and Roger Evans, mercer.

1722 The bailiffs of last year served as *Aldermen,* viz.—John Myddelton,
and David Williams.—*Bailiffs,* Thomas Roberts, William Knowles.

1723, July 2, David Lloyd, attorney-at-
law, *vice* .... Thomas Jones, ironmonger, dead.

Aldermen, Robert Wynne, Esq., David Lloyd, gent. The *bailiffs* of last
year were re-elected.

1724 *Aldermen,* Edward Lloyd, Esq., Thomas Lloyd.—*Bailiffs,* John
Ffoulkes, sen., John Myddelton.

1724, Nov. 2, Richard Lloyd, gent., *vice* Thomas Twiston, tanner, dead.

1725, Sept. 29, David Williams of
Lodge, jun., gentleman, *vice* ...... Edward Brereton (of Borras) Esq.
                          (late M.P.) deceased.

Aldermen, Thomas Roberts, John Myddelton.—*Bailiffs,* Richard Heaton,
Richard Lloyd.

Mr Bailiff Lloyd died before the expiration of the civic year, and
Hugh Hughes, tanner, otherwise styled " gentleman, was elected
common-councilman and bailiff in his place and stead," on the 24th
June, 1726.

1726 *Aldermen,* Richard Heaton, Hugh Hughes.—*Bailiffs,* Roger Evans,
David Williams, jun., gents.

1727 *Aldermen,* the bailiffs of last year elected aldermen; and John
Humphreys, and Thomas Roberts, *Bailiffs.*

1728, Aug. 14, Thomas Price of Glynn,
Esq. *vice* .... Robert Davies of Llannerch, Esq.
                          deceased.

Aldermen, Thomas Price, Esq., John Humphreys, gent.—*Bailiffs,* David
Williams, sen., John Knowles.

1729, Sept. 29, Lynch Salusbury Cotton,
Esq. *vice* .... Richard Heaton, gent. deceased.

Aldermen, John Myddelton of Chirk Castle, Esq., Lynch Salusbury Cotton,
Esq.—*Bailiffs,* David Williams of Lodge, jun., John Myddelton, gent.

1730, April 17, Roderick Lloyd, glover,
vice .... Hugh Hughes, tanner, deceased.

Aldermen, John Myddelton, David Williams.—*Bailiffs,* Roger Evans, Roderick Lloyd. But this Roger Evans died in 1731, as we find in a
record of the municipal election of—

1731, June 30, Peter Vaughan, gent. *vice* Roger Evans, deceased.

Aldermen. John Lloyd, and Thomas Price, Esquires.—*Bailiffs*, Daivd Williams (of Ruthin), Thomas Roberts. Was not this the younger Williams, of Lodge, Denbigh?

1732, *Aldermen*, David Williams, (of Ruthin,) Thomas Roberts. —*Bailiffs* Peter Vaughan, of Bodeiliog, gent., Roderick Lloyd.

1733. There were several elections of capital burgesses this year as,—

1733, April 9, William Myddelton, of Denbigh, Esq. ....: *vice* Robert Myddelton, of Chirk Castle, Esq., deceased.

Same day, John Griffith, of Denbigh Green, ...*vice* John Ffoulkes, mercer, deceased.

1733 August 20, Robert Maurice, of Astrad, Esq....................*vice* Robert Price, deceased.

1733 Michaelmas, *Aldermen*, John Lloyd and William Myddelton, ι Esqrs.—*Bailiffs*, Thomas Price, John Griffith, Esqrs.

1734. The bailiffs of last year made *Aldermen*, and William Knowles and John Hughes, *Bailiffs*.

1735. *Aldermen*, John Myddelton, of Chirk Castle, Esq., and John Myddelton, Gwaenynog, Esq.—*Bailiffs*, Thomas Roberts, David Williams, jun.

1736, March 23, Watkin Wynne, of Voylas, Esq. ....*vice* John Davis, mercer, deceased.

1736 *Aldermen*, the bailiffs of last year.—*Bailiffs*, John Myddelton, Roderick Lloyd.

1737, *Aldermen*, Thomas Price, Esq., John Hughes.—*Bailiffs*, John Knowles, Peter Vaughan.

1738, May 23, Edward Heaton, hat-manufacturer* ....*vice* David Lloyd, gent., deceased.

1738, May 23, Thomas Roberts, jun., grazier, butcher, &c. ....*vice* Roderick Lloyd, deceased.

1738 Sept. 29, Thomas Evans, grocer, *vice* .... John Knowles, glover, deceased.

1738 *Aldermen*, Watkin Wynne, Esq., Peter Vaughan.—*Bailiffs*, David Williams, jun., Richard Heaton.

1739, Sep. 29, John Wynne, of Melai, Esq:...................................*vice* Thomas Roberts, innholder, deceased.

1733 *Aldermen*, the bailiffs of last year.—*Bailiffs*, Thomas Evans, Thomas Roberts.

1740, Sep. 29, John Hosier, gent., *vice* John Lloyd, Esq., deceased.

1740 *Aldermen*, Watkin Wynne and William Myddelton, Esqs.—*Bailiffs*, David Williams, Peter Vaughan.

Mr. Bailiff Williams, disfranchised for a season, together with Thomas Shaw, glover; Humphrey Myddelton, hatter; and

---

* The manufacture of hats was at this time extensively carried on in Denbigh. Heaton was a gentleman by birth, but, according to tradition, served his apprenticeship to a Denbigh hatter, worked afterwards as journeyman in London, and returning home, set up in a large way of business. Many entries in the corporation books are in his beautiful handwriting.

John Lloyd, tanner.) Mr. D. Williams, of Lodge, served as bailiff for the remaining part of this year. Mr. John Hosier, made town-clerk, by patent of George II., given at St. James, 12th March, 1740-1. He seems to have been an entire stranger, active, and perhaps then thought an overbearing and ambitious lawyer. He was three times bailiff and six times alderman.

1741, *Aldermen,* David Williams, (Lodge), Thomas Evans.—*Bailiffs,* John Hosier, Thomas Roberts.

1742, 1743, 1744.—It is unacountable that no municipal election took place for three years. Hosier seems to have had all the business to himself; others apparently refusing to act with him. Few attended the council, or "court of convocation," as it was styled, and even at each succeeding Michaelmas, the great election day, Hosier's endeavours "to form a house," proved a failure.

1745, Sep. 21, Richard Myddelton, of
    Chirk Castle, Esq. ....*vice* Edward Lloyd, of Gwerclas, Esq.
                                      deceased.

      Was this Edward Lloyd, Esq. of Love-lane and Plummog ?

1745, Same day, Rees Ffoulkes, gent.,
    vice .... John Myddelton, gent., deceased.
1745 Same day, John Lloyd, of Coed-
    accas ....*vice* Thomas Roberts.

One knight of the cleaver succeeding another. The same year Hosier was alderman, with Rees Ffoulkes as his colleague, and Peter Vaughan and John Lloyd, *bailiffs.*

1746, Sep, 29, Edward Roberts, tanner,
    vice .... John Chambres, of Plas Cham-
                                  bres, Esq., deceased.

1746 *Aldermen,* John Griffith, of Garn, Esq., John Hosier.—*Bailiffs,* John Lloyd, of Coedaccas, gent., —— Roberts, tanner.

1747, Sept. 29, Robert Jones, apothe-
    cary, *vice* .... John Myddelton of Chirk Castle,
                                  Esq. deceased.

Aldermen, Richard Myddelton and William Myddelton, Esqs.—*Bailiffs,* Edward Roberts, Edward Heaton.

1748,*Sept. 29, Hugh Clough of Plas
    Clough, Esq. *vice*.................... Sir Robert Salusbury Cotton,
                                  Bart. deceased.

Aldermen, Watkin Wynne and Hugh Clough, Esqs.—*Bailiffs,* David Williams, Peter Vaughan.

1749.—No new Aldermen, bailiffs, coroners, leave-lookers, &c., elected, there being "no house" at the Michaelmas convocation, which had been summoned as usual.

* The rent of Acryforwyn settled upon the Grammar School, in 1726, not paid for twenty-one years.

1750 John Price, Doctor-of-Divinity,
vice .... John Hughes, grocer, deceased.
Aldermen, John Price, D.D., Thomas Williams, gent.—*Bailiffs*, John Lloyd, Coedaccas ; Edward Roberts.

Dr. Price was Prebendary of Ely, and was appointed Rector of Denbigh in 1749.—See *A. & M. Denbigh, p. 355.*

Towards the middle of this century, (the 18th) among the common burgesses we find— *Conway of Cotton Hall*, James, John, and Jacob Conway, " gentlemen" ; several *Lloyds of Brynygwynt.—Edwards of Glynn*, John Edwards of Glynn, Esq.—*Davies of Caerhun*, Hugh Davies, Esq.— *Yale of Yale*, David Yale, Esq.—*Wynne of Leeswood*, John Wynne, Esq.—*Lloyd of Rhyl*, Henry Lloyd, Esq. of Rhil—*Wright of Plasissa*, John Wright of Plasissa, Esq.—James Russell Stapleton, Esq., grandfather of the present Field Marshall Lord Viscount. Combermere, who is a native of the Borough of Denbigh.—*Lloyd of Maesannod*, Robert Lloyd, gentleman.—*Jones of Galltfaenan*, John Jones, Esq.—*Paynter of Summer Hill*, John Paynter, Esq.—*Lloyd of Forest*, John Lloyd of fforest, gent.—*Lloyd of Nantglyn*, Peter Lloyd of Nantglyn, gent. —*Jones of Cilygroeslwyd*, James Jones of Ceelygroeslwyd, Esq.—*Griffith of Cefnymwlch*, William Griffith, Esq. of Ceven Amulch, Caernarvon ; besides several *Wynnes of Garthmelio and Plasnewydd, Madockes of Bron-Yew.* In short, some members of almost every patrician family in this part of the kingdom.

1750 Thomas Williams, gentleman, *vice* Robert Jones, apothecary, dead.

1751, *Aldermen*, John Griffith of Garn, Esq., Edward Heaton.—*Bailiffs*, David Williams, John Hosier.

1752, Sept. 29, John Rathbone *vice* ... David Williams (of Ruthin.)

Rathbone is sometimes described as a plumber and glazier, sometimes as glass-merchant, and must have been a person " well to do," with some property. He was, probably, promoted by Hosier.

Aldermen, The bailffs of last year.—*Bailiffs*, Thomas Williams, and John Rathbone.

1753, Aug. 1, Evan Evans, apothecary,
vice .... William Knowles, deceased.
Same day, John Roberts, glover, *vice*   Edward Roberts, deceased.

Aldermen, Thomas Williams, Peter Vaughan.—*Bailiffs*, David Williams, John Hosier.

1754, April 22, John Myddelton of
Gwaenynog, jun. Esq. *vice*......... John Myddelton, Esq. sen. dead.
Same day, John Conway of Astrad, Esq.
vice .... Thomas Lloyd of Aston, Esq.
deceased.

Aldermen, the two newly elected councillors.—*Bailiffs*, John Lloyd, Evan Evans.

1755, Sept. 23, Hugh Lloyd of Coed-y-
     dacoas, *vice* .... David Williams of Lodge, Esq.
                                          deceased.

Aldermen, William Myddelton of Gwaenynog, Esq, Thomas Williams.—
Bailiffs, Peter Vaughan, John Roberts.

Mr Bailiff Vaughan now held the Bull Inn. Harry-ap-Shenkin, and other bellmen, on the night-watch, ordered to go round the town every night, between the hours of eleven o'clock at night and six o'clock in the morning, from the 1st of November to the 1st of March, and use their utmost endeavours to keep the peace, and take care that no robberies, riots, or other misdemeanors were committed, and to lodge all offenders in safe custody. The town was divided into Wards from time immemorial, at least, in the reign of James I., we read of the High or High-street Ward, Lower Ward, Love-lane Ward, and Henllan-street Ward. These were, apparently, the four original suburban wards ; the Old Town, or " Burg," within the walls was called the Castle Ward.

1756, *Aldermen,* the tribunes for this year were Evan Evans, and John Rathbone, and the *Bailiffs,* Thomas Williams, John Lloyd.

1757, Sept. 25, Thomas Edwards, tan-
     ner,*vice*.............. .... Robert Wynne, of Plasnewydd,
                                       Esq. deceased.

Aldermen, John Myddelton, Esq., John Hosier.—*Bailiffs,* Peter Vaughan, Thomas Edwards.

1757, Nov. 2, John Salusbury, grocer,
     vice .... Thomas Evans.

1758, Sept. 29, John Griffith of Garn,
     Esq. (son) *vice*........................ John Griffith, Esq. (father) dead.

Aldermen, Thomas Williams, John Salusbury.—*Bailiffs,* John Rathbone, Hugh Lloyd of Lodge, grazier.

This Hugh Lloyd was not in the council before, unless otherwise " of Coedaccas." This might be decided by examining the signatures.

1759, Sept. 29, Rev. Edward Foulkes,
     clerk, *vice* .... William Myddelton, Esq. dead.

" Alderman Foulkes" was for many years master of the Grammar School, curate of the parish, and lecturer at St. Hilary's Chapel.

Aldermen, the Rev. Edward Foulkes, Thomas Edwards.—*Bailiffs,* John Hosier, John Lloyd.

1660, Sept. 29, Robert Myddelton, Esq.
     vice.................................... Hugh Clough of Glanywern,Esq.
                                       deceased.

Aldermen, John Hosier again tribune with John Lloyd as his colleague.— Rathbone and Vaughan, *Bailiffs.*

The corporate body address King George III. on his accession to the throne.

1761, Sept, 29, Powell Clough of Glany-
wern, Esq. *vice*...................... Thomas Price of Cefnywern Esq.
deceased.

The deceased had been elected as " of Glynn."

Aldermen, John Price, D.D., Thomas Williams.—*Bailiffs,* Hugh Lloyd,
grazier, John Roberts, glover.

The corporate body congratulate the King upon his marriage with
the Princess Charlotte, of Mecklenburg Strelitz.

1762, Sept. 29, John Knowles, glover,
vice.................................... John Rathbone, deceased.
Aldermen, Robert Myddelton, Esq. John Hosier.—*Bailiffs,* Evan Evans,
John Knowles.
1763, Sept. 29, Rev. David Price of
Chirk, *vice*............................. Edward Heaton, gent. deceased.
Aldermen, Thomas Williams, John Salusbury.—*Bailiffs,* Thomas Edwards,
John Lloyd.
1764, Sept. 29, Edward Edwards, (of
Ruthin) grocer, *vice*.................. John Humphrey of Carregypen-
nill, gent. deceased.

This John Humphreys was forty-six years a capital burgess, and
alderman in 1728; probably he had retired to the country in his
old age. But the capital men are almost to a man " called " after
their estates, country seats, or birth-places, although we know that
many of them were professional or commercial men, who held
premises in town, and are sometimes said to be of this " town" or
such " street," or places in the immediate vicinity of the town, as
Lodge, Ystrad, Cotton Hall, Segrwyd, Gwaenynog, &c., &c., as the
reader must have observed.

Aldermen, the Rev. Edward Foulkes, John Hosier.—*Bailiffs,* Peter Vaughan,
John Roberts.
1765, *Aldermen,* John Myddelton, Esq., Thomas Williams.—*Bailiffs,* Evan
Evans, Hugh Lloyd.
1766, Sept. 29, William Simon of Llan-
gollen, gentleman, *vice*............... John Hosier, gent. deceased.
Aldermen, John Price, D.D., Peter Vaughan.—*Bailiffs,* John Lloyd, John
Knowles.

Thomas Williams, gent., appointed town-clerk, in place of John
Hosier, gent., deceased.

1767, April 23, the Rev. Robert Myddel-
ton, clerk, *vice* ..../........ John Conway of Astrad, deceased.
Same day, Peter Vaughan, tanner, *vice* Thomas Edwards, deceased.
1767, Sept. 29, Hugh Stoddart, apothe-
cary, *vice* .... Rees Ffoulkes of Gwerneigron,
Esq. deceased.
Same day, Thomas Roberts, glover, *vice* Thomas Williams, deceased.

Aldermen, John Myddelton, Esq., Hugh Stoddart.—*Bailiffs,* John Roberts, glover, Hugh Lloyd of Lodge.

1768, *Aldermen,* Evan Evans, apothecary, John Salusbury, grocer.—*Bailiffs,* Thomas Roberts, glover, Peter Vaughan, tanner.

1769, Peter Jones (of Ruthin) *vice* ...... Edward Edwards (of Ruthin) deceased.

Aldermen, Rev. John Price, D.D., William Simon, gent —*Bailiffs,* Peter Vaughan of Bodeiliog, John Lloyd of " Coedydaccas."

1770, *Aldermen,* John Lloyd, John Roberts.—*Bailiffs,* Hugh Lloyd, John Knowles.

1771, Sept. 29, Thomas Myddelton of Denbigh Castle, Esq. *vice* .... Hugh Stoddart, deceased.

Aldermen, Thomas Myddelton, Esq. Peter Vaughan, jun.—*Bailiffs,* Evan Evans, William Simon.

1772.—The author could find no record. William Simon was then town-clerk.

1773,*Sept. 29, Richard Heaton, Esq.
      vice .... Sir John Wynne, Bart, deceased.

James Owen must have been elected capital burgess this year.

Aldermen, the Rev. Robert Myddelton, James Owen.—*Bailiffs,* Hugh Lloyd, Thomas Roberts.

1774, *Aldermen,* Evan Evans, Peter Jones.—*Bailiffs,* John Lloyd, John Roberts.

1775, Sept. 29, Richard Kenrick, of Nantclwyd, Esq. *vice*.............. Watkin Wynne, Esq., deceased.

1775 Same day, Rev. EdwardWilliams, clerk *vice*... .... Peter Vaughan, of Bodeiliog, deceased.

This year, Thomas Myddelton, Esq. and William Simon, were elected *aldermen,* John Knowles and Peter Jones, *bailiffs.*

1776, Sept. 29, The Honourable Major-General Taylor *vice*.................. Sir Lynch Salusbury Cotton, Bart· deceased.

Sir Lynch was forty-seven years an active member of the council.

1776 Sept. 29, The Rev. Robert Carter Thelwall, clerk *vice*.................. Powell Clough, Esq., deceased,

. *Aldermen* and *bailiffs.*—This year the same gentlemen were elected as in 1773.

1777, Hugh Vaughan, of Bodeiliog, gent. *vice*............................. John Lloyd, of Coedaccas, deceased.

Aldermen, Thomas Myddelton, Esq. of Denbigh Castle, Hugh Vaughan Bodeiliog.—*Bailiffs,* William Simon, John Knowles.

* A salary of £20 per annum settled upon the town-criership, held then by John Morris, " barber and periwig-maker,"

1777, Sept. 29, Thomas Lloyd, grocer,
vice .... Evan Evans, apothecary, deceased.

It would appear that a Mr Williams (master of the Grammar
School ?) entered an action against the corporation respecting
" *Accar-y-vorwin*," in which the latter lost.   We have a memoran-
dum " of an order in council " for payment of *bills and costs.*

1778.   This year, the *Aldermen* were William Simon and Thomas Lloyd,
Bailiffs, Hugh Lloyd, John Roberts.
1779, *Aldermen*, the Rev. Robert Myddelton, James Owen.—*Bailiffs*,
John Salusbury, John Knowles.

At this time, the town was greatly infested with vagrants, strol-
lers and sturdy beggars, and an officer called a " ban-beggar" was
appointed by the corporation " with power and authority to take
them up, and bring them before the aldermen." The notices (which
still remain) were set up, threatening such characters that they
would be taken up and publicly whipped.
Note.—In 1779, the following gentlemen were admitted common
burgesses, viz., Rich. Myddelton, jun., Esq. ; John Madocks, sen.,
Esq.; Philip Yorke, Esq. ; Bennet Williams, Esq. ; John Vaughan
of Groes, Esq. ; John Ffoulkes, Erriviatt, Esq. ; John Vaughan of
Bodeiliog, gent., &c.

1780, Sept. 29, William Williams, *vice* Thomas Roberts, glover, deceased.

1780 *Aldermen*, William Simon, Thomas Lloyd.—*Bailiffs*, Hugh Vaughan,
John Roberts.

Among the common burgesses sworn, we have, Hugh Hughes
Lloyd, of Gwerclas, Esq., and Dr. Woodville.

1781 *Aldermen*, James Owen, Hugh Lloyd.—*Bailiffs*, John Knowles,
William Williams.

1782, Sept. 29, Edward Knowles, inn-
keeper.............................*vice* John Roberts. glover, deceased.

1782 *Aldermen*, the Rev. R. Myddelton, William Simon.—*Bailiffs*, John
Salusbury, Edward Knowles.

1783, Sept. 29, Richard Myddelton, of
Chirk Castle, jun., Esq. ...... *vice* Robert Myddlelton, of Gwaenynog, Esq., deceased,

1783, *Aldermen*, John Roberts, tanner, Thomas Lloyd, mercer.—*Bailiffs*,
Hugh Lloyd, William Simon.

1784.   Among the common burgesses of this year, we find *Wil-
liams of Bodelwyddan;* John Williams, jun., Esq., of Bodlewithan ;
Richard Tavistock Price ; John Wynne Griffith, and Bennet
Williams, Esquires.

1784, *Aldermen*, John Salusbury, William Simon. — *Bailiffs*, John
Knowles, William Williams.
1785, *Aldermen*, James Owen, John Roberts.—*Bailiffs*, Hugh Lloyd,
Edward Knowles.

X

1786. This year the same aldermen were elected, as in 1782, and the same bailiffs as in 1784.

1787, Sept 29, the Rev. Edward Chambres Jones, clerk .... *vice* Peter Jones, gent., deceased.

1787 *Aldermen*, James Owen, Thomas Lloyd.—*Bailiffs*, Hugh Lloyd, John Roberts.

At this time there were no less than seven clergymen in the council.

1787 Same day, Ellis Roberts of Ruthin
    vice .... John Salusbury, deceased.

1788 The *aldermen* were the Rev. Robert Myddelton, re-elected, and Richard Heaton, Esq.; the *bailiffs* were John Knowles, and Edward Knowles.

1789, Sept. 25, James Roberts, glover,
    vice .... the Rev.R.Carter Thelwall, dead.
Same day, John Roberts of Ruthin, *vice* Ellis Roberts, deceased.

It is a curious fact that Ruthin had for a long period a representative (if we may so speak) in the town-council of Denbigh.

Aldermen, Rev. Robert Myddelton, Richard Heaton, Esq.—*Bailiffs*, Hugh Lloyd, William Simon.
1790 *Aldermen*, Richard Heaton, Esq., James Owen.—*Bailiffs*, the same as in 1786.
1791 *Aldermen*, John Roberts of Goppy, Thomas Lloyd.—*Bailiffs*, William Simon, Edward Knowles.

1792, Michaelmas, William Butler, Esq.
    vice .... John Myddelton, Esq., deceased.
Same day, Edward Roberts, Esq. *vice* Thos. Myddelton, Esq., deceased.
Same day,William Hughes, ironmonger,
    vice .... the Rev. Ed. Foulkes, deceased.
Same day, John Williams of Lodge,
    gentlemen, *vice* .... Hugh Lloyd of Coedaccas, dead.

Aldermen, William Simon, James Owen.—*Bailiffs*, John Knowles, James Roberts.
1793 *Aldermen*, William Simon, Thomas Lloyd.—*Bailiffs*, Edward Knowles, James Roberts.

1794 Michaelmas, the Rev. Robert Myddelton,Doctor-of-Divinity *vice* General Taylor, deceased.
Same day, the Rev. Thomas Clough,
    clerk, *vice*.............................. Richard Heaton, Esq., deceased.
Same day, John Wynne Griffith,Esq *vice* late Alderman James Owen,dead.
Same day, Thomas Lovatt of Chirk, Esq.
    vice....................................... John Griffith, Esq. deceased.

Aldermen, William Simon, John Roberts, Goppy.—*Bailiffs*, Those of last year re-elected.
1795 All the chief officers re-elected.
1796 *Aldermen*, Thomas Lloyd, the Rev. Thomas Clough.—*Bailiffs*, John Knowles, John Williams.

Aldebury Place

FORMERLY THE RESIDENCE OF LORD DE BLAQUIERE.

Muck Dinners.—The right of collecting manure from off the main streets, was declared to be vested in the aldermen for the time being, add this invaluable commodity they farmed to scavengers at a *fair* annual rent, which they expended upon corporation feasts, called " muck dinners," at which municipal hospitality was exhibited in the richest viands, and loyalty flowed in streams of generous wine.

1797 *Aldermen*, the Rev. Thomas Clough, James Roberts.—*Bailiffs*, Edward Knowles, William Hughes.

1798 *Aldermen*, The same as in 1794.—*Bailiffs*, Edward Knowles, William Williams.

1798, Sept.   , John Moore, *vice*......... William Butler, Esq. deceased.
Same day, James Owen, *vice* .... Robert Myddelton.
Same day, Robert Jones, *vice*............ Hugh Vaughan, resigned.
Same day, John Price, *vice* .... Peter Vaughan, resigned.

This Peter Vaughan of Bodeiliog, gentleman, resigned the dignity of town-councilman for the office of town-crier, and consented to pay the corporation fifteen pounds per annum for the crier-ship !

1799 *Aldermen*, the Rev. Thomas Clough, Edward Roberts.—*Bailiffs*, John Knowles, John Price.

Inspectors of Raw Hides appointed.—The corporate body congratulate the king upon his deliverance from the late atrocious and treasonable attempt upon his Majesty's life.

1800 *Aldermen*, Dr. Myddelton, James Roberts.—*Bailiffs*, Edward Knowles, John Price.

The corporation claim one-fourteenth of Denbigh Green, now about to be inclosed.

1801 The Hon. Frederick West, *vice*... (omission)

Aldermen, John Roberts, Goppy, the Rev. Thomas Clough.—*Bailiffs*, John Williams, John Moore.

1802, Sept. 15, Robert Myddelton Biddulph, Esq. *vice* .... Rev. Edward Williams, deceased.
1802, Rev. Roger Clough, clerk, *vice* ... Thos. Lovatt, Esq. deceased.
1802, Sept. 29, The Right Hon. Lord Viscount Kirkwall*vice* .... James Owen, deceased.
Same day, Robert Watkin Wynne, Esq. *vice* .... William Williams, deceased.
1802, Nov. 2, John Owen, grocer, *vice* Richard Myddelton Biddulph Esq. deceased.

Aldermen, Edward Roberts, Esq., Robert Myddelton, D.D.—*Bailiffs*, John Price, Robert Jones.

1803, April 14, John Copner Williams, Esq. *vice* .... Richard Kenrick, Esq. deceased.
1803 Richard Henry Kenrick, Esq. *vice* William Simon, gent. deceased.

* Lord Kirkwall married the eldest daughter of Lord de Blaqniere, who resided at the mansion in Vale-street, near the Railway Station, represented in the accompanying engraving—now the property of Dr. E. Pierce, a town-councillor, magistrate, and coroner.

Neither of the borough sheriffs being present, the one unable to attend through illness, the other out of town, the expedient of swearing in special bailiffs was resorted to, but the legality of this proceeding being afterwards questioned, these two gentlemen were re-elected on the 16th of July following.

An address presented to the king on the declaration of the French War. Companies of volunteers raised in the borough and surrounding parishes; " a public subscription for that purpose opened at Mr Roden's." " The freedom of the borough presented to His Royal Highness Prince William Frederick."

1803 *Aldermen*, John Wynne Griffith, Esq., John Copner Williams, Esq.—*Bailiffs*, William Hughes, John Owen.

Common burgesses—*Anwyl of Hendregyda*, the Rev. Robert Anwyl of Hendregyda, Abergele.

1804, Sept. 4, Hugh Lloyd, grocer, *vice* Arthur Bennet Mesham, Esq. dead. *Aldermen*, those of last year re-elected.—*Bailiffs*, William Hughes, Hugh Lloyd.—Lord Viscount Kirkwall had been elected Alderman, but did not appear to take the oaths.

1805 *Aldermen*, Rev. R. Myddelton, D.D., J. Copner Williams, Esq.— *Bailiffs*, these seem to have been Hugh Lloyd and John Williams, Lodge.

1806 Sept. 29, John Wynne, Esq. (son)
    vice .... Robert Watkin Wynne, Esq. (father) deceased.

Same day, John Williams, tanner, *vice* Edward Knowles, gent. deceased. *Aldermen*, John Wynne Griffith, Esq., William Hughes.—*Bailiffs*, Hugh Lloyd, John Williams, Henblas, (*Denbigh Abbey.*)

The corporate body being opposed to the Roman Catholic Emancipation, address His Majesty King George III., and express the gratitude and admiration with which they were " penetrated " by the recent instance of His Majesty's firm adherence to the Protestant interest.

1807.—The council resolve in the first instance, not to divide the rents of the lands allotted to the body corporate, under the *Act for Inclosing Denbigh Green*, but to expend the same upon public improvements; but having taken high legal opinion, they rescind this resolution, and resolve to divide the money annually among the resident burgesses, as compensation for the loss of the ancient right of common pasture in the Forest of Lleweny, giving each of the bailiffs five pounds in lieu of estrays.* Mr Roberts of Ruthin paid one hundred pounds for his professional services in obtaining the consent of certain parties to the Act. Mr Shone paid for his plan of supplying the town with water, a project which has never been carried into effect.

1807 *Aldermen*, The Rev. Thomas Clough, Hugh Lloyd,—*Bailiffs*, John Williams, Lodge, John Owen.

* In 1601, it was agreed that the borough sheriffs should " paye twentie nobles yearlie into thandes of thaldermen, for am'cim^{ts} and p'ffittes of co^{ts} houlden before them."

1808.—At this time the public mind was agitated with the apprehension of a French invasion, and at a council meeting held upon the 6th of May, Lord Kirkwall proposed, and the Rev. Roger Butler Clough supported an address to the King, expressive of a deep sense of the blessings enjoyed under His Majesty's Government, and of the indignation felt at the unprovoked and unwarrantable aggression of those enemies who sought to deprive this country of those blessings, and threatened His Majesty's kingdoms with invasion, and their (the body corporate's) resolution to redouble their efforts in the national defence.

During several years, there was a dispute and certain litigations between the County and Borough, touching the controul of the highways within the Liberties of Denbigh.

1808 Sept. 29, John Heaton, Esq. *vice* John Owen, deceased. Same day, John Parry, glover, *vice*...... James Roberts, deceased. *Aldermen,* John Copner Williams, John Williams, tanner.—*Bailiffs*, John Williams, Lodge, John Parry, glover.

1809, Jan. 7th.—A new survey of the boundaries of the borough ordered; taking Pontfootmor (a bridge over a small rivulet, on the Mold Road, near the Clwyd) as the radius of the circle which was to be drawn, on all sides, from the High Cross (by the Town Hall), as the centre of the borough; with the view of settling disputes as to who were really resident within the Liberties, and entitled to a share of the rents under the Act of Inclosure.

1809 *Aldermen*, Robert Myddelton, D.D., John Copner Williams, Esq.— *Bailiffs*, Hugh Lloyd, John Williams, Henblas.

This year is remarkable for the great Jubilee rejoicings. On the 25th of October,

THE GRAND JUBILEE PROCESSION
moved in the following order from the Town
Hall, to St. Hilary's Chapel or the High Church;
The Royal Denbigh Militia,
in military order,
The Borough Constabulary,
The Leave-Lookers,
· The Town Crier and Bellman,
The Master of the House of Correction,
The Sheriffs,
The Rector, Curates, and other Clergy,
The Recorder,
The Sergeants-at-mace,
The Aldermen and Common Councilmen,
The Free Burgesses,
The Charity and other Schools,
The Inhabitants and general Public.
An address was presented to His Majesty upon this joyous occasion of his attaining the fiftieth year of his reign, and the

corporation gave a grand banquet to all the burgesses, constabulary, and military. The Egyptian tower, standing upon the lofty summit of Moel-Vamma, was erected in commemoration of the same event.

1810, Sep. 29, John Parry of Tynewydd,
      Esq *vice*.............................. Edward Roberts,Esq. deceased.

1810.—At Midsummer, *The Prince of Wales's Own Regiment of Local Militia*, then embodied and quartered at Denbigh, under the command of Lord Viscount Kirkwall, receives the thanks of the corporation.

1810, Sept. 29, *Aldermen*, John Heaton, John Williams, Henblas.—*Bailiffs*, John Price, grocer, John Parry, glover.

1811, Sept. 29, David Lloyd, Esq. *vice* Thomas Lloyd, grocer, deceased. Same day, Thomas Twiston, tanner, *vice* John Knowles, deceased.
Aldermen. Rev. Thomas Clough, John Heaton, Esq.—*Bailiffs*, Hugh Lloyd, John Parry, Tynewydd.

1812, May 12.—The corporate body address the Prince of Wales upon the assassination of the Hon. Spencer Percival, First Lord of the Treasury. A batch of fifty new burgesses made, at the expense of the corporation, before the general election, in order to secure, as was thought, the seat of Mr Biddulph; the result, however, was the return of Lord Kirkwall by a small majority.

Aldermen, Rev. T. Clough, Hugh Lloyd.—*Bailiffs*, John Williams, Henblas, John Parry, Tynewydd.

1813, Sept. 29, John Hughes, the elder,
      attorney-at-law, *vice* .... John Roberts, Goppy, deceased.
Aldermen, John Copner Williams, John Parry, Tynewydd.—*Bailiffs*, John Williams, John Parry, glover.

1814, Sept. 29, George Cumming, Doctor-
      of-medicine *vice* .... Robt. Myddelton Biddulph, Esq.
                                    M.P. deceased.
Same day, Thomas Hughes, draper, *vice* Rev. Thomas Clough, deceased.
Aldermen, David Lloyd, John Hughes.—*Bailiffs*, Hugh Lloyd, Thomas Hughes, draper.
1815 *Aldermen*, John Hughes, George Cumming, M.D.—*Bailiffs*, The same as in 1809.

1815, Dec. 9, Robert Myddelton of
      Gwaenynog, Esq. *vice*.............. Dr. Myddelton (father) deceased.

During the winter, the water-course from Lenten Pool, to the bridge at the entrance into Henllan-street, was covered in, so that fairs and markets for horses and swine might be held there. Stallions forbidden to be exhibited in the public streets. At this time the town was lighted (with oil) by " *the Lamp Society*," the corporation granting the society a small sum annually towards furnishing and repairing and lighting the lamps. Members of the council to wear gowns of the same colour and quality as those worn by the corporation functionaries of the City of Chester.

1816, Sept. 28, Samuel Edwardes, Esq.
  attorney-at-law, & town-clerk, *vice* John Price, deceased.
Aldermen, Those of last year re-elected.—*Bailiffs*, John Parry, Denbigh town, John Parry, Tynewydd.

An address presented to His Royal Highness the Prince of Wales, then Regent, assuring him that they had heard with indignation and regret of the outrageous attack which had been made upon His Royal Highness' person, &c., and their hopes that " the perpetrators of this daring assault " might speedily receive the punishment " due to so heinous a transgression." This memorial is only valuable in point of history, so far as the memorialists further assure His Royal Highness that although the lower classes of the people in this district were labouring under distress in consequence of the late and defective harvest, the great difficulty in procuring employment, through the unexampled depreciation in the price of all kinds of farming stock, and the total stagnation in the sale of all kinds of agricultural produce, yet they were universally loyal and steady in their allegiance, &c.

1817, Feb. 12, Robert Parry, glover, *vice* John Parry, glover, deceased.
1817, Feb. 17, Rev. Robert Chambres
    Chambres of Llysmeirchion, *vice* Rev. Edward Chambres Chambres, deceased.
1817, March 17, David Hughes, surgeon,
    vice .... William Hughes, gent. deceased.
Aldermen, Hugh Lloyd, Robert Myddelton, Esqrs.—*Bailiffs*, John Williams, Henblas, John Parry.

Feb. 17th, 1817.—The court order an application to be made for some ancient charters of the corporation said to have been discovered by Mr Robt. Humphreys Jones of Ruthin.
Nov. 22nd.—An address of condolence presented to the Prince Regent, on the lamented death of the Princess Charlotte of Wales.

1818 *Aldermen*, Samuel Edwardes, Esq. Hugh Lloyd.—*Bailiffs*, David Hughes, Robert Parry.

Dec. 28th, 1818.—An address of condolence presented to the Prince Regent on the demise of his illustrious mother, Queen Charlotte.

1819 *Aldermen*, John Wynne Griffith, Esq. M.P., John Copner Williams, Esq.—*Bailiffs*, John Williams, Henblas, John Parry, Tynewydd.
1820 April 15, Howell Powell Clough,
    of Brookhouse, Esq. *vice* .... John Moore, deceased.
1820 John Price, Esq. *vice* .... Lord Viscount Kirkwall, dead.

Here, commencing Corporation Book III., we have the usual—

Proclamation on the Election of Capital Burgesses.

Oyez! Oyez! Oyez! All manner of persons are required to keep silence while the capital and other burgesses of this Borough of

Denbigh are proceeding to elect two capital burgesses of the said Borough, in the room and stead of the late John Moore of Denbigh, surgeon, deceased; and the late Honourable John Hamilton Fitzmaurice, commonly called Lord Viscount Kirkwall, who were capital burgesses of this Borough.

Oyez! Oyez! Oyez! I give this public Notice, that the capital and other burgesses of the borough of Denbigh, are now proceeding in the Town Hall to elect two capital burgesses of the same borough, in the room and stead of the late John Moore, surgeon, deceased; and of the late Honourable John Hamilton Fitzmaurice, commonly called Lord Viscount Kirkwall, deceased, who were capital burgesses of this borough; And that all persons having a right to be present at such election may attend the same, if they think proper.

Oyez! Oyez! Oyez! Howell Powell Clough, of Brookhouse, gentleman, having been proposed to be elected a capital burgess of this Borough, instead of the late John Moore of Denbigh, surgeon, deceased, late a capital burgess of the same Borough, I give this public Notice that any burgess demanding a poll may come forward and do so and he shall be heard.

Does any one demand a Poll ?

Does any one demand a Poll ?

Does any one demand a Poll ?

Oyez! Oyez! Oyez! John Price, Esq. of Denbigh, having been proposed to be elected a capital burgess of this Borough, instead of the late Honourable John Hamilton Fitzmaurice, commonly called Lord Viscount Kirkwall, deceased, late a capital burgess of the same Borough, I give this public Notice that any burgess demanding a poll, may come forward and do so, and he shall be heard at the Town Hall where the election is proceeding.

But Mr Councillor Price did not take the oaths until September 13th, 1821.

1820 *Aldermen,* John Heaton, David Lloyd.—*Bailiffs,* Howell Powell Clough, Thomas Hughes.

The author often takes the returns from the signatures of the parties themselves, in which case " esquire," " gent." or " gentleman," is by etiquette dropped. And frequently the simple name and surname are given in the case of all chief corporate officers, not being knights or baronets, save when there are two or more individuals of the *same* name " capital men."

Dec. 9th, an address presented to King George IV. on his accession to the throne.

1821 Sept. 13, Richard Lloyd Williams,
　　　　doctor-of-medicine, *vice* .... Robert Jones, deceased.

" Dr. Robert Jones" was a gentleman of considerable reputation in the medical profession, and a capital burgess about twenty-three years.

This year there was a grand municipal procession in celebration of the coronation of George IV. on the 19th of July.

1821 *Aldermen,* (at Michaelmas) John Hughes, Esq. George Cumming, M.D.—*Bailiffs,* John Williams, Henblas, John Price.

1822 *Aldermen,* John Williams, Henblas, John Hughes.—*Bailiffs,* David Hughes, John Price.

1823 *Aldermen,* John Copner Williams, Howell Powell Clough.—*Bailiffs,* Robert Parry, John Price.

In 1824, according to the *Blue Books,* a capital burgess, who was acting as deputy for one of the aldermen, committed one Eliza Jones to gaol for petty larceny. She brought an action against him for false imprisonment, and on a second trial obtained a verdict, at Shrewsbury, which cost the corporation about five hundred pounds. Considerable sums were likewise spent in litigations, in defending the order of the Court of Borough Sessions, in the case of Rice and others.

1824 *Aldermen,* John Williams, John Parry.—*Bailiffs,* Robert Parry, Richard Lloyd Williams.

1825, March 1, Thomas Evans, attorney-
at-law, *vice* .... John Price, Esq. deceased.
Same day, William Chambres Chambres,
Esq. *vice* .... Richard Henry Kenrick, Esq.
deceased.

Aldermen, Richard Lloyd Williams, Thomas Evans —*Bailiffs,* John Williams, William Chambres Chambres.

Sept, 15th, *William Chambres Chambres, Esq.* of Plas Chambres, was elected *alderman,* in place of John Williams, Esq., who refused to act as alderman and borough justice, under a new Beer Act, which inflicted a penalty of one hundred pounds on any justice-of-the-peace, being a maltster, who should sit at a meeting for granting licenses to ale-house keepers. It is almost needless to add that the gentleman thus displaced was engaged in the malting trade.

1826 *Aldermen,* John Hughes, Samuel Edwardes.—*Bailiffs,* Thomas Hughes, David Hughes.

July 15th, 1826, *John Hughes, Esq*, elected *alderman,* in place of Richard Lloyd Williams, Esq., incapacitated by absence.

1827 *Aldermen,* John Hughes, John Parry.—*Bailiffs,* Those of last year re-elected.

1827.—August 13, William Ody finds on the burgess-roll the names of one hundred and fifty-three freemen, whose admissions were not filed upon proper stamps, and the council votes four hundred and fifty-one pounds for stamps, to serve a political and party purpose.—See *Parliamentary Commissioners' Report on Municipal Corporations.* Sept. 29th, the leave-lookers ordered to inspect all slaughter-houses, which were to be used for that purpose alone, carefully cleaned, washed, and properly ventilated; and that no

Y

animal or beast should be housed therein. Hamilton Maxwell, Esq., a common burgess, restores, at his own expense, the Town Hall clock, puts up a fresh bell, and presents the corporation with new maps of the Borough and Liberties; in consideration of which he receives the thanks of the council and a handsome testimonial of plate and money. The sum of sixty pounds a year voted to the aldermen and bailiffs for ordinary corporation dinners. Indeed, as early as the time of Queen Elizabeth we read of their allowances of wine and sugar, for their own refreshment and entertainment of guests. The council refuse paying the clergy the Oatmeal Toll, because Dr. Howard had discontinued the catechetical lectures at St. Hilary's.

1828 *Aldermen*, Thomas Hughes, Thomas Evans,—*Bailiffs*, Hugh Lloyd, Robert Parry.

1828, Nov. 3, James Vaughan Horne,
    attorney-at-law, *vice*.................. David Lloyd, Esq. deceased.

Wednesday, Sept. 9.—The aldermen, recorder, bailiffs, and common-council, preceded by the serjeants-at-mace, meet His Royal Highness Augustus Frederic Duke of Sussex, at a place called the Shearer's Well, on the northern confines of the Borough, where the recorder reads the following address ;—

" SIR—We, the aldermen, bailiffs, and capital burgesses of the borough of Denbigh, assembled by special convocation, beg leave to congratulate your Royal Highness upon your arrival in the Principality. Anxious upon all occasions to testify our loyalty and attachment to the House of Brunswick, under whose mild and constitutional sway, we have enjoyed so many blessings, we eagerly embrace the opportunity which your Royal Highness' visit to us has fortunately afforded to present to your Royal Highness, in the most respectful terms, the freedom of our ancient Corporation, as the most appropriate token of personal regard for so distinguished a member of the Royal Family, we have it in our power to confer. It would have been particularly gratifying to us upon any occasion to have marked your Royal Highness' visit to our ancient borough with every possible respect, but under the peculiar circumstances which now occur, we feel ourselves imperatively bound to acquit ourselves of that obligation, by an ardent feeling of gratitude for the truly courteous and liberal spirit in which your Royal Highness has condescended to honour our national Festival of Eisteddfod with your presence, and by that means so powerfully contributed to increase in splendour and effect those popular attractions which must ensure its eventual success ; and thus promote the combined objects for which this and other meetings of a similar kind have been recently revived. Signed and passed under the seal of the corporation of and in the said Borough, the tenth day of September, 1828."

On the 29th of September, William Lewis Hughes, Esq., (afterwards Lord Dinorben,) John Madocks of Glanywern, Esq., and Sir Edward Mostyn of Talacre, Bart., were sworn common burgesses,

Sir Edward was president of the Royal Eisteddvod at Denbigh, as above, and it is observable that he was a Roman Catholic.

1829, Sept. 29, John Williams, Doctor-
    of-Medicine, *vice* .... John Roberts (of Ruthin) dead.
Aldermen, Hugh Lloyd, James V. Horne.—*Bailiffs*, Thomas Hughes, Robert Parry.

Five guineas voted annually to the organist and choir of St. Hilary's Chapel.

1830, July 17, Thomas Hughes, attor-
    ney-at-law, *vice* .... John Hughes, Esq. deceased.
Same day, Charles Sankey, banker, *vice* John Parry, Esq. deceased.

It is observable that Mr Sankey was the only Roman Catholic that has sat in the council since the Reformation.

Sept. 21.—The council decides to give a Grand Coronation Banquet (on the accession of William IV.) to all the resident burgesses, officials, &c.

1830 *Aldermen*, Samuel Edwardes, John Williams, M.D.—*Bailiffs*, Thomas Hughes, Charles Sankey.
1831 *Aldermen*, Samuel Edwardes, Charles Sankey,—*Bailiffs*, Dr. Williams, Thomas Evans.

In the same volume we have the names of the recorders, treasurers, coroners, leave-lookers, constables, town-criers, serjeants-at-mace, &c., during the foregoing period of 334 years.

CONCLUDING REMARKS.

These remarks are confined to omissions in, or criticisms upon, the former work.

Family of Peake.—This correction of Chapter xxiii. (*Ancient and Modern Denbigh,*) has been forwarded to us by Richard Peake, Esq., Wirewoods Green, Chepstow.

" The burgages (or the lands whereon built) granted by Henry de Lacy in his charter (c. 1284,) were probably in possession of the family until 1818, when some cottages in Peake Lane, and a chief rent of eight shillings on an adjoining burgage, granted away in 1569, by Hugh Peake, were sold.

There can be but little doubt that the Peakes and other ' hereditary ' tenants of 1334, inherited from private grants of Lacy, lands not alluded to in his charter.*

According to *Williams' Aberconwy*, Hugh, sheriff for Carnarvonshire in 1546 and 1552, and Richard, sheriff in 1576, were the last Peakes of that place. There appears to be no recorded pedigree of this (no doubt) branch. There is no trace of any Peakes in Lan-

---

* There is, however, no proof of this.—*The Author.*

cashire, though there can be but little doubt that they came thence. Their earliest recorded alliance is with Hulton, deriving thence, from Pontefract and Brierley, individuals of these three names, and of nine others, derived from Lancashire or Yorkshire places, had similar grants by the same charter, and the English families about Denbigh generally, had names of the same origin, as, Heaton, Rosindale, and Salebury. There is Peck mill-house, and several Pykes in Lancashire; there was the chace of Peek, and there is the Peak headland, in Yorkshire; and the continuation of the Derby Peak borders Lancashire, Yorkshire, and Staffordshire. The surname was early in Yorkshire, but not with the Denbigh arms.

Peke, Peek, Peck, Peake, simply implies derivation from a place so named by the Saxons. The Derby district Pech became *ke*, about the time such local surnames became hereditary (c. 1200), but there is no proof of any family of Pech, Pic, (surnames existing in 1066–1121) having become *ke*. Peche of Kent became Peché, there rebus a Peach with *e* on it. Ric. de Pek, custos Bolsover, 1190-5, (Leland) was probably Pec. Peche.

1183 is the earliest date of the surname Peke (county Durham) and the arms borne in the counties of York, Derby, Norfolk, Lincoln, Hereford and Kent, &c., allude more or less to each other, but *not* to the Denbigh Arms.

The name was in Staffordshire in 1343, has continued, and is now common there,—the arms 'quarterly or a gu, a griffin's head counter-changed,' were possibly there borne, and perhaps allude to Denbigh, as does " checky arg. and sab. a saltire ermine," quartered by Patten, for Peake of Bowden, Cheshire. The Denbigh arms " varied" are assigned in a seventeenth century MS. to Devon and Bedfordshire, (Edward Peake endowed a school at Biggleswade in 1557) also to Pecke, of Berkshire, with the Denbigh crest. The crest of the Eastern Counties family was " a Lion's head erased, pierced with an arrow," the Navy family's crest is " a Lion's head erased, with a cross on the neck." " A Lion's head erased," with arms " argt. a saltire gules," is to Peak in dictionaries, all more or less alluding to Denbigh.

The Denbigh crest, called " a leopard's face," is on 1600 glass, clearly a lion's, and is thence copied in the Henllan window. *Leopart* in old French means 'a lion passant.' The head is, therefore in fact, a lion's front face, as is the mark on plate, ante 1823. (on plate marks Arch: Journal 1852, by Mr. Octavius Morgan.)

For the marriage of Peake and Hulton, p. 194: *See pedigrees College of Arms, &c. Baines' Lancashire* of Hulton of Hulton. Baines (in error) makes Pontefract, the Baron Lacy himself; but it is curious that the arms quartered with Peake in Elizabeth's time for Pontefract are the original " Lacy," without the label, but with a bordure. The arms of Rosindale (traced to 1441,) " quarterly," of Heaton, " bend sable," and Peake " saltire, or one bend crossing another, with more or less sable, (in each Elizabethan variety) all point to the same origin, though Henry de Lacy, clearly bore the lion rampant purpure. *See the beautiful seal, and Charter, in this work.* Perthewig (as suggested by me.—*Archæologia Cambrensis,* 1849, p. 66.) was probably derived, like most other places, from the nature of its situation, " bush wood," * 'the doe a rebus,' and the tradition from seeing the doe. The nearest tenement is "Berth-bach," and the ground between described by the 1691 deponents, as full of thorns, gorse, &c. Coedwig is four miles west.

The deponent, p. 196, was aged 80; it should read " father and mother of H.P. the complainant's grandfather, also to his said grandfather, and after his decease, to H.P., complainant's father, at the time and after complainant was born."

The J.C.W. p. 197 calls his grandmother, sister to Mrs. Peake.

The Wynnes of Coed Coch, descend from this Throgmorton alliance. *See also Anwyl. p.* 197 *&* 198.

Page 198. This tablet replaced in 1844, by the writer. This Elizabeth Heaton's daughter was a Garnett, wife of Hugh Peake, the father of the Elizabeth Peake.

The last regular resident at Perthewig was Hugh P. who died there S. P. 1697.†—His brother John was in the army at the siege of Tangiers. The three next generations, Hugh, Thomas, and Thomas, where in the profession of the law, the last being the late Mr. Serjeant Peake, the latter's children and grandchildren are the only known descendants of the Lleweny, or Perthewig family.

Their early alliances are explained in the Henllan window. and for those further interested in genealogy, a pedigree will be found in *Burke's Landed Gentry,* 1844 & 1857, and at the *College of Arms.*

The quarterings in Henllan window,‡ are Hulton (from the 1441 authority,) Pontefract, Newport, Brierley, Clare, or Clarke, Elizabethan authority.—'Garnett,' modern alliance, 'Budgen' (on an escutcheon of pretence.) The arms of Peake (though only traced to about 1570,) are of the oldest and simplest kind; arms then granted became more complicated.

Peake does not come within the fifty most common names, which list (Registrar's return,) ends with Shaw, and has in it 16th, 19th and 25th, Wood, Green, and Hill, four similar local surnames.

Tracings from the signature of every generation, from Hugh Peake, in 1569, shew in favor of Henry of Mayneva, and his brother William, in 1631, until 1740. •

* I cannot see why *Perthewig,* may not be simply derived from *Perth,* a bush, shady bush, (for we speak of " oysgod perth, &c) and, *ewig* a doe; that is, in strict accordance with the (Welsh) *law* for the formation of compound words, the doe's bush or doebush, not " bush-doe." But qy. if Perthewig be perth-y-wig, the forest bush, or brake, as Bachegraig is Bach-y-graig ? The article *y* anciently was written *e.—The Author.*

† Tablet at Henllan; part of this inscription is now worne off; it was " leaving no issue, to continue the name of his ancestors, who has lived there in credit for many generations."

‡ From Ward and Nixon, designed by Charles Winston, Esq.

This plate illustrates the possible origin of the arms of Peake ;
the arms of other English families, in Lleweny, having apparently
the same origin. The first shield represents the original arms of
Henry de Lacy ; (his grandfather John the first Earl of Lincoln, who
died 1240, having had a *baton* instead of a *bend.*) ' Henry certainly
used the "Lion rampant purpure" to Denbigh Charter (1284 ?), and
at Carlaverock 1300 ; and it would appear that John had used it;
see *Ormerod's Cheshire*, 1,¶514, and *Heylin's Help*.

The second shield is found quartered with Peake (time of Elizabeth) for *John de Pontefract* (1284–1300 c.), which John, in *Baines'*
Lancashire, the pedigree of Hulton, appears (in error, no doubt) as
the Baron *John de Lacy*, grandfather of the first Earl, above; but
Pontefract was the Lacies' property, and these arms are *clearly*
allusive. The fourth shield exists on glass, and stone, Henllan,
Whitchurch, and in MSS., (all time of Elizabeth) as then used by the
family. The sixth was " seen in some " by Holmes in 1625. The
seventh exists in glass and MSS., (time Elizabeth) as then used by
the family, and since that time has been and is now used *or*
gules. The ninth was borne by a Peake ; probably of Staffordshire,
and points to the same origin.

The arms of Rosindale and Heaton confirm my suggestion, viz.,
quarterly or and *azure*, four roebucks trippant, counterchanged,
Whitchurch, and MSS. (time of Elizabeth), and argent on *a bend*
Sable, three bull's heads, sometimes three deer's heads.

Hulton and Salusbury's Lion, may or may not allude to Lacys.

All the above appear old : are in Elizabethan pedigrees as then
inherited; the seals alluded to in Lacy's charter possibly had arms
on. I trace representations of Hulton's and Rosindale's to 1441.
with the inscription given, p. 145, (*Harl. MSS.* 2129.)—*A. & M.*
Denbigh.

The Chambre Family.—A very old Latin pedigree of the family,
which is now in the possession of Robert Chambre Vaughan, Esq.,
of Burlton Hall, Salop, and traces the descent of the Salopian
branch up through nineteen generations.

    " *Ex Chartâ Arthuri de Petton in Com. Salop, Arm.*
        29 *Septembris, Anno* 1623."

Henricus de Lacy, Comes Lincoln. Constabularius Cestriæ, Dno.
de Roos & Rewiniock, concessit Johanni Chambre, camerario, pro
homagia & servitio suo. duas Carucatas terræ cum pertinertiis in
Lleweny. This Lacy died 1310.

" Johannes de Chambre," says our informant, " the first name in
the annexed pedigree, is stated in a very old, but exceedingly mu-
tilated account of the family of Chambre, to have been descended
from ' John de la Chambre, a nobelle Normane, whoe ent'red
Englaunde in yᵉ traine of Kinge Williame yᵉ Conqueroure, had two
Sonnes, Step * * * * and a da * * * * Mau * * * *' Much
that follows is quite ellegible." Of the first John de Chambre of

Salisbury Place.

FORMERLY THE RESIDENCE OF LORD DE BLAQUIERE.

Denbigh, we read that he came here with De Lacy, and had two allotments of Land in Lleweny, for his homage and service.

JOHANNES DE CHAMBRE,

Who was married to " *Ellena* dau. of Lodwick de la More."

Henricus Chambre,═Jana filia Blethine Vychan.

In the same generation we have Walter Chambre of the county of York.

Joshua Chambre,═Katharina filia Edmundi Churlton de Powis.

His brothers were Miles Chambre, alias Miles the Steward of Scotland, and Ludovicus Chambre of Ellesmere. in Com. Salop.

Morgan Chambre,═Anne daughter of Hen: Ferrers.

He had four brothers, Henry, Francis, Gawen, and Egidius Chambre, married to a daughter of Powell de Whittington. And a sister, Cecilia, wife of Madoc-ap-Evan.

Samuel Chambre,═* * * daughter Tho. Newport Miles.

In the same generation we have Stephen, Andrew, Catherine and Dorothy Chambre.

Anthony Chambre═Anne dau. to Peter de Cûw (?)

Hugh Chambre,═ * * * dau. of George Ravenscroft of Denbigh.

He had a brother William Chambre.

William Chambre,═Katherine dau. and heir to Jenkin Pigott.

He had two brothers; John Chambre, D.D., Dean of St. Stephen's, Westminster, who died in 1549: and Hugh Chambres Miles, who espoused * * * dau. and heir to Griffith Vaughan of Powis.

Henry Chambers, son and heir═ * * * dau. of William Dutton, of the Co. of Chester.

He had two brothers; Robert Chambre, who married Elizabeth Hookes; and Jenkin Chambre, of Burlton, in the Co. of Salop, father of Richard Chambre of Petton, in the same county, whose descendant afterwards sold Petton estate; and a sister Margaret, wife of Thomas Conway.

Robert Chambres, son and heir═Agneta dau. and heir to Hugh Duckworth.

Robert Chambres,═Margarita, dau. to Foulk Salusbury, second son of Thomas Salusbury, knt.

John Chambres,═Dorothy, dau. to Edward Goodman, of Ruthin.

Henry Chambres,═Agneta, dau. to Foulk-ap-Tho-
mas-ap-Grono.

John Chambres of Plas Chambres═Anne, dau. to Charles Myddelton of Denbigh.

Charles Chambres,═Ellen, dau. to Edward Griffith
of Henllan.

The Chambres of Salop, are descended from—
Jenkin Chambre of Burlton, third son.

Richard Chambre of Petton═Maria, dau. to John Hill of Hill
Court, Salop, father to Michael
Chambre, bailiff of Shrewsbury,
in 1583, and 1593.

The elder branch became allied to many " families of worship,"
especially to the Grosvenors, ancestors of the present Marquis of
Westminster.

John Chambre, son of Jenkin Chambre, above named, purchased
lands in the Lordships of Lappington, Wem, &c. He lived in 24
Henry VIII. The male line became extinct in the fifth generation,
but the heiress married Philip Vaughan of Burlton, Esq., grandfather
of Thomas Vaughan of Burlton and Plas Thomas, Esq., who married
Lowry Nanney, daughter of William Wynne, (Nanney,) Esq., of
Maes-y-Neuadd, Co. of Merioneth, by whom he had issue Robert
Chambre Vaughan, Esq., the living inheritor of the estates of
Burlton and Woodyate, married to Anna, daughter of the Hon.
Edw. Massy :—issue, John Nanney Chambre Vaughan, eldest son
and heir apparent.

─────

The Dryhurst Family.—There is an emblazoned pedigree of the
Dryhursts, drawn up about the year 1629, by some person who
evidently understood heraldry. This interesting relic is now in the
possession of J. Jones, Esq., of Groes, and is still almost entire. It
traces the family up through thirteen generations; and in order to
avoid typographical difficulties and " spare our space," we give a
part of it in that order.

1st generation.—* * * ert * * * rst of * * * gh lived * * * Ed.
III., 1354. The stars denote the portion torn away. When entire, it must, we presume, have been " Robert Drihurst of Denbigh,
lived 27 Edward III."

2nd generation.—Henry Drihurste of Denbigh, lived 5 R. 2
(Richard II) anno 1382.

3rd generation.—John Drihurst of Denbigh, lived 9 H. V. A° 1421.

4th generation.—Rawling Drihurst of Denbigh, lived 24 H. VI., A° 1446. He married Emma, daughter of Robt. fflecher of Denbigh.

5th generation.—Raphe or Raffe Drihurst of Denbigh, lived 23 E. IV. A° 1483. He married Jonnett, daughter and heire to Henry Huntington of Huntington Wood, neere Chester. She was paternally descended from John Wall alias Walley of " Wyrall," in Cheshire; and maternally from John Warwick, Lord of Upton, in the same county.

6th generation.—Thomas Drihurst of Denbighe, 24 H. VII. 1509. He married Cicely, daughter and heire to Thomas de Cottingham. She had no land by reason of a gift and composition of her father for being married out of Chester.

7th generation.—Hugh Drihurst of Denbigh, married and had nineteen children by Lucy, daughter and sole heire to Robt. Grimsdiche of Ruthland, by Agnes, daughter to Hugh Dutton of Denbigh.

8th generation.—1, *Robert Drihurst* of Chester, second sonne, who married Margaret, da. and heire of Robt. * estwick, alderman of Chester, by whom he had one daughter, who had two husbands; John (Robt. *Holme*) Wright of Chester, draper; Robt. Jonnes of Chester, glover. The issue of her first marriage was Robt. Wright of Chester; and of the second marriage John Jonnes, and Alexander Jonnes. 2, *Piers Drihurst*, fourth sonne, married Sina, daughter of John-ap-Thomas-ap-Richard of Denbigh, (of Oswestry *Holme,*)but died without issue. 3, *Richard Drihurst* of Denbigh, fifth sonne, (father of Richard Drihurst of Chester,) married Janne, daughter and heire of John Bridlington of Denbigh. 4, *Grace Drihurst*, who married Henry Conway of Rithland. 5, *Janne Drihurst*, who married Richard Myddelton of Denbigh, by whom she had Alderman Sir Hugh Myddelton, Sir Thomas Myddelton, knt., &c. Lord Mayor of London, and several other children; see monumental brass at Whitchurch. 6, *Thomas Drihurst* of Denbigh, (eldest sonne, *Holme,*) married Janne, da. to John Salisbury, Chamberlayne of Northwales, whose descent is given thus :—Salisb * * Leweney (Lleweni) gave th * * in Denb * * Abbey * * * 1304 * * 1389.—Henry Salusbury of Lleweney, s'named the Blacke, who married Nest. da. and heire to Kenwrick Sais-ap-Ithel Vychan of Northop. William Salisbury of Lleweney, who married Margaret da. and heire to dd. ap Kenrick-ap-Phillipe ffichdan. Raphe Salisbury of Lleweney, married Margaret, da. and heire to Jevan ap Cadowgan ap Llowarch Vychan. Henry Salisbury of Lleweney, Esq. married Agnes, da. and heire to John Curties, sonne of Sir Arthur Curties, knight. Ould Thomas Salusbury of Lleweney, Esq., married Elizabeth, daughter to Sr John Don' of Vtkington, knight. Sr Thomas Salisbury, knighted at Blackfeild, 4

Z

E. IV. married Jannett da. to William Vaughan of Pentryn, Esq., Chamberlayne of Northwales.   John Salisbury, Chamberlayne of Northwales, father of Janne S. who married Thomas Drihurst. 7, *Elizabeth Drihurst*, who married Robt. (Richard, *Holme*) Ashton of Denbigh, father to William Ashton.

9th generation.—John Drihurst of Denbigh, who married Janne, daughter to John Lathom of Denbigh.   Lucey Drihurst married John Stanney (Stearmer, *Holme*) of Oswestry.

10th generation.—1, *Hugh Drihurst*, of Denbigh, A° 1629, who married Janne, daughter to Thomas ap John Conway of Potrevan, Esq.   2, *Thomas Drihurst* of Denbigh, second sonne married Grace dau. to Henry Knowsley of Brynwyllan, * *   3, *Robert Drihurst*. 4, *John Drihurst*.   5, *William Drihurst*.   6, *Richard Drihurst*. They had also several daughters, viz :—1, *Janne Drihurst*, married Roger Conway * * (sonne and heire) to John ayr (?) Conway.   2, *Lucy Drihurst*, married Richard Lloid, alias Rossendale of Denbigh.   3, *Cicely Drihurst*, married to Richard * * * Esq., by whom she had issue * * * m. Barbara, yᵉ dau. of Joⁿ Thelwal of Bathavorne, Esq.   *John*, m. yᵉ dau. of Simon Ashpoole, and died in Holland.   *Rich.* Bachelor of Divinitie.   *Roger* * * * *   *Gaynor* m. Joⁿ Edds of Keuen-y-wern.   *Katherine*, m. Thomas Knowsley. * * * * m. Rich. Blodwel of Oswestrie.   *Jane*, m. Joⁿ Lloyd of Bomgay, in Montgomeryshire.   *Dorithie*, m. Eubule Evans, and * * * died younge.   *Mary Drihurst* married Rich. Clough of Lleweney Green, and had issue, Rich. Cloughe of Lleweney Green, who married Jane, daughter to Mr John Lloyd of Moylvrey, by whom he had *Richard*, who m. Luce, da. to Thomas Humphreys, Esq., and *John* m. dau. of Joⁿ Vaughan, Esq. (of Groes).   Richard Clough, sen. had likewise by this Mary Drihurst, Humfrey, William, John, and Hugh Clough ; Annie, Emme, Mary, Jane, and Grace Clough.   *Ellen Drihurst* married George Langford.   *Luce Drihurst* first married Mr John Lloyd of (Fox) Hall ; and after to Capt. Piers Salusbury, Esq.; and had issue Jane and Lowry. Jane first married Henry Roberts, by whom she had issue Jane and Elizabeth ; and afterwards to William Doulben, Esq., by whom she had issue Richard, (?) John, Mary, David, Barbara, William, (?) Richard, (?) Lumley, William, (?) and Emey.

11th generation.—Thomas Drihurst had issue, Thomas, Richard, John, Grace, and Jane, who married Henry Lathom.   Hugh Drihurst, also son of John, had issue, John Drihurst, sonne and heire, 1629, Hugh and Petter Drihurst, and Mary, Lucey, and Anne.

Thomas Drihurst, brother to Hugh, was father to Thomas Drihurst, (of Denbigh,) and Richard Drihurst of Denbigh, dyer, who married Anne, daughter to Ffoulke Salusbury.

The only lineal male descendant of this family now remaining at Denbigh (1859), is Hugh Drihurst, mason, who is upwards of eighty

years of age, who is a son of Robert Drihurst, son of Edward Drihurst, but can trace no higher traditionally.

The Clough Family.—In the author's former work, many interesting facts respecting the Cloughs were omitted. The following is
an abridged pedigree of this patrician family—patrician so far, at
least, as concerns the history of this very old municipality.

Richard Clough, *(Rissiart Clŵch Hên.)* of Denbigh, who lived
in the reigns of Henry VII. and Henry VIII., and whose second
wife was a daughter of Humphrey Holland. See notice of the
Hollands of Hendrefawr, Abergele, Vaerdre, Kinmel, Terdain, Denbigh, &c. *(A. & M. Denbigh, p. 200.)*

Sir Richard Clough, Knight of the Sepulchre.

He travelled much abroad and was Knighted at Jerusalem, afterwards became a partner of Sir Thomas Gresham, *(Lord Mayor of
London,)* and factor to Queen Elizabeth. He built Bachegraig
Hall, and Plas Clough, Denbigh, and died at Antwerp, whence his
heart was brought in a silver urn to Denbigh. He married the
celebrated Catherine (Tudor) of Berain, in the Lordship of Denbigh, a nearer relative of Queen Elizabeth, who was her guardian.

Roger Salusbury,=Ann, born in 1568,	Mary, to whom Sir Richard gave May-
son of Sir John y to whom Sir R. gave	nan Abbey, now possessed by her de-
Bodiau, by Jane Bachegraig, posses-	scendant, Spencer Wynne, third Baron
Myddelton. sed by her celebrated	Newborough.
descendant, Hester	
Lynch Piozzi.	

Richard Clough,
Born at Antwerp, Sheriff of the Borough of Denbigh in
1596, to whom Sir Richard gave Plas Clough, possessed
by the representative of the family in 1856. He was
educated at Hart Hall, Oxford, and married Mary, daughter of Alderman John Drihurst of Denbigh, by Jane
Lathom, dau. of John Lathom of Denbigh.

William Clough, Borough Sheriff in 1618, and alderman
1620, who married Mary, dau. of John Vaughan of Groes.

John Clough, Alderman of Denbigh 1667, who married
Susanna, dau. and heir of Owen Smith, Esq. Co. Carnarvon.

Hugh Clough of Plas Clough, who married Anne, eldest,
dau. of Thomas Williams, Esq., of Halkin Hall.

Hugh Clough, educated at Brazenose College, Oxford,
1726, married Catherine dau. and heir of Henry Powell,

Esq., of Glanywern, by whom he had thirteen children, three of whom were—

Richard, born in 1753, B.A. of Oriel.Coll. High Sheriff of Denbigh in 1782, married Patty, dau. of James Butler, of Warminghurst, Esq.

Richard Butler Clough, born in 1781, Plas Clough sold Glanywern.—Minydon, died in 1844. He was married to Catherine, daughter of the Rev. Roger Clough.

Roger, born in 1759, Canon of St. Asaph, Rector of Llansannan, Vicar of Corwen, who married Jemima, dau. and coheir of James Butler, Esq., of Warminghurst Park, Sussex, by Martha Dolben, descended from the Dolbens of Segrwyd.

The last-named · Canon Clough had ten children: The Rev. Roger Butler Clough, Vicar of Corwen, born in 1762; James B. Clough of Liverpool, merchant; Charles Butler Clough, late Dean of St. Asaph, who was married to Sydney, dau. of Edward Jones, Esq. of Wepre Hall, Flint; Frederic B. Clough, Recorder of Ruthin; Alfred Butler Clough, B.D., F.A.S. Rector of Buranston (1860), born 1796, married Sarah, dau. of R. H. Lamb, Esq., of Bragborough Hall, Northampton, having numerous issue.

Thomas, born in 1756, Canon of St Asaph, Rector of Denbigh, Vicar of Nantglyn, who got Halkin Hall, died 1823. He was married to Dorothea, dau. of Hedd Lloyd, Esq. of Havodunos.

Thomas Hugh Clough, of Havodunos, married to Caroline, dau. of R. Price, Esq. of Rhiwlas.

Among the MSS. in Christ Church Library, Oxford, are some fine poems, by that eminent bard, William Kynwal, in his own handwriting; as, " *Kowyd. marwnad am y Mastr Rhisiart Klŵch, marchog o Ved. Krist,*" an Elegiac Ode for Master Richard Clough, knight of Christ's Sepulchre; another entitled, " *Kowyd. i yrru y 'long i nol Mr Ric. Klŵch a Meistres Katrin adref o Denmark,*" an Ode to send the ship to fetch Mr Richard Clough and Mistress Katherine home from Denmark; and a third, called, " *Kowyd' i groessawu meistres Katrin adref pan fu tu hwnt i'r môr,*" an Ode to welcome Mistress Katherine home when she was beyond the sea; with an equally quaint description of the arms borne by them.— " *Pais Maister Rissiart Klŵch, marchog o Ved. Krist, a Meistres Katrin i wraic, aeres Tudur ap Robt. Y Bais honn sy yn ber pali yn arwydokau priodas deilwng rrwng Mr Rissiart Klŵch a Meistres Katrin. Penn y ki y syd. o rann Kowirdeb yn i wassanaeth dros y pryin's. Y Kroessau o rann santeid'rwyd. pan vu ynghaersalem. Y 'lew a'r kled'yf o rann i fenter a chalon.*" Our translation shall differ but little from that of the immortal Tegid.—" The ' coat,' of Master Richard Clough, knight of the Sepulchre of Christ, and

Mistress Catherine his wife, heiress of Tudor ap Robert:—This coat is per pale, to signify a worthy marriage between Master Richard Clough and Mistress Catherine. The dog's head because of his sincerity in the service of the princess ; the crosses because of holiness when he was at Jerusalem ; the lion and sword because of his daring and heart." The silver urn which contained the heart of the patriotic knight was coveted and stolen by some Iscariot.

N.B.—*L* and *d* with a dot, denote *ll* and *dd*, in the original.

It is scarcely possible to conceive anything more graphic and humorous than the following description of a ship.

I.

" Kowyd 'i yrru y 'long i nol mʳ ric Klŵch a meistres Katrin adref o Dengmark," i.e. An Ode to send the Ship to fetch Mr Richard Clough and Mrs Catherine home from Denmark. (Copied by the late Ioan Tegid, from the original MS. of William Cynval, in Christ Church Library, Oxford, fol. 11.)

Y llong a geidw llu yngod : îs y môr glas a mawr glod.
Kafell goed' ystafell gau : krud hun uwch kwrr y tonnau.
Gŵydd heli, gwŷdd a Goelion : gwiber dec aber y donn.
Ystyd a chyrt estud chwyrn : wyd waisc hwyad, wysc heiyrn
Yscw'l ing 'n yscîl angor : yscrîn mwdwl eithin môr.
Ysclêd wyllt neu 'sceled wyd : yscâl ledw, yscol ydwyd. [dw'r.
Kafn gorddic kefn y garwddw'r : kwrn uwch gwelw, donn kornchwigl
Klwyd ar gais yn kludo 'r gwyr : kist dull sad kastell sawdwyr.
Gwaisc oergnu burw gwascargnwd : gwennol ffrom ar ganol ffrwd.
Elor gyrt i lu ar g'oedd : olmari 'n hwylio moroedd.
Klau uwch dw'r, clochdy oerwynt : kassec wyllt yn keissio gwynt.
Vn o ffrom wyd, a ffriw march : a ffroen gau, a ffrwyn gowarch.
Prennol a geidw Duw 'r Prynwr : poenffustia 'r daith pennffestr dw'r.
Bregia drwy y berw eigiawn : buwch môr wyd a baich mawr iawn.
Taith oervaith, tuthia arw-vôr : ty annedd mewn tonnoedd môr.
Kyrch burlamp kowarch barlwr : kyfeiria 'r daith, kyfrwy 'r dwr.
Yna hwylia ʍ helynt : â'th hwyl wenn, ac o'th ol wynt.
Dos beunydd, bydd Duw 'n dy bart : drossodd at y mastr Rissiart.
A thynn oll, ni'th ynnillir : a markia hafn Dengmark hir.
Kyrch wr hael, kowirwych hedd : Klŵch eginyn kloch Gwynedd.
A dwc i'r wlad, na'd yn ol : wawr grysswenn, i wraic rassol.
Klaer veistres gynnes i gwedd : Katrin benn kytrann bonedd.
Y mae i'r ddau—mawredd oedd : ordr maer ar dir a moroedd.
Pa ynys ? pwy a enwai ? pa sir na bo 'i tir ne 'i tai ?
Dithau gida Duw weithian : dec aur lwyth, a'i dwc i'r lann.
Ail wyt, trum heli tremynt : arʲ y llanw gwyllt, i'r llong gynt.
Boddes Duw—bu ddwys y dic : braw gan wyn berw gwenwynic.
Y byd i gyd (bowyd gau) : baich adwyth am bechodau.
Ni ddiengodd, hwyliodd helynt : nid doeth, o gof, ond wyth gynt.
A llong Noe wrth ollwng nawdd : wych obaith ! a'i achubawdd.
Tithau lestr, taith hwylustec : torr wrth dy fron y donn dec.

A novia hwlk henaviaid : y berw o nwyf, heb roi naid.
Eiste',—ymddwc yn wastad : escud vodd, a llusc dy vad.
A rred y dwr, 'rryd y donn : â marchog i'r Duw Meirchion.
Arwain y mab a rran medd : awdwr gwin i dir Gwynedd.
A'i da 'n llawn ynod yn llwyth : y del i wraig a'i dylwyth.
Dof innau, difai annedd : dawn oll ym wyd, dunnell medd.
I'th aros draw, uthr ystryd : arth vawr, i borth y Voryd.
Siwrneia 'n hawdd nawdd Duw nef : sawdwraic, a brysia adref.

Free Translation.

Thou ship design'd a crew to keep,
'Neath the blue surface of the deep ;
Chamber of wood, a narrow cell,
Cradle of sleep, rock'd by the swell.
Goose of the brine, or pinion'd wood ;
A spotted viper of the flood ;
A duck, which moor'd in eddies rides,
With stilts, and cords, and knots, and slides.
A moor-cot in the distance lost,
A skate on ice, or skillet toss'd ;
An oval dish, a ladder rais'd
To climb above the wat'ry waste.
A tower on the floods adrift,
A lapwing on the waters swift ;
A raft which oft a host transports,
A coffer built like soldiers' forts.
A skimmer of the foaming deep,
As swallows o'er the cool brooks sweep ;
A bier which beams and cords sustain,
An alm-chest, steering o'er the main.
The cold wind's belfry of the seas,
The ocean-horse that scents the breeze ;
A prancing, plunging steed untrain'd,
Restive in hempen halters rein'd.

Frail bark ! may God thy treasure save,
Belabour on, and stem the wave.
Thy course through boiling surges tear,
Sea-cow ! thy pond'rous burden bear.
Tho' long and rough the passage be,
And cold the mansion of the sea,
Trim lamps thy canvas parlour light,
Sit ! saddle of the stream, aright.
Direct thy course through smoother seas,
Thy white sail spread to catch the breeze.
May God each day thy pilot be
To " Master Richard " o'er the sea ;
Pull up ! escape the pirate's hand,
Mark well the hav'n of Denmark's land.

Bring back in peace that man whose name
Is Clough, green branch of Gwynedd's fame.
Fetch home to Wales, leave not behind
That wife so gracious, fair, and kind.
Mistress of hearts so warm and good,
Catherine of noblest race and blood.
Each has, at pleasure and command
A mayor's rule o'er sea and land.
What isle? what shire? or who relates
Where they've not houses or estates?
Come, O Ship! at God's command,
This golden treasure safely land.
Be like that ancient craft of God,
On the wild current of the Flood
When vengeance burst upon the world,
And men to dark perdition hurl'd;
When boiling seas o'er mountains swept,
Eight souls in Noah's ship escap'd.

But thou the placid ocean plough
In ripples breaking on thy prow;
Glide smoothly on, dark hulk antique,
Nor roll in fits, nor leap in freak.
On glassy tide-waves sit afloat,
And gently tow thy little boat.
O'er gliding currents spread thy wing;
The knight to old Dymeirchion bring.
Safe home that son of Cambria lead,—
Dispenser of the wine and mead.[1]
His wife, and suite, bring back in health,
Thy precious cargo—their fair wealth.
Then shall my steps to those halls lead
Where gifts abound, and tuns of mead—
Yes, I will come, Great Northern Bear![2]
To Voryd Port, and wait thee there.
Thy course be short! by God's help come,
My Heroine, O haste thee home.

GLANMOR.

The following is another Elegy by Simwnt Fychan.

II.

MARWNAD RICHARD CLWCH.
(O waith Simwnt Fychan.)

Braw a droes, oer bryder sydd: briw dwfn fal i bu 'r defnydd.
Braw anial, briwo Ynys: Brydain a Llundain a'i llys.

1, Mead, (written in Welsh *medd*, but always pronounced " *meth*," the *th* as in *Seth*, sharp,) was a favourite beverage with the ancients, next to wine in repute, and made of honey. 2, An idea probably suggested by the fact of its being homeward bound from the North Sea; although its name may have been the *Great Bear*, or " *Yr Arth Vawr*."

Aeth yr Iessu â'i thryssor : a gwres darn o Loegr a'i stôr.
Marw ddoe hydd, mae'r waedd heddyw : Mastr Clwch, holl Westmi'ster
Am Rissiart tymmor yssig : yn mro drwch Cymru a drig. [a'i clyw.
Trist a'r llif, trostaw ar lled : trwy gwyn i'w 'r tir i ganed.
Y mae dynion am danaw : heb iachâu trwy Ddinbych draw.
Garw gwyn y' Machegraig oedd : gan vdlef i genedloedd,
Lliaws o'r rhyw llâs y rhain : llesmeiria 'r llys y' Merain.
Troes hiraeth tros i oror : tarrio y mae tu hwnt i'r môr.
Yn Nhroia 'roedd bloedd o'r blaen : a'r eilmodd sy'n yr Almaen.
Ein hynys llâs yn unawr : am y braw fu 'n Hambrw fawr.
Gwae Anwarp a thir Gwynedd : gau ar bur farchog o'r bedd.
Gwae bawb trwy och, gwae bob trem : gau ar sêl groes Gaersalem.
Ef a'n llâs am wr trasyth : fe aeth y bangc ar feth byth.
Hanner marsiant Brenhiniaeth : hynnu yn ol hwnn äi 'n waeth.
Hwnn fu 'mddiriaid llwyrblaid lles : hynod Râs ein Brenhines.
Diau rhann fawr o'i daoedd : dann i law yn dwyn elw oedd.
Mewn golud mann i gwelwn : megis Siôb oedd ymgais hwnn.
Ni roe hwnn, heuai 'r henaur—bu ras yw rudd—bris ar aur.
E dalodd rhwng i dylwyth : i ordro lles, aur dri llwyth.
Ifor ydoedd i frodyr : weithian a wnaeth hwnn yn wyr.
A'i genedl hoff, gnawdol had : i gyd a roes ar godiad.
Prynodd diroedd, fab breunerth : prynodd a welodd ar werth.
Ni fynnodd hyd yn Fenis[1] : un mann heb roe mwy na 'i bris.
Adeilodd cyfleodd lys : adail wenn a dâl ynys.
Gwnai fal Berwig[2] neu Fwlen[3] : gaer galch y' Machegraig wenn.
Main nadd fal y mynnodd fo : main Anwarp y mae 'n yno.
Main a gwydd mann y gwedda : *marblystôns*[4] iw 'r mowr-blas da.
Eiddil wedd, hynn a wyddir : wrth hwnn oedd twr Nimroth[5] hir.
Oes oerfraw y llys eurfron : eissiaw 'n hwy oes yn honn.
Troes wedi fyn'd fal trist fâr : trwy niwl, i Gatrin alar.
Oeres hynn oll Farsia 'n[6] iaith : aeres Tudur wastadiaith.
Graddloer wylo ei grudd wylch : gwiw heulwen frig Heilin Frych.
Essyllt dduwiol ddefosiwn : ydoedd hi 'n ddiweddu hwnn.
Da, a ni wnaeth Duw o nef : dyn wiwdraul, i ddwyn adref.
Da, o'i cyrph eill dau i caid : dwy loer megis dail euraid.
Moliant dygiant diogel : mawr i Ann a Mari êl.
Er marw gwr mawr i gariad : (amhwyllai lu) ymhell o'i wlad.
Gyrrodd yw fro, wr gwrdd fraint : ag arwydd att i geraint.
I galon (wr haelfron rwydd) wenn a yrrai yn arwydd.
Arwydd hael iraidd hoewlonn : arwydd hallt i rai oedd honn.
Arwydd serch cowirddwys oedd : ar i wlad, gwrol ydoedd.
Gwir yw ni yrrwyd o Grêd : ag arwydd cynn gywired.
I'r Eglwys Wenn, arogl saint : i gyrroedd, galon gowraint.
Aed yr enaid, air wiwnawdd : a fu 'n honn i nef yn hawdd.

Transcribed by W. W. E. Wynn, Esq. of Penniarth, M.P., from
the Porkington MSS., No. 2, a volume containing for the most part

1, Venice. 2, Berwick-upon-Tweed. 3, Boulogne. 4, Marblestones. 5, Birs
Nimroud. 6, Marsia, queen of Cyhelin, the 24th King of Ancient Britain.

Elegies and Laudatory Poems upon various ancestors of the Porkington family, amongst which are several by the celebrated Hugh Morris, not to be found in his printed works.

Simunt Vychan, was an eminent poet and gentleman of property of Llanelidan, who obtained the degree of chief bard, at the Royal Eisteddvod, held at Caerwys, in A.D. 1567.

III.

An Elegiac Poem on the death of Sir Richard Clough, who was the first of the name.—See his life in Pennant's Wales, and Fuller's British Worthies. (The original was published some years back, by the Poet Backwell.)

O God! how overflowing this year
Are the waters of Noah[1] over our earth,
God has inflicted a stroke upon us :
God knows how to impose a heavy penalty,
The loss of a saint, who was in unison with good men,
Sank Denbigh under a load of ice.
  Master Richard, a mighty treasure,
Having fallen down, caused a destitute void.
Master Clough was great for the munificence of his gifts
Even among those who were masters of praise *(laudis compotes)*.
I grieve, ah me!
To see the country so sorrowful after him :
Alas, alas! for the hour, a hundred times alas !
Alas! Jesus! there is a cause, a great one ;
The county is chilled. *Duw o'r saig,*[2]
A cold terrible burden to Bachegraig,[3]
There is after him an increasing sorrow,
A chillness in yonder unhappy *Berain,*[4]
Alas! for the surviving Catherine's affliction,
The disconsolate appearance of his honourable wife ;
The best of women, the daughter of a Squire,[5]
Of the boldness of a hawk[6] the grandchild of a *knight.*
Woe to her heart of eminent liberality ;
Woe to *her family of noble[7] blood,*
Her children in prosperity and respect,
From the same *Lion,*[8] the grandchildren[9] of Llywarch,
May the Divine Jesus long grant them his grace :

1, Cf. Hor. I. 2, " Grave ne rediret seculum Pyrrhæ." 2, The dish or cup. 3, *Bachegraig*, the name of his country seat near Denbigh, built by him A.D. 1567. 4, *Berain*, the seat of his wife Catherine Tudor, commonly called Catherine of Berain, which place descended with the Lleweni estate to the heirs of her first husband, Sir John Salusbury. 5, Tudyr ap Robert of Berain. 6. Qualem ministrum, &c.; *Sir Roland Veilleville*, of Britany, natural son of Hen. VII., Governor of Beaumaris Castle, whose only daughter and heiress was married to Tudyr ap Robert of Berain.—(*See Note p.* 138, *Angharad Llwyd's Hist. of Anglesea.*) 7, She was great granddaughter to Owen Tudor, by Queen Katherine of France, widow of Hen. V. of England, and was third cousin to Queen Eliz. who was her guardian. 8, Perhaps alluding to the lion rampant, argent, arms of her

2 A

And may the two daughters be united to two knights,
We praise them ; they are worthy of it :
Anne[10] and Mary[11] are our greatness.
If long life be granted them, we shall be gratified
To hear of Clough's rising posterity.
May they prosper more and more :
The fame of ancient *Llyr's*[12] daughters was inferior to their's,
Their family connections, like vines,[13] shall be interwoven
So as to spread all over *Gwynedd*.[14]
May the privilege be a comfort to the *brothers*,
To the sisters,[15] and their kindred.
Let Richard depart to Jesus,
We shall go to his brother above (he being gone above:)
Master *William*[16] a mighty dispenser[17] of hospitality,
Will in his stead gain a noble fame,
You shall hear Clough named as a chief,
Independent, powerful, and cheerful.
    The God of heaven in his goodness
Gave us, and took away from us, a good man.

  The age of Jesus the ruler,
  When the noble chief died,   }   *Ob : July* 26,
  Ten times seven, a perfect number, }   *A.D.* 1570.
  And a thousand and a half.   }

I'w[18] *fyw odiaeth ef ydoedd*   }   *The meaning of these lines*
Faen tros Iaen[19] *mor Ventrus oedd,* }   *is to me inexplicable.*
    Some support the weak
With their powerful gold and silver,
And then treat them with severity (as being dependants,)
But he treated no one in such a manner,
He with his old gold and silver
Assisted the weak, with a truly noble liberality.
God unsparingly gave him
The goods of this world as a gift.
He could command, it was believed,
The gold of the Bank,[20] with the mere word of his mouth :

family. 9, Or descendants, *nepotes*. 10, Ann was married to Roger, son of Sir John Salusbury of Lleweni, and was heiress of Bachegraig, which was left by Mrs Piozzi, their lineal descendant, to the late Sir John Salusbury. 11, Mary was married to Wm. Wynn of Melai, ancestor of the present Lord Newborough, who inherits from her the Abbey of Maynan. 12, King Lear. 13, Cf. Psalm 128, 3. 14, North Wales. 15, Sir Richard's son married a Drihurst of Denbigh, a family connected with the old Myddeltons, (*See Drihurst pedigree in British Museum, p.* 3,) and lived at Plas Clough, Co. Denbigh, possessed by Sir Richard's descendant in the 7th generation. 16, William was the 2nd son. Sir Richard the 5th son of Richard Hen. (or the old) temp. Hen. VIII. The eldest settled at Dunham Massey, Co. Cestr. The 3rd Humphrey ob. s.p. The 4th Hugh built the Grove House, Denbigh, A.D. 1574 ; and a sister was married to Griff. Sponne or Spenne, of Denbigh. 17, Or bursar. 18, The sense in these lines is not clear. 19, In life he was remarkable ; as a stone over the ice, in enterprise was he. In every adventure he was rapid as a stone over the ice. " *Faen tros Iaen*," is an old Welsh adage. 20, Pennant states that his

His word was firm *in grace*, (and gracious, courteous.)
And was a greater security than a seal for an island,
The course of his prosperity[21] *was full of grace,*
It is God's grace that bringeth a man prosperity.
He was very firm as the Seker[22]
And unshaken under his *Bince.*[23]
   He had been at the tomb[24] of Christ, the sight was solemn,
Under the sun of Jerusalem.
He was very renowned as chief of all
At Antwerp[25] for a time.
How was the object of our regard, our head,
The noblest tree of our forest, cut down in *Hambro!*[26]
The north country, the cause of our lengthening regret!
Alas! for us now: thither he went:
A furnace void of light is that dire country,
A wrathful furnace, a hellish, cheerless land.
   God grants the thread of life,
And allots the duration of its existence:
No man can prolong life for an hour,
Nor his kind friend gain for him two;
He died,—we grieve to know it,
And Atropos supplanted him.
His body the earth possesses,
But his soul,—the Redeemer.   *JOHN TUDOR,
                       one of the Choral of St. Asaph.

   Translated from the Welsh, by Morris Williams, *(Nicander,)* of
Jesus College, Oxford, now Rector of Llanrhyddlad.

IV.

WELCOME TO CATHERINE TUDOR.

   " Kowydd i groessawu y meistres Katrin adref pann fu tuwnt ir
mor val y kair gwybod wrth y kowydd."
Katrin law ruddwin roddiad: Kares wyth lu kroesso i'th wlad.

wealth was so great, that "Efe a aeth yn Clough," or he is become a Clough
grew into a Proverb, on the attainment of riches by any person. 21, Fuller says " How much the New Church in Denbigh is beholding to his bounty, I
am not as yet certainly informed. This is true, that he gave the impropriation
of Kilken, in Flintshire, with £100 per annum, to the Free School in Denbigh,
and if the same at this day be aliened, I question whether repentance, without
restitution, will secure such as are the causers thereof." And Pennant calls
him joint founder of the Royal Exchange, with Sir Thos. Gresham. 22, Ex-
chequer? or Royal Exchange, of which he was co-founder with Sir Thomas
Gresham. 23, Princess? 24, Having made a pilgrimage to Jerusalem; he was
created Knight of the Holy Sepulchre, and assumed the five crosses for his arms.
25, Pennant says that he was buried at Antwerp, save his right hand and heart,
which were to be placed in an urn in Whitchurch (St. Marcellus, Denbigh), upon
the coffin of the last inheritor of his property. 26, Hamburg, and not Edinbro,
as a note in the original says.—*Notes chiefly by the Rev. A. B. Clough, B.D.*

   • John Tudor of Wigfair in Rhôs, Denbighshire, was John Conway's domestic
bard. He was a skilful Herald, and satirised the views of the age very freely.
—*Note to Wynn's Hist. of Gwydir Family.*

Dwc y bel, di gel y gwedd : Drwy synwyr, meistres Wynedd.
Aeres Dudur, loer eirwir : ap Rhobert hael halbert hir.
Wyr Syr Rolant dda i ddur : O Frytaen' dda, frwd dan ddur.
Aeth vwch dir a'th wych dorriad : Em iaith dec dy vam a'th dad.
O du 'r tad gwych' leuad gain, Em wiw bur y mae, Berain.
O'th vam reiol mèrch Rolant : Aeres y Buwmares' bant.
Hwyliaist megis vn helynt : Elen verch Goel lanfraich gynt.
Honn a gerddodd, henw gwirddoeth : Y mor ar tir, ddyn îr ddoeth.
Yno, drwy nerth Duw o'r nef : Or daith hydr y doeth adref.
Ac val hynn gwiwvawl henwi : Wrth ystad yr aethost di.
Gida 'th wr, mewn kyflwr kain, Gwir lendyd, i gaer Lundain.
O Lundain, hardd riain hael : I'r Galais,' eurloer gulael.   [fawr.
A thrwy Ffraingk, winvaingk iawnvawr, Hofflowndres vod, i Fflandis
O Frebant,' gwarant geirwir : Iawn tro pell, i Antwarp hir.
Ac ywch wedi, gwych ydoedd : Yn yr Yssbaen wrssib' oedd.
Yn Hambrw, uffern henbryd ! O vewn Dengmark, bark y byd.
Ing dic y rhwng i deugwr : Ofer dim ! y bu farw d'wr.
Ac i'r ystad at Grist wynn : Yn aeth ef wrth i ofyn.
A chwi a ddoeth, eigr goeth gain : I Loegr yn ddyn weddw liwgain.'
Yno bu uwch yn unawr : A gwiwras maith groessaw mawr.
A'th glod aeth golud weithion, O'r vn sud drwy'r ynys honn,
Oddyno yn ddi anair, Orau dyn, heb wyro d'air,
Doeth i'th ty (ch) hun, y fun fain, Drwy fowredd i dre Ferain.
Llem fu r floedd lle ir oedd heb wrid, Llann-ufudd yn llawn ofid.
Deubeth oedd, diobaith haint ! Dec eurwawr, ar dy geraint.
Eissiau y rrawc yn îs Rhos, A hiraeth yn ych aros.
Ness ych ddyfod i'r frodir, Ni thoddes rhew tew (n) y tir.
Y gaeaf fu dragowydd, A rhif serch yr haf y sydd.
Kyw ffol' yn lle (r) kyffyloc, Kannaid gwrs, kaned y gog.
Yma i(r) byd ! bo mawr a bach, O lawn bwyll lawen bellach.
Iawn drwy Wynedd dirionwych, Ag onor' klod ganu (r) klych.
Adolwc, bennes dalaur,' Dyn loew wych ! dan wiail aur.
Fry na ddos hael linos lan, Varn well o Verain allan.

WILLIAM KYNWAL.

Copied from a Welsh Manuscript (f. 11) in Christ Church Library, Oxford, January 29, 1839.

(Signed) TEGID.

V. ·

ELEGY TO CLOUGH.

" Kowydd marwnad am y Mastr Rhissiart Klŵch marchog o Vedd Krist."

(Although there are some fine " touches and strokes," in the fol-

---

a Robert with the long halberd. b Bretagne in France. c Beaumaris, of which Catherine was heiress. d Helena, mother of Constantine the Great. e Calais. f Brebant. g They were worshipped in Spain. h The barbarous word " *dynes*," was not then used ; *dyn* was of both genders, as, " Dyn glan," a handsome man ; " Dyn lân," a fair woman. i The cuckoo in place of the woodcock—spring after long winter. j Honour. k With a gold frontlet.

lowing poem, there is, on the whole, much waste of words. Like the last, it is a wild extravagant effusion, and as such, curious.)

Bu ddu'r hin, bydd rhew ennyd, Bob rhan o bedwar bann byd;
Mair ŵyr! mor llwyr i'n llas, Marw dwrn a mur y d'yrnas.
O'i restio*a* bu fawr dristwch—Aes wart clau Mr Rissiart Clŵch.
Dirwywyd lle, y mae 'n draoer, Dinbych wenn dau ebwch oer!
Byd hwyrnos, bowyd hirnych, Bryn o ia yw Berain wych.
Gwae lu gweled, gwal Gwlen,*b* Grug o ia 'm Machegraig wenn.
Ni wnn fann, drwy gwynfan draw, Na bo trist y byd trostaw.
A fu 'rioed, rhyfawr adwy ! Och Iesu! vyth achos vwy ?
Dir gyllaeth, drud yw'r golled, Dirwy, hyll gri, drwy holl Gred.
Gwae o'i gofal gogyfoed, Calon ei wraig lân yrioed.
Meistres Katrin, llin wellâu, Merch Dudur, mor wych deidiau.
Wylaw, Duw fu ddialwr, Ydyw i gwaith wedi i gwr.
Iesu a ad a'i had i'w hol Y Loer ddisseml urddassol.
Hon yw 'r iawn, henwer yna, I'w thai teg am ei thad da.
Einioes a gaiff, bennaig*c* gwin, I'r llys, bur iarlles Berain.
Achwyn i'w ol, gwych iawn oedd, Am Rissiart y mae'r oesoedd.
Od aeth Ef i nef, yn wâr,—I'w genedl yn rhy gynnar,—
Iawn a roes, y mae'n rasol, O'i lin Ef oleuni i'w ol:
Dwy aeres o'r un dorriad, Draw 'n hir i gadw tir i lad.
Un yw Ann hael, mae'n wenn hi, Ar elw mawr; ail yw Mari.
Yn vyw hapus, vwy hepil, O waed yr rhai'n y daw'r hil.
Ni adan', dwy hynodwawr, Uchod lin Klychiaid i lawr.
Diryfedd iownwedd yna, Dyfu o had i tad da.
Ef fynnodd i'w vyw ennyd, Wellau ar bawb oll o'r byd,
Yn gedyrn hwnn a gododd, I bobl; rhoe gan' *nobl* yn rhodd.
I'w frodyr doe, bu frwydr dydd, A chwerw gwyn i'w chwiorydd.
Yr oedd deg, hardd diwygiad! Yn aeron teg o'r un tad.
Oed Iesu fu, dewis fodd, Di gam, pan y degymmodd,
Pymtheg cant, tyfiant ofer, Pum saith ddwywaith, mae'n daith deg.*d*
William Klŵch a'i lymwaew clau, O'r llu gwyr yw 'r llew gorau.
Bu benn Kapdenn*e* i'r brenin, Bu ddewr draw, val baedd i'r drin.
Iawn ddedly hwn yn ddidlawd, E geidw y fro gwedi i frawd.
Tomas, Wmffrai, Huw dduwiol, A Rhobart rwyddwart*f*; ar ol.
Ann, Alis, rhoen' win eilwaith, Ac Elin deg, Luned iaith.
Llyna imp pell a wnai i part, Llawn o ras, now-llin Rissiart.
Dyna wiwlu dan wylaw, Dwyn i brawd a wnai y braw.
Gannthaw 'r oedd lle y gwnaeth i ran, Gowaeth dugset waith diogan,
Ni ddug hwnn, o ddig kynnar, Wrth arian rann y gwann gwâr.
Er hen aur hwnn ni yrrai, Neb yn wir o'i tir ne'i tai.
Y da a rodd, nid ar wall, Hael pur i helpio arall.
A'i dryssor ef a drwssiawdd, Ei dŷ 'n y nef, dyna nawdd,   [Salem.*j*
Bu'n Rhufain sain',*g* bu 'n nhref Sem,*h* Bu 'nghôr Sawl*i* bu 'nghaer

a From *arrest*, arrestio. *b* Wall of Cologne. *c* Chief or leader. *d* A.D. 1570.
e Captain, chief captain. *f* The riches of a duke. *g* Rome of Saints.
h The town of Shem, probably *tref* here has the *old* sense, distinct territory, patrimony, &c.; the ity *Zama* at the head of the Tigris, is by some said to be so called, from the patriarch *Shem*. *i* Saul's Chapel. *j* Or, Caersalem, Jerusalem.

Bu ar vedd Krist, bur vodd kred, Pell gynnyrch, bu lle e'i ganed.
Ef fu lle 'r aeth, velly 'r oedd, Oes nafd Iesu i nefoed,
Ac ymhob gwlad, breiniad brau, Ufudd wr ef oedd orau.
Ki gorff sydd gynnyrch gwynwaith, Obry o vewn Hambrw vaith.
A'i galon, hawdd i'n goeliaw, Kbwch drom ! yn Ninbych draw.
A'i enaid at frenhinoedd, Aeth i nef, penaeth in oedd.

WILLIAM KYNWAL.

The Salusbury Family.—For further notice of this illustrious
family see Lleweny.   But perhaps nothing could be more truly
laughable than the following method of proving a man a gentleman.

"This is truly coppied from the originall, wch was made for Mr
Foulke Salisbury, to be produced for him in the Earle Marshalls
Courte, in a sute betwixt him and Samuel Martyn of Chester Marchant, there dependinge beinge for scandalous words spoken against
the nation in generall, & the Salisburies in generall, & him the sayd
Foulke Salisbury in particular, by the said Martyn ; to wch I am
wittnesse & procured the same descent."

Rand. Holme of Chester, aldr., Deputy to the Office of Armes.

To all xtain people to whom this present writing shall come to
be seene or read, Greetings, in our Lord God Everlastinge, Know
ye that whereas Mr Foulke Salisbury, one of the 24 aldermen of the
Citty of Chester, and also one of his Majesties Coroners for the sayd
citty is desirous to have a Certyficate of his descent, that the same
may appeare by good Testimony, for to remayne vpon record for
his future posterity, & also to cleare all doubtes and questions, that
ether now are or hereafter may arise conserninge his progeny, hath
requested vs his kinsmen, beinge descended of the same blood &
familey, vnder our hands for to certyfie the truth therof, by this
our Testimoniall to wch his lawfull request and desier wee have
yealded, as Christian Charity byndeth vs thereunto, to declare and
relate the same, when and so often as wee be therunto desired,
Wherfore we doe Certyfie that the sayd Mr Foulke Salisbury was
borne at Evenighted in the County of Denbigh and was second
sonne by birth, but now heyre, to Henry Salisbury, of Evenighted
aforsayd, in the County of Denbigh, gent., lawfully begotton of
Margery his wife, dau. to Peirs Salisbury of Llanrayder, in the sayd
County gent., wch sayd Henry dyed in Chester, 6 October 1637,
beinge of great age ; and was youngest sonne to Foulke Salisbury
of Maes Kadarne in the said County gent., lawfully begotten by
Morvith his wife, daughter of Meredith Lloyd of Havodynos, in the
County of Carnarvon esq., and the forsayd Foulke Salisbury was 3
sonne to Peires Salisbury of Bachymbydd, or Ruge, in the County of
Denbigh, esquier, lawfully begotten by Margret his first wife, daughter
and heyre to Evan ap Holl. ap Rees of Ruge, in the sayd County,
esq^{r.} & the sayd Peires Salisbury was sonne and heyre to John
Salisbury of Bachymbydd, in the county aforsayd Esqr. lawfully

begotton of Lowrey his wife; dau. and heyre to Robt. ap Meredith ap Tudyr Esq˙˙ & the sayd John Salisbury was a younger sonne of Thomas Salisbury Hên of Lleweny in the County of Denbigh, esq˙˙ and brother to S˙˙ Thomas Salisbury; who was knighted at Blackheathfield 1464, of whom is descended S˙˙ Thomas Salisbury of Lleweny baronett now liuinge, both beinge lawfully begotton of the body of Ellen daughter to S˙˙ John Done of Vtkington in the County of Chester Kt. & the sayd Tho: Salisbury Hên was sonne and heyre to Henry Salisbury of Lleweny esq˙˙ lawfully begott of Agnes daughter and heyre of S˙˙ John Curteys, Kt. & the sayd Henry was sonne and heyre to Rafe or Rawlyn Salisbury, sonne annd heyre to William, sonne and heyre to Henry, sonne & heyre to S˙˙ John, sonne & heyre to Thomas, sonne and heyre to Alexander, sonne & heyre to Adam Salusbury, all whos matches remayne to be seene in the severall pedegrees of the said famileys, from w⁽ᶜʰ⁾ this lyne mentioned in this Certyficate was carfully and diligently extracted, at the request of the sayd Foulke Salisbury, and for more verity herof, wee haue herunto subscribed our names the 14ᵗʰ day of November 1638.

Thos. Powell of Berkhead, baronett. John Conway Kt. de Botry Dan. Thomas Myddelton Kt. de Chirk. Roger Mostyn Kt. de Mostyn. Thomas Mostyn Kt. de Cilken. Simon Thelwall de Placeward, Esq. William Wynne de Llanvayre, Esq. John Lloyd de Llanrayder, Esq. Peter Evans of Northop, Esq. Hugh Nanny of Nanny, Esq. John Lloyd of Ruedock, Esq. William Salisbury of Ruge, Esq. John Salisbury of Bachegrigh, Esq. John Salisbury of Bachegrigh, Esq. his sone. William Salisbury of Llanyrader, Esq. William Thomas of Carnarvon, Esq. John Jeffreys of Royton, Esq. William Conway of Perthekensey Esq. Edward Conway of Sughton. Hugh Parry of Chester, Doctor. Rouland Griffeth of Carnarvon. John Powell of Llwynskotog. Jenkin Conway. John Lloyd of Llanynys. Foulke Salisbury of Denbigh. Thomas Salisbury of Denbigh. John Thelwall of Ruthen. Gabriell Goodman of Ruthen. John Eaton of Lleeswood, Esq. Thomas Mostyn of Rhed, Esq. Piers Conway of Ruthland, Esq. Rich. Perry of Combe, Esq. Peter Wynne of Tythen, Esq. Thos. Salisbury of Ledbrooke, Esq. Hugh Lloyd of Foxhole, Esq. Jarratt Eyton of Eyton, Esq. Edward Norris of Speake, Esq.

CHAPTER XIV.

DE BECKELE'S SURVEY RESUMED—LIBERTIES OF THE BOROUGH
OF DENBIGH—TOWNSHIPS OF LLEWENY, YSTRAD CANON, GALLT-
FAENAN, GWAENYNOG, ETC.—EXTENT AND VALUATION—TENANTRY
OF ENGLISH COLONY, CUSTOMS, ETC.

THE TOWNSHIP OF LLEWENY,

WITH its hamlets of Newburgh and Polflat, (names now unknown,)
and the Park contained 4,560 acres of land and waste, in three free,
and eighteen bond gavels.

The free gavels paid 2s. 11½d. tunc-rent, and 15s. 2¼d. for provision for the Prince.

Six of the free gavels were escheats. Each tenant paid the lord
for butter 3d., for provision for prince,s servants 1s. 5¾d., for horses
and men 5d., for the raglot 4d., repair of houses 1d., mill 4d., three
days' reaping in harvest 4½d., for foresters 4d., for satellites of the
peace, if not fed 4d., for stallions and grooms 1d., for dogs 1d., for
penmackewe and "gweision bychan" ½d., at the feast of All Saint's.
For making or repairing hedges 1d., at the feast of St. Philip and
St. James. For every plough 8d. The property of intestate persons went to the lord, the Church, and the raglot, as elsewhere.
On the marriage of a daughter or bondwoman, the lord had 5s. from
each tenant, and from husbands of wives who committed adultery,
5s.,* for "letherwite" 5s. *Total*, tunc 4s. 1½d., Prince's servants
38s. 5½d., horses and men 10s. 10d., raglot 8s. 8d,, houses and mills
10s. 10d., harvest work 9s. 9d., stallions and grooms 23d., dogs 23d.,
penmackewe, &c., 11½d.

There were twenty-six bond tenants, of whom twenty-three had
houses.

Eight oxgangs of ten acres each, were held by Richard de Orel,
Henry del Frith (three), Robert de Hulton, sen.; Alice, widow of
Thomas de Salbury (two), William de Duckworth, Robert Skipton,
William de Sonderlond and Alice his wife, and William del Mos.

---

* Their relief and fine was less by one half than that of other tenants.—(*See p.* 45.)

And William del Forlond, Radulph le Heende, Matilda del Bouk, Hugh and John sons of Robert de Pontefract, William de Hibernia, William Thorstell, Robert de Castelford, William, Roger, and Hugh de Sonderlond, Robert Wyberleye, Nicholas son of Ham . . . . and William Bassket, held in all 15 acres and 10 perches, for 12s. 0½d.

And William and John de Swinemor, held in " Thloyn and Kilkedyk," 108 acres 3 roods, by knight's service for 1s.; Roger de Pannton and Elen his wife 40 acres for 2d., the heirs of Thomas de Pontefract 80 acres in " Athlevaynan," for 4d.; Robert de Pontefract, and Richard de Duerdew, 320 acres for 8d.; the heirs of John de Camera, 160 acres for 8d.; Henry de Ferour 80 acres for 4d., Richard de Shoreworth 80 acres for 4d., and the wife of William Basket 15 acres for 1d. These were to keep ward at the castle, in time of war, for forty days, at their own expense, and do suit at court.

And Henry de Totenhale, Joan daughter of Ralphe de Totenhale, Adam de Blakeburne, Peter de Hennde and Ralph his son, Richard del Peek, Henry de Runcorne, John de Kylford, Adam son of Hugh (Kylford?) Henry son of Adam de Salesbury,* Thomas de Crace, Adam le Heende, Richard de Foute, Robert de Frauncis, Robert son of Adam le Foute, Adam le Longe, Robert le Foute, Robert Sutor, John le Mareschal, Roger and William de Sonderlond, John de Salesbury,† William de Lanton, Adam son of John le Salter, Hugh de Hodreshale, Margaret and Alice daughters of William de Henglewode, Richard de Decer, William Balle, Richard son of John de Romworth, Richard le Cartwright, William le Lannergh, Robert de Plesynton, William del Mos, Robert de Bispham, Simon le Turnor, William le Barkere, David Backerue, Nicholas son of Hamon, John Shadde, John de Stokton Henry del Spen, Alice Verdon (at Garthmeiller), Roger de Pieutre, Robert de Hulton, sen., Robert de Lannergh, John de Hylton, William le Bordwere, William son of William de Lanton, Henry de Symunduston and Joan his wife,

---

* Nine acres for 7s. 4d. His father Adam probably came from *Salebury*, or Salesbury, (Salebury Hall or Court) in Lancashire, and is *said* to have been captain of the garrison at Denbigh Castle, under Henry III. although it is more reasonable to suppose that he came with De Lacy. Gilbert de Salebury, (of Clitheroe,) living 42 Henry III. had a son called Adam. And Salebury first belonged to the Salesburies or Salusburies, who now claim to have originally come from Saltzbury, in Germany. † Twenty acres 3½ roods for 19s. 4½d.

2 B

Adomara daughter of Roger Carles, Richard de Orel, Robert de Shoresworthe, Richard le Bordhewer and Thomas his son, William de Lanton, John de Stadhurst, William son of Michael le Ruddehech (*Rhydderch?*) and his daughter Margaret, John de Swinbourne, Thomas de Halghton and Agnes his wife, Thomas de Hulton, Robert Bercare and Margaret his wife, Richard son of Robert de Hulton, Thomas son of Richard del Peek, lve Skot, John de Conwey, Richard de Cumberbache, Robert Kay, John de Rheved, Richard de Birchynshawe, Elias Stell, William de Rachedale and Eden his wife, Adam le Norssove, Ralph de Bridlyngton, John de Gamesleye, Alice la Seimestre, Henry de Westmorland, William Throstle, William son of Hugh del Frith, Adam de Leweny, and Kichard son of Benedict, pay altogether, £61 5s. 4¼d. for two messuages, eleven " toffs," one curtilage, 1559 acres, 23½ perches, eight " *places*" two " cloughs," and two " bouks," of land.

Robert de Hulton paid two shillings annually for permission to dig turf and grindstones in the lord's mine there. And Richard del Peek farmed Lleweny and Henllan mills, for £7 10s. a-year, and paid for license to have a fulling mill on his land 13s. 4d. Total, £8 3s. 4d.

Newburgh.—And there is a hamlet within the bounds of Lleweny called Newburgh, containing sixteen " places," held by Richard son of Robert de Romworth, Elias Steel, Ralph de Cumberbache, William de Stonyfeld, Isabella de Hendebury, Cecilia Ribchestre, and William de Romworth, for 19s, 9¼d. annually, altogether.

Lleweny Park.—And there is a park at Lleweny, which, from the time of the Earl of Lancaster, has been arrented at 12d. per acre, for which John Faber, Richard de Birchynshawe, Elias Steel, Isabella de Hendebury, William son of Hugh del Frith, Roger the son of Adam de Sunderlond, William de Hendebury, Thomas Balle, Hugh del Frith, William Throstele, Elias Englepeny, John de Stokton, Richard de Romworth, Ralph de Cumberbache, Adam de Hendebury, William de Kailly, Richard del Peek, Robert and Richard de Hulton, Robert de Westmorland, Adam de Wyrhale, Robert le Roper, Adam son of Isolda and Matilda his wife, John de Hoghton, Henry Danney, Thurstan de Orell, Robert le Knappe, Henry del Spen, Thomas de Lonnesdale, Henry de Cliderowe, William Basket, John de Pontefract, Robert de Wyberleye, Alan de Craven, Adam le Taillor, Richard de Wode, Henry Gryme, and John le Reved, pay £25 13s. 0¾d. and one mite, annually, for 513 acres and 12 perches of land.

Garthysnodiog.—And there is a " place" of land and wood called Garthisnodyok, containing 215 acres, besides an allowance of nine acres, held by William de Dukkeworth, Thomas le Shepherd, Juliana and Isabella de Hallum,* Henry de Clyderowe, John le Mereer, Richard de Dydesbury, Jordan de Byngeleye, Robert de Halton, John de Gayte, Adam and William Moody, Robert de Wickwere, Henry de Runcorne, Thomas Irvento, Thomas de Steyford, Ralph son of Nicholas, William Russell, Peter le Heende, John le Chapeman, Henry de Yokshale, and Thomas Bateman, for £8 18s. per annum. It is remarkable that there is no mention of the present townships of Upper and Lower Bannister.

Polflat.—A "furlong " of land, near the great fishpond of the manor, called the Polflat, " rendered " 58s. 11¼d. and one mite annually, and was held by William de Schereworth, John le Reved, Roger del Peak, Juliana and Isabella de Hallum, John de Mostyn, Thomas de Steynford, Thurstan de Orel, Thomas Irvento, William Russell, Nicholas de Chadewyk, William de Hereford, William de Dydesbury, Robert de Wyberleye, William de Basket, William de Swynmour, and Henry de Heton, whose holdings together made 41 acres, 1½ roods, 4¼ perches. From the description, *Polflat* could not have been identical with the present *Bowflat.*

Denbigh Green or Common.—There were also 937 acres 25 perches, in roads and wastes, in which the tenants of Lleweny, Astret Canon, and the Burg of Denbigh, had common of pasture by grant of the Earl of Lincoln. And 225 acres 3½ roods of land, of which the lord took no profit. Total revenue from Lleweny £116 5s.

TOWNSHIP OF ASTRET CANON.

This township consisted of four gavels, and rendered 6s. 11¼d. tunc-rent, and 36s. 11d. provision for the prince's servants ; being all held by free tenants. The whole came into the lord's hands by escheat and exchange. The manor of Kilforn takes in 208 acres, 18

* These two maiden ladies had various and considerable holdings here and elsewhere.

perches; the Little Park, under Denbigh Castle, 55 acres, 1½ roods 5 perches; the domain of Astret Owen, 14½ acres 4 perches; Llewey Park incloses 113¼ acres 26 perches; roads and wastes 30 acres 17 perches.

William del Mos, Adam de Rossyndale, John de Swinemor, John son of William Egglyne, Richard de Termory, and John de Lonnesdale, hold three oxgangs for 10s. a-year, and 50 acres for which they pay no rent. And William Curteys, John de Moston, Adam le Carpenter, William and John de Swinemor, John Egglyne, Thomas de Hulton, Alexander Danney, William de Wode, John de Hoghton, Jordan de Byngeleye, Henry Grym, Thomas and John de Lonnesdale, and Richard de Bayton, hold 62 acres of land, in all, for 47s. 6d. per annum. Besides 50 acres 20 perches whereof the lord takes no profit. Total value of Astret Canon, £5 1s. 4¾d.

TOWNSHIP OF ATHLEVAYNAN.

The free tenants of Galltvaenan paid 7¼d. tunc, and 3s. 10¼d. yearly for the prince's servants. The (Welsh) bond tenants paid 17s. 0¾d. yearly for the customs enumerated under other townships. And the tenants on the lord's land, which contained 272 acres 1 rood 5 perches, paid as rent, £7 7s. 0½d. per annum. And 24d. was rendered by one tenant for having the weir of his water-mill upon the lord's soil.

Le Graba, (now called *Nant-y-crabas?*) was formerly a separate wood of the prince, containing 94½ acres 30 perches; but now 29½ acres 34 perches were inclosed in Moilleywick Park, and John de Kylford held 34 acres for 12s. 8d. per annum, with common of pasture for all his cattle, by charter from the Earl of Lincoln. The rest was held for 7s. 8d. by Richard de Wyckwere, William Raven, and Henry de Runcorne. These also paid 20d. yearly for the herbage of a small patch of common.

"*Bronnskip*" is described as a hamlet in the occupation of English tenants, containing 120½ acres 25 perches; of which 5½ acres 25 perches were inclosed in Moilewyk Park. Robert de Pontefract and Richard de Averdue, held 105¼ acres by ward of the Castle of Denbigh. The remainder was rented by John de Kylford, Thomas de Irulham, and John de Rossyndale for 7s. 7½d. per annum. Total revenue for Galltvaenan £10 1s. 2¼d.

WENNENOK WYNTUS.·

Four tenants held one eighth and one forty-eighth part of the hamlet of Gwaenynog Wyntus (Bach?) rendering 4½d. " tung " annually. They did no service, but came to court, when reasonably summoned, and followed the prince with his army. But John de Kylford, Henry de Runcorne, Robert de Wickwere, and John his son, William and Robert de Wyberley and William Raven, rented 98 acres 1 perch for 58s. 2d. per annum. Waste, 19 acres 1½ rood, rendering the lord no profit. Lord's portion, 117 acres 1½ rood 8 perches. Total extent of this hamlet, 137 acres 1½ rood 16 perches.

WENNENOK CANON.

This hamlet belonged to the township of Astret Canon, and contained 238 acres 1½ rood 10 perches of land, wood, and waste. It came " entire " into the lord's hands by escheat and exchange. Hugh, William, and Thomas Pygot, Thomas de Clayton, Henry son of Hugh le Carter, Richard de Wyberlegh, John le Chapman, Hugh le Beere, Hugh le Carter, Robert de Rossyndale, Adam son of William Cocus, Adam de Haywode, and Cecilia de Rachedale held 153 acres 3 roods 15 perches, for £4 9s. 8½d. per annum. The wastes, woods, and hills, whose soil was almost valueless, comprehended 72 acres 1½ rood 3½ perches, which brought the lord 5s. annually, as common pasture. Total annual value of both hamlets, £7 3s. 3d.

CONCLUDING REMARKS.

Those who are acquainted with the locality and present community must have read the foregoing Chapter with astonishment. We naturally ask, but in vain, what has become of the descendants of this host of English settlers ?

The Heaton Family.—Heaton, alias " Heton," is the only English name, (on the long and tedious list,) now connected by residence with the locality. This one family, now represented by J. R. Heaton, Esq., of Plas Heaton, still holds its patrimony and position among the leading gentry of the neighbourhood. They derive, according to *Lewis Dwn's Visitation*, from Alexander Heaton,* Lord of Heaton in Lancashire, who settled in Wales in the reign of

* Plas Hettwn, or Old Heaton Hall, on the north of the town of Denbigh, under Parc Prys.

Edward I.   The figures denote the generations, = marriages, in the following pedigree:—

1, Alex. Heaton aforesaid; 2, Sir Charles Heaton, knt.; 3, Harri Heaton; 4, Harri Heaton; 5, Harri Heaton; 6, Harri Heaton.— One of these four *Harrys*—probably the first or second—is here presumed to have been the same individual as "Henry de Heton," one of the free tenants at the "Plotflat" of Lleweny.—7, Jenkin Heaton, living in the time of Edward IV.; 8, Harri Heaton,=Ann Myddelton; 9, Harri Heaton,=Dows or Douce, daughter of Richard Buckley; 10, Harri Heaton,=Alice Lloyd of Foxhall; 11, Harri Heaton; 12, Harry Heaton, living 2 Elizabeth; Richard Heaton,=Elizabeth Wynne of Voelas; 14, Richard Herton;=Isabel Lloyd of Foxhall; 15, Huw Heaton,=Elizabeth Pigot; 16, Richard Heaton,=Elizabeth Davies of Denbigh; 17, John Heaton, =Margaret Adamson; 18, Richard Heaton,=Sarah Venables; 19, the late John Heaton, Esq., High Sheriff in 1837, died in 1855. But it will be seen that "John de Heton" was tenant in the township of Grugor, in A.D. 1334.—*John Heaton, Esq.*, had *issue* by Elizabeth his *first wife*, sister of William Jones, Esq., of Hartsheath Park, Mold:—1, Sarah Elizabeth, deceased; 2, John Richard, 37th Regt. Foot, and Brevet Lieut. Colonel, a magistrate for the county of Denbigh; 3, Charles Wilson, (Rev.) B.D., a Fellow of Jesus College, Oxford, lately Junior Proctor; 4, Hugh Edward, (M.A.) formerly a Scholar of Jesus College, Oxford, now vicar of Bettws-yn-Rhos, = Catherine Maria Craven. *By his second wife*, Anne Eliza, sister to the present Lord Henniker:—1, Mary; 2 Anne Eliza,=Reginald, R. Walpole, Esq., and died Nov. 1853; 3, Emily Margaret; 4, Frances; 5, Anne Maria, died Nov., 1851; 6, William Henniker,=Henrietta Mary Anderson; 7, Frederick Luxmoore, B.A.; 8, Arthur, Lieut. in the 15th Regt.; 9, Llewelyn Francis; 10, Jessy.

————

The Salusbury Family, so illustrious for ages in the annals of Denbigh, has no longer any connection with the place.   True it is that two or three plebeian families around have, somehow or other, inherited the name.   And De Beckele throws very little light upon "the mythological origin of the Salusburies."   He says nothing in confirmation or contradiction of their alleged descent from "the Royal House of Bavaria."   With him they, like all the rest, were no more than free tenants, holding, between the whole family, something less than forty acres of land.   It may, indeed, be possible that "Adam de Lewenny," who held 13 acres 3½ roods for 4s., was a Salesbury, Salsbury, or Salbury.   And had these held anything more, by charter or otherwise, it is most probable that our author would have recorded the "grant," as in the case of others. How they became so truly great he furnishes us with no means of deciding. It is certain, however, that the Wars of the Roses, in breaking up the old feudal system, swamped the Norman nobility, and brought up new elements to the surface of society. As the ancient patrician families of Rome derived their origin from gods and demigods, so there is much of " myth " and fable in the earlier portions of of the pedigrees of our present noble and gentle families. There is no doubt, however, that the greater part of the Salusbury Pedigree is true, as will appear in the following hitherto unpublished poems, copied for this work by the Rev. R. Williams, M.A., of Llangadwaladyr, the learned author of the *History of Aberconway, Dictionary of Eminent Welshmen,* &c. The first is a laudatory poem to Sir Thomas Salusbury, (son of Thomas Salusbury Hên,) who greatly distinguished himself at the Battle of Blackheath, (June 23rd, 1497,) against the pretender Perkin Warbeck, for which he was knighted on the field by Henry VII. His first wife was Jonnet, daughter and heir of Edmund Vaughan of Penrhyn, Chamberlain of North Wales. She died Sept. 4th, 1427. His second wife's name was also Jonnet—or Jenette, made executrix of his will, dated Dec. 26th, 1504. He died in January, 1505, and was buried in the Chapel of the Carmelites at Denbigh.

" COWYDD I SYR THOMAS SALSBURY."

Ystiward Rrôs a dart rhudd ; iechyd eryr i'ch deurudd.
Gyrr di yno'r gwŷr danad : gwnewch y tir fal y gwnai'ch tad.
Syr Tomas, aer wyt yma : Salbri, dos yw lwybrau da.
Mae'n d'ammod am Hen Domas :[1] Rosier[2] iwch, aros i ras.
Y màn uchaf mewn iachoedd ; isel eb ryw Salbri oedd.
Kof o Arthur kaf wrthych : Curtais[3] gynt câryt, was gwych.
Ni ddug neb yn ddigon abyl : bleth fân-aur eb wyth Fenabyl.[4]
Na tharrier oni'th eurid : ni bu'r Don eb euro i dîd.
I'th law rhoed, a thaler hwn : ar gledd deitl Arglwydd Dyttwn.
Rhyw'ch mam, rhai ucha 'y Môn : a rhyw Lloegr o'i holl eigion.
Mae had Gwilym[6] hyd Gwlem :[7] mòr wych oedd hil Marchudd Hên.
Ni bu lwyth, er Noe[8] a'i blant, Brynffanigl[9] eb ran ffynniant.

1, *Old* Thomas Salusbury. 2, Roger Salusbury. 3, Sir Arthur Curteis. 4, The Venables. 5, Lord Dutton. 6, Probably, Sir William Manderville, whose daughter and heir married an ancestor of the Salusburies. 7, Cologne. 8, Noah, 9, A very ancient manor near Abergele, supposed to have been first founded by Marchudd Hên, or ap Conan, founder of the eighth noble or patrician tribe of North Wales. His descendants were Lords of Abergele, and one is even styled " *Princeps Opergelei,*" Prince of Abergele, From these Henry VII. descended.

Oes bron a gais brennau gwin ? ond o'r Bryn y daw'r brenin ?
Rhyw yt ddyn ar hyd dy ddur : ros aur tîd rhyw Syr Tudur.[10]
Llew Stanlai[11] llys dy-hen lwyth ; Lletty hen ieirll Hwttwn[12] wyth.
Eurwyd eiltu o'r Daltwn[13] : eurer o hil orwyr hwn.
O waith deubeth i'th dybiwyd : y llew a'r oen, felly'r wyd.
Nid aethoch yn adwythig ; yn dân neu ddur, ond yn ddig.
Dewrach oeddyt i orwyllt : a glewach gynt no'r gwalch gwyllt.
Rhan y ddau mewn rhinwedd dda : rry lonydd 'r hylew yna.
Galw dy nerth i'r golyd, Non : gyrr yn sochach gyrn-sythion.
Gwr i'th wlad, a'i gwŷr i'th law : gâd i'n tir gyd anturiaw.
Aro di fyth ar dy fainc : na warafyn wŷr iefainc.
Am wrolaeth gwas'naethwr : o chair er gwerth chware'r gwr.
Dyn a ddêl dan i ddwylaw ; dewr drud, a wrandewir draw.
Dial o'r tu dalier tant : dysc iddyn' nad yscwyddant.
Deuair sy raid i dyall : gair mam, gair llysfam yw'r llall.
Clyw'r iawn, rhag coelio'r annoeth : cronna dy ddig, gwrando ddoeth.
Gwell yw sôn na gwall synwyr : deg nog un, digon a'i gŵyr.
Ond a'th gâr, un doeth gwrol : ac union yt, gwna'n i ol.
O gwnewch i wr egni chwyrn : nyni gyd a wnai'n gedyrn.
Mae'r wlad a chariad i chwi : maent dy wraidd bob man trwyddi.
Rhagor oedd rhyw a gwreiddyn : rhywiogrwydd uwch rhawg arddyn.
Gwnaethoch ar ginio wythwaith : weilgi o win, ŵyl a gwaith.
Doe ni ddyblwyd yn ddwybleth : dy lys eb waed Elisabeth.
Ni bu grwn Pilstwn[14] eb had : nid un ddail dau'n y ddwywlad.
Nid îr llwyn derw Lleweni : a Bers eb ail Barsabi.
Merch rasol y' mraich Rossier : mae'n aros hon mwy no'r ser.

" Ond o'r Bryn y daw 'r brenin ?" that is, does not the king come from the House
of Brynffanigyl ?" Henry the Seventh, King of England, &c., was the son of
Edmund Earl of Richmond, son of Owen ap Meredith, and of Queen Catherine,
his wife, daughter of Charles VI. King of France. This Owen was son of Meredith ap Tudor ap Gronow ap Tudor ap Gronow, ap Ednyfed or Ednoved Vychan,
Baron of Brinfenigle in Denbighland, Lord of Cricketh, Chief Justice and Chief
Councillor to Llewelyn ap Iorwerth, &c., Prince of all Wales. And in the time
of Prince Llewelyn, grew a variance between King John of England and the said
Prince, whereupon Ednoved, with the Prince's host and men of war, and also a
number of his own people, met the English Lords in a morning, at what time
these English Lords were hostied and slain ; and immediately brought their heads,
being yet bloody, to the said Prince Llewelyn. The Prince, seeing the same,
caused Ednoved Vychan, from henceforth to bear in his arms or shield, three
bloody heads in token of his victory, where he had borne in his arms before a
Saracen's head ; and so ever after this Ednoved bore the said arms, his son, and
his son's sons, &c. And this Ednoved wedded Gwenllian daughter to Rhys,
Prince of South Wales, and had issue by her, Gronow, &c. Ednoved Vychan had
in Wales divers goodly houses, royally adorned with turrets and garrets ; some
in Anglesea, some other in Caernarvonshire, and some in Denbighland ; but his
chiefest manor-house was in the Commote of Crythin, &c., which was a royal
palace, now decayed for want of reparation. Also he builded there a chappel in
the worship of Our Lady, and had license of the Pope for evermore to sing Divine
Service therein for his soul, and his ancestors and progenitor's souls always ; and
had authority to give his tythes and offerings to his chaplain there serving.
Ednoved Vychan was son to Kyner ap Ier. ap Gugan ap Marchudd,, which was
one of the Fifteen Tribes of North Wales, and son of Cynan ap Elfyn ap Môr, ap
Mynan ap Ispwis ap Newintyrch ap Ispwis ap Cadrod, Caluhvynydd, Earl of

Rroi'n hawdd i haur a wnai hi : rraid oedd, a rrowied iddi.
Seigiau rroddion suwgwr rruddaur : * * * * * * * *
Mwnai mewn llaw meinwen : elsai byth yn Elsbeth wenn.
Ffrydiau gwin Sain' ffraid Gwynedd: ffriw deg iawn i phryd a'i gwedd. '
Eraill aur a'r llaw arian : ewch at hon llwyth Chitnai¹⁵ lân.
Gwaed Owain (gwraidd a geidw'n gras): Glyndwfr * * * lin Defras.¹⁶
Awdlai Rydderch, dâl ruddawr : Iarll Straens,¹⁷ ar y llestri aur,
Dy Gwynedd hyd Deganwy : Ty Elen gwaed dwylan Gwy.
Ty'r Fychans¹⁸ torf o iachoedd : towys gwaed Tywysog oedd.
Elsbeth o F"redydd Gethin : ac o Rys Gryc, aur yscrîn.
Gwaed Raglan a gyd-dreiglir : a Llechryd—oll iachau'r tir.
Gwaed Hergest o goed Teirgwent : gem aur Dafydd Gam o Went.
Pennaf nith pan fo'n wythiaith : Penfro—Iarll pennaf o'r iaith.
Eluned hael Went yw hi : ar lin aer o Leweni.
Rroed ym win rrad a mwnai : Rossier, llaw iarll roes aur llai.
* * * * * *
Kyrchais i wlad y tad tau : kyrch gwin ac aur chweugeiniau.
Mae da weddill ym deuddwrn : am na ä d'aur mewn un dwrn.
Ni bu balf i neb o'r byd : a'i llanwai'n well ennyd.
Llawer dyn, rrag lleihau'r da : nes ar unwaith nis rranna.
A dreulir hyd yr elawr : ni bydd ym oes eb dda mawr.
I'ch byw aur ywch a bery : er na bu fraib ar neb fry.
Ond wyd lân at haeloni : ni bu lân o'n blaen ni.
Byth, ac â phawb i'th goffâu : bid d'oes, eb wybod eisiau.
Byw yt wr, be oed derwen : Odid byw wedi dy ben.

TUDUR ALED A'I KANT.

This poem must have been written about the close of the fifteenth century, upon the marriage of Roger Salusbury, (who was created knight banneret by Henry VIII. in 1550,) and Elizabeth Puleston of Berse, near Wrexham, sister to Sir John Puleston of Havody- wern, although addressed to Sir Thomas Salusbury, the father, and having special reference to some military movement of the day. The poet supplicates him, in consideration of his years, and the valour he had displayed in his younger days, to remain at home on the bench, most probably as alderman of Denbigh, and allow

Dunstable and Lord of Northampton, ap Cynwyd Cynwydion, ap Cynvelyn ap Arthwys ap Morydd ap Cynaw, ap Coel Godeboc, King of Britain, of whom King Henry the Seventh, descended lineally by issue male, and is son to the said Coel in the thirty-first degree, as it is *approved* by old chronicles in Wales, &c. Such was the description or "return" of the Royal Commissioners. Sir John Leiaf, priest; Guttin Owen, Griffydd ap Llewelyn ap Ier. Vychan, Madoc ap Llewelyn ap Howell, Robert ap Howell ap Thomas, John King, with many others, at the King's Majesty's costs and charges. The Abbot of Llanegwestle, and Dr. Owen Pool, Canon of Herf, *overseers.*—*See Wynne's History of Wales.* These trace Henry's lineage up to *Brutus*, who, they say, first inherited this island and called it Britain. 10, Sir Tudor Trevor, Earl of Hereford. 11, The Stanleys of (12) Hooton. 13, The Daltons. 14, Puleston of Bersham. 15, Chitney. 16, Devreaux. 17, Earl le Strange. 18, The Vaughans of Penrhyn.

younger men to take up arms. Nothing could be more admirable
than the tact which the poet shows in approaching a high-minded,
haughty-spirited and irritable, but generous and munificent patron, or
the candour and boldness which he interweaves with praise and flat-
tery. But it is very remarkable that, although he seems careful to
enumerate all the " Salusbury alliances," there is not a word said here,
or in *Holme's* Pedigree of Alderman Foulk Salusbury, about their
original descent from the Royal House of Bavaria.

There is no doubt that the Salusburies took an active part in the
Wars of the Roses, and that this fact, and their marriages with the
richest heiresses in the country, at a time when so many heirs male
fell in the field, conduced to the aggrandizement of the family. Sir
Thomas Salusbury and Sir Rhys ap Thomas were among the principal instruments in setting Henry VII. securely on his throne, and
in crushing to extinction the embers of that domestic feud which
had raged so furiously for thirty years. To this the couplet alludes,

" T'wyso'r wyt ti a Syr Rys
Yr iau flaen i'r Fel Ynys"

in the following very fine poem. The orthography of the original
should, however, have been followed by the copyist.

Kowydd i Syr Thomas Salsbury.

Pwy yw blaenor pobyl y Wennol,[1] Pen bras y deyrnas yn Dôl ?
Ystiward Ros a dyrr ystrin, Salbri wyn dros lu brenin.
Syr Tomas a'r het emoc, Mal Syr Galath[2] maels a'r gloc.
Don yn cael aur dan wain cledd, Dyttwn rhoed yt anrhydedd.
Deo yn gwybod yn gobaith, D' angel da yn deongl dy waith.
Gwraidd dawn a gyrydd d' wyneb ; Gorey braens[3] wyt garbron Sieb.[4]
Gwayw Rowling o'r gwrol-waed, Gosod y drwg is dy draed.
Darfuan' bawb—derfyn byrr ; Diflaswyd dy faleiswyr.
O d'oedd wg yw wadu' ddant, O d'oes gwg nid ysgogant.
Wrth falais ar ath faliawdd ; Eiriach y neb archo nawdd.
Os ufydd y dysyfwn, Ufuddhewch i faddau hyn.
Od äi lid yn dy liw iach, Ef a pwyll a fo pellach.
Anian y tân ynot ti, Mewn oed dyddiau mynn doddi.
Na yrr d' ofn ar y difeilch ; Dy ofn a fydd dwfn i feilch.
Gwindai Rôn[5] gennyd a red, Gwledd Sin[6] Arglwyddes Sioned.
Mwythau, seigiau 'r tywysogion, Ar i gwledd, merch Arglwydd Mon.
Wedy gwr wyd o gariad ; Wedi gwraig ydyw o gred.
Tir Lleweni, troell Ionawr, Tad medd y cynteidie mawr.

1, Llys y Wennol," Wennol Court, Whitedale Court, an epithet applied to
Lleweny. 2, One of the Knights of King Arthur. 3, A branch. 4, Cheapside,
as some say. 5, The *Rhone*, whence his wines came. 6, It is difficult to say

Teg yw lled dy gellidion, O led a hyd y wlad hon.
Wyth ager tân i'th gwrt oedd ; O wres powdwr Siep⁷ ydoedd.
Cwn, gweilch, gwyr, yn cowain gwin ; Cyrchu cic ceirw i'ch cegin.
y ·· f ·· d cerdd dafod yn dau, Cerdd dant, penceirddiaid, wyntau.
Gwr a cherdd a gyrch urddas, Godechgar⁸ wyf gyda gras.
Ar fy mharch y rhof fy mhwys, Am rhydit y'mharadwys.
Fal Nanmor⁹ o flaen unmaeth, Tan rent i'r Towyn ir aeth ;
Dafydd¹⁰ faer rhydd Ifor Hael, Iolo¹¹ doeth i wlad Ithael.
Gyda chwi î gyd o chaf, Feistrolaeth, f'oes a dreuliaf.
Ni fwriadwn fawr rodiaw¹² A gwr fall hyn gar fy llaw.
Hawdd i cawn fonheddig gwyr, Gyd a'ch urddas gyd chwarddwyr.
Llew nod Llęweni ydwyd, Llawn ddyrnod cerdd dafod wyd. ·
Mwy no maen mwya' 'n y mor, Mwy na chraic—mynwch ragor.
Ni ostyngir nes d'angau, Bo iawn a chain ben ych iau.
Ni roi bin er i bonedd, Ni thynn dyn wrth yn dy wedd.
Twyso 'r wyt ti a Syr Rys, Yr iau flaen i'r Fel Ynys.¹³
Y radd oreu ar Ddewrion, Fu erioed gradd y Ford gron.
Ni bu erioed yn i bric, O *Round Tabl* yr un tebic.
Ni wn dy radd yn iawn draw, Ond i'r angel yn dringaw.
Yr oedd twts¹⁴ arwydd y tân, I'th rudd fal na'th ddiwreiddian'
Chwyn ŷd, ond ych hun ydynt ; Chwi piau 'r aur, a chopr ynt.
Chwchwi yn gaer chwechan gwryd, A chwi sy ben chwech oes byd.

TUDYR ALED A'I CANT.

ELEGY TO SIR THOMAS SALUSBURY.

The masterly poem given next, is from the pen of the talented Tudor Aled. It is, perhaps, necessary to add that after the final triumph of the Lancastrians, many notorious Yorkists, who escaped the scaffold, became exiles and outlaws, skulking in the yet impenetrable forests and inaccessible caves of the Welsh Mountains, where they took up the life of banditti or robbers ; and it appears that Sir Thomas Salusbury made it his business to hunt them out, and bring them to justice, as well as to impeach the more secret friends of the fallen House of York. There is an allusion to this in the following poem.

Owdl-farwnad Thomas Salsbury, Marchog urddol.

Gwae holl Gred trymmed tromwedd,—am erchwyn
Y marchog o'r Gogledd ;
Cloi 'r bwrdd, a'r clai ar y bedd,
Cau Lleweni, cell Wynedd.

---

which is intended, the *Seine* in France, or *Ais*, alms, gifts; feast of charity. 7, A cheap, a mart. 8, Loving to skulk. 9, The Poet Nanmor. 10, David ap Gwilym. 11, Iolo Goch. 12, Wander about. 13, The Isle of Honey, Britain: 14, Touch, flash of " choler," another allusion to the hero's fiery temper.

Gwynedd am yn gwledd y mae'n gloff,
Marw llew'r *prins*,[1] mae 'r lloer eb priff ;
Marw 'n pen, a'n capten, a'n cyff ;
Marw Salbri ym, a'r sêl braff.

Marwed Syr Thomas mau oerion—fronnau
    Am frenin marchogion ;
    Marw iachoedd mawr Marchudd Môn,
    Marw edryd ymerodrion.

Os marw ef, Iesu ! mae 'r wyd[2]
Yn llwyn o ynnill i waed ;
Mae o'r un cyff mawr o'n coed
Yn wydd iefainc ymddifaid.

Ymddifad o'r tad yw 'r tir—a'i cestyll
    Rhac gostwng y teirsir ;
    O flodau afaleudir,[3]
    Impier o'r rryw emprwr hir.

Empriwyr o eryr Aram—sy egin
    Siacop, Isaac, Abram ;
    Oes merch ? Arglwyddes, hi mam ;
    Oes meibion ? Dynion dinam.

Tad, brodyr, neiaint, plant aeth mewn hiraeth[4]—a cheraint
    Chwiorydd ym penaeth ;
    Cwyn am i ddwyn ym oedd waeth
    Cwyno adladd cenedlaeth.

Bu adladd nowradd o'i nerth,
Bu ddw'r Noe yn boddi'r North ;
Ba ryw swn ? ai 'r wybr a syrth ?
Bu ddiaspat[5] eb ddosparth.

Diaspat gwaeddiat digwyddaw—tyrau
    A'r cateri[6] yn syrthiaw ;
    Dayar oedd yn diwreiddiaw,
    Dan ebwch drom Dinbech draw.

Draw yr aeth dirwy ar wythwin,[7]
Darfu oeri 'r dorf werin ;
Darfu pen y dref[8] a'i post[9]
Darfu 'r gost ar fara gwin.

Darfu 'n diarfu. Deo irfyw !
Darfu am barch dra fo 'm byw :
Dra fo'm byw, deryw[10] dwyrain—a gogledd
    Diryfedd yd Rufain.
    Doe 'n dirwywyd yn druain—
    Dinbech drist dan y baich drain.

1, The Prince, Henry VII. 2, Tree, hence the English word *wood*. 3, The Vale of Clwyd, which was even then celebrated for its apple trees and orchards. 4, This line must be the forgery of some ignorant copyist. 5, A scream or wild cry. 6, Great spreading, sturdy oaks, hill-forts. 7, Flowing wine. 8, The town of Denbigh. 9, Stay, pillar, prop, support. 10, Shall utter a dismal cry. 11,

Ar ddrain, ac ar fain er f'anwyl—yr wyf
    I ba le ir af uchelwyl ?
    Dydd oer ydoedd i arwyl ;
    Die Ystwyll gwin distill gŵyl.[11]

Llyma oer Wiliau lle mae 'r alaeth ;
Llwyr yw briw adfyd llawer browdfaeth ;
Lle odidogach, lle daw dugiaeth
Ni chae iarll yw roi no chôr[12] lle'r aeth.
Na brenin yn sîn wasanaeth—harddach
Na gwledd degach no'i gladdedigaeth.

Mae aro yn taro ? mae 'r anturiaeth ?
Maneg ar aliwns[13] mewn gwroliaeth ?
Methodd, maluriodd milwriaeth—y byd
Mae 'n erchwyn y gyd mewn arch yn gaeth.

Llawen yw cedeirn llawn hoccediaeth ;
O'i rym y dygynt rwymedigaeth,
A llawer eraill o herwriaeth
A gyrchai o'r coed i garchar caeth ;
Yn Nghred ni weled unoliaeth—Gwalchmai[14]
Wr well a fedrai roi llyfodraeth.

Am i fawr golled mae f'argyllaeth[15],
Am rydid ym oes, am ryw dadmaeth,
A mhen, a'm perchen, a'm nenbren aeth,
A'm hoedyl wedi, a'm hadeiladaeth.

Y'mherigl yr wyf o'm hiraeth—bob awr—
Yr af ar f' elawr o'i farwolaeth
Mae 'r fynwes ym ar fwn y saeth,
Eb fy stôr Wiliau, eb feistrolaeth,
Eb allu dros hyn, eb well dros waeth,
Eb windai—mowrdrai mordraeth !—longlwythau
Eb amyl ffrwythau, eb fwythau, eb faeth !

Yn iach na helwyr, na chynhaliaeth ;
Na meirch o arial,[16] na marchwriaeth ;
Na gweilch yw harwain, na gwalchwriaeth ;
Na chŵn awyddus, na chynyddiaeth.
Nà cheision mwy sôn am wasanaeth—gwledd,
Na chôg i wynedd na cheginiaeth.

Gwynedd ! anrrydedd, rredwn—etto wyr
    At i aer y cyrchwn ;
    Os berr fu oes y barwn,
    Oes hir i arglwyddes hwn.

Twelfth day, last day of a feast, when the wine ebbs, runs short. 12, The Abbey of Denbigh, here described as a fit resting-place for a duke or earl. The funeral ceremony, and burial feast, were not surpassed at the obsequies of a king. 13, Aliens. 14, One of the golden-tongued knights of King Arthur's Court. 15. Deep, painful anxiety, torture of mind. 16, Invigorating exercises, field sports.

Am hwn i gwaeddwn, am i gweddwed,
Ni bu lawenydd yn y blaned ;
Ni roed o'm synwyr, y Dâm[17] Sioned,
Gwyn i dri marchog gan dair merched.

Cowir Esyllt gynt, Crused—Siwsan—
Er cwyn i Drystan, wraic cyn dristed,
Rroi alusenau ym rreol Sioned,
Rroi gynau gwynion rhag yn gwaned.
Rroi cyn y ddwyawr, rrai cyn ddued,
Rroi cwyr a menic, rroi cri o'i myned,
Rroi cwyn rrai a'i cant,
Araith oer a thant,
A wnant—methasaut o'i mwythused.

Gwae eigion y'mron i merwined !
Gandryll o waeddi gan dra lludded.
O'm dwyais heddiw im diswydded,
Anodd ymaros yn ddiymwared
Yn ddiddawn ddiddym,
Eb rodd, eb rym,
Eb addwyn feistr ym, eb dda 'n fystred.
Mawr ydd wy'n wylo—Merddin Aled !

Mawr ydyw 'r achos, Mair edryched.
Myn Crist, mannau croes,
Man trist ym troes,
Mae oriau f'einioes ym ar fyned.

Diryfedd trostaw,
Trwy fodd tristed.
Oedd ym gwynaw
Dydd ym ganed.
Duc hwn, Deo ! cwynwn,
Deo ! oll, dyallwn,
Deo ! ni a'i gallwn dan y golled.

Ni bu arm aruthr,[18] eb roi ymwared,
Gandryll o weiddi gan dra lludded,
Can awyr wyth-ryll[19] cyn aruthred,
Can eirth o'i rrwymmau cyn orthymmed,
Can Droia unwaith cyn druaned !

Nid cwyn, cwyn canwr,
Nid byd, byd eb wr,
Wrth gwyn concwerwr wythgan caered.
O bwy cawn lunio neb cyn laned ?
O bwy cawn ddethol neb cyn ddoethed ?
Nac un o'r sessiwn cyn rasussed ?
Nac un ar elyn cyn wroled ?

Ni bydd na hydd na hawc,[20]
Na llew galluawc,

Na blaidd cynddeiriawc, blwydd cyn ddewred,
Yn i arwyddion un a rodded
O fewn y darian faen a dorred
Lleuad newyddian, llew dinodded
Ai thynu deirgwaith yn y darged.[n]
Am nad oedd mewn dur
Teirmil côt armur[22]
Accw 'n nydd Arthur cyn ddiwarthed.[23]
*   *   *   *
O gẃyn i briddo cyn ebrwydded!
*   *   *

TUDUR ALED A'I CANT, A.D. 1505.

AN EULOGY UPON " JOHN Y BODIAU."

Popular tradition relates so many incredible stories of the marvellous strength of " Syr Jobn y Bodiau," that the following,
written by a contemporary, and protegê of the family, is highly
interesting to all Welsh readers.   It will be seen that the poet fully
corroborates what tradition narrates of his extraordinary muscular
powers ; his bow and arrows are described to be such as no other man
could handle — no other man born could bend and string, the
" yew-tree," of which the former was made, while the latter are
compared to " long aspens."   There was no spear, even the most
" fearful," which he could not break, and at " throwing the bar " his
feats of strength were equally astonishing.   The poet also says he
wondered how any lady could have given birth to such an offspring ;
that his bones seemed to be made of steel; that among a host he
was the object of universal attraction, at whom the wise as well as
fools marvelled.   His person is described as equally remarkable for
comeliness and grace.   In temper he was a lamb; in courage a lion,
" brave and wise."   He was but young when he became a page in
the court of Henry VIII., and followed that prince on his expedition
into France.

Cowydd Moliant John Salusbury.

Troes undyn at ras hendaid,[1] A gras Syr Tomas y taid.
Sion ffriw at asenau Ffranc, Sy lew braf Salbri iefanc.
Llwyn gwin Lleweni gan-oes, Grwn o dir gorau yn d'oes.
Mae ar ych claim euro'ch dedd, O'r llwyn arall o Wynedd.
Oes, gwr at ras y goron, Oes, fab arglwyddes o Fôn.
Cawn d'ofyn can do iefainc, Cwrtiwr ffres[2] curyt wyr Frainc.

17, Dame Jannette.   18, An omen.   19, Easily rent, or bursting.   20, A hawk.
21, The lion and three crescents.   22 Coat of Arms.   23, Less tarnished.

1, " Thomas Salbri Hên," whose " grace " he imitated.   2, A fresh courtier.

Ni ddaw dull newydd i dir ; Nes dy gisgoedd nis dysgir.[3]
Tros Wythwyr[4] tarria i seuthu, Tri bys llew,[5] trwy beisiau llu.
Dyn a byw pur dan bop bys, Dwyn dreigiau[6] dau dy wregys.
Ni chauwyd yw, na choed iach Dan figwrn dyn fywiogach ;
Nid ynelodd dan aelawd, Ond egin oedd yn dy guawd.
Rrwymo pren yr heimp[7] yr wyd, Nes yt eni[8] nys tynwyd,
Yw yn olwyn a nelir, A thynu yn hwn aethnen hir.
Tynny saeth at einioes hydd, Ef a'r ewen[9] yn friwydd.
Dy fwaf, praff o dŵf, pren, Dan ddau wlw[10] ddaw'n ddolen.
Crynoyt y ddeucorn attoch, Cnot clau, fal pe cenit cloch.[11]
Pe llai hwp y llew hapus, Oes bren yw nis briwai 'n us ?[12]
Oes gwayn aruthr nas gŵyrych ? Aml oedd gamp y meuludd[13] gwych.
Ni bu 'r troed dau y bar trwm, Eb drithro a ba'i drathrwm.
Oes un grafanc, Sion, gryfach, A edy rwn o dir iach ?
Bar hauarn nis byrrhenir, Er gado i hyd ergyd hir.[14]
Ryfeddais yr haf eddyw, Yn dy faint eni dy fyw ;
O ganed dur dan gnawd dyn[15] Yn hop braich y mab brychwyn.
Dwg nerth, mae degni wrthyd, Drwy dy gorph dur wyd i gyd.
Doetha' ffriw hyd eitha' Ffrainc, Diddicca carw deuddeccainc.[16]
Dewr a chall wyt, drych y llu, Doeth ag ynfyd a'th ganfu.

    Ef a'th gâr un fyth o gred, A'th wyl[17] unwaith a'th laned.
Mae i'th air, y mab mwythais main, Oes breuder Ynys Brydain.
I'th galondit fo aeth glander, Fal y pysc ne afal per.
Fal oen wrth dy foliannu ; Fal llew yn ymafael a llu.
Eithr anos yw d' aros di, Nog aros naw o gowri.
Cawr Trolop,[18] cwrtiwr hylew, Calyn y llys calon llew.
Eb *ddowt*, o byddy waytiwr, O waitio 'n iawn ti ei 'n wr.
O bu dwn y byd unwaith, Torri oes hwnt Harri Saith.
Seithfed H. i'th fywyd oedd, Obru yn henwau 'r brenhinoedd.
H. arall yt sy Harri, Wyth yw 'r dyn a'th eura di.[19]

Tudur Aled a'i cant.

An Ode of Praise to Foulk Salusbury, First Protestant Dean of St. Asaph.

    Dean Salusbury was uncle to Sir John y Bodiau, and was the first Dean of St. Asaph who formally protested against the supre-

---

3, He became the model of fashion to all gentlemen in Wales. 4, The inhabitants of the Isle of Wight. 5, The lion on his shield. 6, Fiery darts. 7, Rhimp. 8, *Nes dy eni*, until thou wert born ; "*Nes yt eni*," or "*it eni*," is now in the active voice. 9, Ywen, a yew tree. 10, A noose, or running knot. 11, *Cyn sowndied a'r gloch*," is a common Welsh saying ; here the bowstring is said to be like a bell-rope on the stretch in ringing. 12, there was no bow of yew which he could not break in pieces. 13, One armed in mail. 14, the allusion is to the feat of throwing a bar of iron with the foot. 15, Freckled by the sun. 16, An allusion to his *twelve* fingers ; as tradition says he had two thumbs on each hand and two great toes on each foot. 17, For *wêl*. 18, He excelled even Sir Andrew Trollope, a captain under the Earl of Warwick, when governor of Calais; a man of great strength, valour, and wisdom. 19, He was afterwards made knight by Henry VIII. as the poet prophesied; was constable of Denbigh Castle in 1530, afterwards chancellor, chamberlain, and M.P. for the county, in the reigns of Henry VIII. Edward VI. and Queen Mary.

macy of the Pope. He is described in the following clever little poem as having succeeded, in property and influence, another great Salusbury. As a dignitary of the Church, he is compared to a lantern or lamp, giving the countries brightness; and the precious words which came, as a preacher, from his heart, are compared to wheat; his eloquence to wine; and his worth to a sapphire.

Cowydd moliant Ffowk Salsbury, Dean Llan Elwy.

D'ynill oedd, a dwyn y llall: Dyn ir fu 'r Deon arall.
I'th duedd, o'th edewir, Ni byddwn wyl heb ddyn ir.
Ni wnai Ddeon yn Wynedd iach, Ar gŵyr lun o'r gwyr lanach.[1]
Lawnter wyt, fal enaid rhydd, I roi gloywder i'n gwledydd.
Mae 'n olau yma 'r wlad, Er marw 'r llew mawr â lleuad.
Am yr adec (mawr ydwyt), Blin, a ddaeth blaen newydd yt.
Os un lloer sy 'n lle arall, Diwedd lloer ydoedd y llall.
Y newid aeth yn y dur, Ni newitia 'n y natur.
Ni ddoe galon ddigeliat, Yn nwy ais dyn, nes yw dat.[2]
Tân coed wyt i un cadarn, Triacl o bydd treiglo barn.
Gwin dy iaith, gan y doethion, Gwerthfawr ynt pob gair o'th fron.
Gwr llên llwyd[3] ger llaw Lladin, Gwenith fydd a gawn o'th fin.
Synwyr a gras, hyn yw 'r gwraidd, Saffyr faen Asa[4] ffurfiaidd.
Aelod a phen, y wlad Ffwc, At Ili[5] wyt a'i olwc.
At arwyddion, het ruddaur, Nid un lle 'th roed yn llythr aur.
Ff: a godir Ffwc ydwyt; S: i le braisc Salbri wyt.
Goleuaist di, wrth gael ystad, Genau 'r llew gwyn a'r lleuad.
Tywynwch Gwrt y Wennol, Ne farned ef yrry 'n d' ol'
Cap a rydd i'r cop ruddaur;[6] Carw a'i gyrn mewn crug aur.
Coron Iork[7] i wr o'n iaith,[8] Coroni Cae hir unwaith.
Cyn teirawr cenad Harri, Caniataed het Caint[9] iti.

TUDUR ALED A'I CANT, ABOUT A.D. 1511.

The Myddelton Family.—In addition to what the author has recorded elsewhere of this eminent local family, it may be as well to say that Richard Myddelton, governor of Denbigh Castle, in the time of Edward VI. and Queen Mary, and lieutenant to the Earl of Leicester, in the reign of Elizabeth, who lies interred in the porch, at Whitchurch, Denbigh, in his will, proved ". 26 ffeb. 1577," makes request to be buried in the Parish Church of Denbigh, and directs his executors to sell Galch-hill Park, &c., and from the proceeds, to give his sons, Foulk, Richard, Robert, and Piers, £40 a-piece. And to his daughters, Barbara, Ellen, and Alice, 100 marks each. He leaves to his grandson John, son of Richard Myddelton, his

1, The Salusburies were generally persons of light of sandy complexion, and consequently fair. 2, " Nes yw dat," nes i'w lle, more just, upright, &c., " Gormod *ddât*, digïon o *ddat*, &c." are common sayings, or more like his *father*. 3, Becoming gray over his Latin. 4, St. Asaph. 5, Ely, of which place he contemplated being bishop. 6, His golden hair. 7, The crown of York, the archiepiscopal mitre. 8, The Dean was a Welsh speaking dignitary. 9, The archiepiscopal hat of Canterbury which the poet hoped Henry VIII. would confer upon him.

property at Llansannan, " except the house wherein dwelleth" his
(testator's) brother Thomas; leaves his house to Piers Lloyd, (a
town-councillor in 1597,) subject to a yearly rent of twenty shillings
to John Myddelton; gives his son Charles £20, and to his
daughters, Lucy, Ellen, and Barbara, his " horses, oxen, kyne, and
sheep." The *executors* were his sons, Simon and Thomas, and his
son-in-law, Thomas Evans;—*witnesses*, Thomas Myddelton, David
Myddelton, Piers Lloid, and others.   This will seems to have
been disputed, (see page 128 of this work.)   It does not appear
which of the Myddeltons was, according to Lord Burleigh's note,
(page 117,) to pay the merchants VIII. *m*. (£8,000) in A.D. 1590.

The Davies of Llannerch,&c.—The Davies also of Gwasanau, Mold;
and Llwyni, Abergele; were of the Tribe of March, deriving from
Kynric Evell, Lord of Eglwysegle, who bore for his arms gules on
a bend, argent, lion passant, sable; and was descended from Meredith Prince of Powis, and through him from Roderic the Great.
" Madame Davies," is described as Gwasanau and Llwyni.   This
must have been a minor branch.   Owen Davies of Llwyni, a maternal ancestor of the writer of this paragraph, sold Bryn-Llwyni,
about the close of the seventeenth century, and became afterwards
tenant at Bodoryn.   ——

Other Mediæval Poems found about Denbigh.

The author is in possession of many other fine poems of the
fifteenth and sixteenth centuries, which, so far as he knows, have
never been published.   Several of these were found at Gwaenynog,
and placed in his hands by the late Capt. Myddelton.   To the Welsh
philologist they are most interesting, not only on account of their
poetical merit, but because they serve to illustrate the state of the
Ancient British Tongue, and the character of its poetry, in the
reign of the Tudors, and tend to throw more or less light upon the
dark mysterious annals of the Wars of the Roses.   Others exhibit
the political, social, moral, and religious state of Wales and England
before the Reformation.   Manuscript copies of the poems are, indeed, to be found amongst the collections of the admirers of Welsh
mediæval poetry in other parts of Wales.   The following is a beautiful poem, written during the war in Wales between the adherents
of the Houses of York and Lancaster.

I.
Kowydd Arglwydd Herbert.

(*Written when three hostile armies penetrated into North Wales, Denbigh was
burnt, and the country laid waste.*)

Trillu ddaeth i Gymru gynt: trwy Wynedd y trowenynt.
Llu 'r Pil,[1] llu 'r Arglwydd William:[2] llu Vepwnt, bu hwnt baham ?
Teirffordd hawdd ; tir Offa hen : siwrnai William Sarn Helen.

Arglwydd Herbert, a'th gerti : a'th lu, Deo,[3] a'th lywio di !
Glaw gynt a gai lu ac ost : hindda weithian pan ddaethost.
Dewiniais y Kaet Wynedd : a dwyn Môn i'r dyn a'i medd.
Berw Lloegr ! bwrw i llygaid : O keisiwch Harddlech ei kaid.
Chwedl Bonfras[4] a g'as i gyd : blaenvain vu i'r bobl ynvyd.
Chwedl blaenvain, bobl druain! dro : Bonfras, Arglwydd ar Benfro.[5]
Ba well kastell rrag kystec : pan fwriwyd wal Penfro deg ?
Bwriaist ergydiaist godwm : ben karrec kynneu i'r kwm.
Ni ddaliawdd i chlawdd uch lann : uwch Harddlech mwy no chorlan.
Ni'th ery na thy na thwr : na chankaer mwy no chwnkwr.[6]
Tair kad aeth o'r teirgwlad tau : trwy Wynedd val taranau.
Tair plaid yn gapdeiniaid ynn : teirmil a nowmil yn Jwmyn.[7]
Dy frodyr, milwyr y medd : dy genedl i doi Gwynedd.
Dy werin oll dewrion ynt : drwy goedydd dreigiau ydynt.
Dringai lle nid elai da : dy rwyddfarch dorr y Widdva.
Torres dy wyr, tair ystâl : trwy Wynedd a'r tir anial.
Tros greigiau mae d' olau di : tir âr y gwnaent Eryri.
Od ennynaist dân ennyd : trwy ladd ac ymladd i gyd.
Dyrnod anuvudd-dod vu : darnio Gwynedd a'i dyrnu.
O bu 'r tir, Herbert wrawl : heb gredu val y bu Bawl.[8]
E vu ar Bawl veiau 'r byd : e ddiveiodd i vowyd.
Chwithau na vyddwch weithian : greulon wrth ddynion â thân.
Na ladd weilch a wnai wledd ynn : Gwynedd, val Pedr y gwenyn.
Na vwrw dreth ar Vôn draw : ni aller ei chynnulliaw.
Na vriw Wynedd yn vranar : na'd i Vôn vyned ar vâr.
N'ad y gweiniaid i gwynaw : na brad na lledrad rrac llanw.
N'ad trwy Wynedd blant Rronwen:[9] na phlant Hors yn y F'flint hên.
N'ad v' arglwydd swydd i un Sais : na 'i bardwn i bwrdais.
Barna 'n iawn, brenin o'n iaith : bwrw 'n tân i braint uniaith.
Kymmer o wŷr Kymru 'rowron : bob kwnstabl o Venstabl i Vôn.
Dwc Vorganwc a Gwynedd : gwna 'n un o Gonwy i Nedd.
O digia Lloegr a'i dugiaid : Kymry a dry yn dy raid.

GUTTO'R GLYNN A.D. 1468.

From what the poet states, (that the walls of Harddlech had not
stood more than the fence of a sheepfold,) it must be understood
that that stronghold was taken by assault, a fact which does not

1, Mustered at Peel in South Wales. 2, Sir William Herbert, afterwards
Earl of Pembroke. 3, *Duw*, God. 4, The robust and tall, a cognomen in which
he seems to have delighted, from the fact that his euglogiat repeats it,—"Chwedl
Bonfras a ga's i gyd," i.e. he obtained all that he spoke of, achieved by the expedition all that he had promised. " Blaenvain vu i'r bobl ynvyd," i.e. " Too
keen for those who played the fool by their insurrection in favour of Henry
Earl of Richmond. 5, "Bonfras Arglwydd ar Penfro," " Bonfras Lord over Pembroke." The Welsh commonly called individuals Sirs, Lords, Earls, &c., when
those personages had no such *titles*, by the laws of England; this was specially
done in courtesy to representatives of families known to be of the ancient *nobility*
of Wales, and was a " trait," characteristic of their veneration of ancestry, loyalty,
and nationality. 5, A concourse, concurrence, concert in action, a faction. 6,
Yewmen, bowmen, archers, so called because they were armed with bows of yew.
7, St. Paul. 8, Rhonwen, Rowena, sister of Hengist. 9, Horsa, the Saxon leader.

quite agree with what that very talented writer, Mr Morgan of
Tregynnon, relates in his able "Memoir of the Herberts," (*Cam-
brian Journal, Sept.* 1857.) "Henry V., after the conquest of
France, continued to treat with Glyndwr, A. D. 1416, as actual
sovereign of Wales; consequently his son, Henry, was never nominated or crowned Prince of Wales. After the death of his son
Griffith at the the battle of Grismont, Glyndwr had devolved the
succession on his cousin, Meredith ap Tudor, whose claims were
now embodied in his great-grandson, the boy Harry Tudor. Edward VI., as Earl of March, and lineal descendant of Gwladus, the
only daughter of Llewelyn the Great, was considered by a great
part of the Cymry to have a sounder claim than the Tudors,
&c. When he succeeded, on the death of his father, A.D. 1461, &c.
to the claims of the House of York, all Siluria, under the influence
of Sir William (Herbert) and the vast ramifications of his family,
declared at once in his favour. The same year, Jasper Tudor, Lancastrian Earl of Pembroke, landed in North Wales, took Denbigh
Castle, and, by a forced march, nearly made himself master of
the young king's person, at Flint," &c. The king was in Denbigh
Castle, at the time when Pembroke attacked, and, according to
some, set the place in flames. Hence, the name, " Pembroke's
Hill," as some call it, on the North side of the town. But Denbigh
was likewise burnt in A. D. 1468, by the Yorkists—(*See A. & M.
Denbigh, p.* 37 *and* 85-86.) " On the first intelligence of Jasper's
disembarkation," says Mr Morgan, " Sir William, and his brother
Risiart Hîr, of Colebrook, marched northward. The battle took
place on the banks of the Alun, and terminated in the defeat of
Jasper, who effected a retreat to the coast, threw part of his forces
into Harlech Castle, under Sir David ap Einion, and with the remainder sailed for Pembrokeshire. Here, levying fresh forces, he
marched with his usual expedition, &c., to the disastrous field of
Mortimer's Cross, &c." When young Harry Tudor had fled to
Bretagne in France, " Sir William and his brother," says our
author, "penetrated by one of the most extraordinary marches in
military history, through the mountainous region of North Wales,
and formed the seige of Harlech Castle. The line is still known as
' *Ile Herbert*,' and passes through the strongest fastnesses of the
highlands, then occupied by the partizans of the Tudors, &c."
According to the foregoing poem, which must be the right version
of the story, the hostile armies entered North Wales by three dif-

ferent routes. Sir William took his march along the ancient Roman Road, called Sarn Helen. But the difficulties encountered in penetrating into the fastnesses of " the Snowdonian Alps " are in no way exaggerated, for our poet tells us that Herbert's followers were all brave as dragons, cutting through the woods; his horse climbing the very sides of Snowdon; his track was to be traced over rocks, and that they actually ploughed up the Eryri, the Eagle mountains of Snowdonia. The poet expostulates with his hero to spare the Welsh, and not lay the country waste with fire and sword, but to expel the children of Rowena, and sons of Horsa, meaning the English constables, freemen, &c., and should that displease the " dukes of England," the Welsh would, he assured him, all turn to his standard.

II.

Kowydd yn dangos val y bu y maes Mambri.

(An Ode describing what took place at Banbury Field)

Dawns o Bowls !¹ doe 'n ysbeiliwyd : dwyn yr holl dynion i'r rhwyd.
Dawns gwyr dinas y gwarrai : dawns yr ieirll dae 'n asswy rai.
Duw-Llun y bu gwaed a lladd : dydd ymliw, diwedd ymladd.
Duw a dduc y dydd Dduw-Iau : Iarll Dwywent a'r holl deiau.
Marchoc a las Dduw-Merchyr : mwy i ladd no mil o wŷr.
Syr Rissiart in sae 'r Iessu : wrtho er lladd Northwyr llu.
Duw-Mawrth gwae ni am Domas : Duw-Llun gyd a'i vrawd y llas.
Dwyn yr Iarll a'i bedwar-llu : dydd y varn, anrhydedd vu.
Arglwydd difwynswydd Defnsir : a ffoes, ni chaffas oes hir.
Bradwyr a droes, brwydr a drwc : Banbri i'r Iarll o Benbrwc.
Kaed drygkiu am y drin draw : karliaid a wnaeth y curlaw.
Ymladd tost am laddiad hwn : Awn ar hynt i Norhantwn.²
Awn oll i ddial yn jaith : ar ddannedd y Nordd uniaith.³
A dyludwn hyd Lydaw :⁴ dan draed y kyffredin draw.
Ef a'r gwŷr a vu ar gam : oll i dd——l yn lladd *William.*
O rroed lle bu anrrydedd : ar fwnwgl iarll arf neu gledd.
Och Fair ! gnodach⁵ fu arwain : aerwy mawr o aur a main.
Doe ddoeth, dan y blaned ddu : drwy 'r Vâl draw i ryvelu.
Och vinnau ! uwch yw v' anhun : nad 3rhoe 'n i dir i hun.

1, " Dawns o Bowls " is a very dark phrase. " Bowls " cannot mean " St. Paul's " in London. Does it mean that war is like a game at tenis-ball, mere " hap hazard ?" But the poet adds, " dawns yr ieirll," the dance of the earls, from which it would appear that this fatal conflict, so serious in its national result, originated at some ball. We know that the Earl of Pembroke and his brother, " Risiart Hir," had challenged the " King-maker " to single combat, with either of them, upon the Tilting-ground at Smithfield, but although they offered to fight with one hand, against his two, Warwick declined it, and no wonder, for these Titan brothers were about seven feet each in stature and equally renowned for strength and courage. Or, which is more likely, the reference here is to the quarrel which took place the night before the battle, between the Earl of Pembroke and Lord Stafford, Earl of Devonshire, who is also mentioned. 2, Northampton. 3, Monoglot Northmen, those who spoke but one language—Englishmen from Lancashire, &c. 4, Bretagne in France, where

Ymddiried i'r dynged wan : a'i twyllodd o Went allan.
Tair merched taer Tynghed (hon⁵) : y sy 'n dwyn oes y dynion.
Un a gyneil gogeilyn : arall a nŷdd—dydd pob dyn.
Trydydd yn torri edau : er lladd Iarll a llu Dduw-Iau.
Mynnwn fy mod, a'm annos : yn torri pen Atropôs.⁷
Nŷdd oes hir yn nydd y Sais : neud rrann i'r tair a henwais.
Os gwir i blant Alis⁸ gau : draeturiaid⁹ dorri tyrau.
Ni ddoe 'r iangwyr, ni ddringynt : i dai 'r gwr, nac yw dir gynt.
Gwinllan fu Raglan i'r jaith : gwae ni wyl i gwin eilwaith.
Gwae oer ! gwelais ar Galan : gynnal gwledd ar ganol glann.
Gwae ! ac eisio rrodio rhawc : Gwent dlawd, oedd gynt oludawc.
I varw oedd well i vardd iach : eb i bwyll, no byw bellach.
Merddin wyllt am i urddas : annhorvyn aeth i'r glynn glas.
Af yn wyllt o fewn elltydd : i eiste rrwng clustiau 'r hydd.¹⁰
Ef am las i a'm nassiwn : yn awr y llas yr Iarll hwnn.
Kymro oedd yn ffrwyno Ffraink : kam-ryol Kymru jevaink.
Ofn i bawb tra vu yn byd : yn iach ofn oni chyfyd.
Ymgyrchu i Gymbru, a gan' : ymsaethu 'Mhowys weithian.
Doed aliwns, nis didolir : o dônt, pwy a'i lludd, i dir.
Llvscant wyr, lloscant i tai : lladdwyd y gwr a'i lluddiai.
Trawst etto rracc trais yttyw : tra gader, Syr Roesier yw.
Tri maib Iarll, os trwm y byd : tri a ostwng y tristyd.
Un o'e hil yn Neheu-wlad : a gyrraedd dwyn gradd i dad.
Iarll oedd Gymbru oll iddo : Iarll oe vab arall a vo.—GUTTO'R GLYNN.

           I'll run distracted 'mid the rocks,
           Sit 'twixt the ears of the hind.

This battle was a most disastrous event to the Welsh, five thousand of whom fell that day, and their two generals, having performed prodigies of valour, were taken and executed at Northampton. The "treachery" to which the poet alludes was the "dirty work," the defection of the Earl of Devonshire, with his 6,000 archers; or the stratagem performed by a Lancastrian officer in displaying, on a neighbouring hill, the colours of the absent King-maker, and raising the shout, "Warwick! Warwick!" The Welsh, who were on the point of carrying the third hill, conceiving themselves suddenly surrounded by overwhelming numbers, and entrapped by the desertion of the Earl of Devonshire's division, were thrown into a panic, and put to flight, slain, or taken. The Earl of Devonshire, who according to the poet, "fled, but was not long allowed to live," had his head struck off upon the nearest mile-stone to the town of Bridgewater. The battle is said to have been fought on the 26th of July, 1468. According to the poem, Thomas Herbert was slain upon "Monday, the last day of the battle," at his brother's side. The knight slain on Wednesday, and whose death was a greater calamity than the loss of a thousand men, must be Sir Richard Herbert, who "stuck to the last," to his brother's colours, and slew a host of Northmen.

This giant is said to have slain, with his pole-axe, seven score men before he was taken. The Earl himself (with several other Welshmen) was executed on Thursday. The "flash" about these giant brothers kissing each other, and laying their necks side by side on the block is not therefore true to *time.* Our poet says that the Earl marched out of South Wales with a blind reliance upon fate, and that he must have taken the field under the direction of a dark planet.

CHAPTER XV.

DE BECKLELE'S SURVEY CONTINUED—THE REMAINING PART OF
THE COMMOTE OF ISALED—NANTGLYN, PRYS, EREIVIAD, BODEILIOG,
LLECHRYD, BODYSGAW, MAESYCAE, CARWEDFYNYDD, DINCADFAEL,
BERAIN, TALYBRYN, TWYSOG, AND TALDRACH — VALUATION
AND CUSTOMS — HENLLAN, NANTGLYN, LLANNEFYDD — ANCIENT
FAMILIES, ETC.

Nanthlyn Canon, with the hamlet of Pennaukyngy, contained
564¾ acres, from which the lord had 7s. 8½d., besides 9s. for the
herbage of a small wood, and 5s. 4d. from Kenet Routh for the lord's
share of a corn mill, and a fulling-mill. Hugh Pygot and several
Welsh tenants appear on the list. The rest was allowed (in
exchange?) to the *priodorion*, or (original) free natives of Astret
Canon.

Nanthyn Santorum (Nantglyn y Saint) rendered 6s. 5d. annually
for tung, treth, dogs, penmackew, &c. David Vaghan, John de
Ribchestre, Tegen 'le Wrek Feriad (Tegain Wraig Offeiriad, Tegain
the priest's wife, although Romish priests* were forbidden to marry),
Kendal Goch, Eignon Loyd, Kenet Routh, and Jevan Vaghan,
paid the lord 38s. 2½d. annually, and the commonalty 11s. for the
herbage of the woods and wastes.

Prees (Prys,† small or dwarf wood) with its hamlets, contained
8878 acres, 1½ rood, besides a desert tract of common pasture for
all the tenants of Roes, Rewaynock, and Kaymerch. In the time
of the princes, before it was forfeited, the hereditary tenants paid
20s. 0d½. tunc-rent. The free tenants now (temp. De Beckele)
pay 9s. 6½d. tunc-rent, and the bondsmen render £7 13s. 4½d. for
about 380 acres of arable and grass land, a small meadow, and a

---

* Some say the clergy in Wales opposed celebacy, for a great length of time.
But where marriage was forbidden, a priest was formerly allowed to have a
concubine, provided he did not keep her publicly at his house, or go to her
so openly as to cause a scandal. " *Clerici beneficiati, aut in sacris ordidibus con-
stituti, in hospitis suis publice tenere concubinas non audeant, nec etiam alibi cum
scandalo accessum habeant ad eas.*"—Lyndwood l. iii. tit, ii p. 126.

† *Parc Prys*, vulgarly called " *Park Pierce*," on the north side of Denbigh.

turbary, the community (all Welsh) give £6 for the herbage of the lord's share of the desert; he has also 50s. annually for the water-mill.

Eryvyot (Eriviatt or Ereiviad) contains 2465¼ acres of land, wood, and waste. The Wilberle family and William Raven, Henry Runcorne, Adam Titharista, Michael de Cestr. (of Chester), Atha Jevan Capellanus, Thomas Yrulham, three Rossyndales, John de Kylford, Adam the son of Bronnrobyn (Brynrobin), Teg. Loyt, Robt. son of Hamon, John Tepel, Robert and John de Wykewere, William Raven, William Scot, Alice wife of William de Cruce and her son Henry de Cruce, Henry Modreshale, and Robert son of Adam the Miller, render for tung, butter, provision for the Prince and his servants, horses, raglot, stallions, grooms, dogs, penmack- ey and weision bychain, building houses, mill, and autumn works, £2 13s. 3d. per annum. Divers free natives of Denbigh, Lleweny, Astret Canon, and Berain, have had in exchange for their patrimo- nies 645 acres, 9 perches, and the tenants above-named paid yearly £11 4s. 11¾d., for nearly 458½ acres of land, one house, three cottages, and one garden; 50s. for the herbage of the woods and wastes, and 54s. rent of a water-mill.

The hamlet of Bodoyllok (*Bodeiliog*) containing 174¼ acres, belonged to Astret Canon. About 53¼ acres, were rented for 31s. 3¾d. annually, to Matilda de Plesynton, Peter de Twysilton, Alan le Carpenter, Henry de Redefern, Henry le Mortermaker, Jevan and Eignon Loyt; besides 2s. for herbage.

The township of Leghred (*Llechryd*) was held by Welsh tenants in three "lecta," containing 460½ acres. The Prince had 8s. 3¼d.' and the lord 13s. 5d. rent of his share, and 8s. for the year's herbage.

The township of Boydneskau (*Bodysgaw*) *with the hamlet of Messekay* (*Maesycae*) contains 721¼ acres. The third part, called Gavell Kendalo ap Talhaern (*Gavael Cynddelw ap Talhaiarn*) held by free tenants, and the remainder, called Wele Kenrek ap Talhaern and Wele Tudur ap Talhaern, was in the tenure of bond tenants. Thomas de Whitacre, William de Waverham, Henry de Lynesey, Madoc and Kenet Vaghan, John son of Thomas the Miller, and Robert son of William de Bulkelegh, paid the lord yearly

£6 5s. 4¼d. for about 318¼ acres. The services of the bondsmen were valued at 8s. 3¼d. per annum. The lord had also 10s. for the year's herbage. And 29s. 9½d. rent of 73½ acres at Messekay, held by Margaret Brodfot (*Broadfoot*), John le Fisher, Henry de Billing, and William de Waverham.

The ˙ *township of Caerueduemuth* (*Carwedfynydd*) consisted of 9¼ gavels, and was wholly in the hands of free tenants, who paid 10s. 0¼d. tung, and 69s. 5¾d. as provision for the prince. It contained upwards of 1094½ acres, of which 325¼ belonged to the lord, who had 47s. 6d. annually. But more than one half was allowed to the (original) free natives of "Astret Canon and Beryn." The lord's portion of the herbage was charged at 26s. 8d. per annum to the commonalty.

The *township of Dyncaduell (Dincadvael)*,—One half of this township was mortgaged by Hoydyl ap Ithel to Prince Llewelyn ap Iorwerth for £12, &c., and that prince gave this mortgage to a certain lady-love of his called Tanguestell Goch, who sold the same to a certain Canon ap Lauwarch, whose descendants hold the same moiety to this day. Tunc-rent, 2s. 4¾d. It contained 263 acres—odd. The lord had 5s. from the waste.

The *township of Beryn (Berain)* contained 737 acres, 22 poles, in 7½ gavels, the whole of which was in the lord's hands, and was an English settlement held by Thomas and Adam Faber, Robert de Suytale, Richard Whitacre, John, Richard, and Robert Gamesley, John de Symunston, Roger, Henry, and Adam de Clifton, Robert de Plesynton, Henry Byllyng, Thomas de Mostone and Thomas his son, William, Henry, and Roger de Shadde, Richard de Halton, Robert de Walton, Thomas de Whitacre, John Wade, William son of Hugh del Broke, Henry de Clyderowe, Adam de Frodesham, William and John Buckele, Margery and Simon de Hallum, John de Whytacre and his wife, Thomas de Whytacre, Matilda daughter of Richard de Golden, John son of Thomas de Heende, Margery and Richard Brodfot, Robert de Hulton, sen., and John Shenyngton, who paid £13 9s. 0½d. annually for 420¼ acres. The (Welsh) bondmen paid £1 3s. 7d. and one mite, in lieu of various services. Water-mill rent 66s. 8d., common 6s. 8d.

The *township of Talabryn, (Talybryn,)* contained 560 acres 1½ rood,
2 E

14 perches.   Rent £8 6s. 0¼d., services and tung 4s. 8¼d., common
6s. 8d.. but which the tenants claimed to have by a grant from the
Earl of Lincoln.

The township of Penporghethl, (Penporchell,) a purely Welsh
settlement, of 1048½ acres, tunc-rent and services 16s. 5d., acreages
32s. 6¼d., herbage of woods, &c., 25s.   Divers tenants of Lleweny,
Astret Canon, Beryn, &c., claimed the rest, in exchange for their
inheritances.

The township of Twyssok, (Twysog) was, under the princes, held
by bond tenants, who paid 7s. 6d. tung, services 4s. 10¼d.; present
rent 48s. 10¼d. for one messuage, and 104 acres 3½ roods 16 perches,
the rest was allowed to the *priodorion* of Denbigh and Lleweny in
exchange.   Herbage 12s. yearly.

The township of Taldrogh (Taldrach.)—In the time of the princes, one-half of this township was held by the descendants of Seisel
ap Canon, *(Seisyllt ab Cynan)* and the other half by bond tenants,
who rendered 12d. for " tung," and 18s. 9½d. annually for services,
&c.   The lord's portion of the whole " vill," which contained above
364½ acres, was 155 acres 39 poles, besides the portion allotted to
the freemen of Lleweny.   Blethin le Bowere, and Robert de Grene-
feld, paid 30s. 1d. for 62 acres 1¼ rood.   The lord took no profit
from the rest, except 10s. yearly for the herbage.

GENERALITIES.

It appears that in the time of the princes, it was the custom to
make provision for one stallion and one groom of the prince, for one day
and one night, not only at, or on account of the house of every freeman
who had no under-tenants ; but, for the house of every free tenant,
and also for the house of every native of this commote ; and this
custom was valued at 2½d. per house, in an old survey.   But now
they only paid one penny each yearly, at the Feast of the Exaltation
of the Holy Cross.   Nevertheless, in the eighth year of Edward
III. there were 126 freemen who " had houses over their heads,"
and of these, 13 had 74 free under tenants, so that the custom, was
then worth 15s. 7d. per annum.   And there were 56 natives who
had " houses over their heads," and their provision was worth
4s. 8d. per annum.   The free tenants of Wyryon Pythle, (Wyrion
Pyllau ? *wyrion* for descendants,) and Wyryon Rimon, in Prees,

were excepted, because they paid this custom in Ros Ughdulas, &c.
So also the priodorion of Nantglyn y Saint.

And in the time of the princes all the freemen and natives of this
commote, (see error, page 58, in confining the duty to those of
Taldrach alone,) were accustomed to construct and maintain at
their own cost, a hall, chamber, wardrobe, chapel, wash-house, &c.,
for the prince at Denbigh. *" Omnes liberi et nativi istius commoti
solebant construere et sustinere sumptibus eorum, apud Dynbiegh,
pro principe, unam aulam, unam cameram, cum gardroba ; et
unam capellam, et etiam unam loteleriam, et unam pistrinam. Et
etiam facere et sustinere sepes circa curiam principis, &c.* And
now since the time of the Earl of Lincoln, they paid 1d. yearly for
building houses; except the grandchildren of Pythle, and the grandchildren of Rimon in Prees.

Value of other customs, &c.—Office and fees of the raglot £6 10s.,
judge 35s., ringild £6, chief-forester £7 4s. 4d., serjeant of the
peace 64s., raglot of avowries and rent of men in avowry 66s. 8d.,
amobrage, "merchet and heywite," with fees £8 10s. Total,
£35 10s. Reliefs, chattels of intestates, escheats, and perquisites
of courts £53 6s. 8d. Perquisites of forest-courts, dead and fall
wood, loppings, bees, and honey £6 4s. Herbage of the waste of
Hauodelwe, (*Havodelwy,*) 650 acres, 20s. Waste of Galgheved,
374 acres, 20s. Total, 40s. Tung 54s. 9¾d. and one mite, butter
27s. 10d., castle guard 3s. 7d., prince's servants £6 2s. 1¾d. and one
mite, from free tenants; and £4 5s. 9½d. from bond tenants; for two
horses and two men 24s. 7d., raglot's horse, stallions and grooms
20s. 3d.; dogs 20s. 5d., penmack and "wession byghain" 10s. 2½d.,
crunnocks (*crynogau*) of oats 9s. 4d., buildings, &c., houses 20s.,
mills 19s. 8d., "ardreth" 37s. 6¼d., harvest work 22s. 1⅛d., "treth"
(tax) 2s. 4¼d. Sum total of all the farms £276 18s. 3¾d., forest
herbage £4 11s. So the value of the Commote of Issalet was
£394 17s. 6¼d. yearly, which might be raised to £34 11s. 9½d. more.

CONCLUDING REMARKS.

HENLLAN, which should, perhaps, have been noticed in the foregoing chapter, is an outlying municipal suburb of Denbigh
mentioned in *Pope Nicholas's Taxation* (A.D. 1291), as a chapel
belonging to the Cathedral of St. Asaph. *"Henllan est capella*

Cathedralis Eccl. Prebend. Decane, 20 *marc.*" In the return made
to Archbishop Parker (A.D. 1560), we have " *Henllan, Humfredus
Martevalls-water, presbyter, vicar. residens.*" The present church,
an ugly modern substitute for the ancient chapel, stands at some
distance from the old steeple; a fact which has afforded some
disciple of Dean Swift an occasion to perpetrate a libel upon the
peaceable and good villagers, thus :—

> " Henllan church and Henllan steeple,
> Are true emblems of the people ;
> All at variance—where 's the wonder,
> When church and steeple are asunder ? "

The old chapel contained many very ancient memorials, see
A. & M. Denbigh, p. 195, and further notice of the Peakes in
this work. There are some fine monuments in the present church;
the oldest are those of Hugh Peake A.D. 1601, Agnes Peake A.D.
1618, William Vaughan (of Groes) A.D. 1661. Here also lie past
generations of the Ffoulkeses of Eriviatt, Salusburies and Joneses
of Galltfaenan, Davieses of Llannerch, Griffiths of Garn, Hea-
tons of Plas Heaton, &c.*

NANTGLYN.—In the return of A.D. 1560, we find " *Nanclyn—
Dominus Johannes de Nanclyn, presbyter, vicar, residens.*" There
are no old monuments except the following :—

> Hic jacet Corpus
> Mar. Wynn uxor John's
> Wynn de Garthm.[1] Arm
> et fil Owen Price de Garthe[2]
> ac Nantmeth.[3] W. Wynn de Me.[4]
> fil et Mar fil Ric. Clough Merc.
> Copt. Gresh. et sa. sep. ord. E.Q.
> et Cathar. de Berain. Sepult.
> 19 die januar. Ano. Dom. 1682.

> Hic etiam humat : est corpus
> ja. fil johns et Mar. Wynn Supra
> ex uxor Fulk Wynn de Nantglyn
> Can. Genek.
> ib. die Mart Ano. Dom. 1701.
> R.P.

The church is a small edifice of no architectural pretensions.

* The new district churches of Trefnant and Bylchau, are handsome structures;
indeed, the former is a superb little edifice.

1, Garthmeilio. 2, Garthewin. 3, Nantmel. 4, Melai.

Here repose the ashes of the learned and great Dr. Owen Pughe, his eminent son Aneurin Owen, Esq., and excellent grandson William Owen, Esq.; and the Welsh poet and grammarian Robert Davies, commonly called "The Bard of Nantglyn." This secluded glen also gave birth to "Dr. David Samwell," who accompanied Captain Cook in his voyage round the world, and to the celebrated actress Mrs. Jordan.

LLANNEFYDD, supposed (by Browne Willis) to be the "Llandyd" of the *Taxatio* (1291) of which it is said—"*Est capel. Cath. Eccl. Prebend. Athael Vachan*," who was then the chancellor. In 1560, "John Lewes (was) vicar of Llanevith." The author had no reply respecting the monumental inscriptions, &c. The church (lately "restored") commands a fine view of the distant sea. The old manor-house of Berain is still standing, and the remains of a very ancient military work crowning the hill called Moel-y-Gaer.

The whole of Isaled is hilly, with many fertile little vales and glens, sheltered woody nooks, and some "hungry hill-tops," as Camden would have said. It is well watered, especially the western part, a clay-slate region. There is a broad belt of shell-limestone, and some under-lying free-stone in the neighbourhood of Denbigh, in the eastern and northern parts.

Ffoulkes of Eriviatt.—This is a very ancient family (descended in the male line from Marchudd, founder of the Eighth Royal Tribe of North Wales), now represented by Major Jocelyn Ffoulkes,—married to Mary Anne, eldest daughter of Sir William Beauchamp, Bart., of Langley Park, Norfolk. The surname Ffoulkes was first assumed about A.D. 1572, by John Wyn ap Fowk (of Eriviatt) ap Thomas ap Gronwy ap Ievan ap Einion ap Ednyfed ap David Llwyd ap Iorwerth ap Tegwared ap Iddon or Ithon, ap Idnerth ap Edryd ap Jonathan Prince of Abergele, who died A.D. 856. The late John Powell Efoulkes, Esq., brother to Henry Ffoulkes, D.D., principal of Jesus College, Oxford (maternally descended from the Cloughs of Glanywern,) was also father to the Rev. Henry Powell Ffoulkes, M.A., of Llandysil, Edmund Salusbury Ffoulkes, late fellow of Jesus College, Oxford; and to William Wynne Ffoulkes, Esq., barrister on the North Wales circuit, who is well-known in the antiquarian world.

CHAPTER XVI.

DE BECKELE'S SURVEY CONTINUED—COMMOTE OF ISDULAS—
DINORBEN FAWR, KINMEL, TYLGARTH, BODROCHWYN, MEIFOD,
CEGIDOG, DINORBEN BACH, FAERDRE, ST. GEORGE, HENDREGYDA,
SERIOR, NANT, PENIARTH, ABERGELE—ITS HISTORY, ANTIQUITIES,
ETC.—VALUATION, CUSTOMS, ETC.

"ROOS ISDULAS."

THE lord had nothing anciently belonging to the lordship here,
but the manor of " Dynnorbyn Vaur," (*Dinorben Fawr*.)

The township of Wykewere, (now *Wigfair*,) *with Kylmail and
Bodroghyn*.—Grono ap Madoc Vaghan, and other free tenants, apparently of the same family, paid 6s. 11¼d. tunc-rent. The Welsh
bond tenants paid 18s. 8¾d. annually as provision for the prince.
Other bondmen of Wyckewere, and Bodroghyn, paid 2s. 3¾d. tunc-
rent. Also for rent of hens at the Nativity of our Lord 8d. or eight
hens, forty-two days' work in autumn 5s. 6d., four vessels of butter
or 13s. 4d., for prince's servants 8s. 1¼d., raglot's horse 13½d., other
horses and men 8s. 4d., release of offices 10s. The "vill" of
Wykewere contained 1072 acres 3½ roods of land, wood, and waste,
the *hamlet of Kylmail (Kinmel)* 160½ acres, and Boydroghyn 1340
acres, in all 2573 acres 1½ rood. Of this, the lord's portion by escheat, was 1638 acres 1½ rood. The allowance to divers priodorion
of Lleweny and Astret Canon, in exchange for their old patrimonies,
was 175 acres 3 roods. Hugh de Hulton, Llewelyn ap Eignon
Goch, Ithel Loyd ap Cad, Rees and Kenet ap Moiller (*Meilir* or
Maelor ?) and Gron. Vaghan, held one "place" of 219 acres 1¼
rood 15 perches, for which they " rendered " 112s. 2d. The commonalty also paid 13s. 4d. for the herbage of 227 acres 3 roods 15
perches of common. And there was a water-mill there, the eighth
part of which belonged to the lord,* held by Heilin ap Watte for
6s. 8d. per annum, besides 8s. 4d. for the attachment of a weir.

* This mill must have been on the Elwy. It was probably the " original"
of the present Wigfair mill.

At Plasnewydd Cefnmeiriadog, said to be the first house in the country "roofed with stone," that is, *slated*, is the following inscription upon a fine oak wainscoting, "*Anno Domini* 1583, *Æta. Ætatis mei Fulconi ap Rob.* 43. *G. H. Deum Time.*"

Bodroghyn.—Here Wladus vergh Edenowyn, Eignon and David Loyd, Heilin ap Eignon Goch, and Eignon Voyl paid 54s. 8d. for 139 acres 1 rood of land, and 26¼ acres 32 perches of waste, and the community 55s. for the herbage of the rest of the lord's portion. There was also a water-mill here, the twelfth part of which belonged to the lord, and was let at 16d. per annum. The origin of the Bodrochwyn mill, its small rent, compared with that of Wickwer mill, arising no doubt from a deficient supply of water.*

Kilmail.—Eignon Loyd and other tenants at Kinmel paid 28s. 9½d. for 46½ acres ¼ rood of land, and the commonalty 4s. yearly for the herbage of the lord's waste.

The township of Meyvyot (Meivod) contained 360 acres, and was held by free and bond Welsh tenants, who paid 4s.2d. tung, 3½ vessels of butter or 25s., and 75 dishes of meal or 3s. 1½d., and 15 thraves of oats or 5s. to the prince, year by year. About 60 acres had fallen to the lord as escheat, and 21 acres by default of tenants. Of this 50 acres ¼ rood were let to Welsh tenants for 15s. 3¾d. per annum. The rest of the lord's share brought in 10s. 2d. yearly, as pasture. And there was a water-mill here let at £6 10s. This was the original Meivod Mill, and the *high* rent (for that age) proves it to have been an important mill, being then, as now, amply supplied with water.

The township of Kylkydyok (Ceigdog, St. George,) contained 245 acres of land and waste. The Welsh tenants paid 3s. 5¼d. tunc-rent; and 3½ vessels and the 40th part of a vessel of butter or 10s. 11d., and three dishes 3¼ vessels of meal, 6½ thraves of oats or 2s. 2d., and 9 hens worth 1d. each, and 27 days' reaping in harvest or 3s. 4¼d. every year to the prince. The lord's portion containing 98 acres 6 perches, of which one tuthyn *(tyddyn)*, one house, and 4 places—87 acres 7 perches were let for 54s. 6d. to Eden ap Madoc

* Bodrochwyn was the palace of Braint Hir, founder of one of the Welsh tribes. The great caves in the Dolben Rocks, and the ruin of Capel Mair, and Bedd y Cawr at Cefnmeiriadog, are worth a visit.

and David ap M. Vaghan, Margery de Clyderowe, John de Pontefract, Leuky wrek (wraig) David, and David Vaghan, Porthour;
and the rest went to the advantage of the tenants.

The township of Dynorbyn Vaghan (Dinorben Bach) contained
163 acres, for a part of which certain Welsh tenants paid 14½d. tung,
and to the prince 4 vessels of butter, the 8th part, the 16th part,
and the 32nd part of a vessel, or 14s. 0¾d.; and 42 dishes of meal
or 21¼d.; and 8½ thraves of oats, and one-fourth part of a thrave or
2s. 11d. yearly. The lord's part consisted of 42 acres 1½ rood 10
perches let for 14s. 6d. The community also paid 5s. 6d. annually for
the herbage of the rest.

The township of Taldragh, (now *Tylgarth* or *Tulgarth*,) contained 62 acres of land, held by Yockyn de Tilgart, and bond tenants,
whose rents and customs were valued at 21s. 11d. per annum. It
appears that in consequence of a dearth (on failure of crops) the
tenants here had migrated, leaving their tenements in the lord's
hands, who had re-let them to others, at the above rents, payable
at the Pentecost, and the Feast of St. Michael the Archangel.

The manor of Dynorbyn Vaur (Dinorben Vawr).—The site of
the manor of Dinorbyn, in which there is one good grange, and
another almost laid waste, except the green inclosure, one granary
or barn, and one byre or cowhouse, and one dilapidated shed for
hay and forage, containing altogether 2 acres and 1 perch, and
the easements of the houses and court are worth 5s. per annum.
And there is one ruinous dovecot here, which if repaired, would be
worth 6s. 8d. per annum.   Total, 11s. 6d.   The whole of the
arable land was 243 acres 3½ roods 15 perches, which was worth
£13 11s. 5d. per annum; meadow land 22 acres 33 perches, worth
60s. 8d.   Other pasture, 72 acres 32 perches, worth £4 6s. 0¼d.;
waste, called *Pendinas*, covered with worthless brushwood, 14s.
Adam Anneisone, Adam the son of Richard, John de Rothlan (John
of Ruddlan), and Richard del Nant rented 28 acres 1½ rood, at
33s. 6d. a-year.   Perquisites of the courts 13s. 4d.   Total value of
the manor, £24 10s. 7¼d. per annum.—Dinorben was, therefore, an
old " decayed " manor, five hundred years back, and is the site of a
military fortification or camp, whose origin history has not recorded.
All the " *dins* " or " *dyns*," are of very high antiquity ; they are rem-

nants of the pre-historic age. Among *Englynion Beddau Ynys Prydain,* we have

"Bed Ketin henben 〔 Bedd Cetin *unben ?*
En aeluit Dynorben." 〕 Yn aelwyd Dinorben:

If the last version be the correct one, we may translate it—

The grave of king Ketin
In the hearth of " Dinorbin."

"Hearth" probably alludes to his "funeral pile," the "burning" made for him.

The hamlet of Mayrdreve (now *Vardre* or *Y Faerdref.*) There was also a certain hamlet called Mayrdreve, belonging to the manor of Dynorbyn, which in the time of the princes was wholly in the hands of bond tenants; and now the occupiers rendered 35s. 10d. annually. And William Cam, John de Rothelon, John de Ponte-fract, Robert de Castleford, and others, paid 25s. 8d. for 38½ acres of this hamlet. So the manor aforesaid, with this hamlet, was worth £27 17s. 1¼d. per annum. In after ages, this was the patri-mony of the Hollands,—also of Hendrevawr and Kinmel.*

St. George is a lovely village, resting on the lap of a woody hill, commanding a magnificent view of sea and land. The princely do-main of Kinmel with its wooded parks, immediately on the right the extensive plain into which the Vale of Clwyd spreads seaward, with the navigable and tidal river—from Voryd to Rhudd-lan Castle—the towns of Rhyl, and Abergele—the long line of the Yale Hills in the eastern background, and the wide blue sea on the north dotted over with the white sail of ships bound to and from all parts of the world, form a panorama which cannot well be ex-celled in any part of Wales. In the *Taxation* of A. D. 1291, St. George occurs as " *Kegydawc, VI. marc. and 30d.*"; in the return of A.D. 1560, as " *Ganiat,*" *(Dolganad)* "*alias Kegidock, Dominus John ap Ellis, rector. residens.*" The advowson formerly belonged to the Lords of Denbigh, and the living is still in the gift of the Queen as lady of the manor. In the days of bygone superstition, the woods called Coedymeibion, Parcymeirch, Nantddu, &c., were the noted haunts of ghosts, sprites, and fairies, and it was popularly

* The late William Lewis Hughes, Esq. of Kinmel, was created Baron of Dinorben, but leaving no issue male, the title died with him. The estate passed to his nephew Hugh Robert Hughes, Esq , the present proprietor.

2 F

believed that the "imprint" of the shoes of St. George's horse
were left on some of the coping-stones of the churchyard-wall, ever
since his terrible conflict here with the dragon.   There is a very
perfect remnant of an ancient military work crowning the conical
hill, called Parc-y-meirch, so named say some of our guide books,
(upon what authority we know not,) because Owen Gwynedd's horse
(soldiers) occupied this strong post during his war with Henry II.
of England, and tradition says that it was the signal station of the
Welsh aidecamps, when the battles of Rhuddlan Marsh were fought.
There is a remarkable spring in Nantddu, powerful in winter, but
cut off in summer.

    The township of Hendregeda (Hendregyda) contained 1299 acres
of land, wood, and waste, held by free tenants in two "*lecta*" (*wele*
or *wely*).   The first "wele" was divided into six gavels, and the
second into four.   These tenants, who were all Welsh, paid 7s. 6d.
"tung" yearly.   The lord's share, was 275 acres 1½ rood, of
which 139 acres 1 rood, and 6 acres of meadow, were let to English
and Welsh tenants, among whom were John de Pontefract, Dionisius
de Bathe, Henry Talbot, Thomas Brown, Agnes de Stretton, and
Wenthlian daughter and heir of Robert de Borebathe, Wenthlian Goz
(Goch), David Trewe, and Ithel Coch, who paid 105s. 5¾d. yearly.
And the commonalty paid 17s. 1½d. for the herbage of the wastes.
And there was a mill there common to the lord and the coheirs of the
township.   The fourth part of this mill belonged to the lord, and
the community held it to farm.   There was another mill called
(Melin) Bragod, which belonged to the lord and was held by
Dionisius do Bagh, and Henry de Clyderowe, at a rent of 66s. 8d. a
year.—It becomes a question, Were these two mills on the rivulet
which runs through Abergele town?   It is remarkable that De
Beckele does not tell us whether these were *water* or wind-mills.   Let
the *original* water-mill called Melin-y-dre be one, and there stands
upon the summit of a high hill to the south-east by south of the
town, the remarkable ruin of a small round tower, now serving as a
landmark for ships at sea, which tradition says was once a wind-mill,
and hence the hill goes by the name of "Allt-y-felin-wynt," or
Windmill Hill.   It has two entrances, north and south, and once
had four windows in the upper storey, and a fire-place.   It was per-

haps intended to be thirty feet high, but, unlike our modern mill towers, it does not taper upwards so as to form the frustrum of a cone. The masonry is rough limestone rubble, with some brick-work imbedded in mortar hardened by the chemical consolidation of ages. There was only one mill in A.D. 1311, and that described as at Abergele.

The hamlet of Seriör, which formerly belonged to Grono ap Hei-lin Seye, (Sais?) who died contrary to the peace, contained 206 acres 1 rood of land, wood and waste, nów arrented to Welsh tenants, who paid 68s. 9d. per annum, for the whole; being, for the above reason, the lord's escheat.

The township of Dynhengroen, (or Dynheugron, qy. Dinhengron, the ancient round fort?) contained 872 acres, held in 24 gavels; of which 17½ gavels were held by free, and the rest by bond tenants—Yevan ap Wylkyn Lloyd, Eignon and Yevan Vaghan, who paid 11s. 5¾d. tung, and 29s. 11¼d. for provision for the prince. The bond gavels in the lord's hands, paid 20½d tunc-rent, 4d. for hens, and 2s. 4d. for autumn or harvest work. The lord's portion consisted of 311 acres 25 perches. And of the *hamlet called Dynand*, (*Dunant, Deunant,* otherwise *Nant Dinhengroen,* now *Nant* and *Nentydd*,) containing 120 acres, the lord had 42 acres 3 roods of land, &c. And there was also another *hamlet* called *Pennarth*, (*Peniarth*,) containing 477 acres, of which the lord had 170½ acres 12 perches of wood and waste. Madoc Vaghan, Yevan Goch, Eignon Hydyr, and other Welsh tenants, held one tithin, (*tyddyn*,) 230 acres 1½ rood 5 perches, for 104s. 1¼d. yearly. The community also paid the lord 10s. yearly for the herbage of one waste, and 5s. for another common. Also in

The hamlet of Pennart,* 20 acres 1 rood held by Welsh tenants for 6s. 4½d. a year, and 149 acres 3 roods 12 perches, belonging to the lord, for which the community paid 16s. 4d. per annum. And there was a water-mill here (which must have been on the river Dulas, or on the tributary stream passing Peniarth Fawr. Query, Melin y Cwymp?) the third part and the 32nd part of which belonged to the lord, and was held by Eden Duy, who paid 10s. a year for the lord's share.

* Now Peniarth Fawr and Peniarth Bach.

The townships of Garthewin and Trovarth.—These belong to Isdulas, and are given in the Inquisition of A.D. 1311, but omitted here. The former, sometimes called " *Trovert,*" belongs to Llanfair-Talhaiarn, the latter to

BETTWS-YN-RHOS,* which contains five townships;—*Peniarth, Bodlyman, Maesegwig, Cilcen, and Trovarth.* The old church was taken down in 1838, and the present neat structure raised upon the same site. The oldest decipherable tomb is the one erected in memory of John Vaughan of Pantglas, date A.D. 1661. Indeed, there are no antiquities here, except a tumulus, called *Bedd-y-Can-Wr*, near Frithycastell, Deheufryn, said to be raised over the remains of one hundred men slain in one of the early wars. There were here, as in many other parishes, some curious customs respecting the collection of tithes, as described in a terrier of 1791. " In taking up the tithe-lambs, it has been customary, time out of mind, to have the whole flock in the same fold, and for the owner to choose one first, and the tithe-gatherer the second ; and if there be more than one due for tithe, then the owner chooses another, and the tithe-gatherer chooses the second, and so on. Out of three pigs at a litter, and out of three young geese in a flock, one is paid for tithe, and if there be three and twenty young geese or so many pigs, one only is paid for tithe. In dividing lambs or geese between the rector and vicar, the vicar has the odds, as out of thirteen the vicar had nine, and the rector four; the parish-clerk ' the bell-sheaf.' "

---

* According to some philologists, *Bettws* is an old Celtic word, which signified " something between a mountain and a valley," a hollow, a depressed table-land, an inhabited hospitable nook among barren hills, and nobody now knows what else. Others take *Bettws, Bettus, Bettous,* to be a corruption of *Abbothouse;* or of *Beadhouse,* a sort of oratory, an open house of prayer, where no priest usually officiated, but where wayfarers turned for purposes of devotion. In after times, the covered open porches of churchyards, were substituted for such places of prayer, and the beadhouses became regular chapels. So say some.

On the roadside, nearly half-way to Abergele, stands a cottage called Bryngwyn, which deserves passing notice, as the first door opened to Methodist itinerant preachers in this part of Wales. And here, a long age back, in times of persecution, they were wont to meet, for private religious "fellowship," then vulgarly called " y weddi dowyll," or the dark prayer. They had then no chapels in the country, but went about preaching repentance, chiefly to gay and riotous Sabbath-breakers; on dancing-banks, gipsey-grounds, and highway crossings.

At Abergele, egg-tithe was collected in kind, and there was a tradition that formerly every tenth milking was brought in pails and
placed upon the churchyard-wall. The Rev. Dr. Jones of Penyrallt,
Abergele, was the first to lay the foundation of a charity school
here, for teaching the principles of the Christian Faith and the
Welsh Language for ever. The schoolmaster, (who should be the
sexton for the time being, if qualified and willing,) was to have
half-a-crown when the child had learned his horn-book, five shillings
when he could master his primer, and 2s. 6d. more when he could
read a chapter or psalm, proper names excepted. This was confined
to five children, but the vicar and parishioners of Bettws provided
for five more, making the master's salary in 1724, £5 per annum!
He was to teach them upon Sundays and holidays, if they could not
come to him on other days, bring them to church twice on the
Lord's day, and keep them from all "dancing-banks," (*tympathau
dawnsio,*) interludes, and all such unlawful assemblies upon the
Sabbath. Every boy who could say his catechism in Lent to have
five shillings. Now there is a large endowment.

ABERGELE.

The township of Abbergelleue, (see p. 107,) contained 1831 acres
3 roods of land, wood, and waste, wholly in the tenure of free
tenants. To a fourth part of this township belonged two whole
hamlets, viz.,

The hamlet of Bodleman, containing 152 acres of land, wood, and
waste; and

The hamlet of Messegewyk, (Maesegwick,) containing 1226 acres
of land, and wood; held by Jevan ap Cad. Vaghan, Jevan ap Eignon Vaghan, Jor. ap Gr. ap Bleth. Ylewell, Gron. ap Beth. and Tudr.
his brother, Yevan Vaghan, Mad. ap Tudr. ap Mad., Jevan ap Eign.
Vaghan, Yevan ap Mad. Vaghan, Mad. ap Eignon Vaghan, ap
Eignon, Ken. Loyd ap Ken. Vaghan, Tudr. Vaghan ap Tudr. Jevan
ap Gron. Vaghan ap Gron., and Tudr. his brother, Day ap Tudr.,
David ap Eign. Vaghan, Mad. ap Eign. Vaghan, who paid 15s. 1¾d.
tung yearly, and 58s. 5¾d. provision for the prince.

The Burg of Abergeleu.—And there were here twenty-nine burgages
(town-houses) and one oven, held by Thomas Brown, John de Pontefract, Robert de Castleford, Henry Talbot, Wenthlian daughter

of Robert de Borebach, Dionisius Wathe, John de Bourghes, Henry
de Jockenhale, Jor. ap Griffud, Adam Arnold and his son Robert,
Simon de Bache, Elias de Borebache, William de Doncaster, Richard
de Wyrhalle, Robert son of Robert de Pontefract, Leweli ap Ple.,
Henry de Clyderowe, Roger de Burches, Agnes de Stratton, and
Margaret de Clyderowe, who paid 20s. 1d. for the same yearly. And
Robert de Castleford, Henry Talbot, John de Pontefract, Adam
Arnald, and Robert his son, and David Sayer, held eight "places" of
land here, and "*tertium partem aule placitorum,*"*at a rent of 16s.10d.
a year. And there was a dovecot near the *Pele* (the Pil or Peel,
from a weir or dam) which Denis de Bathe held to farm together
with the place of the Pele, for 13s. 4d. a year. He also farmed the
tolls of the fairs and markets here for £8 10s. a year. And John
de Pontefract, Thomas Brown, Margaret de Clyderowe, and the heir
of Robert de Borebathe, William Russell, Adam Arnald, John de
Burches, Henry Talbot, Alan de Cravene, Elias Bourebathe, Denis
de Bach, Mad. Martyn, and Richard de Hoyland, held several parcels of land round the town.

GENERALITIES.

The bond tenants rendered 48 hens or 4s. and 36 cribars (*cribyn-
aid*), of oats or 3s. ; and 864 eggs and 36 lambs or 9s. and 168
days' work in harvest or 21s. The bond tenants who did not give
butter, for being exempt from serving the office of reeve, to pay 10s.
Ploughing and harrowing by the bond tenants of Meyvyot, Kilkydok, and Dynorbyn Vaghan, on an average, worth 3s.; brushwood
for repairs of hedges 2s. All the tenants, bond and free, paid the
lord yearly 60s. 8d. for provision for foresters. Total, one year with
another, £17 7s. 7¼d., and one mite. Office of raglot and fees
100s., ringild £4 2s., judge 20s., chief forester 40s., servants of the
peace 60s., advowries and rents of men in advowry 20s.,·amobrages
£10. Total value of offices £26 2s., perquisites and fines of courts
£20, forest courts do. 20s. Value of the manor of Dynorbyn, which

* The third part of the senate-house, or town hall. The author once saw a
very old brass token coined at Abergele. Many years back, a large vase containing ancient coin was found buried near Brynhuddug' on the way to St.
George. According to tradition, the "Harp Inn" occupies the site of the
ancient jail.

was in demesne, £24 10s. 7¼d.—Total, rent, customs, farms, &c., in Isdulas £153 7s. 6¾d. and one mite yearly, ploughing, harrowing, brushwood, forest issues, courts, &c., making it £199 3s. 2¾d. for the whole commote, and it might be made £17 8s. 11d. more yearly.

CONCLUDING REMARKS.

That quaint old writer, Leland, speaking of the region three hundred years ago, says, " Ise Dulesse is good for corne; as whete, rye, peasen, and benes, with verie good free pasture and medois." It is almost wholly a limestone region; bounded on the north by the Irish Sea, on the west by the river Dulas, on the south by the romantic Elwy, and on the east by the conventional line of boundary which divides Denbighshire from Flintshire. Immediately to the south of the town of Abergele stands a very high and steep rock covered with wood to its summit. On the top of this rock is one of the most perfect and almost inaccessible Ancient British (or Roman) fortifications on this island, called Castell-y-Cawr, or Giant's Castle, from which a most magnificent view is obtained—of mountain, plain, and ocean. Here, as others have observed, are some of the largest and most perfect Roman mines in this kingdom. The mountain is cut across by a supposed Roman fosse called Fos-y-bleiddiaid, or the Wolves' fosse, an example of what could be done before the invention of gunpowder, although the chasm may have been produced by primeval earthquake. In driving a level, towards the close of the last century, the miners discovered that the Romans had been deep in the bowels of the earth. " They had followed the vein, where it was large enough to admit a man, and where it opened into a large chamber they had cleared it quite away. Some curious hammers and other tools were found almost decayed to dust, with the golden hilt of a Roman sword." The level which drains these works partly supplies the town with water. The mines at Cae'rgwaith, at the foot of the same hill, are comparatively modern, and were, we believe, very productive until the water became too great for the means of drainage then applicable. A few years since, a considerable sum was expended here upon buildings and powerful machinery; but, some how or other, the works, with every prospect of success, were abandoned. The " bowels " of this great rock have been proved to form a vast magazine of wealth. Some forty years ago, lead was

raised in solid masses of several hundred-weights each, out of a shaft
about a furlong to the east of the last-named spot, but the specula-
tors had not the means to compete with the constant influx of water.
The old mines of Tyddyn Morgan, in the same hill, were wonderfully
productive a century back. It has been handed down to the writer,
amongst family traditions, that hat-fulls of old guineas were then
sported about by the managers on the monthly reckoning days.
These workings are supposed to be exhausted. Still farther west are
the old mines of Cefnogo', so called from one of the largest caverns
in Europe, which has a sort of natural Gothic grand entrance from
the north. Some thirty or forty years back, a large sum was expended in driving a level under this mountain without meeting with
anything worth the research and outlay.

There is a remarkable periodical spring at the foot of Castell y
Cawr, called Ffynnon Ithel; and a perennial spring in the Gwern-
ydd or Fens, near the beach called Y Ffynnawndol, rising in
what is popularly believed to be a bottomless pit. And there was a
tradition that a young man was once ploughing near it, when the
horses took fright, plunged into this " vasty deep," and neither
team nor man was ever more seen.

There is also an insignificant old " holy well " near Bryncoch,
called Efynnon Eflo, (Elfod?) to which crowds formerly flocked every
Easter-Day morning, drank of its sacred water for their soul's
health, and practised hydromancy, to know how long they were
to live.

The great cavern at *Tanyrogo'*, was formerly believed to be
" enchanted " and to contain hidden treasures, guarded by a great
dog of a supernatural species, kept here by the Three Fairy Sisters
whose footmarks were always to be seen in the mud of a small
lodgement of water within the mouth of the cavern. It is also
said that many years ago, in quarrying at Twll-Llwynog (fox-hole)
the fossil remains of gigantic individuals of the human species " an-
tedeluvian giants," were found in crevices of this rock.

The ancient circular camps of *Corddyn Mawr*,* and *Castell y Cawr*
(the ancient *Dinhengron*), overhanging the plain of Abergele,
belong to a system of fortifications of very high antiquity, command-

* Y *Wyddfa*, or observatory, an ancient military watch-post.

ing the hills on both sides of the Vale of Clwyd. And there can
be no question that the present Castle of Denbigh stands on the
former site of one of this series of "camp-works"—the ancient
"*Dinbych*." There was once a small military-work, or tumulus, on
the right bank of the brook, at Abergele, near the Peel; upon
which tradition said a "*castell-pren*," a wooden castle or turret,
once stood. It is still called "the Mount,"—rectius *mound*.

"In the time of the princes" Abergele gave the title of *Lords* to the
representatives of the "Royal House of Brynfanigle." After the Conquest, it was, as we have seen, a small English burg or municipality,
and held its fairs and markets—no doubt by charter from De Lacy or
Edward I. The extraordinary dimensions of the church, and the
fact that it had two or more chapelries, would lead us to suppose
that it was intended for something more than a mere parish
church. We have the name of Elbodius, who was appointed by
the Pope, Archbishop of North Wales, (A.D. 750,) connected with
an endowment of this church—"*A'r Escop Elvod a roddes lain o
dir i'r Ecclwys ar yr avon Geleu*." Bettws-yn-Rhos is commonly
called Bettws Abergele, and in a MS. of Thomas Prys of Plas Yolyn,
an antiquary who flourished about 1560 to 1619, we find "Bettws
was formerly (or ever) a chapel to Abergele. Their feast (wakes)
is on St. Michael's Day as well as in Abergele." It was not so
described in A.D. 1291, for in the Taxation we have "*Bettwe xiv
marc. vicar, ejusdem vi marc. 25d.*" But Llangystenyn was a
chapelry—"*Eccl. de Abergeleu, cum capella sua Langustenin
annex. Prebend. Archidiaconi, et taxatur inferius cum vedem
li marc. vicar, xv marc.*"

The present townships of Abergele are *Tre'rdre', Towyn,**
*Bodoryn, Bottegwal, Hendregyda, Dolganed, Serïor, Brynffanigl,
Nant, Garthgogo, Gwrych* (in which Gwrych Castle Park, &c. is
situated), *and Penrhyn Dulas.*

The following is a list of the vicars of Abergele, since A.D. 1537,
John Gethyn, 1556 John Roberts, 1570 Hugh ab Owen, 1582, John

---

* Upper and Lower Towyn, now dotted all over with cottages, farm-houses,
watering villas, &c., from Pensarn to Voryd, was evidently uninclosed in De
Beckele's time—a sandy plain, diversified with small salt-lakes, called "*crinciau*,"
or creeks.

1611 Richard Lloyd, B.D., 1613 Gabriel Parry, B.D., 1653 Vaughan Thomas Caster (a Presbyterian), 1657 John Connant, D.D., 1662 Henry Pugh, M.A., 1671 David Lloyd, M.A., 1775 William Williams, 1684 David Maurice, 1702 Peter Williams, 1796 John Griffiths, 1716 Thomas Jones, D.D., * * * Lewis Anwyl, * * * * Evan Williams, 1777 William Stoddart,* 1794 Richard Jackson, * * * * * * James Meredith, M.A., now vicar and honorary canon of St. Asaph.

The oldest terrier, only dates from 1710. On the great bell, is the following passage, "*Os meum annunciabit laudem tuam,*" my mouth shall set forth thy praise. Before the others were recast (in 1844), one of them, at least, bore the names of some of the Lloyds of Gwyrch —maternal ancestors of the present Lloyd Hesketh Bamford Hesketh, Esq. Tradition once spoke of a still older bell, called the Great Crack-bell of Abergele, which was heard all over the wide-spread parish, and from a place on the utmost bounds of the present parish of Bettws—upon the mountain plain going to Eglwysfach— called *Vownog Rhydd*, or the free turbary. A silver goblet, bearing the initials — " H. H. P H. L L. H L., 1601," a silver paten presented by Bishop Barrow in 1685, and two plated flagons with "*D.D. Ecclesia Abergele Gul^{mus} Stoddart, A.M., &c., vicarius, A.D.* 1778," constitute the communion service.

There are no very old memorials of the dead. Some of the Hollands of Hendrefawr lie here. " There is a tradition," says Canon Meredith, " that they originally came from England, and settled first in a house called, after their residence, " Llawendai," from the circumstance of their being very merry people, and their incessant fiddling from morning till night. This house is in the township of Dolganed. There is a memorial of the last male of the race, Roger Holland, whose daughter and heir, Catherine Holland, married William Parry, of Llwyn Inne (near Wrexham), Esq., &c." There was once in the churchyard an ornamental "table-tomb" with the inscription—" RHYS AP DAFYDD AP HOWEL

* The *clochyddion*, or parish-clerks, since 1783,—William Parry, previously of Bodoryn, upwards of thirty years, Richard Smallwood, John Vaughan, and William Hughes.

A GLADDED YMMA—ŒDRAN YN HARGLWYDD 1595."
According to tradition, he was owner of Hendre-ucha', and died of
the "cornwyd," or great plague ; hence no sexton would ever open
this grave. The ashes of the celebrated Dr. Maurice of Nant lie
here, under a tomb-stone bearing the arms of Owen Gwynedd and a
laudatory Latin inscription, date 1702, age 76. Tradition also
records that he was a divine of deep learning, a great preacher, and
remarkable for his godliness, but not without some childish crotchets
of faith, one of which was that he should be interred in the most
eastern corner of the churchyard, in order that, as a pastor, he
might rise before his flock at the sound of the trump of judgment.
Over his old fire-place at Nant, is the rather odd inscription :

M.
FVMVS D: A: W: G: MI: 1666.
S.

The Castle is a princely mansion, erected within the last fifty
years, and while the extensive and beautiful park was gradually
being formed, one cottage and farm after another disappeared. Old
Gwrych Hall, of which just a fragment remains, stood close on the
beach ; and here the celebrated Mrs Hemans spent the days of her
childhood.

There has always been a tradition, or popular opinion, that the
original Abergele was overwhelmed by the sea, a calamity believed
to have occurred about the eighth or ninth century. "A stone
tablet without a date, set in the churchyard wall, close to the north
gate, is adduced as a proof of the inroads of the sea. This stone
does not bear on the face of it any signs of great antiquity; but
there a is tradition among old people, that the present one is only a
copy of another of far more ancient date. On the other side of
the wall, there is to be seen a piece of a very old stone with
portions of letters not now decipherable. This is held to be the
original. The inscription on the stone at present in existence runs
thus :—

Yma mae'n gorwedd
Yn mynwent Mihangel
Gwr oedd ei annedd
Dair milldir yn y Gogledd.

The English of which is :

> Here lies
> In the Churchyard of St. Michael
> A man who had his residence
> Three miles to the North."

That is, about two and a half miles out to sea. . The second line is evidently an interpolation. Leave this line out, and you have something like the ancient Welsh verse called "Triban Milwr," The Soldier's Triplet. But might it not have been

> Yma mae'n gorwedd
> Gwr oedd ei annedd
> Yn Morfa Rhianedd—
> Dair milltir i'r gogledd ?

Or the third line might have been the second, for Abergele undoubtedly stands in the remnant of Morfa Rhianedd, a coast plain which once stretched from the Point of Air in Flintshire, round Orme's Head, to the eastern banks of the Conway. The greater part of this region is now deep sea, known to mariners as the Abergele Roads. The remains of forest trees and bog-peat have, from time to time, been grubbed up "near low-water mark," and many fishermen's cots, and even green fields over which our grandsires gamboled, have been washed away by the encroaching sway of the tide.

END.

CONTENTS.

CHAPTER I.

The Lordship of Denbigh fifty years after the Conquest of Wales. De Beckele's Survey. Extent, valuation, tenantry, customs, &c., including the Divisions of the Lordship. Commote of Ceinmyrch, now Cinmerch. Manor of Ystrad Owain. Manor of Cilffwrn, Kilfurn, now Kilford. Tenants, &c. *Concluding Remarks.*—Boundaries and physical features of the Hundreds of Rhos and Rhuvoniog. Uchdalas and Isdulas, Uchaled and Isaled. The Grays, Lacies, Myddeltons, Cottons, Maurices, and Conways. *Antiquities.*—Whitchurch or Eglwys-Wenn, Llys Gwenllian, and Hen Ddinbych in the desert.

CHAPTER II.

Ancient Welsh Laws and Customs. The feudal condition of youth under the Welsh Princes, old statute divisions of land. De Beckele's Survey continued—Segrwyd, tenantry, rents, and services. Segrwyd Park, an English Settlement. Garthynwch, &c. *Concluding Remarks.*—Genealogy of the Dolbens, &c.

CHAPTER III.

De Beckele's Survey continued—Prion, Brynbagyl, Cernyfed, Esceirwen, Postyn, Ysceibion, Bachymbyd, Llwyn, Llawesog, Brynlluarth, Caserwyd, Llech, Cilcedig or Clicedig, &c. Tenantry, rents, customs, services, officers, forests, courts, valuation, &c. *Concluding Remarks.*—Boundaries and natural features, geology, &c., of the " English Commote of Caymergh." Llanrhaiadyr; Cave at Prion, St. Dyfnog's Well, old Church, wonderful preservation of the body of Mrs C. Parry, the Jesse Window and its story, ancient and curious inscriptions, &c. Archæological dispute touching Thomas Plantagenet, Earl of Lancaster, set at rest. Decay and extinction of the English " Colony " here, The Wildings, Peakes, and Birchenshaws, last surviving descendants of the old English settlers. John Birchenshaw Abbot of Chester. A Poem descriptive of his character and times, written about the close of the fifteenth century. Llanynys, &c.

CHAPTER IV,

De Beckele's Survey continued — Commote of Isaled. The Castle, Parks, and Borough of Denbigh. Tenure of land, &c., in the times of the Princes of Wales. English settlers after the Conquest. *Concluding*

CHAPTER XII.

CHAPTER XIII.

CHAPTER XIV.

CHAPTER XV.

CHAPTER XVI.

Wrexham: Printed by George Bayley, " Advertiser " Buildings, Hope-street.

CPSIA information can be obtained at www.ICGtesting.com
Printed in the USA
BVOW022229210313

316186BV00010B/219/P